THE AMERICAN SONGBAG

THE AMERICAN SONGBAG

Carl Sandburg

A Harvest/HBJ Book
Harcourt Brace Jovanovich, Publishers
San Diego   New York   London

Library of Congress Cataloging-in-Publication Data
The American songbag/[compiled by] Carl Sandburg;
introduction by Garrison Keillor.
1 score.
Piano acc.
Originally published in 1927.
ISBN 0-15-605650-X (pbk.)
1. Songs, English—United States. 2. Ballads, English—United
States. 3. Folk-songs, English—United States. 4. Folk music—
United States. I. Sandburg, Carl, 1878–1967.
M1629.A517   1990   90-36804

Printed in the United States of America

C D E F G H I

Dedicated

TO THOSE UNKNOWN SINGERS—WHO MADE SONGS—
OUT OF LOVE, FUN, GRIEF—AND TO THOSE MANY
OTHER SINGERS—WHO KEPT THOSE SONGS AS LIVING
THINGS OF THE HEART AND MIND—OUT OF LOVE,
FUN, GRIEF

INTRODUCTION TO THE 1990 EDITION
by Garrison Keillor

"I am a loafer and a writer and would rather loaf and write, and pick a guitar with the proper vags, than to deliver spoken exhortations before any honorable bodies wheresoever," wrote Carl Sandburg, one of the most industrious writers who ever was and an inveterate exhorter, in 1921. In six years he had published three volumes of poetry — *Chicago Poems, Cornhuskers,* and *Smoke and Steel,* the best work of his life — and was hard at work on his *Rootabaga Stories* (1922), a fourth book of poems, *Slabs of the Sunburnt West* (1922), and the two-volume *Abraham Lincoln: The Prairie Years* (1926) and was assembling *The American Songbag* and pursuing a career as a performing literary man. He was not quite forty.

Sandburg was a writer who loved a crowd. He had worked as a traveling salesman or "canvasser," as it was called in 1900, selling stereoscopic photographs across the country. A few years later he switched to lyceum lecturing, giving inspirational talks for a fee on Walt Whitman (the talks entitled "The Dreamer," "The Poet of Democracy," and "An American Vagabond," three badges that Sandburg proudly wore himself), later adding to his repertoire a lecture on "Blunders of Modern Civilization." As an organizer for the Social Democratic party, Sandburg rode the trains through Wisconsin and Illinois, giving hot socialist sermons. He campaigned for his hero Eugene Debs in the presidential election of 1908, riding aboard Debs's train, The Red Special. ("Debs is superb. Crowded house, all kinds of enthusiasm.") As a lecturer, Sandburg worked schools and colleges, women's clubs, lyceums, and chautauquas for a set fee (by 1921 he was asking $125), but he was sufficiently confident of his drawing power to appear for 50 percent of the receipts (after expenses, with Sandburg handling all the advertising).

From lecturing on Whitman and reading Whitman's poems aloud, Sandburg came to give readings of his own. In 1910 he bought a guitar. And discovered that a poet with a guitar was an even better draw than a poet standing behind a lectern. "I am reading poems and singing Casey Jones, Steamboat Bill, and medleys," he wrote to a friend in 1921. "This whole thing is only in its beginnings, America knowing its songs. . . . It's been amazing to me to see how audiences rise to 'em; how the lowbrows just naturally like Frankie an' Albert while the highbrows, with the explanation that the murder and adultery is less in percentage than in the average grand opera, and it is the equivalent for America of the famous gutter songs of Paris — they get it." That was the year he began seriously collecting songs, for his own use on the platform and then to make this book.

In August 1926 he was putting the songs in order and writing notes to them. The following April he was still at work, trying to cut 338 songs down to one volume. He wrote to Vachel Lindsay, "Just now, I am trying to finish up 'The American Song Bag.' It has mounted beyond all first plans for it. It is not so much my book as that of a thousand other people who have made its 260 colonial, pioneer, railroad, work-gang, hobo, Irish, Negro, Mexican, gutter, Gossamer songs, chants and ditties." By May he had whittled the book down to 255 songs, reluctantly dropping songs he was fond of, such as "Cabahges, Cabeans, and Carotts":

> Some people like rhododendrons
> And some forget-me-nots,
> But what I like best is the dish of ka-beef
> With ca*bahges,* ca*beans,* and *carotts.*

In September he wrote to his publisher Alfred Harcourt that he expected to finish the manuscript by October 1 and to have a condensed edition ready by the middle of October. "I have been sleeping an average of nine hours a night for six weeks and broke training last night for the first time to see the Fight," he wrote, the morning after Gene Tunney defeated Jack Dempsey in Chicago. "I gained in weight; I cut out all meats, liquor, pastries; have handled an ax an hour a day and done puttering work of different kinds another hour and then have laid around lazy whenever I felt like it. Now I believe I can make the grade on the Songbag, and the condensation, on the date named."

To H. L. Mencken, who contributed an arrangement of "The Drunkard's Doom," Sandburg wrote ("Dear Hank"), "An early copy of the Songbag will go to you. The detail work on it nearly killed me. . . ." And, months later: "I said at the beginning it would be a thankless job and my gratification about the book is merely that of a patriot who has seen his duty and done it."

Sandburg was a great cultural patriot and he came along at a time when he was needed. When *The American Songbag* appeared in 1927, schoolteachers and school singing books showed a marked preference for sentimental songs about home and family, that taught a moral, that promoted proper values of patriotism, industry, cleanliness, and reverence for God—a genteel tradition whose maudlin excesses were published the same year in Sigmund Spaeth's valuable *Read 'Em and Weep*—and when teachers referred to "folk song," they meant something like the art songs of Stephen Foster. My father, who attended school then, didn't get to hear about John Henry the steel-driving man; he heard "Work, For the Night Is Coming" and "Paddle Your Own Canoe." He knew some of the songs Sandburg collected—"Red River Valley," "Sweet Betsy from Pike," and "Old Gray Mare," for example—but not "Jay Gould's Daughter" ("Put your head out the window, hear the drivers roll") or "The Roving Gambler" ("She took me in her parlor, she cooled me with her fan") or "Railroad Bill," who shot the lantern out of the brakeman's hand. He didn't know "Frankie and Johnny." When I arrived in school twenty-five years later, a great many more American songs were available to teachers, and to me, thanks to such popularizers of folk song (an odd term, but there you are) as the radio performers Bradley Kincaid and Vernon Dalhart, and thanks especially to *The American Songbag*. A copy sat in the library of our little three-room country school in Brooklyn Park, Minnesota, a cornucopia from which flowed Pretty Polly and Barbara Allen, the elusive Laura of "The Colorado Trail," and "I Ride an Old Paint." We sat in Benson School and sang about old Bill Jones, whose wife died in a poolroom fight, and the dirty little coward who shot Jesse James, and the Erie Canal and the gin getting low, and the-worms-crawl-in-the-worms-crawl-out, and:

> Times getting hard, boys, money's getting scarce.
> If times don't get no better here, bound to leave this place.

From the *Songbag,* beloved to our grade-school teacher, it was a short stop to listening to Burl Ives, then The Kingston Trio, then Pete Seeger, The Weavers, Woody Guthrie, Leadbelly, Cisco Houston, Bill Broonzy, Sonny Terry and Brownie McGhee, Flatt and Scruggs, and The New Lost City Ramblers.

So much is collected here that later became standards: "C. C. Rider," "The John B. Sails," "Foggy, Foggy Dew" (along with a variant, "The Weaver"), "The Jam on Gerry's Rock," "Casey Jones," "I Was Born Almost Ten Thousand Years Ago," "Shenandoah" (as "The Wide Mizzoura"), "The Ship That Never Returned," "Mister Frog Went A-courting," "The Farmer (Is the Man Who Feeds Them All)," "When the Work's All Done This Fall," "The Ballad of the Boll Weevil," and "St. James Infirmary" (as "Those Gambler's Blues," in which it's St. Joe's infirmary). In 1990 it's odd to see these songs without guitar chord symbols, but the genteel book-buying American home of 1927 had a piano, not a guitar, so the songs came with arrangements, which tend to sound a little fragrant and stately today. So do many of Sandburg's notes to the songs, which read like little sales talks, commercials. "This poem, trying to ease heartbreak, uses the simplest of words. They go to a soft, brave melody," he writes about "Careless Love." "Its lyric cry is brief, poignant as Sappho. Its measures are close to silence and to art 'to be overheard rather than heard.'" You assume the song could not have been very well known in 1927 — either that, or Sandburg the old stereoscope salesman and booster of Whitman was unable to publish a song without giving it a little push. His schoolmarmish pitch for "I Ride an Old Paint" strikes you as slightly awkward and warbly, like a bad book report:

> The song smells of saddle leather, sketches ponies and landscapes, and varies in theme from a realistic presentation of the drab Bill Jones and his violent wife to an ethereal prayer and a cry of phantom tone. There is rich poetry in the image of the rider so loving a horse he begs when he dies his bones shall be tied to his horse and the two of them sent wandering with their faces turned west.

What explains lines like these about such a pure classic as "Old Paint"? Was the literate public of 1927 so sheepish about American folk song that they required a pitch for each one ("The power and restraint of art and genius lurk in the lines and melody of this song from the negro hard rock gangs of Georgia and Alabama") or is it the old newspaperman's love of flourish (". . . this song originated in Chicago, the premier meat packing city of the round earth, the continents thereof, and the archipelagoes of the seven seas")? Or is it Sandburg laboring mightily to bring folk art to the masses and save them from commercial exploiters who will sell them the confections of Tin Pan Alley?

This is the side of Sandburg that is faintly embarrassing to us old admirers — Sandburg the persistent salesman, the promoter, the man looking for an angle. He was a writer and performer who always promoted himself well; he designed his own advertising circulars, devised blurbs from favorable reviews, negotiated his own fees and advances, wrote effusive letters to reviewers, talked up his product to booksellers, argued with his publisher the merits of various kinds of display. Would it help *Rootabaga Stories* to get Brentano's to fill a show window with rutabagas? Would a three-compartment cardboard display rack help, each compartment marked for a different age group, all three filled with the same book? Could Harcourt send a copy of *Smoke and Steel* to the Ford Motor Company, pointing out that on page 39 the Model-T is mentioned, and not as a joke but favorably? The question of marketing engaged Sandburg; he took to promotion with great enthusiasm. (The euphony of "Sandburg/Songbag" strikes me as a happy invention of Sandburg the copywriter.) He saw as his competition the versifiers Robert W. Service and Edgar A. Guest, authors respectively of "The Cremation of Sam McGee" and "Home" ("It takes a heap o' livin' in a house t' make it home"), and he set out to beat them, and he did. He sold more books and got his poems into more anthologies and made a bigger impression than they did, and he didn't do it by being demure.

As a young man, Sandburg aimed to start a proletarian magazine to "twist the tail of conventionality, grab social and political fallacies by the scruff of the neck and throw them to the outer whirlwinds" — it would be called *STUFF, A Magazine for the Mob*. As an admirer of Debs, as secretary to Milwaukee's socialist mayor Emil Seidel, Sandburg certainly knew which end the tail of conventionality was attached to. In his Chicago newspapering days his friends were radicals, rebels, famous bohemians. At the Daily News his desk was near Ben Hecht's, whose play *The Front Page* depicted some of the tail-twisting spirit of Chicago journalism; Sandburg's hero was the *Daily News* editor Henry Justin Smith, who said, "I don't want writers, I want fighters." Through Harriet Monroe's *Poetry* magazine Sandburg met the Chicago lawyer and poet Edgar Lee Masters, soon to write *Spoon River Anthology,* who introduced him to Theodore Dreiser, who had just published *The Titan.* They admired Sandburg's work, as did H. L. Mencken and Sinclair Lewis, both of whom contributed songs to this book. In 1927 Sandburg was a member in good standing of the American Anti-Booboisie League.

And yet, in the struggle between the genteel and the genuine, between the highbrows and the People, the academy and the "proper vags," Sandburg had to learn to walk the line if he was going to get ahead. The genuine was what he had to sell, and the genteel was who he had to sell it to. He was a socialist who sided with striking miners and steelworkers and packinghouse workers and sympathized with the Negroes of the South Side, but he was also a romantic individualist in the genteel tradition of the "appreciation" of lower-class life. When he picked up his guitar and sang, "Ah'm goin' whah nobody knows mah name,/Ah'm goin' whar dey don't shovel no snow, Lawd, Lawd, Lawd, Lawd," for his audience of schoolteachers and sensitive young shopkeepers, it was clear to them that Sandburg was not someone who would ever have said ". . . whar dey don't shovel no snow." For a time, in his early twenties, he gentrified his name to "Charles," not only on poems but also in letters to friends. Carl Sandburg was not Joe Hill. When it came to leaving political organizing and the socialists for a career as Whitman lecturer and poet-balladeer, Sandburg did not hesitate.

His steady rise to fame as a poet-troubadour and near-mythic status as Voice of the Common Man was accomplished with considerable campaigning on his part. He became the sort of revered figure whom public schools are named after — more than sixteen in his lifetime. No public school is named after Debs, Dreiser, Mencken, or Lewis, that I'm aware of. Certainly, none were named after them in their lifetime.

Growing up reading and adoring Sandburg, the great bard of the Midwest, listening to recordings of him intoning from his autobiography, singing in his rather wooden baritone, imagining him as a sort of literary cowboy roaming the plains fighting for the good of the common man, I am a little taken aback by the man's attention to business — e.g., his long letter to Howard Clark, the designer of this book, criticizing a sketch for the cover ("The design now is off-key. The letters of 'The' and the scrolls alongside are mainly what's wrong"), enclosing a rough sketch of his own, and adding, "There is strength, value, fiber, stuff (as distinguished from stuffing) inside the book that isn't done right by the cover." Somehow a Man of the People isn't supposed to be so clever as Sandburg was, nor so elaborately humble, nor so entrepreneurial: his introduction to the book reads like a thousand-word blurb ("It is so intensely and vitally American that some who have seen the book have suggested that it should be collateral material with the study of history and geography in schools, colleges, and universities. . . . 'A big bandana bundle of bully ballads for big boys and their best girls,' was the comment of one who read the Table of Contents").

Reading the introduction and the fulsome notes, you see what a useful disguise Man of the People must have been, how adventurous and vital and *interesting* it made him — and how American. When it came to assembling this treasury of the American Authentic, Sandburg collected everybody's oral tradition but his own. You will find black spirituals by the score, cowboy songs, work songs, sea chanties, hobo songs, and even seven songs in Spanish, but you will search in vain for anything that comes from a clean, industrious, pious Swedish immigrant family in Galesburg, Illinois. Nowhere in the book does he mention his own mother or father or grandparents or any songs they taught him. The beautiful immigrant song of longing for the old country, "Hälsa dem där hemma (Greet Those at Home)," universally beloved among Swedes in America, is absent. So is everything else Sandburg learned at home or experienced before he was eighteen. His troubadour persona had no room in it for himself, only for Sailors, Negroes, Hoboes, Prisoners, Workers, the romantic heroes of the American Left. He invented himself as carefully as Bob Dylan did, or Rambling Jack Elliott, or a lot of other people in the folk business.

But having said that about Sandburg, one arrives at the heart of the book, the songs themselves, and there I stop. Somehow they *did* become collateral material in schools, a bundle of American folk treasures laid out for us to look at and to sing. Some of Sandburg's own work survives, much has collapsed, but when he collected these songs, he made himself part of something permanent.

INTRODUCTION TO THE FIRST EDITION

The American Songbag is a ragbag of strips, stripes, and streaks of color from nearly all ends of the earth. The melodies and verses presented here are from diverse regions, from varied human characters and communities, and each is sung differently in different places.

The song history of America, when some day it gets written, will accomplish two things. It will give the feel and atmosphere, the layout and lingo, of regions, of breeds of men, of customs and slogans, in a manner and air not given in regular history, to be read and not sung. And besides, such a history would require that the student sing his way through most of the chapters.

If and when such history is written it will help some on the point registered by a Yankee philosopher that there are persons born and reared in this country who culturally have not yet come over from Europe. The chronicle would include that quaint commentary from the Rio Grande, "In Mexico nobody knows how to sing—and everybody sings!" It would deal with minor incidents, vivid and hilarious. For instance, musical Chicago a few years ago looked with keen interest on a lawsuit. Two composers were each claiming to be the first and only music writer to score the Livery Stable Blues. On the witness stand the plaintiff testified that one evening, long before jazz had become either a vogue or an epidemic, his orchestra was playing in a cabaret, "and a lady dancer started doing some fancy steps, and I picks up a cornet and lets go a few pony neighs at her. The trombone come through with a few horse laughs. Then the banjos, cowbells, and sax puts in a lot of 'terplitations of their own. And that was the first time the Livery Stable Blues was played."

Thus musical history in America already has its traditions and controversies. The origin of jazz is still in a fog of wordy disputation. The years to come will see plenty of argument on other moot matters.

There is presented herein a collection of 280 songs, ballads, ditties, brought together from all regions of America. The music includes not merely airs and melodies, but complete harmonizations or piano accompaniments. It is an All-American affair, marshaling the genius of thousands of original singing Americans.

The book begins with a series of Dramas and Portraits, rich with the human diversity of the United States. There are Tarnished Love Tales Told in Song, or Colonial and Revolutionary Antiques; some of them have the feel of black walnut, of knickerbockers, silver shoe-buckles, and the earliest colonial civilization. Out of the section of Pioneer Memories, one may sing with the human waves that swept across the Alleghanies and settled the Middle West, later taking the Great Plains, the Rocky Mountains, the west coast. That notable distinctive American institution, the black-face minstrel, stands forth in a separate section. There are groups of railroad, hobo, work-gang, steamboat songs. Seven Mexican border songs give the breath of the people above and below the Rio Grande. Tunes and verses are given from the camps of lumberjacks, loggers, and shanty-boys. One section contains ballads chiefly from the southern mountains. One called Kentucky Blazing Star has the largest assemblage of interesting Kentucky ballads and songs that has been put between the covers of any book. Two powerful Great Lakes songs are given, "Bigerlow" and "Red Iron Ore," either of which may yet rival the song of the Volga boatmen. One section is titled Picnic and Hayrack Follies, Close Harmony, and Darn Fool Ditties. The quaver of rare Irish lilts, emigrants to the States, is in The Ould Sod. A little series of exquisite musical fragments, light as gossamer mist, are grouped under the title, Lovely People. The book closes with a list of spirituals called The Road to Heaven.

Probably 100 pieces, strictly folk songs, have never been published; they have been gathered by the compiler and his friends from coast to coast and from the Gulf to Canada. First of all, this is a book of *singable* songs. It is for the library, but it belongs in the music corner of the library, or on the piano, or on the back porch, or at the summer cottage, or at the camp, or wherever people sing songs and want new songs to sing.

There is a human stir throughout the book with the heights and depths to be found in Shakespeare. A wide human procession marches through these pages. The rich and the poor; robbers, murderers, hangmen; fathers and wild boys; mothers with soft words for their babies; workmen on railroads, steamboats, ships; wanderers and lovers of homes, tell what life has done to them. Love and hate in many patterns and designs, heart cries of high and low pitch, are in these verses and tunes. There are low-keyed lyrics, brief as the life of a rose; there are biographies of voyagers that epitomize long novels and thick log-books.

This is precisely the sort of material out of which there may come the great native American grand opera. It is so intensely and vitally American that some who have seen the book have suggested that it should be collateral material with the study of history and geography in schools, colleges, and universities; the pupils or students might *sing* their answers at examination time.

"A big bandana bundle of bully ballads for big boys and their best girls," was the comment of one who read the Table of Contents. Look at its program. Its human turmoil is terrific. Blasphemies from low life and blessings from high life for baritone or soprano are brought together. Puppets wriggle from their yesterdays and testify. Curses, prayers, jigs and jokes, mix here out of the blue mist of the past. It is a volume full of gargoyles and gnomes, a terribly tragic book and one grinningly comic; each page lifts its own mask. It is as ancient as the medieval European ballads brought to the Appalachian Mountains; it is as modern as skyscrapers, the Volstead Act, and the latest oil-well gusher. Though meant to be sung, it can be read and is a glorious anthology of the songs that men have sung in the making of America.

History, we may repeat, runs through this book. Yet it is first of all, we say again, a songbook to be sung rather than read. Music and the human voice command this parade of melodies and lyrics. They speak, murmur, cry, yell, laugh, pray; they take roles; they play parts; in topics, scenes, and "props" they range into anthropology, houses, machines, ships, railroad trains, churches, saloons, picnics, hayrack and steamboat parties, and human strugglers chanting farewell to the frail frameworks of earthly glory. There is patter and jabber of vulgarity, there are falsetto mockers and groaning blasphemies, there is moaning of prayers and tumult and shouting of faiths.

Honest workingmen and hardened criminals sing their lives; beloved vagabonds and miserable miscreants are here; pretty babies and tired mothers, bad boys and anxious fathers, people who are fat, rollicking and gay along with restless and desperate men and women; they stand forth here and in bright ballads or melancholy melodies tell what life has done to them.

The American Songbag comes from the hearts and voices of thousands of men and women. They made new songs, they changed old songs, they carried songs from place to place, they resurrected and kept alive dying and forgotten songs.

Ballad singers of centuries ago and mule-skinners alive and singing today helped make this book. Pioneers, pick and shovel men, teamsters, mountaineers, and people often called ignorant have their hands and voices in this book, along with minstrels, sophisticates, and trained musicians. People of lonesome hills and valleys are joined with "the city slicker," in the panorama of its pages.

The American scene and pageant envisioned by one American singer and touched off in one of his passages is measurably vocal here. "Forever alive, forever forward they go, they go, I know not where they go, but I know that they go toward the best, toward something great."

PREFATORY NOTES

The airs and verses, tunes and words, on the pages herewith, are most of them intended to be sung. A minor portion of them are enduring poems of lyric or narrative value; they are worth reading for the reading's sake, as one communes with books worth while. Yet even with such poems there is an added lighting or tincture given them if the air is hummed or the poem sung to an accompaniment.

A few of the ballads and ditties are too long to be sung, from the first to the last verse, more than once a year. Only by singing, however, will some of the airs and verses open up their best slants and glimpses.

If you like a particular air and would rather sing it in a way you have found or developed yourself, departing from the musical expressions indicated, making such changes as please you at any given moment, you have full authority to do so. We quote an able singer's comment, "Many a modern song the interpreter looks at with a shudder. Riddled with expression marks and even breathing marks, hedged in with arbitrary directions, radiating polyglot colloquialisms, it looks like a barbed-wire entanglement. Singer and accompanist smile at one another, study the song as a whole, and sing it their own way."

Some of our songs are sublime; some are silly. Some tell of lovable eyes and hearts, others tell of crimes learned of in grand opera or read about in daily newspapers or in the classics of literature. They deal with a panorama of events and people, substance and shadow, paunches and fleshpots, as well as filaments of sunset mist. They have roles.

Often a song is a role. The singer acts a part. He or she is a story-teller of a piece of action. Characters or atmosphere are to be delivered. . . . No two artists deliver a role in the same way. Yet all good artists study a song and live with it before performing it. . . . There is something authentic about any person's way of giving a song which has been known, lived with and loved, for many years, by the singer.

Perhaps I should explain that for a number of years I have gone hither and yon over the United States meeting audiences to whom I talked about poetry and art, read my verses, and closed a program with a half- or quarter-hour of songs, giving verbal footnotes with each song. These itineraries have included now about two-thirds of the state universities of the country, audiences ranging from 3,000 people at the University of California to 30 at the Garret Club in Buffalo, New York, and organizations as diverse as the Poetry Society of South Carolina and the Knife and Fork Club of South Bend, Indiana. The songs I gave often reminded listeners of songs of a kindred character they knew entirely or in fragments; or they would refer me to persons who had similar ballads or ditties.

In the arranging of a song I would usually sing it for the composer—and bring out my note-book sketch, a rough affair rapidly penciled and as a document looking rather like a "shivaree" than a quiet wedding. The composer and I usually collaborated on the main design or outline of the harmonization or accompaniment. From then on the work was entirely that of the composer, except in a number of instances when I suggested a different mood, atmosphere or rhythm to meet the requirements of the song as I had customarily heard it. The words "arranger" (abbreviated as Arr.) and "arrangement" are generally employed throughout the book. The musical setting of a song is occasionally an elaborate and accomplished harmonization. Most often, however, the "arrangement" is a simple accompaniment. (If time and circumstance had permitted there would have been included a number of guitar, accordion, and harmonica accompaniments for the portable instruments.)

Special acknowledgments are made to Alfred G. Wathall, to Thorvald Otterström, to Leo Sowerby, and to Hazel Felman for musical settings, for counsel and guidance at points where their technical skill and musical experience was requested.

Alfred G. Wathall wrote the major number of harmonizations; he had the gift of versatility requisite for the treatment of such a varied character of songs. His moods of work and methods of approach have a generous gamut. The ways of his heart and head range from the playboy who pranks as he pleases, who follows the gleam of the whim of the moment whether he happens to have the wishing heart of an innocent child or the tumultuous thoughts of a stranger lost in the solitude of the packed traffic on a big city street. More important yet, Wathall is the cunning technician familiar with all the classics, exercising a gift of showmanship in behalf of a humanity that he loves with laughter and tears. He knows what is verandah and what is ashcan in the realm of music and can mingle them with effective contrast. His "Music Box" and "Arabian Nights" creations for WGN, the *Chicago Tribune* radio station, for which he is the master arranger, have had a remarkably widespread and enthusiastic audience. His "Sultan of Sulu" music was the work of a nineteen-year-old genius. The touch of genius, too, goes for his forty-minute musical setting of that trifling tale from *Rootabaga Stories*, a piece of puppetry called "The Romance of the Rag Doll and the Broom Handle"; as the announcer reads the story there are accompaniments and interspersals of music from a chamber-music orchestra.

Leo Sowerby was twenty-one years old when a Chicago orchestra produced a concerto for 'cello by him entitled "The Irish Washerwoman." He took a favorite folk piece of American country fiddlers, a famous tune of the pioneers, and made an interesting experiment and a daring adventure with it. He was a bandmaster during the World War. Then later he is found doing a happy-go-lucky arrangement for Paul Whiteman's orchestra; it may be an exploit in "jazz" or possibly a construction in "the new music." One definite thing about Sowerby is his ownership of himself, his acceptance of hazards. He is as ready for pioneering and for originality as the new century of which he is a part. One other definite thing is that he does not prize seclusion to the point where he is out of touch with the People. Not "the peepul" of the politicians, nor the customers of Tin Pan Alley, but rather The Folks, the common human stream that has counted immensely in the history of music. We reckon it a privilege that Sowerby could undertake the musical settings for sixteen of our songs.

Thorvald Otterström is a compound of toil, technical knowledge, and genius. I cannot enumerate nor set forth here anything like an outline of the ideas and projects that animate him. He is encyclopedic in scope of knowledge. I cannot mention nor discuss intelligently one of his manuscripts, a scientific treatise of technical phases of music; his writings have to be wrestled with and are tough as mathematics. And his compositions of music have specimens that are yet to be written about, both simply and intricately, as work that has come from a temperament of fire and a hand possessive of master strokes.

Hazel Felman (Mrs. Jacob R. Buchbinder) has rare adaptability of mood and technic, has versatility, and has ranged widely as evidenced in her song air and musical setting of Rudyard Kipling's "Boots," made known to a wide audience through the singing of Reinald Werrenrath, and later a fantastic "March of the Zizzies," based on a breed of small people who make all things zigzag, as told in the affidavits of *Rootabaga Stories*. She is adaptive, pictorial, imaginative.

We could write a considerable little book about the ways of our composers, the contralto of Elizabeth Carpenter Marshall crooning her airs to the verses of Dorothy K. Aldis; she is as obedient to her inner voices as her uncle, John Alden Carpenter. We could mention the unmistakable genius of Henry Joslyn and the fighting stride of some of his cacophonic speculations as played by Stokowski's orchestra on the one hand and Whiteman's on the other.

The versatile Rupert Hughes, writer of novels and short stories, director of photoplays, biographer of musicians, biographer of George Washington, and author of remarkably free and independent essays and inquiries into human credulity, is a composer of music which the house of Schirmer has published. The latter folios include airs and musical settings of three pieces from *Chicago Poems* and *Cornhuskers*. It was natural when I met Hughes in his Southern California home that I should show him the Mexican songs that needed harmonizations for our fiesta.

R. W. Gordon placed at our disposal the resources of his immense collection of old songs that men have sung. His fellowship at Harvard University, his editorship of the *Adventure Magazine* department, "Old Songs That Men Have Sung," and his extended series of articles on American folk songs in the *New York Times*, resulted in his being in touch with a force of contributors and correspondents numbered at upwards of 2,700. His travels from coast to coast, his meanderings in a motor car through the southern states, always seeking old songs or characteristic and significant songs, brought about a collection that is without doubt the largest assemblage of folksong material ever gathered by any one person. On close acquaintance with the thorough character of his service, his intense devotion and anxious concentration in one chosen area of effort, the extent of the data gathered, one realizes that Gordon's work is monumental.

Harry M. Gilbert, half a New Yorker and half a Paducah Kentuckian, was an adviser on points in music, texts, and general drift of the book. Besides his classical training, his musical association with Jess Ricks, the Long Island fiddler, was of advantage in scrutiny of folk songs. Alfred Frankenstein, author of the book *Syncopating Saxophones* and other kit-kats in musical criticism, was an interested counselor from the start.

Alexander Hannah of Pasadena, California, Oliver R. Barrett of Chicago, William H. Richardson of Jersey City, New Jersey, and Dr. Ernest Horn of the College of Education of the University of Iowa, gave the use of scarce books on old minstrel and pioneer songs.

Our illustrations are chiefly from songsters and broadsides of 1840 and 1850. A few are from the *Family Magazine* and *Harper's New Monthly Magazine* of that period. William Gropper is the contributor of four or five skits pertinent to his style and modernist viewpoint. Hans Stengel furnished the silhouette of the author singing and driving a one-horse milk wagon. Diego Rivera of *Mexican Folkways* did the line drawing with his initials on it.

Thanks are due that sterling Brooklyn citizen, W. W. Delaney, who for twenty-two years published twice a year a ten-cent songbook containing the words of about 160 songs in each number. He looked and spoke as the friendliest of men, rich with memories of popular songs, song writers, "pluggers" and publishers. His advice to me, as I wrote it in a note-book riding the subway, was: "You got to get it through your nut there's only a limited amount of people know how to sing those old songs. Take those songs of fifty years ago—who knows how to sing them? who cares about them? The people you're catering to have never heard of them. That's a point you've got to look to."

DIALECT

Dialects in the United States are many and various. The southern states have several; the daily speech and the common idioms of South Carolina, Alabama, and Texas, have differences. The lingo of mountaineers is not the same in all Appalachian regions. The cowboy and the sheep-herder are as far apart in ways of talk as a Chicago newsboy and a Santa Fé brakeman running out of Albuquerque. In putting dialects into print, an author has to consider how it may help those who are to read or sing it. If you know a dialect and have heard it from living people you will not need much help from the butcheries of words, the cleavages, elisions, and apostrophes required for an accurate phonetic record. And those who have *not* heard a certain dialect, who must get acquainted with it and learn to pronounce it from the printed page, may stumble on difficulties. The word "the" in different cases, according to the way it is spoken, would be indicated as (1) the, (2) de, (3) thuh, (4) th', (5) t', (6) d', (7) duh. Or the word "here" would be indicated as (1) here, (2) hyer, (3) hyeah, (4) hyar, (5) hyah, (6) yere, (7) heeyah. Four kinds of the word "the" are in the negro sentence, "*T*' fust ting he knowed *thuh* p'lice had him an' *de* wagon come aroun' *duh* cornah." Three kinds of the word "here" are in the mountaineer sentence, "*Hyeah* comes dis *yere* Bill Brown up dat *hyar* road." Following are two ways of writing a verse of a South Carolina spiritual, one in dialect, the other not:

Stah in de eas', stah in de wes',
Wish dat stah wuz in mah breas',
Chu'ch Ah know yuh gonna miss me w'en Ahm gawn.
W'en Ahm gawn, gawn, gawn,
W'en Ahm gawn to come no mo',
Chu'ch, Ah know yuh gonna miss me w'en Ahm gawn.

Star in the east, star in the west,
Wish that star was in my breast,
Church, I know you're going to miss me when I'm gone.
When I'm gone, gone, gone,
When I'm gone to come no more,
Church, I know you're going to miss me when I'm gone.

AN AMERICAN BOOKSHELF OF SONG

An interesting list of books to go on an American Bookshelf of Song could be named. It would include such volumes in recent years as *Cowboy Songs and Other Frontier Ballads* (Macmillan & Co.), by John A. Lomax; *American Songs and Ballads* (Charles Scribner's Sons), by Louise A. Pound; *American-English Folk-Songs Collected in the Southern Appalachians* (G. Schirmer), by Cecil J. Sharp; *Folk-Songs of the South* (Harvard University Press,) edited by John Harrington Cox; *Ballads and Songs of the Shanty-Boy* (Harvard University Press), by Franz Rickaby; *On the Trail of Negro Folk Songs* (Harvard University Press, by Dorothy Scarborough; *The Flying Cloud*, published by the compiler, M. C. Dean, Virginia, Minnesota; *Frontier Ballads: Songs from Lawless Lands* (Doubleday, Page & Co.), by Charles J. Finger; *The Book of Navy Songs* (Doubleday, Page & Co.), collected by The Trident Literary Society of the United States Naval Academy and arranged by Joseph W. Crosley; *Singing Soldiers* (Scribner's), by John J. Niles; *Negro Workaday Songs* (University of North Carolina Press), by Howard W. Odum and Guy B. Johnson; *Mellows: Work Songs, Street Cries. and Spirituals* (A. & C. Boni), by R. Emmet Kennedy; *Roll and Go: Songs of American Sailormen* (The Bobbs-Merrill Company), by Joanna Colcord; *The Land of Poco Tiempo* (Scribner's), by Charles Lummis; *Blues* (A. & C. Boni), by W. C. Handy, with introduction by Abbe Niles; *Texas and Southwestern Love* (Number VI of Publications of the Texas Folk Lore Society), edited by J. Frank Dobie.

Files of the *Journal of the American Folk Lore Society*, and such freshly original publications as those of the Texas Folk Lore Society, contain considerable folk-song material, much of it priceless. Besides her volume, *The American Indians and Their Music* (The Womans Press), Frances Densmore has presented a superb array of studies of the Red Man as a singer in her volumes published by the Bureau of Ethnology, Smithsonian Institution; the songs in this field require an exceptional practice and technic. The literature on the negro spiritual and its songbooks has steadily grown and is well itemized in *The Negro Year Book*. For a gallantly bantering treatment of American song during the past century and a half, with merriment over the changing fads, fashions, foibles, and formulas of commercialized song, Sigmund Spaeth's volume, *Read 'Em and Weep* (Doubleday, Page & Co.), is worth having.

TOO LATE TO CLASSIFY

While our book was nearly ready for press, and prefatory notes about finished, I rambled through 1,300 pages of *The Universal Songster*, published in London 1826–28, and found there a piece which should have been included in our folio of songs known among the Lincolns and Hankses. Dennis Hanks, a cousin of Abraham Lincoln, when queried by W. H. Herndon as to what songs were known to their families in southern Indiana in the 1820's, mentioned one about "The turban'd Turk, who scorns the world and struts about with his whiskers curled." The first time I met the words of this song was in the above-named book, where its title and text appear as follows:

None Can Love Like an Irishman
(Collins)

The turban'd Turk, who scorns the world,
May strut about with his whiskers curled,
Keep a hundred wives under lock and key,
For nobody else but himself to see;
Yet long may he pray with his Alcoran
Before he can love like an Irishman.

The gay Monsieur, a slave no more,
The solemn Don, the soft Signor,
The Dutch Mynheer, so full of pride,
The Russian, Prussian, Swede beside—
They all may do whate'er they can,
But they'll never love like an Irishman.

The London folks themselves beguile,
And think they please in a capital style;
Yet let them ask, as they cross the street,
Of any young virgin they happen to meet,
And I know she'll say, from behind her fan,
That there's none can love like an Irishman.

By what ways this ditty, or lines of it, traveled to southern Indiana and was popular in cornfields and at cross-roads, we may leave to later investigation. It is evidence that metropolitan songs may take long migrations.

Also we add here another verse of the song "I Met Her in the Garden Where the Praties Grow" in the folio The Ould Sod. It goes—

And now that we are married
  And we're blessed with children three,
Two girls just like their mother
  And the boy the image of me—
We'll raise them up so neatly
  In the way they ought to go
So they'll not forget the garden
  Where the praties grow.

Strictly, we have a book that is unfinished, that has oddments and remainders, that has tatters and remnants, elsewhere and far away in many ports and valleys.

DATA CONCERNING THE COMPOSERS AND WRITERS OF MUSICAL SETTINGS, HARMONIZATIONS, AND ACCOMPANIMENTS

COLLINS, EDWARD—Pianist, composer, Chicago. Born, Joliet, Ill. Studied piano with a sister, later with Rudolph Ganz. Studied composition under Engelbert Humperdinck and others at Royal Academy, Berlin. Toured the United States with Ernestine Schumann-Heink, 1912–13. Assistant conductor, Century Opera Company, New York, 1913–14; Wagner festival, Bayreuth, 1914. Has appeared as piano soloist and guest conductor with Chicago and St. Louis Symphony Orchestras. Has composed many works for piano and for orchestra. Member of faculty, Chicago Musical College.

CRAWFORD, RUTH PORTER—Composer, Chicago. Born, East Liverpool, Ohio. Studied piano under Vallborg Collett, Jacksonville, Fla., Bertha Foster, Miami, Louise Robyn and Djane Lavoie-Herz, Chicago. Studied theory under Adolph Weidig, Chicago. Member of faculty, American Conservatory, Chicago. Composer of violin sonata, suite for small orchestra, suite for wind instruments and piano, "Tom Thumb" suite for piano solo, songs, preludes for piano. Member, board of directors, Pro Musica Society, Chicago, non-resident advisory board, New Music Society of California, Sigma Alpha Iota.

EDSON, CHARLES FARWELL—Bass, Chicago. Born, San Francisco. Studied under Frederick Buck, Ella G. Richards, L. G. Gottschalk, and others. Début, Los Angeles, with Los Angeles opera. Sang with Ferris Hartman Opera Company. Conducts private vocal studio in Chicago. Has also appeared as actor. Composer of songs. Member, Gamut Club, Los Angeles, Society of American Musicians.

FARWELL, ARTHUR—Composer. Born, St. Paul, Minn. Studied engineering at Massachusetts Institute of Technology. Studied music under Homer Norris in Boston, Engelbert Humperdinck and Hans Pfitzner, in Germany, and Alexandre Guilmant in Paris. Member of faculty, Cornell University, 1899–1901. Established Wa-Wan Press, publishing native American works, 1901, continuing publication to 1908. Correspondent, *Musical America*, 1909–15. Has taught at Settlement Music School, New York, and at University of California. Has made extensive studies of American folk music. Composer of many works on folk themes—*American Indian Melodies, Folk Songs of West and South, From Mesa and Plain*, etc., all for piano solo, and music for pageants and plays. Founder and director, Theater of the Stars, Big Bear Lake.

FELMAN, HAZEL (Mrs. J. R. Buchbinder)—Composer, Chicago. Born, Joliet, Illinois. Studied under Thorvald Otterström. Numerous songs, including setting of Kipling's "Boots." Concerto for piano and orchestra. "Legend" for violin and piano. "March of the Zizzies." Residence, 1137 E. 50th St., Chicago, Illinois.

GILBERT, HARRY M.—Organist, pianist, New York. Born, Paducah, Ky. Studied under Alberto Jonás, Hans Pfitzner, Max Landow, and others, in New York and Berlin. Organist and choir director, Fifth Avenue Presbyterian Church, New York. Conductor, Society of American Singers and Gilbert Singers. Director, Eveready Hour. Has appeared as soloist on tour with David Bispham, Maud Powell, Pablo Casals, Geraldine Farrar, and others. Composer of songs, piano pieces, and church music.

GOODMAN, LILLIAN ROSEDALE (Mrs. Mark Goodman)—Born, Mitchell, S. D. Graduate Institute of Musical Art, New York. Studied in Europe under Buzzi-Peccia. Singer with Coit-Alber Chautauqua bureau; in duo program at French theater, New York; under Shubert direction in *Hello Alexander* and *Red Pepper;* headliner in vaudeville concert program; composer of many songs, including Cherie I Love You, My Heart is Sad, Love's Like the Robin, Mammy's Precious Pickaninny, I Found You, If I Could Look Into Your Eyes. Head of musical booking bureau, Capital Building, Chicago, Ill.

JOSLYN, HENRY—Composer, violinist, conductor, New York City. Born, Elmira, New York. Symphonic suite, "Native Moments," produced by Stokowski and Philadelphia Orchestra; Ganz and St. Louis Symphony Orchestra; Stock and Chicago Symphony Orchestra; Nathaniel Finston and Sunday Symphony Concerts, Chicago Theatre (première). Symphonic silhouette, "American Sky Lines," produced by Paul Whiteman's orchestra, the composer conducting. Other compositions: three symphonies—"War," "Pythagoras," "The Symphony of the Low-Downs"; "Red White and Blues" Symphony (for Paul Whiteman); symphonic odes—"Eulogy," "Joy," "The Day of Days"; symphonic suites—"The Seven Ages of Man," "The Melting Pot," "Symphony Miniature," "Mitchie-Gaunee," "Fairy Tales"; tone-poems—"Down Wind," "Prairie," "Chicago"; concertos for piano, violin, 'cello, viola (for Louis Bailly); string quartet in C Minor; string pieces—"Elation," "Once Upon a Time," "Tryst."

KENNEDY, R. EMMET—Author, pianist. Born, Gretna, Louisiana. Author of three books of sketches with negro folk music: "Black Cameos," "Mellows," "Runes and Cadences;" and a novel, *Gritny People*. In reply to certain queries, Mr. Kennedy makes free to declare: "My voice is a cross between a tenor cricket and a baritone lizard. Studied under myself and God. Name of present and former managers: R. Emmet Kennedy."

LYCHENHEIM, MARION—Pianist, Chicago. Born, Philadelphia. Studied under Mrs. Crosby Adams, Max Kramm, Heniot Levy, Jan Chiapusso, Adolph Weidig, and others. Début, Chicago, 1915. Has appeared as soloist and accompanist with Adolph Weidig, Francis Macmillen, Lionel Tertis, Jacques Gordon, Florence Macbeth, Willy Burmester, and others. Composer of string quartet; trio for violin, viola, and piano; fugues for piano, children's songs, violin and violoncello pieces. Member, Musicians' Club of Women, Lake View Musical Society, Musical Guild, MacDowell Club.

MARSHALL, ELIZABETH CARPENTER (Mrs. Thomas L. Marshall)—Composer, Lake Forest, Illinois. Born, Winnetka, Illinois. Studied under Horace Middleton, Ralph Lawton, Adolph Weidig, Thorvald Otterström, Marta Milinowski, and Luigi Gulli. Niece of John Alden Carpenter. Compositions for violin, piano, voice. Musical settings for Dorothy Aldis' children's poems. Residence, 11 Scott St., Lake Forest, Ill.

NEMKOVSKY, MOLLIE (Mrs. Ben Abramson)—Pianist, Chicago. Studied under Karl Reckzeh. Played in concert in Northwest States, Canada and Alaska under direction of Dominion Concert Bureau. Accompanist of her brother, Sol Nemkovsky, violinist, in concerts.

OTTERSTRÖM, THORVALD—Composer, pianist, Chicago. Born, Copenhagen, Denmark. Studied under Sofie Wenter, St. Petersburg, Russia. Devoted to composition and theory. Orchestral compositions performed by Chicago, Philadelphia, New York and Copenhagen Symphony Orchestras. Violin and piano sonata and 'cello piano sonata premières in Chicago, 1913 and 1915. Piano solo compositions, 24 preludes and fugues and 6 concert studies, played by numerous artists in United States and Europe. Author of theoretical works. Residence, 1400 E. 59th St., Chicago, Illinois.

PARKS, HENRY FRANCIS—Organist, conductor, Chicago. Born, Louisville, Ky. Studied under Leo Sowerby, Karl Schmidt, Fisher Thompson, Ignacio Lazcano, George Rogovoy, and others. Has played and conducted at many theaters in the West and Middle West. Conducted Butte Symphony Orchestra, Butte, Mont. Taught at MacPhail School, Minneapolis, and conducted Minneapolis Lyceum Symphony Orchestra, 1924–25. Member of faculty, Chicago Musical College; contributor to *Band, Orchestra, Melody*, and other periodicals. Author, *The Jazzology of Organ Playing; The Modern Theater Organ*. Member, American Guild of Organists, American Federation of Musicians.

SOWERBY, LEO—Composer, Chicago. Born, Grand Rapids, Mich., 1895. Studied piano under Calvin Lampert, theory under Arthur Olaf Andersen, American Conservatory, Chicago. Bandmaster in United States army, 1918–19; taught theory at American Conservatory to 1921. Was first American composer to win the Prix de Rome, 1921, and lived at American Academy in Rome, 1921–23. At present, teacher of theory, American Conservatory, Gunn School, Chicago, and organist and choirmaster, St. James Episcopal Church, Chicago. Composer of symphony, concertos for piano, for violin, and for violoncello, arrangements of folk tunes for symphony orchestra, symphonic poems, "King Estmere" for two pianos and orchestra, and "Medieval Poem" for organ and orchestra, many smaller works for string quartet, solo instruments, organ, voice, and jazz orchestra.

WATHALL, ALFRED GEORGE—Composer, violinist, pianist, organist, conductor; Chicago, Illinois. Born, Bulwell, near Nottingham, England. Came to America with parents in 1890. Studied under Franz Esser, William Middelschulte, Peter Christian Lutkin; and in London, England, under Sir Charles Villiers Stanford and Sir Frederick Bridge. At the age of twenty he composed the music for George Ade's musical comedy, *The Sultan of Sulu*, which ran continuously for seven seasons. Member of faculty, Northwestern University School of Music, for ten years. Composed and conducted cantata, "Alice Brand," Evanston, 1903. Other compositions include two operettas and many songs. As master-arranger and composer for WGN, the *Chicago Tribune* radio station, 1926 and 1927, put on the air original musical experiments such as a Rhapsody for voices and orchestra, based on the popular tune Valencia; and a setting of Sandburg's Rootabaga story, "The Wedding of the Rag Doll and the Broom Handle."

Apologia

I APOLOGIZE FOR THE IMPERFECTIONS IN THIS WORK. I BELIEVE
NO ONE ELSE IS NOW, OR EVER WILL BE, SO DEEPLY AWARE AND
SO THOROUGHLY AND WIDELY CONSCIOUS OF THE IMPERFECTIONS
IN THESE PAGES. I SHOULD LIKE TO HAVE TAKEN TEN, TWENTY,
THIRTY YEARS MORE IN THE PREPARATION OF THIS VOLUME.

MANY CONSIDERATIONS WHICH HAVE GOVERNED THE SELEC-
TION OF MATERIAL, AND THE METHODS OF PRESENTATION, ARE
NOT WORTH SETTING FORTH IN A FOREWORD, DECLARATION, OR
ARGUMENT; THEY WOULD HAVE VALUE CHIEFLY AND ONLY TO
THOSE WHO ALREADY UNDERSTAND SOMEWHAT THE LABYRINTHS,
THE TWISTED PATHWAYS, AND ROADS OF LIFE, OUT OF WHICH
THIS BOOK ISSUES.

THE BOOK WAS BEGUN IN DEPTHS OF HUMILITY, AND ENDED
LIKEWISE WITH THE MURMUR, "GOD BE MERCIFUL TO ME, A
SINNER." IT IS A BOOK FOR SINNERS, AND FOR LOVERS OF HUMAN-
ITY. I APOLOGIZE TO THEM FOR THE SINS OF THE BOOK AND THAT
IT LOVES MUCH BUT NOT ENOUGH.

CARL SANDBURG.

Chicago, 1927

TABLE OF CONTENTS

TABLE OF CONTENTS

DRAMAS AND PORTRAITS

The world grows more majestic but man diminishes. Why is this?—We carry within us greater things than the Greeks, but we ourselves are smaller. It is a strange result. . . . The whole secret of remaining young in spite of years, and even of gray hairs, is to cherish enthusiasm in one's self by poetry, by contemplation, by charity. . . . The modern haunters of Parnassus carve urns of agate and of onyx; but inside the urns what is there? Ashes. Their work lacks feeling, seriousness, sincerity, and pathos—in a word, soul and moral life. I cannot bring myself to sympathize with such a way of understanding poetry. The talent shown is astonishing, but stuff and matter are wanting. It is an effort of the imagination to stand alone—a substitute for everything else. We find metaphors, rhymes, music, color, but not man, not humanity. Poetry of this factitious kind may beguile one at twenty, but what can one make of it at fifty? It reminds me of Pergamos, Alexandria, of all the epochs of decadence when beauty of form hid poverty of thought and exhaustion of feeling. I strongly share the repugnance which this poetical school arouses in simple people. It is as though it only cared to please the world-worn, the over-subtle, the corrupted, while it ignores all normal healthy life, virtuous habits, pure affections, steady labor, honesty, and duty. It is an affectation, and because it is an affectation the school is struck with sterility. The reader desires in the poet something better than a juggler in rhyme, or a conjurer in verse; he looks to find in him a painter of life, a being who thinks, loves, and has a conscience, who feels passion and repentance.   FREDERICK AMIEL.

HE'S GONE AWAY

This is an arrangement from a song heard by Charles Rockwood of Geneva, Illinois, during a two-year residence in a mountain valley of North Carolina. It stages its own little drama and characters. The mountain called Yandro was the high one of this valley. A "desrick," Mr. Rockwood was told, is a word for our shack or shanty. The song is of British origin, marked with mountaineer and southern negro influences. Other mountain places in the southern states have their song about going away ten thousand miles; this one weaves in the exceptional theme of the white doves flying from bough to bough and mating, "so why not me with mine?" Mr. Sowerby was lighted with a rich enthusiasm about this song and has met its shaded tones with an accompaniment that travels in fine companionship with the singer.

Arr. L. S.

I'm goin' a-way for to stay a lit-tle while, But I'm comin' back if I go ten thou-sand miles. Oh, who will tie your shoes? And who will glove your hands? And who will kiss your ru-by lips when I am gone? Oh, it's

4

HE'S GONE AWAY

while, But he's com-in' back if he goes ten thou-sand miles. . I'll go

build me a des-rick on Yan-dro's high hill, Where the wild beasts won't bother me

nor hear my sad cry; For he's gone, he's gone a-way for to stay a lit-tle

while, But he's com-in' back if he goes ten thou-sand miles. . . . . .

HE'S GONE AWAY

I'm goin' away for to stay a little while,
But I'm comin' back if I go ten thousand miles.
Oh, who will tie your shoes?
And who will glove your hands?
And who will kiss your ruby lips when I am gone?

Oh, it's pappy'll tie my shoes,
And mammy'll glove my hands,
And you will kiss my ruby lips when you come back!

Oh, he's gone, he's gone away,
For to stay a little while;
But he's comin' back if he goes ten thousand miles.

Look away, look away, look away over Yandro,
On Yandro's high hill, where them white doves are flyin'
From bough to bough and a-matin' with their mates,
So why not me with mine?

For he's gone, oh he's gone away
For to stay a little while,
But he's comin' back if he goes ten thousand miles.

I'll go build me a desrick on Yandro's high hill,
Where the wild beasts won't bother me nor hear my sad cry;
For he's gone, he's gone away for to stay a little while,
But he's comin' back if he goes ten thousand miles.

BOLL WEEVIL SONG

A boll weevil couple, arriving in a cotton field in the springtime, will have, by the end of summer, more than twelve million descendants to carry on the family traditions. So it is estimated. They are a species of creatures among whom there is no talk at all about "the first families." The billion dollar devastations of this little eater of cotton crops are of America's traditions of tragedy. J. Russell Smith, the geographer, says the economic loss caused by the boll weevil equals in amount that of the four year war in the 'sixties. John Lomax first sang this for the present writer, and of four different airs and sets of words the Lomax version is the most important; the other boll weevil songs are worth printing, however, for artistic and scientific purposes. I have known this song for eight years, since the year John Lomax and his family lived in Indian Hill, Illinois, and it never loses its strange overtones, with its smiling commentary on the bug that baffles the wit of man, with its whimsical point that while the boll weevil can make a home anywhere the negro, son of man, hath not where to lay his head, and with its intimation, perhaps, that in our mortal life neither the individual human creature, nor the big human family shall ever find a lasting home on the earth. Elements, weather, crop gambling, fate, Lady Luck, flit in the backgrounds. It is a paradoxical blend of moods: quickstep and dirge, hilarious defiance and bowed resignation.

Arr. H. F.

Lively with overtones of pathos

Oh, de boll wee-vil am a lit-tle black bug, Come from Mex-i-co, dey say, Come all de way to Tex-as jus' a-look-in' foh a place to stay, Jus' a-look-in' foh a

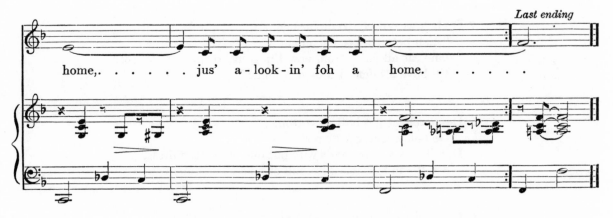

1 Oh, de boll weevil am a little black bug,
   Come from Mexico, dey say,
   Come all de way to Texas, jus' a-lookin' foh a place to stay,
   Jus' a-lookin' foh a home, jus' a-lookin' foh a home.

2 De first time I seen de boll weevil,
   He was a-settin' on de square.
   De next time I seen de boll weevil, he had all of his family dere.
   Jus' a-lookin' foh a home, jus' a-lookin' foh a home.

3 De farmer say to de weevil:
   "What make yo' head so red?"
   De weevil say to de farmer, "It's a wondah I ain't dead,
   A-lookin' foh a home, jus' a-lookin' foh a home."

4 De farmer take de boll weevil,
   An' he put him in de hot san'.
   De weevil say: "Dis is mighty hot, but I'll stan' it like a man,
   Dis'll be my home, it'll be my home."

5 De farmer take de boll weevil,
   An' he put him in a lump of ice;
   De boll weevil say to de farmer: "Dis is mighty cool and nice,
   It'll be my home, dis'll be my home."

6 De farmer take de boll weevil,
   An' he put him in de fire.
   De boll weevil say to de farmer: "Here I are, here I are,
   Dis'll be my home, dis'll be my home."

9

7 De boll weevil say to de farmer:
  "You better leave me alone;
I done eat all yo' cotton, now I'm goin' to start on yo' corn,
  I'll have a home, I'll have a home."

8 De merchant got half de cotton,
  De boll weevil got de res'.
Didn't leave de farmer's wife but one old cotton dress,
  An' it's full of holes, it's full of holes.

9 De farmer say to de merchant:
  "We's in an awful fix;
De boll weevil et all de cotton up an' lef' us only sticks,
  We's got no home, we's got no home."

10 De farmer say to de merchant:
  "We ain't made but only one bale,
And befoh we'll give yo' dat one we'll fight and go to jail,
  We'll have a home, we'll have a home."

11 De cap'n say to de missus:
  "What d' you t'ink o' dat?
De boll weevil done make a nes' in my bes' Sunday hat,
  Goin' to have a home, goin' to have a home."

12 An' if anybody should ax you
  Who it was dat make dis song,
Jus' tell 'em 'twas a big buck niggah wid a paih o' blue duckin's on,
  Ain' got no home, ain' got no home.

MOANISH LADY!

This offshoot of the spiritual, "Mourner, You Shall be Free," has been widely known for many years among barber shop harmonizers. The other stanzas of the barber shop version, however, are so lackadaisical that they don't do justice to the stately cadence of that solemn promise that when the good Lord shall call you home you shall be free. Any one requiring foolish verses for this air can easily improvise as silly ones as have been left out here. The music is too superbly serious to have cheap lines.

Arr. H. F. P.

I RIDE AN OLD PAINT

This arrangement is from a song made known by Margaret Larkin of Las Vegas, New Mexico, who intones her own poems or sings cowboy and Mexican songs to a skilled guitar strumming, and by Linn Riggs, poet and playwright, of Oklahoma in particular and the Southwest in general. The song came to them at Santa Fe from a buckaroo who was last heard of as heading for the Border with friends in both Tucson and El Paso. The song smells of saddle leather, sketches ponies and landscapes, and varies in theme from a realistic presentation of the drab Bill Jones and his violent wife to an ethereal prayer and a cry of phantom tone. There is rich poetry in the image of the rider so loving a horse he begs when he dies his bones shall be tied to his horse and the two of them sent wandering with their faces turned west.

Arr. H. F.

I ride an old Paint, I lead an old Dan, I'm goin' to Mon-tan' for to throw the hool-i-an. They feed in the cou-lees, they wa-ter in the draw, Their tails are all mat-ted, their backs are all raw. Ride a-round, lit-tle do-gies, Ride a-

I RIDE AN OLD PAINT

round them slow, For the fier - y and snuf - fy are a - rar - in' to go.

1 I ride an old Paint, I lead an old Dan,
   I'm goin' to Montan' for to throw the hoolian.
   They feed in the coulees, they water in the draw,
   Their tails are all matted, their backs are all raw.

      Ride around, little dogies,
      Ride around them slow,
      For the fiery and snuffy are a-rarin' to go.

2 Old Bill Jones had two daughters and a song,
   One went to Denver and the other went wrong.
   His wife she died in a poolroom fight,
   Still he sings from mornin' till night.

      Ride around, little dogies,
      Ride around them slow,
      For the fiery and snuffy are a-rarin' to go.

3 Oh, when I die, take my saddle from the wall,
   Put it on my pony, lead him out of his stall.
   Tie my bones to his back, turn our faces to the West,
   And we'll ride the prairie that we love the best.

      Ride around, little dogies,
      Ride around them slow,
      For the fiery and snuffy are a-rarin' to go.

FOGGY, FOGGY DEW

This arrangement is from a song rather widely known, which I heard first from Arthur Sutherland and his bold buccaneers at the Eclectic Club of Wesleyan University. A middle verse is censored from this version as being out of key and probably an interpolation. At least, it is what they call apocryphal and of the twilight zone. Observers as diverse as Sinclair Lewis, Sherwood Anderson, Arthur T. Vance and D. W. Griffith say this song is a great condensed novel of real life. After hearing it sung with a guitar at Schlogl's one evening in Chicago, D. W. Griffith telegraphed two days later from New York to Lloyd Lewis in Chicago, "Send verses Foggy Dew stop tune haunts me but am not sure of words stop please do this as I am haunted by the song."

FOGGY, FOGGY DEW

win - ter   time And in   the sum -mer,   too; . And the on - ly, on - ly thing   I

did   that was wrong Was   to keep her from the fog - gy, fog - gy   dew. . 2. Oh,

1 When I was a bach'lor, I lived by myself,
   I worked at the weaver's trade;
   The only, only thing I did that was wrong
   Was to woo a fair young maid.
   I wooed her in the winter-time
   And in the summer, too;
   And the only, only thing I did that was wrong,
   Was to keep her from the foggy, foggy dew.

2 Oh, I am a bach'lor, I live with my son;
   We work at the weaver's trade;
   And ev'ry single time I look into his eyes
   He reminds me of the fair young maid.
   He reminds me of the winter-time
   And of the summer too;
   And the many, many times that I held her in my arms,
   Just to keep her from the foggy, foggy dew.

WAILLIE, WAILLIE!

An arrangement of an old-time British piece as made known by Daniel Read and Isadora Bennett Read of Chicago, Illinois, and Columbia, South Carolina. Its stately diction might be compared to certain laced ladies and ruffled gentlemen imprisoned in fine porcelain works of England a century or two ago. It is a deep heart cry, too profound and prolonged to be called poignant, yet shaken with memory of passion.

Arr. H. J.

16

wail - lie, But love is bon - nie A lit - tle while When

it . . is new. But it grows old . . . . .

And wax-eth cold, ... And fades a - way like eve - ning dew.

When cockle shells turn silver bells,
Then will my love return to me.
When roses blow, in wintry snow,
Then will my love return to me.
Oh, waillie! waillie!
But love is bonnie
A little while when it is new!
But it grows old and waxeth cold,
And fades away like evening dew.

DIS MORNIN', DIS EVENIN', SO SOON

This arrangement is from the ballad as sung by Nancy Barnhart, painter and etcher, of St. Louis. It is a monotone of life in songtones of dusk colors and rhythms that emerge from shadows. The final verse is a scenario for a pantomime.

Arr. H. F.

Not too fast

Tell old Bill, when he leaves home dis morn-in', . Tell old Bill, when

he leaves home dis eve-nin', . Tell old Bill, when he leaves home, To

let dem down-town coons a-lone, Dis morn-in', dis eve-nin', so soon.

8va sotto

DIS MORNIN', DIS EVENIN', SO SOON

1 Tell old Bill, when he leaves home dis mornin',
Tell old Bill, when he leaves home dis evenin',
Tell old Bill, when he leaves home,
To let dem down-town coons alone
Dis mornin', dis evenin', so soon.

2 Bill left by de alley gate dis mornin',
Bill left by de alley gate dis evenin',
Bill left by de alley gate,
Old Sal says: Now don' be late,
Dis mornin', dis evenin', so soon.

3 Bill's wife was a bakin' bread dis mornin',
Bill's wife was a bakin' bread dis evenin',
Bill's wife was a bakin' bread,
When she got word dat Bill was dead
Dis mornin', dis evenin', so soon.

4 O dear, dat can't be so, dis mornin',
O dear, dat can't be so, dis evenin',
O dear, dat can't be so;
For Bill left home 'bout a hour ago,
Dis mornin', dis evenin', so soon.

5 O dear, dat cannot be, dis mornin',
O dear, dat cannot be, dis evenin',
O dear, dat cannot be,
Dey shoot my husband in de firs' degree,
Dis mornin', dis evenin', so soon.

6 Dey brought Bill home in a hurry-up wagon dis mornin',
Dey brought Bill home in a hurry-up wagon dis evenin,'
Dey brought Bill home in a hurry-up wagon,
Dey brought Bill home wid his toes a-draggin',
Dis mornin'. dis evenin', so soon.

OH, BURY ME NOT ON THE LONE PRAIRIE

This arrangement is from a song known to boys of the Crossroads Club at the University of Oregon. After a recital and reception there one evening three years ago, we held a song and story session lasting till five o'clock in the morning. Nearly all nations and the seven seas were represented. A contingent from the Black Hills of South Dakota sang this version of The Cowboy's Lament. They put their arms on each other's shoulders, stood in a circle, and cried the lines almost as a ritual from lonesome flat lands, the arms on each other's shoulders signifying that no matter how tough life might be they could meet it if they stood together. They pronounced "wind" with a long "i" as in "find" or "blind," and said the cowhands always sang it in that classical manner.

Arr. H. F.

1 Oh, bury me not on the lone prairie,
  Where the wild kiyotes will howl o'er me;
  Where the rattlesnakes hiss and the wind blows free,
  Oh, bury me not on the lone prairie!

2 They heeded not his dying prayer,
  They buried him there on the lone prairie,
  In a little box just six by three,
  His bones now rot on the lone prairie.

20

CARELESS LOVE

This poem, trying to ease heartbreak, uses the simplest of words. They go to a soft, brave melody. R. W. Gordon, from whose handsome collection this comes, says it reckons among authentic folk fabrics; he has heard it with slight variations in several southern regions. Its lyric cry is brief, poignant as Sappho. Its measures are close to silence and to art "to be overheard rather than heard."

Arr. A. G. W.

1 Love, oh love, oh careless love,
Love, oh love, oh careless love,
It's love, oh love, oh careless love,
You see what love has done for me.

2 Sorrow, sorrow, to my heart,
Sorrow, sorrow, to my heart,
Sorrow, sorrow, to my heart,
When me and my true love have to part.

3 It's a pity that we ever met,
It's a pity that we ever met,
It's a pity that we ever met,
For those good times we'll never forget.

4 Now my money's spent and gone,
Now my money's spent and gone,
Now my money's spent and gone,
You passed my door a-singing a song.

5 Oh I love my mama and my papa too,
Oh I love my mama and my papa too,
Oh I love my mama and my papa too,
But I'd leave them both and go with you.

6 Oh I cried last night and the night before,
Oh I cried last night and the night before,
Oh I cried last night and the night before,
Going to cry to-night and I'll cry no more.

7 Oh ain't it enough to break my heart,
Oh ain't it enough to break my heart,
Oh ain't it enough to break my heart,
To see my man with another sweetheart.

8 Oh it's done and broke this heart of mine,
Oh it's done and broke this heart of mine,
Oh it's done and broke this heart of mine,
And it'll break that heart of yours some time.

THE JOHN B. SAILS

John T. McCutcheon, cartoonist and kindly philosopher, and his wife Evelyn Shaw McCutcheon, mother and poet, learned to sing this on their Treasure Island in the West Indies. They tell of it, "Time and usage have given this song almost the dignity of a national anthem around Nassau. The weathered ribs of the historic craft lie imbedded in the sand at Governor's Harbor, whence an expedition, especially sent up for the purpose in 1926, extracted a knee of horseflesh and a ring-bolt. These relics are now preserved and built into the Watch Tower, designed by Mr. Howard Shaw and built on our southern coast a couple of points east by north of the star Canopus."

Arr. A. G. W.

Oh, we come on the sloop John B., My gran'-fad-der an' me.

Round Nas-sau Town we did roam, Drink-ing all night, we got in a

fight, I feel so break-up I want to go home!

REFRAIN

Poco f

So hoist up the *John B.* sails, See how de main - s'l set,

Send for de Capt'n a-shore, Lem-me go home! Lem-me go home! ..... Lem-me go

home! .... I feel so break-up I want to go home! .., ...

1 Oh, we come on the sloop *John B.*,
My gran'fadder an' me.
Round Nassau Town we did roam,
Drinking all night, we got in a fight,
I feel so break-up I want to go home!

REFRAIN

So hoist up the *John B.* sails,
See how de main-s'l set,
Send for de Capt'n ashore, Lemme go home!
Lemme go home! Lemme go home!
I feel so break-up I want to go home!

2 De first mate he got drunk,
Break up de people's trunk.
Constable come aboard an' take him away.
Mr. Johnstone, please let me alone.
I feel so break-up I want to go home! *Refrain*

3 De poor cook he got fits,
Tro' 'way all de grits,
Den he took an' eat up all o' my corn!
Lemme go home, I want to go home!
Dis is de worst trip since I been born! *Refrain*

23

JOHN HENRY

In southern work camp gangs, John Henry is the strong man, or the ridiculous man, or anyhow the man worth talking about, having a myth character somewhat like that of Paul Bunyan in work gangs of the Big Woods of the North. He is related to John Hardy, as balladry goes, but wears brighter bandannas. The harmonization is by Thorvald Otterstrom: it is massive in its pounding and evokes the atmosphere in which the powerful titan, John Henry, "does his stuff."

Arr. T. O.

John Hen-ry tol' his cap'-n' Dat a man wuz a na-tu-ral

man, An' be-fo' he'd let dat steam drill beat him down He'd fall dead

wid a ham-mer in his han', He'd fall dead wid a ham-mer in his han'.

24

JOHN HENRY

1 John Henry tol' his cap'n
  Dat a man wuz a natural man,
  An' befo' he'd let dat steam drill run him down,
  He'd fall dead wid a hammer in his han',
  He'd fall dead wid a hammer in his han'.

2 Cap'n he sez to John Henry:
  " Gonna bring me a steam drill 'round;
  Take that steel drill out on the job,
  Gonna whop that steel on down,
  Gonna whop that steel on down."

3 John Henry sez to his cap'n:
  " Send me a twelve-poun' hammer aroun',
  A twelve-poun' hammer wid a fo'-foot handle,
  An' I beat yo' steam drill down,
  An' I beat yo' steam drill down."

4 John Henry sez to his shaker:
  " Niggah, why don' yo' sing?
  I'm throwin' twelve poun' from my hips on
    down,
  Jes' lissen to de col' steel ring,
  Jes' lissen to de col' steel ring! "

5 John Henry went down de railroad
  Wid a twelve-poun' hammer by his side,
  He walked down de track but he didn' come
    back,
  'Cause he laid down his hammer an' he died,
  'Cause he laid down his hammer an' he died.

6 John Henry hammered in de mountains,
  De mountains wuz so high.
  De las' words I heard de pore boy say:
  " Gimme a cool drink o' watah fo' I die,
  Gimme a cool drink o' watah fo' I die! "

7 John Henry had a little baby,
  Hel' him in de palm of his han'.
  De las' words I heard de pore boy say:
  " Son, yo're gonna be a steel-drivin' man,
  Son, yo're gonna be a steel-drivin' man! "

8 John Henry had a 'ooman,
  De dress she wo' wuz blue.
  De las' words I heard de pore gal say:
  " John Henry, I ben true to yo',
  John Henry, I ben true to yo'."

9 John Henry had a li'l 'ooman,
  De dress she wo' wuz brown.
  De las' words I heard de pore gal say:
  " I'm goin' w'eah mah man went down,
  I'm goin' w'eah mah man went down! "

10 John Henry had anothah 'ooman,
  De dress she wo' wuz red.
  De las' words I heard de pore gal say:
  " I'm goin' w'eah mah man drapt daid,
  I'm goin' w'eah mah man drapt daid! "

11 John Henry had a li'l 'ooman,
  Her name wuz Polly Ann.
  On de day John Henry he drap daid
  Polly Ann hammered steel like a man,
  Polly Ann hammered steel like a man.

12 W'eah did yo' git dat dress!
  W'eah did you git dose shoes so fine?
  Got dat dress f'm off a railroad man,
  An' shoes f'm a driver in a mine,
  An' shoes f'm a driver in a mine.

MIDNIGHT SPECIAL

This arrangement is from the song as rendered by midnight prowlers in Dallas and Fort Worth, Texas. It is impressionistic in style, delivering the substance of two lives in brief array. We see the man behind the bars looking out toward Roberta, who carries a document given her by some politician or precinct worker. The warden tells her, probably, the day is not Visitor's Day. As her man considers that he has twenty years yet to serve, he cries out that he would rather be under the wheels of a fast midnight train.

Arr. H. J.

Yon - der come Ro - ber - ta! . . Tell me how do you know? . . .

. . By de col - or of her a - pron . . an' de dress she wo'.

Um - ber - el - la on her shoul - der, . . . piece o' pa - per in her han', ...

Yonder come Roberta!   Tell me how do you know?
By de color ob her apron and de dress she wo'.
　　Umberella on her shoulder, piece o' paper in her han',
　　She says to de cap'n:　" I want my man!"
Let de Midnight Special shine a light on me,
Oh twenty long years in de pen-i-ten-tiar-y!

ALICE B.

This is arranged from the ballad as sung by Arthur Sutherland and the buccaneers of the Eclectic Club of Wesleyan University. Sutherland, who is the son of a lawyer in Rochester, New York, first heard of Alice B. when he was with the American Relief Expedition in Armenia, riding on top of a box car to Constantinople with a friend who came from New Orleans, Louisiana, and who in that gulf port one day paid $1.50 to a hobo to sing Alice B. as he, the hobo, had just heard it a few days previously in Memphis from a negro just arriving from Galveston, Texas. This is as far back as we have to date traced the Alice B. ballad. Though the verses have wicked and violent events for a theme, they point a moral and adorn a tale in their conclusion. In a sense it is propaganda in favor of the Volstead Act.

Arr. A. G. W.

Oh I'm goin' out West, . . down on the Ri - o Grande, Sing -in'

fare-thee, O my hon-ey, O my hon-ey, fare -thee-well! I'm goin' out West, . down

on the Ri - o Grande, And it's fare-thee, O my hon - ey, fare - thee-well!

ALICE B.

1 I'm goin' out West, down on the Rio Grande,
   Singin' fare-thee, O my honey, O my honey, fare-thee-well!
   I'm goin' out West, down on the Rio Grande,
   And it's fare-thee, O my honey, fare-thee-well!

2 The twenty-fifth of September, Martin F. a man tall and slender,
   He was the man who committed that most terrible deed.
   On a Sunday morning, with hardly any warning,
   He shot and killed his high-brown Alice B.

3 Martin F. was a coward, he run, O how he did run!
   In his hand he carried a smokin' forty-one;
   He ran up to de co't, says: " Judge, I committed that terrible crime,
   And now I'm ready for to serve my ninety-and-nine."

4 Alice B. like a baby lay on her dyin' bed.
   She says: " Mammy, I want you to take care of my little girl.
   Keep her feet from slippin' through, 'cause I love her, 'deed I do,
   An' I hopes to meet her in that other worl'."

5 De judge held co't de very next day;
   Martin F. refused, absolutely refused, to testify.
   He says: " Judge, I killed my baby, my Alice B.,
   And now that I killed her I'm all ready to die."

6 " She was a good woman, an' I loved her, 'deed I did.
   We had such good times, together all the time;
   Till one night I went out, got filled with nigger gin,
   An' when I saw her I completely los' my min'."

7 Then come all you rounders, an' all you high-browns too,
   Take heed to what dis man has done.
   You may go out some night, get filled with squirrel rum,
   An' do the very same thing that Martin has done.

8 Then I'm goin' out West, down on the Rio Grande,
   Singin' fare-thee, O my honey, O my honey, fare-thee-well!
   I'm goin' out West, down on the Rio Grande,
   Singin' fare-thee, O my honey, fare-thee-well!

PO' BOY

Po' Boy is a jail song in Oklahoma and Texas. It is also heard among post-graduates from jail in the federal penitentiary at Leavenworth, Kansas. We are left to infer that if the "po' boy" had made a safe getaway after taking a bag of mail from the baggage car, the woman in the case would not have run away with another man but would have stayed with him to enjoy the loot. The lilt of the song is almost gay throughout except for the steady beat of the mournful, melodious vocables of "po' boy." The "Katy" train is a reference to the Missouri, Kansas & Texas, or "K.T." railway. Of course, though this is a jail song, it is sung by many who are free and "outside."

Arr. L. R. G.

My mam-my's in the cold, cold ground; My dad-dy went a - way; My . sis - ter mar-ried a . . gam - blin' man; And now I've gone a - stray. . . . I sit here in the pris - on; I do the best I can; But I get to think-in' of the

wom - an I love; She ran a - way with an-oth - er man. . . . .

Chorus

She ran a - way with an-oth - er man, po' boy, She ran a - way with an-oth - er

man; I get to think-in' of the wom - an I love .

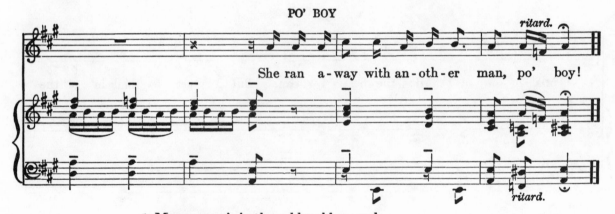

She ran a-way with an-oth-er man, po' boy!

1 My mammy's in the cold, cold ground;
My daddy went away;
My sister married a gamblin' man;
And now I've gone astray.
I sit here in the prison;
I do the best I can;
But I get to thinkin' of the woman I love;
She ran away with another man.

Chorus: She ran away with another man, po' boy,
She ran away with another man.
I get to thinkin' of the woman I love;
She ran away with another man.

2 Away out on the prairie,
I stopped that Katy train;
I took the mail from the baggage car;
And walked away in the rain.
They got the bloodhounds on me,
And chased me up a tree;
And then they said, " Come down, my boy,
And go to the penitentiaree."

Chorus: She ran away with another man, po' boy, **etc.**

3 " Oh, mister judge, oh, mister judge,
What are you going to do to me? "
" If the jury finds you guilty, my boy,
I'm going to send you to the penitentiaree."
They took me to the railroad station;
A train came rolling by;
I looked in the window, saw the woman I love;
Hung down my head and cried.

Chorus: Hung down my head in shame, po' boy,
Hung down my head and cried;
I looked in the window, saw the woman I love,
Hung down my head and cried, po' boy!

THE OULD SOD

AS I WAS WALKIN' DOWN WEXFORD STREET

This should be sung easily and casually to begin with, but in the end it is a Celtic "crying out loud." The mood or tone seems to be of that important Irish drama, "The White Headed Boy," where there is trouble for everybody with nobody to blame, or all at fault. This lilt, too, is from Mother McKinley, formerly of McKinley, Iowa, and later of Chicago.

Arr. L. R. G.

As I was walkin' down Wex-ford Street Me fa-ther's house I chanc't to meet; Me a-ged fa-ther stood in the dure, An' me sis-ter stood on the flure, . . While me ten-der moth-er her hair she ture.

As I was walkin' down Wexford Street
Me father's house I chanc't to meet;
Me aged father stood in the dure,
An' me sister stood on the flure,
While me tender mother her hair she ture.

35

SH–TA–RA–DAH–DEY

(IRISH LULLABY)

This little croon is an impromptu, made up in some hour when a man or woman holding a baby, or rocking a cradle, needed hushing words for a hushing tune. Of course, the statistical information that a dollar a day is all they pay for work on the boulevard does not interest a sleepy child, but as crooned by Robert E. Lee, of the *Chicago Tribune*, the word "boul-e-vard" has comforting and soothing quality. Lee heard the song from an Irishman in charge of the railroad station at Wallingford, Iowa. While selling passenger tickets, or making out way-bills, or figuring freight demurrage, or hustling trunks off and on baggage cars, or piling crates of eggs, "the agent" would ease his heart with this lullaby.

Arr. E. C.

36

dol - lar a day is all they pay For work on the boul - e - vard.

senza cresc.

Sh - ta - ra - dah - dey, sh - ta - dey, Times is might - y hard, . . A

ppp

dol - lar a day is all they pay For work on the boul - e - vard. . . . .

Sh-ta-ra-dah-dey, sh-ta-dey,
Times is mighty hard.
A dollar a day is all they pay
For work on the boulevard.
Sh-ta-ra-dah-dey, sh-ta-dey,
Times is mighty hard.
A dollar a day is all they pay
For work on the boulevard.
Sh-ta-ra-dah-dey, sh-ta-dey,
Times is mighty hard.
A dollar a day is all they pay
For work on the boulevard.

37

SHE SAID THE SAME TO ME

A briefly etched love story is here, with only a first chapter, leaving the middle and ending chapters untold. There may be other verses telling of marriage and children, or of fate that ran otherwise. It is a true Irish lilt, and was sung by folks from the Ould Sod who settled in Iowa. This version is from Mother McKinley of the family from whom the town of McKinley, Iowa, was named.

Arr. A. G. W.

'Twas in the month of Au-gust, . or the mid-dle of Ju - ly, . . One

eve - ning I went walk-ing, . . a fair maid-en I did spy; . . She was

melanconico

mourn-in' for her true love, who was in A - mer - i - kee, . . . Agh,

38

div - il   a word   I   said   to   her, and   she   said   the   same   to   me! . .

'Twas in the month of August, or the middle of July,
One evening I went walking, a fair maiden I did spy;
She was mournin' for her true love, who was in Amerikee,
Agh, divil a word I said to her, and she said the same to me!

WHO'S THE PRETTY GIRL MILKIN' THE COW?

The fragment here is probably a make-over, a distillation, from an Irish song of lesser grace and melody. Bob Lee sang this for me, but wasn't sure he had the words right; he would see the traffic policeman, Tom Burke, and be sure; and Burke said, "Why should ye be wantin' that little song? It's old. Everybody knows it."

Arr. A. G. W.

O 'twas on a bright mornin' in summer
When I first heard her voice singin' low
As he said to a colleen beside him:
"Who's the pretty girl milkin' the cow?"

40

GIVE ME THREE GRAINS OF CORN, MOTHER

Sometimes it happens that a maudlin, drivelling song published elaborately as sheet music undergoes a transformation. It mellows and sweetens as it is passed on and sung in new ways. Harsh contours are worn down, jagged edges smoothed. This is the case with "Three Grains of Corn." I have an 1848 original of the sheet music; it is long; it prolongs desolation beyond endurance or healthy art. The latter quality is not found in the variants known among midwest pioneers. Of several versions, the most appealing to me is one from the Franz Rickaby collection, communicated by Mrs. C. A. Yoder of Bloomington, Indiana. I have gone to this song in certain moods and found it sickly with melancholy, not worth singing. Again, in other moods, I have gone to it and found it a gaunt little human drama with a melody carrying some of the tone color of dark, vivid Irish hearts.

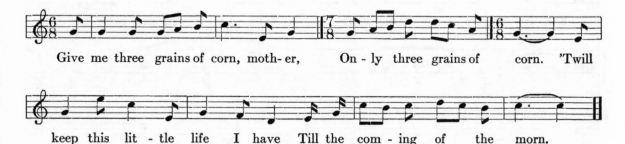

Give me three grains of corn, moth-er, On-ly three grains of corn. 'Twill keep this lit-tle life I have Till the com-ing of the morn.

1 Give me three grains of corn, mother
Only three grains of corn.
'Twill keep what little life I have
Till the coming of the morn.

2 For I'm dying of hunger and cold, mother
Dying of hunger and cold,
And the agony of such a death
My lips have never told.

3 Oh, what has old Ireland done, mother,
Oh, what has old Ireland done,
That the world looks on and sees them starve,
Perishing one by one?

4 There is many a brave heart, mother,
That is dying of hunger and cold,
While only across the channel, mother,
Thousands are rolling their gold.

5 Oh, how can I look to you, mother,
Oh, how can I look to you
For bread to feed your starving child
When you are starving too?

6 For I read the famine on your cheek
And in your eyes so wild,
And I felt it in your bony hand
When you laid it on your child.

7 It has gnawed like a wolf at my heart, mother,
A wolf that was fierce for blood,
All the livelong day and the night beside,
Gnawing for lack of food.

8 I dreamed of bread in my sleep, mother,
The sight was heaven to see.
I awoke with an eager and famishing lip
And you had no bread for me.

KEVIN BARRY

Tongues of love and hate, breaths of passion and suffering, all mingled with a strange bitter-sweet, are in this song out of the violent events in Ireland. Probably all wars and revolutions produce figures like Kevin Barry, though seldom do they have such adequate songs as memorials. In Nashville, Tennessee, one may look at the statue of Sam Davis, who died refusing to turn informer and thus save his life. Davis has a statue in bronze; Kevin Barry has a song. These verses and their wistful, longing melody are from Irish boys and girls in Chicago who learned the ballad on the Ould Sod.

Arr. M. N.

Ear - ly   on   a Mon - day morn - ing, High up - on   the gal - lows tree,

Kev - in Bar - ry gave his young life   For the cause   of lib - er - ty.

1 Early on a Monday morning,
  High upon the gallows tree,
  Kevin Barry gave his young life
  For the cause of liberty.

2 Only a lad of eighteen summers,
  Still there's no one can deny,
  As he walked to death that morning
  Nobly held his head up high.

3 Another martyr for old Ireland,
  Another murder for the crown,
  Brutal laws to crush the Irish
  Could not keep their spirits down.

42

4 Lads like Barry are no cowards.
  From their foes they do not fly;
  For their bravery always has been
  Ireland's cause to live or die.

5 "Kevin Barry, do not leave us,
  On the scaffold you must die!"
  Cried his broken-hearted mother
  As she bade her son good-bye.

6 Kevin turned to her in silence
  Saying, "Mother, do not weep,
  For it's all for dear old Ireland
  And it's all for freedom's sake."

7 Just before he faced the hangman
  In his lonely prison cell,
  The Black and Tans tortured Barry,
  Just because he wouldn't tell

8 The names of his brave comrades,
  And other things they wished to know.
  "Turn informer and we'll free you."
  But Kevin proudly answered "No!

9 "Shoot me like a soldier.
  Do not hang me like a dog,
  For I fought to free old Ireland
  On that still September morn.

10 "All around the little bakery
   Where we fought them hand to hand,
   Shoot me like a brave soldier,
   For I fought for Ireland."

THE SON OF A GAMBOLIER

Misery with a light-hearted lilt . . . . a far-flung companion of roving men.

I'm a ram-bling wretch of pov - er - ty, from Tip - 'ry town I came. 'Twas
Refrain: Then com-bine your hum-ble dit - ties as from tav-ern to tav-ern we steer; Like

po - ver - ty com-pelled me first to go out in the rain; In all sorts of
ev - e - ry hon - est fel-low, I drinks my la - ger beer; Like ev - 'ry hon-

wea - ther, be it wet or be it dry, I am bound to get my live - li- hood, or
est fel - low, I takes my whis-key clear, I'm a ram-bling wretch of pov er - ty, and the

D.C. REFRAIN *(Conclusion of* REFRAIN*)*

lay me down and die.
son of a gam-bo-lier. I'm a son of a, son of a, son of a, son of a, son of a gam-bo - lier.

1 I'm a rambling wretch of poverty, from Tip'ry town I came.
   'Twas poverty compelled me first to go out in the rain;
   In all sorts of weather, be it wet or be it dry,
   I am bound to get my livelihood or lay me down and die.

   Refrain:
      Then combine your humble ditties as from tavern to tavern we steer;
      Like every honest fellow, I drinks my lager beer;
      Like every jolly fellow, I takes my whiskey clear,
      I'm a rambling wretch of poverty, and the son of a gambolier —
      I'm the son of a, son of a, son of a, son of a, son of a gambolier.

2 I once was tall and handsome, and was so very neat;
   They thought I was too good to live, most good enough to eat;
   But now I'm old my coat is torn, and poverty holds me fast.
   And every girl turns up her nose as I go wandering past.
   Refrain:

3 I'm a rambling wretch of poverty, from Tip'ry town I came;
   My coat I bought from an old Jew shop way down in Maiden Lane;
   My hat I got from a sailor lad just eighteen years ago,
   And my shoes I picked from an old dust heap, which every one shunned but me!
   Refrain:

MINSTREL SONGS

I WISH I WAS SINGLE AGAIN

A lawyer with a larger divorce practice than he can handle conveniently tells us that half the time when divorced men marry again they pick the same kind of a wrong woman a second time. However that may be today, it seems that the minstrels of a generation past won wide popular success with a song voicing the troubles of a man who made the same mistake twice. The ditty spread to mountains and prairies. The version here is one that Edwin Ford Piper heard in Nebraska when a boy.

Arr. H. G.

1. When I was sin - gle, O then, O then, When I was sin - gle, O then, When I was sin - gle, my mon - ey did jin - gle, I wish I was sin - gle a - gain, a - gain, And I wish I was sin - gle a - gain. . .

1 When I was single, O then, O then,
When I was single, O then,
When I was single, my money did jingle,
I wish I was single again, again,
And I wish I was single again.

2 I married me a wife, O then, O then,
I married me a wife, O then,
I married me a wife, she's the plague of my life
And I wish I was single again, again,
And I wish I was single again.

3 My wife she died, O then, O then,
My wife she died, O then,
My wife she died, and then I cried,
To think I was single again, again,
To think I was single again.

4 I married another, the devil's grandmother,
I wish I was single again,
For when I was single, my money did jingle,
I wish I was single again, again,
I wish I was single again.

47

WALKY–TALKY JENNY

This has the saunter and the swagger of the southern mountaineers when they are having a luminous good time. Its style is comic rather than humorous; it has dangerous moods; its eyes have odd twinkles from under the hat brim; it says to the city slicker, "You all better looka out, we might be tellin' you to not let the sun go down on you hereabouts." This version of "Walky-Talky Jenny" came from H. Luke Stancil of Pickens County, Georgia. He wrote the verses and monologues on the porch of the Holden home in Athens, Georgia, a house which is the residence of a niece and grandniece of Alexander Stephens. Long ago, perhaps before the Civil War, a minstrel troupe played one-night stands in the valley towns, performed with this song, and it was picked up by the mountaineers and made into what we have here. The mingling of comic bucolic monologue with song lines and chorus was a minstrel feature.

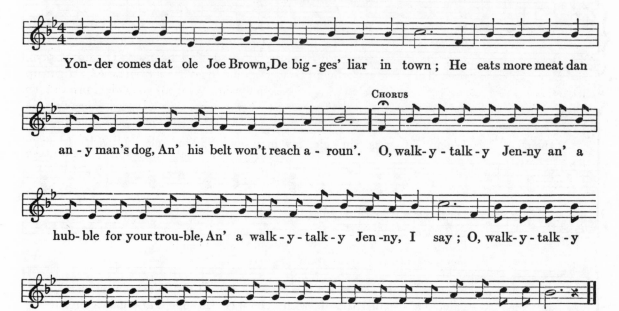

Yon- der comes dat ole Joe Brown, De big - ges' liar in town; He eats more meat dan an - y man's dog, An' his belt won't reach a - roun'. O, walk- y - talk - y Jen-ny an' a hub- ble for your trou-ble, An' a walk - y - talk - y Jen -ny, I say; O, walk- y - talk - y Jen -ny an' a hub-ble for your trou-ble, I'm a nig - ger from de state of Al - a- bam!

Yonder comes dat ole Joe Brown,
De bigges' liar in town;
He eats more meat dan any man's dog,
An' his belt won' reach aroun'.

Sing Chorus
O, walky-talky Jenny an' a hubble for your trouble,
An' a walky-talky Jenny, I say;
O, walky-talky Jenny an' a hubble for your trouble,
I'm a nigger from de state of Alabam!

I went down de road de udder day, I did, I did, so I did. When I got down dere I seed an ole man settin' on de bank o' de road, an' I says, "Hey! ole man, what time is it?" He said, "'Bout one o'clock," an' about dat time he knocked me down twice 'fore I could get up once. I said, "Ole man, I sho' would hate to pass yo' house 'bout twelve o'clock. If you eber do cross my path agin I'm gwine-a make you . . ."

Sing Chorus
O, walky-talky Jenny an' a hubble for your trouble,
An' a walky-talky Jenny, I say;
O, walky-talky Jenny an' a hubble for your trouble,
I'm a nigger from de state of Alabam!

I went on down de road a little fudder, I did, I did, so I did. I got down dere an' I seed a great big fine house afire. Dat house sho' was a-burnin' up. I got up a little closer an' seed somebody settin' up on top o' dat air house. I got up a little closer an' seed it was ole Aunt Dinah. I says, "Ole gal, yo' sho' am in a mell of a hess. I wonder how yo' gwine to git down from dere." I got up a little closer an' stuck a plank up to de side o' de house an' said, "Ole gal, yo' slide down dat air plank!" Here she come, a-slidin' down into my arms. When she got down dere, she made a face at me. I says, "Ole gal, what am de matter wid you?" She says, "I don' know, mister, dere musta been a little nail in dat air plank, mighta scratched me a little as I come down." I says, "Ole gal, yo' de bigges' fool I eber did see. If you eber do cross my path agin, I'm gwine-a make you . . ."

Sing Chorus
O, walky-talky Jenny an' a hubble for your trouble,
An' a walky-talky Jenny, I say;
O, walky-talky Jenny an' a hubble for your trouble,
I'm a nigger from de state of Alabam!

I went on down de road a little fudder, I did, I did, so I did. I went down in my corn patch to see how my field was a-growin'. I got down dere an' along come a punkin runnin' along, an' he picked up a calf in his mouth an' trotted off wid it. I went back to de house an' dere stood my baby in de door wid my wife in her arms. I stood dere a few minutes an' here come a little ole bark around de house a-doggin'. I put my pocket down in my hand, pulled out my tail an' cut his knife off. "Ole dog, if you eber do cross my path agin, I'm gwine-a make you . . ."

Sing Chorus
O, walky-talky Jenny an' a hubble for your trouble,
An' a walky-talky Jenny, I say;
O, walky-talky Jenny an' a hubble for your trouble,
I'm a nigger from de state of Alabam!

49

HAYSEED

The minstrels always enjoyed giving their audiences songs about the accidents and calamities that country people met with in the large cities.   Out of many songs having to do with the ignorant ones who blew out the gas, and the adventures of "hayseeds" in the big city, we present one with a don't-care tune.   It is communicated by Mrs. William Pitt Abbott of Duluth, Minnesota.

Arr. A. G. W.

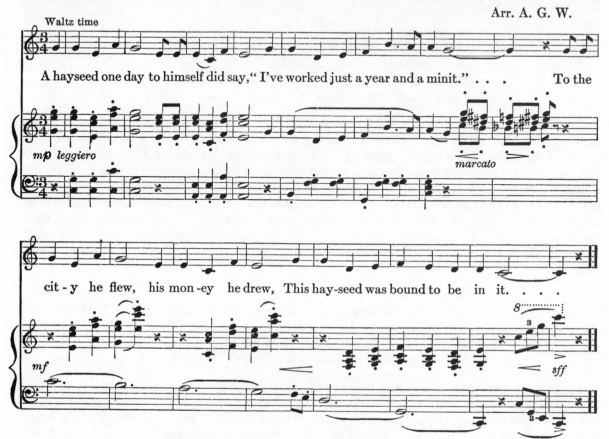

A hayseed one day to himself did say," I've worked just a year and a minit." . . .   To the

cit-y he flew, his mon-ey he drew, This hay-seed was bound to be in it. . . .

1 A hayseed one day to himself did say,
  " I've worked just a year and a minit."
  To the city he flew, his money he drew,
  This hayseed was bound to be in it.

2 He went to a hotel, he engaged him a room;
  It cost him five dollars a minit.
  But he did not care, he had money to spare;
  This hayseed was bound to be in it.

3 He went to his room, he blew out the gas,
  He pulled down the bed and got in it.
  Next morning at nine, in a coffin of pine
  This hayseed was strictly dead in it.

GOOD-BY LIZA JANE

When the Rutledge & Rogers mammoth and mastodonic circus travelled the mid-west many years ago, this minstrel song was on the program of its concerts. We give it here from the recollection of C. W. Loutzenhiser of Chicago, who was a boy at the time. The drollery and the mathematics of the nonsense here will stand comparison with some of the best in "Alice in Wonderland." Also, with some of the worst in "Hostetter's Almanac."

Arr. A. G. W.

Our horse fell down the well a-round be-hind the sta-ble, Well he did-n't fall clear down but he fell, fell, fell, fell, fell, fell, As far as he was a-ble. Oh! it's good-by Li-za Jane.

1 Our horse fell down the well around behind the stable,
Our horse fell down the well around behind the stable,
Well he didn't fall clear down but he fell, fell, fell, fell, fell, fell,
As far as he was able. Oh! it's good-by Liza Jane.

2 Our goose swallowed a snail, and his eyes stuck out with wonder,
Our goose swallowed a snail, and his eyes stuck out with wonder,
For the horns grew through his tail, tail, tail, tail, tail, tail,
And bust it all asunder. Oh! it's good-by Liza Jane.

3 My gal crossed the bridge, so she wouldn't get her feet wet,
My gal crossed the bridge, so she wouldn't get her feet wet,
Well she didn't cross the bridge, but she would, would, would, would, would, would,
But the bridge it wasn't built yet. Oh! it's good-by Liza Jane.

WIZARD OIL

Earlier than 1880 patent medicine men and their wagons were traveling. Kickápoo Indian Sagwa as a spring tonic and Kickapoo Snake Oil for rheumatism and neuralgia were bespoken and proclaimed by dancing and shouting Indians. The Wizard Oil remedies had their merits sung by slick-tongued comedians with banjos. Flaring gasoline lamps lighted their faces as the throngs surged about listening to the promises made to the sick, lame, sore. Harry E. Randall of San Diego, California, heard the Wizard Oil mountebanks in Illinois in the late 1870's, and the following is a text and air communicated through Neeta Marquis of Los Angeles, California.

Arr. H. F. P.

Like a big city slicker

Oh! I love to trav - el far and near through-out my na -tive land;

I love to sell as I go 'long, and take the cash in hand.

I love to cure all in dis - tress that hap - pen in my way,

52

And you bet-ter be-lieve I feel quite fine when folks rush up and say:

"I'll take an-oth-er bot-tle of Wiz-ard . Oil, I'll take an-oth-er bot-tle or

two; I'll take an-oth-er bottle of Wiz-ard Oil, I'll take anoth-er bottle or two."

Oh! I love to travel far and near throughout my native land;
I love to sell as I go 'long, and take the cash in hand.
I love to cure all in distress that happen in my way,
And you better believe I feel quite fine when folks rush up and say:

Chorus:

> "I'll take another bottle of Wizard Oil,
> I'll take another bottle or two;
> I'll take another bottle of Wizard Oil,
> I'll take another bottle or two."

Now, listen to what I'm going to say, and don't you think I'm jesting
When I tell you for your aches and pains that Wizard Oil's the best thing.
It's healing and it's soothing, it's refreshing and it's thriving,
The proof of which, wherever it's sold the people all are thriving.

Spoken:

That's so! Wherever Wizard Oil is used, the people always thrive. I never get up
to sell the second time in a town but I'm interrupted by the sweet silvery voice of a
young lady or the sonorous tones of a gentleman. They rush up to me with a half-
dollar in their hands and soon I hear their sweet exclamations, which sound very
much like:

"I'll take another bottle of Wizard Oil,
I'll take another bottle or two!
I'll take another bottle of Wizard Oil,
I'll take another bottle or two!"

Once while selling 'way out West in the State of Illinois,
The people all came running up to see what made the noise.
The merchants laughed in their counting rooms, the farmers laughed a-hoeing.
Amongst the rest a Dutchman came, a-puffing and a-blowing.

Spoken:

"Mein Gottin Himmel, vot a country und vot a peoples! Stab me in the back mit a
double-barrelled bootjack, he's the same man I saw in Chicago last week! I buys von
bottle of oil of him, I takes him home, und py dam, he's good stuff! So . . .

"I'll take another bottle of Wizard Oil,
I'll take another bottle or two!
I'll take another bottle of Wizard Oil,
I'll take another bottle or two!"

Soon after this a lady came up, just fresh from the Em'rald Isle.
Says she, "Mister, if you will, I'll spake wid you a while!"
Says I, "Certainly, madam, don't be afraid. Let's hear what you have to say.
Are you sick, or lame, or going blind, or what's the matter, I pray?"

Spoken:

"No, no, it's me husband, bad luck to the lazy divil! Divil the bit of work has he
done for the past six months. He lies in bed till ten in the mornin', and I think your
oil a profitable quality to pull the lazy divil out of bed. So . . .

"I'll take another bottle of Wizard Oil,
I'll take another bottle or two!
I'll take another bottle of Wizard Oil,
I'll take another bottle or two!"

TARNISHED LOVE TALES or COLONIAL AND REVOLUTIONARY ANTIQUES

It may be considered remarkable, that it was not till English literature had reached its highest point of refinement—it was not until the days of Addison and Pope, or, still later, of Gray and Goldsmith—that the rude ballad poetry of the people became an object of interest to the learned. In the *Spectator*, Addison first drew the attention of what was then called the "polite world" to the merits of the ballad of Chevy-Chase; but he did so in the apologetic strain of one who was fully prepared for the said world being surprised at him taking under his protection anything so vulgar, or even humble. He introduces the ballad much in the manner that the fastidious yet generous Guy Mannering may be supposed to have introduced to his lettered friends the hearty borderer, Dandie Dinmont, with his spattered jack-boots and shaggy drednought:—there was no denying the rough and startling exterior, but many excellent qualities were to be found under it. Up to this time, the traditionary ballads of the country were held to be of so rude a character as to be scarcely amenable to the rules of literary criticism; no historical value seems to have been attached to them; and with the exception of some plodding Pepys, who, for his own gratification, stitched and preserved his "Penny Garlands," no endeavor was made to rescue them from the perishable breath of oral tradition, or the fragile security of the pedlar's broadside.

ALEXANDER WHITELAW in *Book of Scottish Ballads*.

The handing on of songs by oral tradition has become more and more curtailed. It is far from extinct, and it is not to be expected that it will ever completely die out from the human race; but with the spread of literacy, the increasing circulation of printed matter, the introduction of phonographs, and the removal of old-time isolation, through the agency of railroads, automobiles, and (in these days) of airplanes, the singing of traditional songs plays a lessened role.

American folk-song as a whole has been imported from the Old World. This is becoming less true, but it still holds. Folk-songs are still brought across the Atlantic by newcomers; and a large percentage of the most striking and persistent pieces current in America are derived from Old World originals, English, Scottish, or Irish. Many survive which were brought over long ago, or they enter in new form with some shipload of immigrants. Songs recently imported still win foothold and then wander from community to community.

LOUISE POUND in *American Songs and Ballads*.

BARBRA ALLEN

Hard-hearted Barbra Allen is a girl who figures in hundreds of ballads. In nearly all of them Willie dies for love of her and she, with a wasted heart, goes into the grave beside him. That is the story. But the last verse has a sequel. The rose rises from one grave, the briar from the other; the two climb to the top of the old church tower and there intertwine. So ends the story. It has been told and sung in hundreds of dialects. Usually the tune is stale, flat, monotonous. The one given here has long been a favorite of mine and the friend who gave it to me, H. L. Davis, the Oregon poet who came from the mountains of Georgia. The text is from the R. W. Gordon collection. Sometimes, in the singing of this song, I get the feel of old, gnarled, thornapple trees and white crab-apple blossoms printed momentarily on a blue sky, of evanescent things, of the paradox of tender and cruel forces operating together in life. Perhaps something of that paradox working in the hearts of people has kept the Barbra Allen story alive and singing through three centuries and more.

In Lon-don Cit-y where I once did dwell, there's where I got my learn-ing, I fell in love with a pret-ty young girl, Her name was Bar-bra Al-len.

1 In London City where I once did dwell, there's where I got my learning,
  I fell in love with a pretty young girl, her name was Barbra Allen.

2 I courted her for seven long years, she said she would not have me;
  Then straightway home as I could go and liken to a dying.

3 I wrote her a letter on my death bed, I wrote it slow and moving;
  "Go take this letter to my old true love and tell her I am dying."

4 She took the letter in her lily-white hand, she read it slow and moving;
  "Go take this letter back to him, and tell him I am coming."

5 As she passed by his dying bed she saw his pale lips quivering;
  "No better, no better I'll ever be until I get Barbra Allen."

6 As she passed by his dying bed; "You're very sick and almost dying,
  No better, no better you will ever be, for you can't get Barbra Allen."

7 As she went down the long stair steps she heard the death bell toning,
  And every bell appeared to say, "Hard-hearted Barbra Allen!"

8 As she went down the long piney walk she heard some small birds singing,
  And every bird appeared to say, "Hard-hearted Barbra Allen!"

9 She looked to the East, she looked to the West, she saw the pale corpse coming
  "Go bring them pale corpse unto me, and let me gaze upon them.

10 Oh, mama, mama, go make my bed, go make it soft and narrow!
   Sweet Willie died today for me, I'll die for him tomorrow!"

11 They buried Sweet Willie in the old church yard, they buried Miss Barbra beside him;
   And out of his grave there sprang a red rose, and out of hers a briar.

12 They grew to the top of the old church tower, they could not grow any higher,
   They hooked, they tied in a true love's knot, red rose around the briar.

THE FROZEN GIRL

An old ballad is often like an old silver dagger or an old brass pistol; it is rusty, or greenish; it is ominous with ancient fates still operating today. Thus with Charlotte, who was worth looking at, who was very fair, who "laughed like a gypsy queen," we are told. The tarnished tale of her love and death on a winter night is to be found in the balladry of all the peoples of northern Europe. As a ballad it was born where nights are bitter cold in the hard winters. It is a puppet play, told instead of acted, but told in an easy narrative tune. The dramatic players are three: (1) Charlottie, the heroine who dies; (2) Charles, who loves her; (3) the ruthless, icy weather. In America this is among ballads known in all the areas into which the English settlers spread; it is of mountain and prairie. The text here is from Isadora Bennett Read as heard in an isolated mountain region of Georgia; the tune is from Dr. James Lattimore Himrod of Chicago, author of "Johnny Appleseed," who as a boy in southern Indiana heard his mother sing of "the frozen girl." Here and elsewhere it may be noted, the mountain people take priveleges with the King's English, especially in moments of stress and distress. At that "monoment" may be a dramatic vocable as good as "monument."

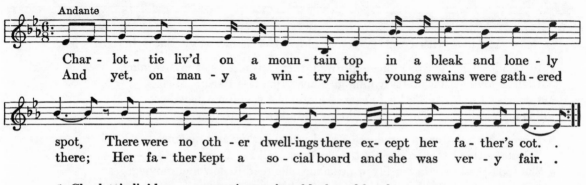

Char - lot - tie liv'd on a moun - tain top in a bleak and lone - ly
And yet, on man - y a win - try night, young swains were gath - ered

spot, There were no oth - er dwell-ings there ex - cept her fa - ther's cot. .
there; Her fa - ther kept a so - cial board and she was ver - y fair. .

1 Charlottie liv'd on a mountain top in a bleak and lonely spot,
There were no other dwellings there except her father's cot.
And yet, on many a wintry night, young swains were gathered there;
Her father kept a social board and she was very fair.

2 On a New Year's Eve as the sun went down, far looked her wishful eye
Out from the frosty window pane as a merry sleigh dashed by.
At a village fifteen miles away was to be a ball that night,
And though the air was piercing cold her heart was warm and light.

3 How brightly gleamed her laughing eye, as a well known voice she heard;
And dashing up to the cottage door her lover's sleigh appeared.
"Oh, daughter dear," her mother cried, "This blanket round you fold,
Tonight is a dreadful one, you'll get your death of cold."

4 "Oh, nay, oh nay!" Charlottie cried, as she laughed like a gypsy queen,
"To ride in blankets muffled up I never would be seen;
My silken cloak is quite enough, you know 'tis lined throughout,
And there's my silken scarf to twine my head and neck about."

5 Her bonnet and her gloves were on, she leaped into the sleigh,
And swiftly they sped down the mountain side and o'er the hills away.
With muffled beat so silently five miles at length were passed,
When Charles with a few and shivering words the silence broke at last.

6 "Such a dreadful night, I never saw, the reins I scarce can hold,"
Charlottie faintly then replied, "I am exceeding cold."
He cracked his whip, he urged his steed much faster than before;
And thus five other weary miles in silence were passed o'er.

7 Said Charles: "How fast the shivering ice is gathering on my brow,"
And Charlott' then more faintly cried, "I'm growing warmer now."
Thus on they rode through frosty air and the glittering cold starlight,
Until at last the village lamps and the ballroom came in sight.

8 They reached the door and Charles sprang out, he reached his hand to her,
"Why set you there like a monoment that has no power to stir?"
He called her once, he called her twice, she answered not a word;
He asked her for her hands again, but still she never stirred.

9 He took her hand in his, — 'twas cold and hard as any stone;
He tore the mantle from her face, the cold stars o'er it shone.
Then quickly to the lighted hall her lifeless form he bore;
Charlottie's eyes had closed for aye, her voice was heard no more.

10 And there he sat down by her side, while bitter tears did flow
And cried, "My own, my charming bride, 'tis you may never know."
He twined his arms around her neck, he kissed her marble brow;
His thoughts flew back to where she said, "I'm growing warmer now."

PRETTY POLLY

Murder is evil but what shall we say of six murders of young women for the sake of their "costly clothing"? We are told here and in ancient Scandinavian ballads of a man who drowned six women. But the seventh and last of his brides foiled him and sent him to his death. With all her strength she "pushed him into the sea" and that was his end. The piece is an ancient one, a Scottish text of it, "May Colvin," appearing in David Herd's collection published in 1776. In English ballad books and broadsides it has been variously titled "The Old Beau," "The Outlandish Knight," "False Sir John," and "May Colleen." It is heard in variants in nearly all the Appalachian regions. This version is from the R. W. Gordon collection.

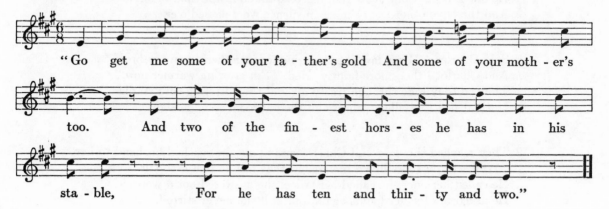

"Go get me some of your fa-ther's gold And some of your moth-er's too. And two of the fin-est hors-es he has in his sta-ble, For he has ten and thir-ty and two."

1 "Go get me some of your father's gold
And some of your mother's too,
And two of the finest horses he has in his stable,
For he has ten and thirty and two."

2 She got him some of her father's gold
And some of her mother's too,
And two of the finest horses he had in his stable,
For he had ten and thirty and two.

3 Then she jumped on the noble brown,
And he on the dappled gray,
And they rode till they came to the side of the sea,
Two long hours before it was day.

4 "Let me help you down, my Pretty Polly;
Let me help you down," said he.
"For it's six kings' daughters I have drowned here,
And the seventh you shall be."

5 "Now strip yourself, my Pretty Polly;
Now strip yourself," said he;
"Your clothing is too fine and over-costly
To rot in the sand of the sea."

60

6 "You turn your back to the leaves of the trees,
   And your face to the sands of the sea;
   'Tis a pity such a false-hearted man as you
   A naked woman should see!"

7 He turned his back to the leaves of the trees,
   And his face to the sand of the sea;
   And with all the strength that Pretty Polly had
   She pushed him into the sea.

8 "Come, lend me your hand, my Pretty Polly;
   Come, lend me your hand," said he,
   "And I will be your waiting-boy,
   And will wait upon you night and day."

9 "Lie there, lie there, you false-hearted man!
   Lie there, lie there," said she;
   "As six kings' daughters you've drowned here,
   Then the seventh you shall be!"

10 Then she jumped on the noble brown,
   And led the dappled gray,
   And rode till she came to her father's hall,
   Two long hours before it was day.

11 Then up bespoke her Poll Parrot,
   Sitting in his cage so gay,
   "Why do you travel, my Pretty Polly,
   So long before it is day?"

12 Then up bespoke her old father,
   Lying in his room so gay,
   "Why do you chatter, my pretty parrot,
   So long before it is day?"

13 "The cat was around and about my cage,
   And I could not get it away
   So I called unto Miss Pretty Polly
   To drive the cat away."

14 "Well turned, well turned, my pretty parrot,
   Well turned, well turned for me;
   Thy cage shall be made of handbeaten gold,
   Thy door of the finest ivory."

COMMON BILL

Women keep songs alive that men would let die. R. W. Gordon and others find "Common Bill" sung almost exclusively by women. It is not a man's song. The way of a maid with a man, the stratagems and maneuvers of women, their changing moods and fertile excuses are presented in the progress of this sketch dealing with Bill and the woman who was good to him, who could have been mean but who had mercy in her heart. Verses and melody here are from Mary O. Eddy and her neighbors of Perrysville, Ohio.

Arr. A. G. W.

I will tell you of a fel-low, Of a fel-low I have seen;

Who is nei-ther white nor yel-low, But is al-to-geth-er green; And his

name it is-n't charm-ing, For it's on-ly com-mon Bill, And he

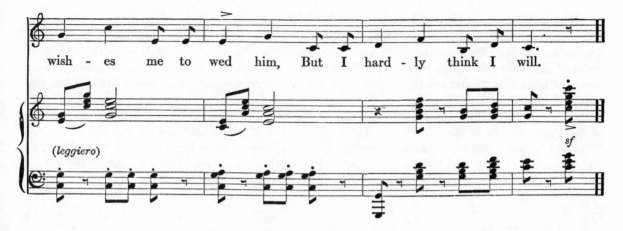

wish - es me to wed him, But I hard - ly think I will.

(leggiero)

sf

1 I will tell you of a fellow,
    Of a fellow I have seen;
  Who is neither white nor yellow,
    But is altogether green;
  And his name it isn't charming,
    For it's only common Bill,
  And he wishes me to wed him,
    But I hardly think I will.

2 He was here the other night,
    And he made so long a stay
  I began to think the gump-head
    Would never go away;
  Oh, he talked of devotion,
    Of devotion pure and bright,
  And don't you think the fool-killer
    He nearly stayed all night.

3 And he wants me for to wed him,
    And the very deuce is in it,
  For he says if I refuse him
    He cannot live a minute;
  And you know the blessed Bible
    It teaches not to kill,
  And I've thought the matter over,
    And I guess I'll marry Bill.

LITTLE SCOTCH–EE

The little drama presented here is as somber with groaning shadows as certain scenes from the plays of Shakespeare or those chapters in the Bible dealing with Samson and Delilah or the woman known as Jezebel. Sung deliberately and with understanding of its implications, delivered as a series of character roles and situations having contrast, it has the pride of an ancient tapestry, with gashes of knife thrusts and splotches of red that are on second look found to be dry blood. We are indebted for this text to Reed Smith of the University of South Carolina and his original work in "The Traditional Ballad and Its South Carolina Survivals," published by the Extension Division of the University of South Carolina. The ballad is hoary, of many variants, sometimes called "Young Hunting," known in America usually as "Lord Henry," "Love Henry," or "Loving Henry." This specimen of "The Old Scotch Well," or "Little Scotch-ee," is from Miss Tressie Pierce of Columbia, South Carolina, who learned it in Alexander County, North Carolina.

1 "Light, light, light, my little Scotch-ee,
    And stay all night with me;
  I have a bed of the very, very best,
    I'll give it up to thee,
    I'll give it up to thee."

2 "I cannot light, and I will not light,
    And stay all night with thee;
  For there's a girl in the old Scotch Yard,
    This night a-waiting for me,
    This night a-waiting for me."

3 "You cannot light, and you will not light,
    But from me you'll never part;"
  She took a pen-knife from her side,
    And pierced him in the heart,
    And pierced him in the heart.

64

4 She called unto her little lady miss,
    "Come unto me I say;
For there's a dead man in my bed,
    Come carry him away,
    Come carry him away."

5 She called unto her little lady miss,
    "Count the hours, one, two, three;
Are the chickens a-crowing for the middle of the night,
    Or are they a-crowing for day,
    Or are they a-crowing for day?"

6 Some took him by the lily-white hand,
    Some took him by the feet,
And threw him into a new-dug well,
    Some forty feet deep,
    Some forty feet deep.

7 "Light, light, light, my little birdie,
    And settle on my knee;
I have a cage of the very, very best,
    I'll give it up to thee,
    I'll give it up to thee."

8 "I cannot light, and I will not light,
    And settle on your knee;
For I'm afraid you will sarve me like you sarved
    Your little Scotch-ee,
    Your little Scotch-ee."

THE HOUSE CARPENTER

This is among the hoary and tarnished keepsakes of the ballad world. In the days before there were daily newspapers, or even weekly "intelligencers," schools were few, and people who could read and write were scarce. Then ballads flourished, and ballad singers were in every tavern where men drank ale, and in every hay or rye field where men gathered the crops. The House Carpenter, in style, story, method, has some of the leading characteristics of many of the oldest ballads. Of course, repeating the last two lines of every verse as indicated in the music here, is not necessary at all. Leave out the last two lines if you like, but don't forget that among antiques this song is as quaint to some of us as a mezzotint portrait in the lid of a snuff box of one of General Washington's staff officers.

"I have just come from the salt, [salt sea, And 'twas
all on ac-count of thee; For I've had an of-fer of a
king's daugh-ter fair, And she fain would have mar-ried me; For I've
had an of-fer of a king's daughter fair, And she fain would have mar-ried me."

1 "I have just come from the salt, salt sea,
  And 'twas all on account of thee;
For I've had an offer of a king's daughter fair,
  And she fain would have married me."
    (Repeat the last two lines in each verse)

2 "If you've had an offer of a king's daughter fair,
  I think you're much to blame;
For I've lately been married to a house carpenter,
  And I think he's a nice young man."

3 "If you'll forsake your house carpenter,
  And come along with me,
I will take you to where the grass grows green,
  On the banks of Italy."

4 "If I'd forsake my house carpenter,
  And go along with you,
And you'd have nothing to support me upon,
  Oh, then what would I do?"

66

5 "I have three ships upon the main,
   All sailing for dry land,
And twenty-five jolly sailor lads
   That you can have at your command."

6 She dressed herself in rich array,
   All from her golden store,
And as she walked the streets all 'round,
   She shone like a glittering star.

7 She called her baby unto her,
   And gave it kisses three,
Saying, "Stay at home, my pretty little babe,
   And be your father's company."

8 We had not sailed more than two weeks,
   I'm sure it was not three,
Till this fair maid began to weep,
   And she wept most bitterly.

9 "Oh, why do you weep, my pretty maid?
   Do you weep for your golden store,
Or do you weep for your house carpenter
   Which you never shall see any more?"

10 "I do not weep for my house carpenter,
   Or for my golden store,
But I do weep for my pretty little babe
   Which I never shall see any more."

11 We had not sailed more than three weeks,
   I'm sure it was not four,
Till our gallant ship she sprang a leak,
   And she sank to rise no more.

12 Once around went our gallant ship,
   Twice around went she,
Three times around went our gallant ship,
   And she sank to the bottom of the sea.

13 Oh, cursed be the sea-going train,
   And all the sailors' lives,
For the robbing of the house carpenter,
   And the taking away of his wife.

A PRETTY FAIR MAID

Occasionally the verses of a song make a good story if only read, and not sung at all. In the case of "A Pretty Fair Maid" there is a whimsically sweet air going with an oddly spoken story. What lively, old, old-fashioned gossip we have here!

Arr. E. M.

A PRETTY FAIR MAID

1 A pretty fair maid all in a garden,
    A sailor boy came passing by;
  He stepped aside and thus addressed her,
    Saying, "Pretty fair maid, won't you be my bride?"

2 "I have a sweetheart on the ocean,
    For seven long years has been to sea,
  And if he stays for seven years longer
    No other man shall marry me."

3 "Perhaps your sweetheart he is drownded,
    Perhaps he's in some battle slain,
  Perhaps he's to some pretty girl married,
    And he shall ne'er return again."

4 "Oh! if my sweetheart he is drownded,
    Or if he's in some battle slain,
  Or if he's to some pretty girl married,
    I'll love the girl that married him."

5 "My sweetheart he is neither drownded
    Nor is he in some battle slain,
  Nor is he to some pretty girl married,
    For he is by my side again."

6 He put his hands in both his pockets,
    His fingers they were long and slim,
  And unto me he drew a gold locket,
    And to my feet his knees did bend.

7 "I have six ships all on the ocean,
    And they are loaded to the brim,
  And if I'm worthy of such a young lady,
    I care not if they sink or swim."

LORD LOVEL

Among the most widespread ballads in the United States is "Lord Lovel." The version here is from the collection of Reed Smith of the University of South Carolina; the melody is from W. R. Dehon and the text from Caroline S. Dickinson. The mood and way of this song is peculiar. It is to be sung and not read. Why this is so, Mr. Smith explains in this note: "'Lord Lovel' clearly shows how necessary it is to deal with ballads as songs and not merely as poems. The text of 'Lord Lovel' is sad and mournful. The tune, however, is lilting and rollicking, and with the triple repetition of the last word of the fourth line, turns the tear into a smile. The difference between reading it as a poem and singing it as a song is the difference between tragedy and comedy."

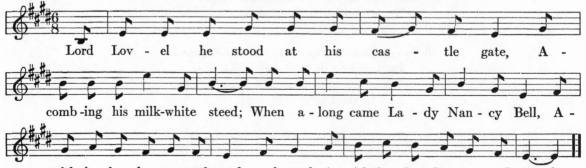

Lord Lov-el he stood at his cas-tle gate, A-comb-ing his milk-white steed; When a-long came La-dy Nan-cy Bell, A-wish-ing her lov-er good speed, speed, speed, A-wish-ing her lov-er good speed.

1 Lord Lovel he stood at his castle gate,
   A-combing his milk-white steed;
When along came Lady Nancy Bell,
   A-wishing her lover good speed, speed,
   speed,
   A-wishing her lover good speed.

2 "Oh where are you going, Lord Lovel?" she
      said;
   "Oh where are you going?" said she.
"I'm going, my dear Lady Nancy Bell,
   Strange countries for to see, see, see,
   Strange countries for to see."

3 "When will you be back, Lord Lovel?" she
      said;
   "When will you be back?" said she.
"In a year or two or three at the most
   I'll return to my Lady Nancee-cee, cee,
   I'll return to my Lady Nancee."

4 He'd not been gone but a year and a day,
   Strange countries for to see,
When languishing thoughts came into his
   mind
Lady Nancy Bell he would see.

5 He rode and he rode on his milk-white steed,
   Till he reached fair London Town;

And there he heard St. Varney's bell
   And the people all mourning around.

6 "Is any one dead?" Lord Lovel he said;
   "Is any one dead?" said he.
"A lady is dead," the people all said,
   "And they call her Lady Nancy."

7 He ordered the grave to be opened forthwith,
   The shroud to be folded down;
And then he kissed her clay-cold lips
   Till the tears came trickling down.

8 Lady Nancy she died as it might be today,
   Lord Lovel he died tomorrow.
Lady Nancy she died of pure, pure grief,
   Lord Lovel he died of sorrow.

9 Lady Nancy was laid in St. Clement's
      churchyard,
   Lord Lovel was buried close by her;
And out of her bosom there grew a red rose,
   And out of his backbone a briar.

10 They grew and they grew on the old church
      tower,
   Till they couldn't grow up any higher;
And there they tied in a true lover's knot,
   For all true lovers to admire.

THE QUAKER'S WOOING

The Quakers were ever a stubborn people — of sweet ways and deep faiths. The men wore black hats with broad brims, the women wore black bonnets with white facings. Their love-making may have had some of the rich though simple tinting in this old English tune and verses. Something about it is as genuine as the wood grain of an unvarnished, black walnut, four-post bed. This comes from Miss Harriet Louise Abbott of Bethel, Ohio, as communicated to Mary O. Eddy.

"I had a true love but she left me, Oh, oh, oh, oh, And I now am bro-ken heart-ed, Oh, oh, oh, oh." "Well, if she's gone I would-n't mind her, .. Fol de rol de hey ding di do, You'll soon find one that'll prove much kind-er, Fol de rol de hey ding day. (2. I've a)

1 "I had a true love but she left me,
    Oh, oh, oh, oh,
And I now am broken-hearted,
    Oh, oh, oh, oh."
"Well, if she's gone I wouldn't mind her,
    Fol de rol de hey ding di do,
You'll soon find one that'll prove much kinder,
    Fol de rol de hey ding day."

2 "I've a house and forty servants,
    Oh, oh, oh, oh,
And thee may be the mistress of them,
    Oh, oh, oh, oh."
"I'll not do your scolding for you,
    Fol de rol de hey ding di do,
'Deed I feel myself above you,
    Fol de rol de hey ding day."

3 "I've a ring worth twenty shillings,
    Oh, oh, oh, oh,
And thee may wear it, if thee's willing,
    Oh, oh, oh, oh."
"What care I for rings or money,
    Fol de rol de hey ding di do,
I'm for the man who calls me honey,
    Fol de rol de hey ding day."

71

THE MAID FREED FROM THE GALLOWS

One time long ago, it seems, the law came down on a young woman. And she was to be hanged. And her father came, her mother, her brother, sister, aunt, uncle, cousins. Yet not one would help her with gold or fee. They all wanted her hanged. Then came her true love and he freed her from the gallows; he slacked the hangman's rope. So goes the story. We do not know just how many centuries it has been going. The text and tune here are from the admirable Reed Smith Ballads published by the University of South Carolina.

"Slack your rope, hangs-a-man, O slack it for a-while; I think I see my fa-ther com-ing, Rid-ing man-y a mile." "O fa-ther, have you brought me gold? Or have you paid my fee? Or have you come to see me hang-ing On the gal-lows tree?" "I have not brought you gold; I have not paid your fee; But I have come to see you hang-ing On the gal-lows tree."

1 "Slack your rope, hangs-a-man,
   O slack it for a while;
I think I see my father coming,
   Riding many a mile."
"O father, have you brought me gold?
   Or have you paid my fee?
Or have you come to see me hanging
   On the gallows-tree?"
"I have not brought you gold;
   I have not paid your fee;
But I have come to see you hanging
   On the gallows-tree."

2 "Slack your rope, hangs-a-man,
   O slack it for a while;
I think I see my mother coming,
   Riding many a mile."
"O mother, have you brought me gold?
   Or have you paid my fee?
Or have you come to see me hanging

   On the gallows-tree?"
"I have not brought you gold;
   I have not paid your fee;
But I have come to see you hanging
   On the gallows-tree."
(And so on for brother, sister, aunt, uncle, cousin, etc.)

3 "Slack your rope, hangs-a-man,
   O slack it for a while;
I think I see my true-love coming
   Riding many a mile."
"O true-love, have you brought me gold?
   Or have you paid my fee?
Or have you come to see me hanging
   On the gallows-tree?"
"Yes, I have brought you gold;
   Yes, I have paid your fee;
Nor have I come to see you hanging
   On the gallows-tree."

FRANKIE AND HER MAN

FRANKIE AND ALBERT

A Frankie song is like a grand opera rôle; interpretations vary. The Leighton brothers run a gamut of emotions; John Lomax delivers a quizzically mournful monotone; Sig Spaeth vocalizes it like a gnome riding a gnu with gnats mellifluously. The maxim, "Life is a tragedy to those who feel, a comedy to those who think," may go for viewpoints on this ballad. It is stark and fierce, it is serio-comic, or it is blah-blah — as you like it.

If America has a classical gutter song, it is the one that tells of Frankie and her man. Josie, Sadie, Lillie, Annie, are a few of her aliases; she has many. Prof. H. M. Belden of the University of Missouri showed me sixteen Frankie songs, all having the same story though a few are located in the back country and in bayous instead of the big city. Then I met up with R. W. Gordon; he has 110 Frankie songs, and is still picking up new ones. R. Emmett Kennedy in his remarkably thorough and valuable book, "Mellows" has a song, "My Baby in a Guinea Blue Gown," which belongs in the Frankie discussion because its tune may have been the grandfather of the most widely known Frankie melodies. The Frankie and Albert song, as partly given here, was common along the Mississippi river and among railroad men of the middle west as early as 1888. It is a simple and mournful air, of the short and simple annals of the poor. The Frankie and Johnny song is of later development, with notes of violence and flashes of exasperation. The Frankie Blues came still later, and with its "blue" notes is, of course, "meaner" as a song. In many colleges are groups who sing Frankie songs in ragtime manner, with lackadaisical verses. As our American culture advances, it may be that classes will take up the Frankie songs as seriously as a play by Molière or a Restoration comedy or the Provençal ballads of France. It may be said that the Frankie songs, at best, are an American parallel of certain European ballads of low life, that are rendered by important musical artists from the Continent for enthusiastic audiences in Carnegie Hall, New York, or Orchestra Hall, Chicago. Some day, perhaps, we may arrive at a better common understanding of our own art resources and how to use them. While the Frankie story deals with crime, violence, murder, adultery, its percentage in these respects is a good deal less than in the average grand opera.

Lastly, for those about to sing this piece, we should note that in several places, in San Francisco, Omaha, Fort Worth, Fort Smith, Fort Scott and Dubuque the verse about the man under the doctor's care crying, "Roll me over easy," or "Turn me over, doctor," has no tune; all present joining in a wide, wild, disconnected wailing. Also, we note, by alternating the names of Albert and Johnny, or Frankie, Josie, Sadie, any verse of any song goes for all. The air of version II of Frankie and Johnny, carries all the verses of version I, exept that the repeat, "so wrong" isn't used. While it may seem a discrepancy that Frankie, threatened with the electric chair, ends her days on the gallows, it should also be understood that several versions of the song picture her starting to join a county chain gang, wearing a ball and chain attached to one of her ankles.

FRANKIE AND ALBERT

Arr. E. C.

Frankie and Albert were sweethearts, ev'ry - bod - y knows, Frank-ie spent a hun-dred dol - lars just to get her man some clothes; He was her man, ... but he done her wrong. . . . . . .

1 Frankie and Albert were sweethearts, everybody knows,
   Frankie spent a hundred dollars just to get her man some clothes;
     He was her man, but he done her wrong.

2 Frankie went down to the corner, took along a can,
   Says to the lovin' bartender, "Has you seen my lovin' man?
     He is my man, but he's doin' me wrong."

3 "Well, I ain't gonna tell you no story, ain't gonna tell you no lie,
Albert went by 'bout an hour ago, with a girl called Alice Fry;
      He was your man, but he's doin' you wrong."

4 Frankie's gone from the corner, Frankie ain't gone for fun,
Underneath her apron she's got Albert's gatlin' gun;
      He was her man, but he done her wrong.

5 Albert sees Frankie comin', out the back door he did scoot,
Frankie pulled out the pistol, went roota-de-toot-toot-toot.
      He was her man, but she shot him down.

6 Frankie shot him once, Frankie shot him twice,
Third time that she shot him the bullet took his life;
      He was her man, but he done her wrong.

7 When Frankie shot Albert, he fell down on his knees,
Looked up at her and said, "Oh, Frankie, please,
      Don't shoot me no mo', don't shoot me no mo'."

8 "Oh, turn me over, doctor; turn me over slow,
Turn me over on my right side, 'cause the bullet am hurtin' me so.
      I was her man, but I done her wrong."

9 Now it's rubber-tired carriages, decorated hack,
Eleven men went to the graveyard, and only ten come back:
      He was her man, but he's dead and gone.

10 Frankie was a-standin' on the corner, watchin' de hearse go by,
Throwed her arms into the air, "Oh, let me lie
      By the side of my man, what done me wrong."

11 Frankie went to the graveyard, bowed down on her knees,
"Speak one word to me, Albert, an' give my heart some ease.
      You was my man, but I done you wrong."

12 Sheriff arrested Frankie, took her to the county jail,
Locked her up in a dungeon cell, and throwed the keys away.
      She shot her man, said he done her wrong.

13 Judge tried lil' Frankie, under an electric fan;
Judge says, "Yo' free woman now, go kill yourself anothah man.
      He was yo' man, now he's dead an' gone."

I

FRANKIE AND JOHNNY

Arr. E. C.

Frank-ie and John-ny were lov-ers, . O lord-y how they could love.

Swore to be true to each oth - er, . true as the stars a-

bove; He was her man but he done her wrong, so wrong.

II

FRANKIE AND JOHNNY

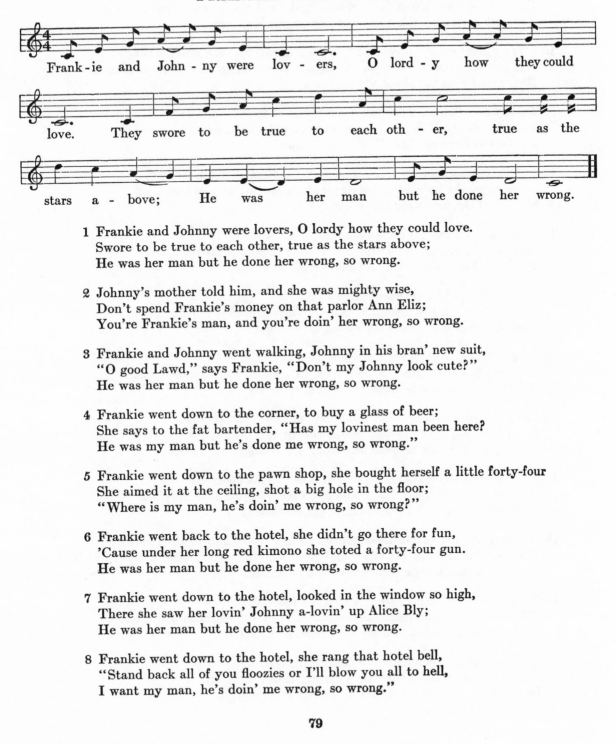

Frank-ie and John-ny were lov-ers, O lord-y how they could
love. They swore to be true to each oth-er, true as the
stars a-bove; He was her man but he done her wrong.

1 Frankie and Johnny were lovers, O lordy how they could love.
   Swore to be true to each other, true as the stars above;
   He was her man but he done her wrong, so wrong.

2 Johnny's mother told him, and she was mighty wise,
   Don't spend Frankie's money on that parlor Ann Eliz;
   You're Frankie's man, and you're doin' her wrong, so wrong.

3 Frankie and Johnny went walking, Johnny in his bran' new suit,
   "O good Lawd," says Frankie, "Don't my Johnny look cute?"
   He was her man but he done her wrong, so wrong.

4 Frankie went down to the corner, to buy a glass of beer;
   She says to the fat bartender, "Has my lovinest man been here?
   He was my man but he's done me wrong, so wrong."

5 Frankie went down to the pawn shop, she bought herself a little forty-four
   She aimed it at the ceiling, shot a big hole in the floor;
   "Where is my man, he's doin' me wrong, so wrong?"

6 Frankie went back to the hotel, she didn't go there for fun,
   'Cause under her long red kimono she toted a forty-four gun.
   He was her man but he done her wrong, so wrong.

7 Frankie went down to the hotel, looked in the window so high,
   There she saw her lovin' Johnny a-lovin' up Alice Bly;
   He was her man but he done her wrong, so wrong.

8 Frankie went down to the hotel, she rang that hotel bell,
   "Stand back all of you floozies or I'll blow you all to hell,
   I want my man, he's doin' me wrong, so wrong."

9 Frankie threw back her kimono, she took out her forty-four.
Root-a-toot-toot, three times she shot, right through that hardwood floor,
She shot her man, 'cause he done her wrong, so wrong.

10 Johnny grabbed off his Stetson, "O good Lawd, Frankie, don't shoot."
But Frankie put her finger on the trigger, and the gun went roota-toot-toot,
He was her man but she shot him down.

11 Johnny saw Frankie a comin', down the backstairs he did scoot;
Frankie had the little gun out, let him have it rooty-de-toot;
For he was her man, but she shot him down.

12 Johnny he mounted the staircase, cried, "O Frankie don't shoot!"
Three times she pulled the forty-four gun a rooty-toot-toot-toot-toot,
She nailed the man what threw her down.

13 "Roll me over easy, roll me over slow,
Roll me over easy, boys, 'cause my wounds they hurt me so,
But I was her man, and I done her wrong, so wrong."

14 "Oh my baby, kiss me once before I go.
Turn me over on my right side, doctor, where de bullet hurt me so.
I was her man but I done her wrong, so wrong."

15 Johnny he was a gambler, he gambled for the gain.
The very last words he ever said were, "High-low Jack and the game."
He was her man but he done her wrong, so wrong.

16 Bring out your long black coffin, bring out your funeral clo'es;
Bring back Johnny's mother; to the churchyard Johnny goes.
He was her man but he done her wrong, so wrong.

17 Frankie went to his coffin, she looked down on his face.
She said, "O Lawd, have mercy on me, I wish I could take his place,
He was my man, and I done him wrong, so wrong."

18 Oh bring on your rubber-tired hearses, bring on your rubber-tired hacks,
They're takin' Johnny to the buryin' groun' an' they won't bring a bit of him back;
He was her man but he done her wrong, so wrong.

19 Frankie stood on the corner to watch the funeral go by;
"Bring back my poor dead Johnny to me," to the undertaker she did say,
"He was my man, but he done me wrong, so wrong."

20 Frankie heard a rumbling away down in the ground,
Maybe it was little Johnny where she had shot him down.
He was her man and she done him wrong, so wrong.

21 Frankie went to Mrs. Halcomb, she fell down on her knees,
   She said, "Mrs. Halcomb, forgive me, forgive me, if you please,
   For I've killed my man what done me wrong, so wrong."

22 "Forgive you, Frankie darling, forgive you I never can.
   Forgive you, Frankie darling, for killing your only man,
   Oh he was your man tho' he done you wrong, so wrong."

23 Frankie said to the warden, "What are they goin' to do?"
   The warden he said to Frankie, "It's the electric chair for you,
   You shot your man tho' he done you wrong, so wrong."

24 The sheriff came around in the morning, said it was all for the best,
   He said her lover Johnny was nothin' but a doggone pest.
   He was her man but he done her wrong, so wrong.

25 The judge said to the jury, "It's as plain as plain can be;
   This woman shot her lover, it's murder in the second degree,
   He was her man tho' he done her wrong, so wrong."

26 Now it was not murder in the second degree, and was not murder in the third,
   The woman simply dropped her man, like a hunter drops a bird.
   He was her man but he done her wrong, so wrong.

27 "Oh bring a thousand policemen, bring 'em around today,
   Oh lock me in that dungeon, and throw the keys away,
   I shot my man, 'cause he done me wrong, so wrong."

28 "Yes, put me in that dungeon, oh put me in that cell,
   Put me where the northeast wind blows from the southeast corner of hell.
   I shot my man, 'cause he done me wrong, so wrong."

29 Frankie mounted to the scaffold as calm as a girl can be,
   And turning her eyes to heaven, she said, "Good Lord, I am coming to Thee.
   He was my man, but he done me wrong, so wrong."

FRANKIE BLUES

Not fast

Arr. E. C.

Frank - ie was a good wom - an, . Ev - 'ry bo - dy knows, Gave

for - ty - one dol - lars to buy Al - bert A suit of clothes;

"Yes, he's my man, ... but he done me wrong." . . .

1 Frankie was a good woman,
   Ev'rybody knows,
   Gave forty-one dollars to buy Albert
   A suit of clothes:
   "Yes, he's my man, but he done me wrong."

2 Frankie went to the corner,
   Took a forty-four gun,
   Shot her Albert a-rooty-ti-toot,
   And away he tried to run:
   "He was my man, but he done me wrong."

3 "Roll me over easy,
   Roll me over slow,
   Roll me over on my right side,
   'Cause the bullet hurt me so;
   I was your man, but I done you wrong."

4 Frankie sit in a parlor,
   Cool herself with a fan,
   Tell all the other women and girls,
   "Don't trust any doggone man,
   He'll do you wrong, he'll do you wrong."

JOSIE

The restless sons of Man in the mountains of Kentucky sometimes descend to the plains and live in the big cities, in the centers of wickedness, in the tents of the ungodly, where night is turned into day by the bright lights. When they go back to the mountains sometimes they have songs their lips have learned in strange places. Perhaps one of the children of the mountains learned a Frankie song in one of the cities and brought it back to the mountains where the name of the heroine was changed to Josie. Or, perhaps, it was in the mountains that the first Frankie song was born and the name of the leading character was Josie and it was in the city that her name was changed. When the song history of America is definitively written, we shall know about these things.

Arr. A. G. W.

Jo - sie she's a good girl, as ev - 'ry-bod - y knows, She gave one hun-dred dol - lars for an i - vo - ry suit of clothes; "He is my man, ... but he won't come home." . . . .

84

JOSIE

1 Josie she's a good girl, as everybody knows,
   She gave one hundred dollars for an ivory suit of clothes;
   "He is my man, but he won't come home."

2 She went down the street as far as I could see,
   And every band that she passed by played "Nearer My God to Thee,"
   "Oh, he's my man, but he won't come home."

3 She went down the street, a revolver in her hand,
   Saying, "Stand back, gents and ladies; I'm searching for my man,
   Oh, he's my man, but he won't come home."

4 She stepped into the barroom, and there her husband stood,
   She drew her revolver from her side and shot him thru and thru;
   "He's my man, but he wouldn't come home."

5 She went down to the jail-house, keys all in her hand,
   Saying, "Here, Mr. Jailer, lock me up, for I've shot my man;
   He's my man, but he wouldn't come home."

6 One thing hurt Mrs. Josie, one thing made her cry,
   Standing there in the courthouse door when the hurst (hearse) came rolling by;
   "Oh, he's my man, but he wouldn't come home."

7 "I'm not going to wear no mourning, not going to wear no black,
   But I'll go down to the graveyard and bring my Iva back;
   Oh, he's my man, but he done me wrong."

8 She went down to the graveyard and fell down on her knees,
   And prayed to the Lord in heaven to send her heart some ease;
   "Oh, he's my man, but he wouldn't come home."

9 Sitting in the parlor by an electric fan,
   Pleading with the youngest girl never to marry a gambling man;
   "He'll be your man, but he'll not come home."

SADIE

This is a woman's version of the old story of Frankie and her man. Six young women from six old cities sang it at White Lake, Michigan. They wrap Sadie in a "sky-blue kimono." They have Sadie kill her man, he is hauled to the graveyard, and that's all. No arrest, no murder trial, neither acquittal nor execution. Text and tune here are from Julia Peterson of Ann Arbor.

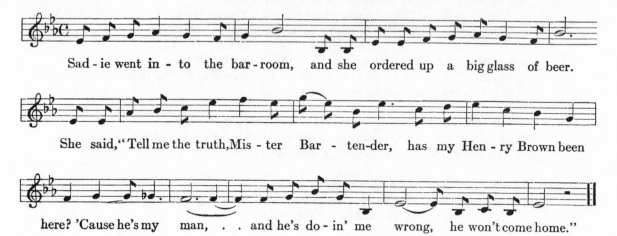

Sad-ie went in-to the bar-room, and she ordered up a big glass of beer.

She said, "Tell me the truth, Mis-ter Bar-ten-der, has my Hen-ry Brown been

here? 'Cause he's my man, . . and he's do-in' me wrong, he won't come home."

1 Sadie went into the bar-room, and she ordered up a big glass of beer.
   She said, "Tell me the truth, Mister Bartender, has my Henry Brown been here?
   'Cause he's my man, and he's doin' me wrong, he won't come home."

2 "Well I ain't goin' to tell you no secrets, and I ain't goin' to tell you no lies,
   But I saw Henry Brown just a moment ago, and I could hardly b'lieve my eyes,
   'Cause he's your man, what's been doin' you wrong, he won't come home."

3 Sadie drank up all her beer, and she ordered up a big glass of gin,
   She said, "Ain't it a shame, Mister Bartender, that I've a-takin' to drinkin' again,
   On account of my man, what's a-doin' me wrong, he wouldn't come home."

4 Sadie went up a dark alley, and she didn't go up there for fun,
   For under her sky-blue kimono, she had a great big forty-four gun,
   On account of her man, what was doin' her wrong, he wouldn't come home.

5 "Roll me over easy, now roll me over slow,
   Oh, roll me over on my right side because my left side hurts me so,
   'Cause I'm Sadie's man, what's a done her wrong, I wouldn't come home."

6 They hauled out the rubber-tired carriage, and they hauled out the rubber-tired hack,
   They were haulin' a guy to the grave-yard, and they weren't gonna haul him back,
   He was Sadie's man, that had done her wrong, he wouldn't come home.

PIONEER MEMORIES

HONOUR TO PIONEERS WHO BROKE SOD THAT
MEN TO COME MIGHT LIVE.

Inscription from state capitol building at
Lincoln, Nebraska

TO THE STARS BY HARD WAYS.

Motto adopted by the State of Kansas

IOWA — THE AFFECTIONS OF HER PEOPLE, LIKE
THE RIVERS OF HER BORDERS, FLOW ON TO AN
INSEPARABLE UNION.

Inscription from the state capitol
building at Des Moines, Iowa

THE COWARDS NEVER STARTED AND THE WEAK
ONES DIED BY THE WAY.

Slogan of the Society of California

THE LITTLE OLD SOD SHANTY

A little girl from western Nebraska, home again after a trip to the East, was asked, "What is the East?" She answered, "The East is where trees come between you and the sky." Early settlers noticed log cabins were scarcer as timber land thinned out going farther west. On the windy, open prairies of the Great Plains, the best house to be had in short order was of sod. A cellar was dug first; long slices of turf were piled around the cellar lines; wooden crosspoles held the sod roof. Ceilings went high or low: tall men put roofs farther from the ground than short men did. In timber country farther east they sang The Little Old Log Cabin in the Lane; its tune was familiar to the lonely "sodbuster" who made this song about his dwelling — in a region where rivers are sometimes a half mile wide and a half inch deep.

Arr. A. G. W.

I am look-ing rath-er seed-y now while hold-ing down my claim, And my
Yet I rath-er like the no-vel-ty of liv-ing in this way, Though my

vict-uals are not al-ways of the best; ... And the mice play shy-ly
bill of fare is al-ways rath-er tame, ... But I'm hap-py as a

round me as I nes-tle down to rest, In my lit-tle old sod shan-ty in the
clam on the land of Un-cle Sam, In my lit-tle old sod shan-ty on my

THE LITTLE OLD SOD SHANTY

West. . . . . . claim. . . . . . The hing - es are of
leath - er and the win-dows have no glass, While the board roof lets the
howl - ing bliz-zards in, ... And I hear the hun - gry ki - yote as he
slinks up through the grass, Round my lit - tle old sod shan -ty on my claim. . . .

THE LITTLE OLD SOD SHANTY

1 I am looking rather seedy now while holding down my claim,
  And my victuals are not always of the best;
  And the mice play shyly round me as I nestle down to rest,
  In my little old sod shanty in the West.
  Yet I rather like the novelty of living in this way,
  Though my bill of fare is always rather tame,
  But I'm happy as a clam on the land of Uncle Sam,
  In my little old sod shanty on my claim.

  Refrain:
  The hinges are of leather and the windows have no glass,
  While the board roof lets the howling blizzards in,
  And I hear the hungry kiyote as he slinks up through the grass,
  Round my little old sod shanty on my claim.

2 O when I left my eastern home, a bachelor so gay,
  To try and win my way to wealth and fame,
  I little thought that I'd come down to burning twisted hay
  In the little old sod shanty on my claim.
  My clothes are plastered o'er with dough, I'm looking like a fright,
  And everything is scattered round the room,
  But I wouldn't give the freedom that I have out in the West
  For the table of the Eastern man's old home.
  Refrain:

3 Still I wish that some kind-hearted girl would pity on me take,
  And relieve me from the mess that I am in;
  The angel, how I'd bless her if this her home she'd make
  In the little old sod shanty on my claim.
  And we would make our fortunes on the prairies of the West,
  Just as happy as two lovers we'd remain;
  We'd forget the trials and troubles we endured at the first,
  In the little old sod shanty on our claim.
  Refrain:

4 And if kindly fate should bless us with now and then an heir,
  To cheer our hearts with honest pride of fame,
  O then we'd be contented for the toil that we had spent
  In the little old sod shanty on our claim.
  When time enough had lapsed and all of those little brats
  To noble man- and womanhood had grown,
  It wouldn't seem half so lonely as around us we should look,
  And see the little old sod shanty on our claim.
  Refrain:

WHERE O WHERE IS OLD ELIJAH?

A widely known song among pioneers in the middle west was this one borrowed, possibly, from the negroes. It might be called a white man's spiritual. Its melody, its half-story elements, its weaving repetitions, make it a good song for company and party singing. And it is one of the best I know of for children and grown-ups to join in on, to loosen up, and to get at each other's voices. This complete version comes to us from Lloyd Lewis, Free Quaker, and former and early resident of Pendleton, Indiana, a man of sterling integrity and many devices.

Arr. L. S.

92

Where O where is old Elijah?
Where O where is old Elijah?
Where O where is old Elijah?
'Way over in the promised land.
  He went up in a fiery chariot,
  He went up in a fiery chariot,
  He went up in a fiery chariot,
  'Way over in the promised land.

Refrain:
By and by we will go and see him,
By and by we will go and see him,
By and by we will go and see him,
'Way over in the promised land.

Where O where are the Hebrew children?
Where O where are the Hebrew children?
Where O where are the Hebrew children?
'Way over in the promised land.
  They went up in a fiery furnace,
  They went up in a fiery furnace,
  They went up in a fiery furnace,
  'Way over in the promised land.

Where O where is the bad boy Absolom?
Where O where is the bad boy Absolom?
Where O where is the bad boy Absolom?
'Way over in the promised land.
  He went up on the spear of Joab,
  He went up on the spear of Joab,
  He went up on the spear of Joab,
  'Way over in the promised land.

Where O where is poor old Daniel?
Where O where is poor old Daniel?
Where O where is poor old Daniel?
'Way over in the promised land.
  He went up in a den of lions,
  He went up in a den of lions,
  He went up in a den of lions,
  'Way over in the promised land.

TURKEY IN THE STRAW

This is the classical American rural tune.   It goes back to "Zip Coon" and early minstrel songs. It has been sung at horses and mules from a million wagons.   It has a thousand verses, if all were gathered.   In the solitudes of tall timbers it has been the companion of berry pickers in summer and squirrel hunters in fall time.   On mornings when the frost was on the pumpkin and the fodder in the shock, when nuts were ripe and winter apples ready for picking, it echoed amid the horizons of the Muskingum river of Ohio and the Ozark foothills of Missouri.   Arguments have been presented that the turkey, the Thanksgiving bird, is more the Yankee national emblem than the eagle. Maybe so.   Anyhow the turkey has a song of the people and the eagle hasn't.   And as a song it smells of hay mows up over barn dance floors, steps around like an apple-faced farmhand, has the whiff of a river breeze when the catfish are biting, and rolls along like a good wagon slicked up with new axlegrease on all four wheels.   It is as American as Andrew Jackson, Johnny Appleseed, and Corn-on-the-Cob.

Text B. was printed by Delaney who tells me this is the earliest stage version he knows of and it is at least fifty years old.   With a little "puckering in" and doubling up, the lines can be adjusted to the harmonized melody.   Text C. is a 1925 ditty from the oil fields of Ohio; Paul Schact, of Columbus, passed it along; like oil strikes, gushers, wildcats, doodlebugs, it is a little mysterious.

Arr. L. S.

As I was a-gwine down the road,   Tired team and a hea-vy load,

Crack my whip and the lead-er sprung; I says day - day to the wa - gon-tongue.

REFRAIN

Tur-key in the straw,   tur-key in the hay,   Roll 'em up and twist 'em up a

high tuck - a - haw, And hit 'em up a tune called Tur-key in the Straw!

2. Went out to milk and I did-n't know now, I milked the goat in-stead of the cow. A

mon - key sit - tin' on a pile of straw A - wink - in' at his moth-er - in - law.

Refrain

Tur-key in the straw, tur - key in the hay, Roll 'em up and twist 'em up a

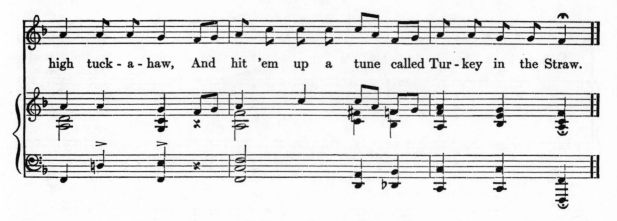

high tuck-a-haw, And hit 'em up a tune called Tur-key in the Straw.

A

1 As I was a-gwine down the road,
  Tired team and a heavy load,
  Crack my whip and the leader sprung;
  I says day-day to the wagon tongue.
    Turkey in the straw, turkey in the hay,
      Roll 'em up and twist 'em up a high tuckahaw,
      And hit 'em up a tune called Turkey in the Straw.

2 Went out to milk and I didn't know how,
  I milked the goat instead of the cow.
  A monkey sittin' on a pile of straw
  A-winkin' at his mother-in-law.
    Turkey in the straw, turkey in the hay, etc.

3 Met Mr. Catfish comin' down stream,
  Says Mr. Catfish, "What does you mean?"
  Caught Mr. Catfish by the snout
  And turned Mr. Catfish wrong side out.
    Turkey in the straw, turkey in the hay, etc.

4 Came to the river and I couldn't get across
  Paid five dollars for an old blind hoss
  Wouldn't go ahead, nor he wouldn't stand still
  So he went up and down like an old saw mill.
    Turkey in the straw, turkey in the hay, etc.

5 As I came down the new cut road
  Met Mr. Bullfrog, met Miss Toad
  And every time Miss Toad would sing
  Ole Bullfrog cut a pigeon wing.
    Turkey in the straw, turkey in the hay, etc.

6 O I jumped in the seat, and I gave a little yell,
The horses run away, broke the wagon all to hell;
Sugar in the gourd and honey in the horn,
I never was so happy since the hour I was born.
Turkey in the straw, turkey in the hay, etc.

B

Went down to New Orleans, got on a fence, Tom Turkey in de buckwheat straw.
Dutchman asked me I talk French, dat's nine points ob de law;
Hit 'em in de head wid a great big brick, Tom Turkey in de buckwheat straw,
Didn't I make dat nigger look sick, dat's nine points ob de law.

Refrain:
Den a turkey in a straw, den a turkey in a straw;
Roll a web of straw 'round to hide de turkey's paw,
And we'll shake 'em up a tune called Turkey in a Straw.

Tobacco am an Ingin weed, Tom Turkey in de buckwheat straw,
From de debil it did seed, dat's nine points ob de law;
Rots your pocket, scents your clothes, Tom Turkey in a buckwheat straw.
Makes a chimbley of your nose, dat's nine points ob de law.
Refrain:

C

Said the tooler to the driller, "Will you dance me a jig?"
"O yes, by golly, if I tear down the rig."
So he took down the wrench that the contractor stole,
And he danced a jig around the ten-inch hole.

WHO WILL SHOE YOUR PRETTY LITTLE FOOT?

One night after I had given my song and guitar recital at Indiana University, I went with Prof. Frank C. Senour to his room and we sang and talked till three o'clock in the morning. He had in his heart and memory a little piece that he called "exquisite"; that is the word. As a boy growing up in Brown County, Indiana, he heard his mother sing it at dish washing and sewing and mending, and sometimes for company. He remembered only the verse given below in text A. R. W. Gordon gave me text B and I went to Alexander Whitelaw's "Book of Scottish Ballads" for text C, where it is titled, "Fair Annie of Lochyran." In another old version, it is known as "The Lass of Loch Royal." A little book could be written around this song and all its ramifications in the past.

Arr. L. S.

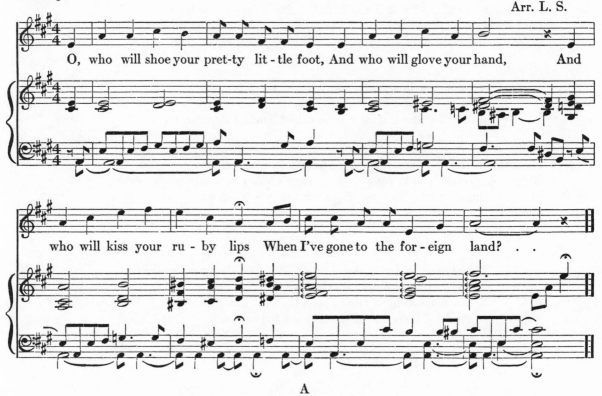

O, who will shoe your pret-ty lit-tle foot, And who will glove your hand, And who will kiss your ru-by lips When I've gone to the for-eign land? . .

A

O, who will shoe your pretty little foot,
And who will glove your hand,
And who will kiss your ruby lips
When I've gone to the foreign land?

B

THE TRUE LOVER'S FAREWELL

"Farewell, farewell, my pretty maid,
Fare-thee-well for a while;
For I'm going away ten thousand miles,
Ten thousand miles from here.

98

2 "Who will shoe your bonny feet,
    And who will glove your hand?
Who will kiss your red, rosy lips,
    While I'm in some foreign land?"

3 "My father will shoe my bonny little feet,
    My mother will glove my hand;
But my red, rosy lips shall go wanting,
    Till you return again."

4 "You know a crow is a coal, coal black,
    And turns to a purple blue;
And if ever I prove false to you,
    I hope my body may melt like dew.

5 "I'll love you till the seas run dry,
    And rocks dissolve by the sun;
I'll love you till the day I die,
    And then you know I'm done."

C

FAIR ANNIE OF LOCHYRAN

1 "O who will shoe my fair foot,
    And who will glove my han'?
And who will lace my middle jimp
    Wi' a new-made London ban'?

2 "Or who will kemb my yellow hair
    Wi' a new-made silver kemb?
Or who'll be father to my young bairn,
    Till love Gregor come hame?"

3 "Your father 'll shoe your fair foot,
    Your mother 'll glove your hand;
Your sister 'll lace your middle jimp
    Wi' a new-made London ban';

4 "Your brethern will kemb your yellow hair
    Wi' a new-made silver kemb;
And the King of Heaven will father your bairn
    Till love Gregor come hame."

99

TEN THOUSAND MILES AWAY

Four times a year for twenty-two years William W. Delaney published at Park Row, New York, his ten-cent songbook, each one with about 170 songs, words only. "On the last page or two," he told me, "I always put a few old ones." A favorite of his, among the old ones, is Ten Thousand Miles Away. "It's a good song, you can have it," he said as I took down the notes. "Some mighty good men have sung it. The songs these days are cheap alongside what we used to have. You can't find tunes now like you could in the old days." And he said, after singing, "It's one people have forgotten. I don't know how old it is. The old men who sang it for me when I was a boy said it was an old song then. And they learned it from old men when they were boys."

Sing I for a brave and a gallant barque, and a stiff and a rattling breeze, A bully crew and a captain true, to carry me o'er the seas; . To carry me o'er the seas, my boys, to my true love so gay-ay-ay, . Who went on a trip in a Government ship ten thousand miles away! .

REFRAIN

Blow, ye winds, hi oh! . A-roaming I will go, . I'll stay no more on England's shore, so let the music play; . I'll start by the morning train . . to cross the raging main, For I'm on the road to my own true love, ten thousand miles away! .

1 Sing I for a brave and a gallant barque, and a stiff and a rattling breeze,
A bully crew, and a Captain, true, to carry me o'er the seas;
To carry me o'er the seas, my boys, to my true love so gay-ay-ay,
Who went on a trip in a Government ship ten thousand miles away!

Refrain:
Blow, ye winds, hi oh! a-roaming I will go,
I'll stay no more on England's shore, so let the music play;
I'll start by the morning train to cross the raging main,
For I'm on the road to my own true love, ten thousand miles away!

2 My true love she was handsome, my true love she was young,
Her eyes were blue as the violet's hue, and silvery was the sound of her tongue;
And silvery was the sound of her tongue, my boys, and, while I sing this lay-ay-ay,
She's a-doing of the grand in a far off land, ten thousand miles away!
Refrain:

3 Dark and dismal was the day when last I seen my Meg,
She'd a Government band around each hand, and another one round her leg;
And another one round her leg, my boys, as the big ship left the bay-ay-ay,
Adieu, said she, remember me, ten thousand miles away!
Refrain:

4 Oh! if I were a sailor lad, or even a bombardier,
I'd hire a boat and go afloat, and straight to my true love steer;
And straight to my true love steer, my boys, where the dancing dolphins play-ay-ay,
And the whales and sharks kick up their larks, ten thousand miles away!
Refrain:

5 The sun may shine through a London fog, or the river run bright and clear,
The ocean's brine be changed to wine, and I forget my beer,
And I forget my beer, my boys, or the landlord's quarter day-ay-ay,
But never will I part from my own sweetheart ten thousand miles away.
Refrain:

101

OLD GRAY MARE

Before the horseless carriage came, in the years when people went buggy-riding, there were more songs about horses than now. Oats for Dobbin was an expense then as gas is at the filling station now. Fodder for the mare and her foal cost money the same as oil, water and new wind shields do today. The horse doctor earned his living as the crack mechanic at the garage does, by fixing the ailing parts. We remember in our school readers the verse from Bayard Taylor, voicing the sentiments of an Arab to his steed, "My beautiful, my beautiful, thou standest so meekly by." The following poem is in a different vein and mood. It is keyed rather to the homely philosophy of an Iowa editor who was asked by a Kansas editor what he wanted on his gravestone. The answer was they could write, "He et what was sot before him." It is not as lofty in manner as the reply of an Iowa farmer asked about his first horse, a two-year-old given him by his father. "How was she? Well, she was stylish but she couldn't stand grief." The melody here is directly appropriated from the negro spiritual, The Old Gray Mare Came Tearin' Out the Wilderness.

Oh, the old gray mare, she ain't what she used to be,

Ain't what she used to be, ain't what she used to be. The old gray mare, she

ain't what she used to be, Man - y long years a - go.

OLD GRAY MARE

Many long years ago, many long years ago. The old gray mare, she ain't what she used to be, Man-y long years a-go.

1 Oh, the old gray mare, she ain't what she used to be,
Ain't what she used to be, ain't what she used to be.
The old gray mare she ain't what she used to be,
    Many long years ago.
Many long years ago, many long years ago,
The old gray mare, she ain't what she used to be,
    Many long years ago.

2 The old gray mare she kicked on the whiffletree,
Kicked on the whiffletree, kicked on the whiffletree.
The old gray mare she kicked on the whiffletree,
    Many long years ago.
Many long years ago, many long years ago,
The old gray mare, she ain't what she used to be,
    Many long years ago.

THE DRUNKARD'S DOOM

"Whiskey!" cried the land rent agitator in a famine year in Ireland. "Whiskey it is that makes ye shoot at the landlords — and miss 'em!" When the Washingtonian Society flourished in the 1840's its basic argument was that George Washington drank liquor but knew when to stop. Later came the saying, "The difference between a barber shop and a saloon is that when a man has had one shave he quits." School children in midwest states in the 1880's carried physiology books with color charts showing the progress of a drunkard's stomach from the pink of health to the raging crimson of delirium tremens. The drink habit, as an insidious destroyer, was presented in church, school, and town opera house, in the play Ten Nights in a Bar Room. The mood of that melodrama is gathered in these six verses of The Drunkard's Doom. Mary O. Eddy heard it from old women who sang it as girls in Ohio when the Temperance Movement was using songs in its crusades. Henry L. Mencken, a chamber music pianist, a composer, a contrapuntalist, a critic of music and the arts in general, writes the harmonization here.

Arr. H. L. M.

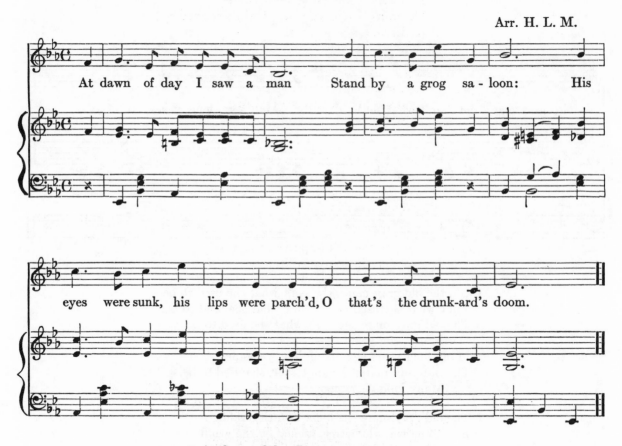

1 At dawn of day I saw a man
  Stand by a grog saloon:
  His eyes were sunk, his lips were parched,
  O that's the drunkard's doom.

104

2 His little son stood by his side,
  And to his father said,
  "Father, mother lies sick at home
  And sister cries for bread."

3 He rose and staggered to the bar
  As oft he'd done before,
  And to the landlord smilingly said,
  "Just fill me one glass more."

4 The cup was filled at his command,
  He drank of the poisoned bowl,
  He drank, while wife and children starved,
  And ruined his own soul.

5 A year had passed, I went that way,
  A hearse stood at the door;
  I paused to ask, and one replied,
  "The drunkard is no more."

6 I saw the hearse move slowly on,
  No wife nor child was there;
  They too had flown to heaven's bright home
  And left a world of care.

7 Now, all young men, a warning take,
  And shun the poisoned bowl;
  'Twill lead you down to hell's dark gate,
  And ruin your own soul.

WHAT WAS YOUR NAME IN THE STATES?

This ditty, of course, is out of the time when fugitives from the East preferred western to eastern climate.

Arr. H. F.

Oh, what was your name in the States? Was it Thomp-son or John-son or Bates? Did you mur-der your wife And fly for your life? Say, what was your name in the States?

Oh, what was your name in the States?
Was it Thompson or Johnson or Bates?
Did you murder your wife
And fly for your life?
Say, what was your name in the States?

SWEET BETSY FROM PIKE

It's four long years since I reached this land,
In search of gold among the rocks and sand;
And yet I'm poor when the truth is told,
I'm a lousy miner,
I'm a lousy miner in search of shining gold.

My sweetheart vowed she'd wait for me
'Till I returned; but don't you see
She's married now, sure, so I am told,
Left her lousy miner,
Left her lousy miner, in search of shining gold.

Oh, land of gold, you did me deceive,
And I intend in thee my bones to leave;
So farewell, home, now my friends grow cold,
I'm a lousy miner,
I'm a lousy miner in search of shining gold.

The verses from a song of California known as The Lousy Miner go to the tune of an older piece The Dark-Eyed Sailor. In Put's Original California Songster, we find the comic and the bitter. Many a line has a sting and a bite in it, a cry of the frustrated fool, sitting in the ashes of defeat and humiliation. There were two ways to reach the goldfields from the Atlantic seaboard or the Mississippi Valley. One was by ship around Cape Horn, the other across the Great Plains by covered wagon. These routes are told of in verses from The Fools of '49 to the tune of Commence, You Darkies All; they give facts in a half-comic manner that, as the testimony piles up, becomes sardonic.

The poor, the old and rotten scows, were advertised to sail
From New Orleans with passengers, but they must pump and bail;
The ships were crowded more than full, and some hung on behind,
And others dived off from the wharf, and swam till they were blind.

> *Refrain:*
> Then they thought of what they had been told,
> When they started after gold,
> That they never in the world would make a pile.

With rusty pork and stinking beef, and rotten, wormy bread,
And captains, too, that never were up as high as the main-mast head,
The steerage passengers would rave and swear that they'd paid their passage,
And wanted something more to eat besides Bologna sausage.

Then they began to cross the plains with oxen, hollowing "haw";
And steamers they began to run as far as Panama,
And there for months the people staid that started after gold,
And some returned disgusted with the lies that had been told.

The people died on every route, they sicken'd and died like sheep,
And those at sea, before they were dead, were launched into the deep;
And those that died while crossing the Plains fared not so well as that,
For a hole was dug and they thrown in, along the miserable Platte.

SWEET BETSY FROM PIKE

The ups and downs of covered wagon life, mixed with romance and ending in divorce, are told in one of the favorite songs of California in the 1850's. Sweet Betsy From Pike has the stuff of a realistic novel. It is droll and don't-care, bleary and leering, as slippery and lackadaisical as some of the comic characters of Shakespeare, or as trifling as the two murderers who are asked, "How came you here?" and who answer, "On our legs." It was a good wagon song. Miles of monotonous scenery would pass to the singing of it. Disappointed prospectors could share their own misery with Betsy and Ike. The last line of each verse could be repeated, for a change, with the fol de rol words, "Tooral lal looral lal, Tooral lal la loo." It was a good wagon song.

1 Oh don't you remember sweet Betsy from Pike,
    Who crossed the big mountains with her lover Ike,
    With two yoke of cattle, a large yellow dog,
    A tall Shanghai rooster, and one spotted hog;

Refrain:
    Saying goodbye, Pike County,
      Farewell for a while;
    We'll come back again
      When we've panned out our pile.

2 One evening quite early, they camped on the Platte,
    'Twas near by the road on a green shady flat;
    Where Betsy, quite tired, laid down to repose,
    While with wonder Ike gazed on his Pike County Rose.
    Refrain:

3 They soon reached the desert, where Betsy gave out
    And down in the sand she lay rolling about;
  While Ike in great tears looked on in surprise,
    Saying, "Betsy get up, you'll get sand in your eyes."
    Refrain:

4 Sweet Betsy got up in a great deal of pain,
    And declared she'd go back to Pike County again.
  Then Ike heaved a sigh and they fondly embraced,
    And she traveled along with his arm 'round her waist.
    Refrain:

5 The Shanghai ran off and the cattle all died,
    The last piece of bacon that morning was fried;
  Poor Ike got discouraged, and Betsy got mad,
    The dog wagged his tail and looked wonderfully sad.
    Refrain:

6 One morning they climbed up a very high hill,
    And with wonder looked down into old Placerville;
  Ike shouted and said, as he cast his eyes down,
    "Sweet Betsy, my darling, we've got to Hangtown."
    Refrain:

7 Long Ike and Sweet Betsy attended a dance,
    Where Ike wore a pair of his Pike County pants,
  Sweet Betsy was covered with ribbons and rings,
    Quoth Ike, "You're an angel, but where are your wings?"
    Refrain:

8 A miner said "Betsy, will you dance with me?"
    "I will, old hoss, if you don't make too free;
  But don't dance me hard.   Do you want to know why?
    Dog on ye, I'm chuck full of strong alkali."
    Refrain:

9 Long Ike and Sweet Betsy got married, of course,
    But Ike getting jealous obtained a divorce;
  And Betsy, well satisfied, said with a shout,
    "Goodbye, you big lummux, I'm glad you backed out,"

    Last Refrain:
    Saying goodbye, dear Isaac,
      Farewell for a while.
    But come back in time
      To replenish my pile.

CALIFORNIA

Shortly after the young congressman, Abraham Lincoln, came home from Washington and settled down again to the practice of law in Springfield, Illinois, there were announcements in newspapers occasionally, such as, "All who are interested in the California expedition will meet at candle-light to-night in the court house." California then was a place to talk about, to guess and wonder about. News came from Sutter's Creek: ten men shook pay dirt through hand screens and found a million dollars apiece in gold nuggets; the San Francisco city council adjourned without setting a date when it would meet again, churches closed their doors, newspapers stopped printing, ships lay in harbor with no sailors, cooks and soldiers ran away from military forts. A free-for-all rush started to the gold diggings: a spade sold for $1,000.00. It was news that made New York and London sit up. Across the Great Plains came wagon trains; in ten miles along the Platte River a traveler counted 459 wagons. At the trail's end was gold and California.

Arr. M. L.

When formed our band, we are all well manned, To jour-ney a-far to the pro-mised land; The gold-en ore is rich in store On the banks of the Sac-ra-men-to shore. Then ho, boys, ho: To Cal-i-for-nia go, There's

110

plen-ty of gold in the world, I'm told, On the banks of the Sac - ra - men -to shore.

1 When formed our band, we are all well manned,
   To journey afar to the promised land;
   The golden ore is rich in store
   On the banks of the Sacramento shore.

   Refrain:
       Then ho, boys, ho! To California go,
       There's plenty of gold in the world, I'm told,
       On the banks of the Sacramento shore.

2 As oft we roam o'er the dark sea's foam,
   We'll not forget kind friends at home,
   But memory kind still brings to mind
   The love of friends we left behind.
   Refrain:

3 We'll expect our share of the coarsest fare,
   And sometimes sleep in the open air,
   On the cold damp ground we'll all sleep sound
   Except when the wolves go howling round.
   Refrain:

4 As we explore to the distant shore,
   Filling our pockets with the shining ore,
   How it will sound as the shout goes round,
   Filling our pockets with a dozen of pounds.
   Refrain:

5 The gold is there almost anywhere;
   We dig it out rich with an iron bar,
   But where it is thick, with spade or pick
   We take out chunks as big as a brick.
   Refrain:

THE BANKS OF SACRAMENTO

Sailing ships took tens of thousands of gold seekers around Cape Horn to San Francisco, later taking thousands of the same passengers back. Many were bitter. A song came on the ships. Sailors sang it. In the goldfields it passed the time over pick and sieve or frying pan or over shirt and trousers having the vermin boiled out. The scramble for claims, belongings, pay dirt, was fierce. What is called "the mortality rate" ran high. They tried to laugh it off, sing it away.

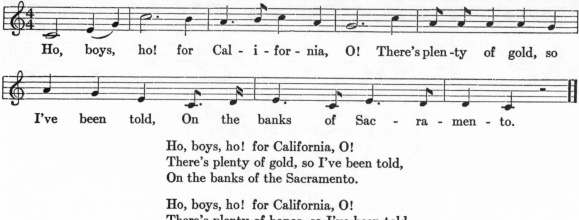

Ho, boys, ho! for Cal - i - for - nia, O! There's plen -ty of gold, so I've been told, On the banks of Sac - ra - men - to.

Ho, boys, ho! for California, O!
There's plenty of gold, so I've been told,
On the banks of the Sacramento.

Ho, boys, ho! for California, O!
There's plenty of bones, so I've been told,
On the banks of the Sacramento.

MONEY

Black-faced banjoists on the wagons of medicine men used to sing a money song with many verses. I remember the following refrain as going with each verse.

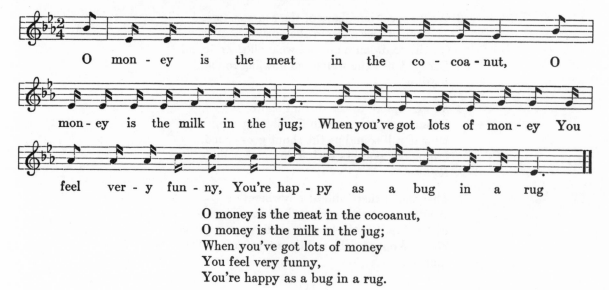

O mon - ey is the meat in the co - coa - nut, O mon - ey is the milk in the jug; When you've got lots of mon - ey You feel ver - y fun - ny, You're hap - py as a bug in a rug

O money is the meat in the cocoanut,
O money is the milk in the jug;
When you've got lots of money
You feel very funny,
You're happy as a bug in a rug.

THE MONKEY'S WEDDING

In many odd corners of America may be heard improvised verses rattled off to this tune of The Monkey's Wedding with nonsense of a similar order, though most often such impromptus are too silly or too irregular for use at gatherings of ordinary citizens. Some old English and Irish jigs have much this same tune.

The mon-key mar-ried the bab-oon's sis-ter, Gave her a ring and then . he . kissed her; He kissed so hard he raised a blis-ter, She set up a yell. The brides-maid stuck on some court-plas-ter, It stuck so . fast it . could-n't stick fast-er; Sure-ly . 'twas a . sad dis-as-ter, But it . soon got well.

1 The monkey married the baboon's sister,
Gave her a ring and then he kissed her;
He kissed so hard he raised a blister,
She set up a yell.
The bridesmaid stuck on some court-plaster,
It stuck so fast it couldn't stick faster;
Surely 'twas a sad disaster,
But it soon got well.

2 What do you think the bride was dressed in?
White gauze veil and a green glass breast-pin,
Red kid shoes quite interestin',
She was quite a belle.
The bridegroom blazed with a blue shirt-collar,
Black silk stock that cost a dollar,
Large false whiskers, the fashion to follow;
He cut a monstrous swell.

3 What do you think they had for supper?
Chestnuts raw and boiled and roasted,
Apples sliced and onions toasted,
Peanuts not a few.
What do you think they had for a fiddle?
An old banjo with a hole in the middle,
A tambourine and a worn-out griddle,
Hurdy-gurdy too.

4 What do you think were the tunes they danced to?
What were the figures they advanced to,
Up and down as they chanced to?
Tails they were too long!
"Duck in the kitchen," "Old Aunt Sally,"
Plain cotillion, "Who keeps Tally?"
Up and down they charge and rally!
Ended is my song.

ROSIE NELL

In the first Oklahoma land rush in the late 'Eighties, was a woman who rode a wild horse and staked out a claim worth having. In the years that came she raised corn, broom corn, alfalfa, soy beans — and three daughters who had freckle faces, hair of a dark gold corn silk, and sweet dispositions. Time passed. The family moved. New York was their home, the address was on Eighty-eighth Street, and the number in the phone book. They were now far from Oklahoma. Yet there came one cold rainy night to their fireside, their steam radiator, a young man who had raised corn, broom corn, alfalfa, and soy beans in Kansas, the next state to Oklahoma and standing on the same big prairie. They sang on that cold rainy night, those people around the steam radiator. And one of the songs was Rosie Nell. "It was a comfort to us in those days of the first Oklahoma land rush," said the woman who rode a wild horse to stake out a claim.

Andantino, quasi allegretto

Arr. A. G. W.

How oft I dream of child-hood days, of tricks we used to play Upon each oth-er when at school, to pass the time a-way. They of-ten wished me
with them, but they al-ways wished in vain; I'd rath-er be with Ro-sie Nell, a-

swing-ing in the lane A-swing-ing in the lane, . a-swing-ing in the

lane, I'd rath - er be with Ro - sie, Nell, a - swing - ing in the

lane, A - swing - ing in the lane, . . a - swing - ing in the

lane, I'd rath - er be with Ro - sie Nell, a - swing-ing in the lane.

1 How oft I dream of childhood days, of tricks we used to play
Upon each other when at school, to pass the time away.
They often wished me with them, but they always wished in vain;
I'd rather be with Rosie Nell, a-swinging in the lane.

Refrain:
    A-swinging in the lane, a-swinging in the lane,
    I'd rather be with Rosie Nell, a-swinging in the lane,
    A-swinging in the lane, a-swinging in the lane,
    I'd rather be with Rosie Nell, a-swinging in the lane.

2 But soon a cloud of sorrow came; a strange young man from town,
Was introduced to Rosie Nell by Aunt Jemima Brown;
She stayed away from school next day, the truth to me was plain;
She'd gone with that young city chap, a-swinging in the lane.
Refrain:

3 Now all young men with tender hearts, pray take advice from me;
Don't be so quick to fall in love, with every girl you see;
For if you do you soon will find, you've only loved in vain;
She'll go off with some other chap, a-swinging in the lane.
Refrain:

CHICKEN REEL

Of all the country fiddlers' tunes I have heard, the old timer Chicken Reel is the favorite that keeps best. Other favorites hold their charm. Over the Sea is friendly and human. Hen Cackle is funny; The Old Town Pump and Speckled Hen, too. Also McLeod's Reel, Irish Washerwoman, Turkey in the Straw, Hell on the Wabash, and Sweet Potatoes Grow in Sandy Land have their points. Yet, the trickiest of all is Chicken Reel. Cunning of musical design, elusive and unexpected in its transitions, it is like a poem that parodies itself, like a cat that walks alone, like a woman who forgets that she has forgotten, like three thistle sifters with thimbles sifting softly through three sieves. Its theme is "Never trouble trouble till trouble troubles you." The tune here was notated by Harry Gilbert from the playing of Jess Ricks, a Long Island, New York, fiddler. Ricks was raised in Taylorville, Illinois, and learned Chicken Reel from Uncle Jim Simpson, a famous barn dance fiddler of Palmer, Illinois.

HANGING OUT THE LINEN CLOTHES

From break of day till set of sun, woman's work is never done. In those days there was linen. And woman took thought about her clothes. Six days she toiled and smoothed and fashioned her linen garb and vestment, and all the time she hoped to look good and seem fair and acceptable in the eyes of her "darling" who, the song says, saw her at work. He regarded her all the more highly because she was a working girl fixing her own clothes. Grandmothers of the present generation of Californians sang this over wash-tubs and ironing boards, over the needles as they stitched and hemmed. Thus we have it from Pauline Jacobson and friends in San Francisco.

Arr. M. L.

'Twas on a Mon-day morn-ing, the first I saw my dar-ling A-
hang-ing out the lin-en clothes, a-hang-ing out the lin-en clothes.

1 'Twas on a Monday morning, the first I saw my darling
A-hanging out the linen clothes, a-hanging out the linen clothes.

2 'Twas on a Tuesday morning, the first I saw my darling
A-taking in the linen clothes, a-taking in the linen clothes.

3 'Twas on a Wednesday morning, the first I saw my darling
A-ironing of the linen clothes, a-ironing of the linen clothes.

4 'Twas on a Thursday morning, the first I saw my darling
A-mending of the linen clothes, a-mending of the linen clothes.

5 'Twas on a Friday morning, the first I saw my darling
A-folding of the linen clothes, a-folding of the linen clothes.

6 'Twas on a Sunday morning, the first I saw my darling,
A-wearing of the linen clothes, a-wearing of the linen clothes.

DOWN, DOWN DERRY DOWN

When children in the old days asked for a story or a song, the older folks sometimes gave both in a ballad such as this, which seems to have been known in Hartfordshire, England, in Massachusetts and Virginia, before it traveled to Illinois and the midwest. There were children heard a father or uncle, a mother or aunt, sing it hundreds of times. "We'll go over to Aunt Mehitable and ask her to sing 'Down, Down Derry Down.'" Eyes were shiny with fascination over the boy hero selling the cow, matching his wits against the robber, and bringing home a horse, bags of gold, and "bright pistols." The line "Down, down derry down," was useful; the singer while giving that line could refresh his recollection about the next verse; in the same moment the children could be guessing about what would happen next; they enjoy such guessing as they also enjoy wondering how many more verses there can be; and naturally, those well acquainted with a long ballad watch and wait for their favorite verses. Text and tune here are from Margery K. Forsythe of Chicago, who tells us, "Down, Down Derry Down was sung in our family before the Revolution. My mother (1860) heard her grandmother (1793) sing it and she in turn remembered it farther back. The first two lines of the third verse were lost and these are impromptu."

Arr. H. F. P.

Oh! La-dies and gen-tle-men, please to draw near; I'll sing of a man who lived in Hard-ford-shire. A fine Hart-ford-shire boy he had for his man to do his busi-ness, his name was called John. Down, Down Der-ry Down.

118

DOWN, DOWN DERRY DOWN

1 Oh! Ladies and gentlemen, please to draw near; I'll sing of a man who lived in Hartfordshire.
A fine Hartfordshire boy he had for his man to do his business, his name was called John.
Down, Down Derry Down (repeat this line after each verse).

2 Bright early one morning he to him did come, saying, "John, take my cow to the fair in the town.
Oh, this very day take my cow to the fair, for she's in good order and her I can spare."

3 So John took the cow and rode to the fair; "I'll make a good bargain," he then did declare.
And on the way there he met with a man and sold him the cow for six pound ten.

4 The man had paid the boy down all the chink, when they went into an ale-house to drink,
And unto the landlady then he did say, "Oh, what shall I do with this money I pray?"

5 "Sew it into your coat lining," then she did say, "Lest you should be robbed upon the highway."
There sat a highwayman a-drinking his wine; he said to himself, "That money is mine."

6 The boy took his leave and away he did go, the highwayman followed soon after also;
He soon overtook him upon the highway, "You're well overtaken, young lad," he did say.

7 "Oh, jump up behind me," the highwayman said; "How far are you going?" replied the young lad.
"About four miles further for all that I know," so he jumped up behind and away they did go.

8 They rode until they came to a dark lane; the highwayman said, "I must tell you now plain,
Deliver your money without any strife, or I will assuredly take your sweet life."

9 The boy, seeing there was no chance for dispute, he jumped from the horse and the money pulled
out.
And from his coat-lining the money pulled out and in the long grass he strewed it about.

10 The highwayman immediately jumped from his horse, but little he judged it was for his loss,
For while he was putting it into his purse, the boy took his leave and rode off with the horse.

11 The highwayman hollooed and bade him to stay, the boy never minded but still rode away,
And unto his master's house he did bring horse, saddle and bridle and many fine thing.

12 On searching the saddle-bags, as we are told, there were ten thousand pounds in silver and gold,
Beside two bright pistols — the boy said, "I trow, I think, my dear master, I've sold well your
cow!"

13 His master smiled when him he had told, saying, "As for a boy you've been very bold,
As for the highwayman, he's lost all his store, let him go a-robbing until he gets more."

THE LANE COUNTY BACHELOR

What is a pioneer? An American poet answered, "A pioneer is a beginner." It was a child-like answer. The pioneers in any country are those who make its beginnings. They begin the trails that later become roads. They stake out land claims, put in crops and start farming. An inscription chiseled on the state capitol building of Nebraska reads, "Honour to pioneers who broke sod that men to come might live." They were strugglers, those who went out on the Great Plains to make homes. They took weeks for the wagon trip west as "movers." Or they rode on "Home-seekers' Excursion Trains," eating from lunch baskets, sleeping on the seats of railroad cars two, three, four nights. Once located on the quarter-section claim, which would be their own land and home if they stayed a few years and farmed it, there was strife and struggle. To get food and clothes, to keep a shelter going that would shut out rain and snow, to outwit the grasshoppers that came to eat crops, to live through bad cooking, blizzards and vermin, was a steady round of strife and struggle. "There's nothing will make a man hard and profane like starving to death on a govern-ment claim," we are told in this song. They had a saying, "The worse things are the better they are." Sometimes the battle wore them down; it was too much. With "nothing to lose and noth-ing to gain," they quit as this bachelor, Frank Bolar, did. "They moved to new parts," was com-mon talk as to neighbors. Or, "they vamoosed, skedaddled." The text here is from Edwin Ford Piper, whose poems of "barbed wire" cover that Iowa and Nebraska territory where cattle used to have free range. There were no fences; then came barbed wire. "My people always sang Lane County Bachelor to the Irish Washerwoman," says Piper. It is a document in jig time.

My name is Frank Bo - lar 'nole bach - 'lor I am, I'm
My house it is built of the na - tion - al soil, The

keep - in' ole bach on an el - e - gant plan. You'll find me out West in the
walls are e - rect - ed ac - cord - ing to Hoyle, The roof has no pitch but is

Coun - ty of Lane, . . Starv - ing to death on a gov - ern - ment claim;
lev - el and plain And I al - ways get wet when it hap - pens to rain.

REFRAIN

But hur - rah for Lane Coun - ty, the land of the free, The

home of the grass-hop - per, bed-bug, and flea, I'll sing loud her prais - es and

boast of her fame While starv - ing to death on my gov - ern - ment claim.

120

1 My name is Frank Bolar, 'nole bachelor I am,
  I'm keepin' ole bach on an elegant plan.
  You'll find me out West in the County of Lane
  Starving to death on a government claim;
  My house it is built of the national soil,
  The walls are erected according to Hoyle,
  The roof has no pitch but is level and plain
  And I always get wet when it happens to rain.

   Refrain:
      But hurrah for Lane County, the land of the free,
      The home of the grasshopper, bedbug, and flea,
      I'll sing loud her praises and boast of her fame
      While starving to death on my government claim.

2 My clothes they are ragged, my language is rough,
  My head is case-hardened, both solid and tough;
  The dough it is scattered all over the room
  And the floor would get scared at the sight of a broom;
  My dishes are dirty and some in the bed
  Covered with sorghum and government bread;
  But I have a good time, and live at my ease
  On common sop-sorghum, old bacon and grease.

   Refrain:
      But hurrah for Lane County, the land of the West,
      Where the farmers and laborers are always at rest,
      Where you've nothing to do but sweetly remain,
      And starve like a man on your government claim.

3 How happy am I when I crawl into bed,
  And a rattlesnake rattles his tail at my head,
  And the gay little centipede, void of all fear
  Crawls over my pillow and into my ear,
  And the nice little bedbug so cheerful and bright,
  Keeps me a-scratching full half of the night,
  And the gay little flea with toes sharp as a tack
  Plays "Why don't you catch me?" all over my back.

   Refrain:
      But hurrah for Lane County, where blizzards arise,
      Where the winds never cease and the flea never dies,
      Where the sun is so hot if in it you remain
      'Twill burn you quite black on your government claim.

121

4 How happy am I on my government claim,
　Where I've nothing to lose and nothing to gain,
　Nothing to eat and nothing to wear,
　Nothing from nothing is honest and square.
　But here I am stuck, and here I must stay,
　My money's all gone and I can't get away;
　There's nothing will make a man hard and profane
　Like starving to death on a government claim.

　　Refrain:
　　Then come to Lane County, there's room for you all,
　　Where the winds never cease and the rains never fall,
　　Come join in the chorus and boast of her fame,
　　While starving to death on your government claim.

5 Now don't get discouraged, ye poor hungry men,
　We're all here as free as a pig in a pen;
　Just stick to your homestead and battle your fleas,
　And pray to your Maker to send you a breeze.
　Now a word to claim-holders who are bound for to stay:
　You may chew your hard-tack till you're toothless and gray,
　But as for me, I'll no longer remain
　And starve like a dog on my government claim.

　　Refrain:
　　Farewell to Lane County, farewell to the West,
　　I'll travel back East to the girl I love best;
　　I'll stop in Missouri and get me a wife,
　　And live on corn dodgers the rest of my life.

KENTUCKY BLAZING STAR

When at the University of Kentucky with my talk and recital, I was told of Gilbert Reynolds Combs, minister of the First Methodist Episcopal Church of Lexington. He came from the mountain people and believes in them as having characters of tragedy and comedy, as having temperament, speech, song and original minds. His talk about the mountain people and his singing of their ballads and ditties is quiet and convincing. Born "on the waters of Cow Creek," he saw life amid the log cabins on the ridges of Pine Mountain and the streams named Troublesome, Cutshin, Hell-fer-Sartain and Kingdom Come. His forefathers for three generations were natives of "Bloody Breathitt" county, tracing back to Scotch-Irish settlers in Virginia before the Revolution. When Combs came down from the mountains in his sixteenth year, he was to see for the first time a railroad train, a telephone, typewriter, fountain pen, bath tub, barber chair, and other items of onrushing civilization. He worked his way through Berea College, was the valedictorian at Kentucky Wesleyan, took post-graduate studies, won an oratory medal at Vanderbilt University, at twenty-seven was ordained a minister and in a few years became one of the leaders, at thirty-six was the pastor of what is regarded as the central and leading church of his Conference. In a corner of his church study Mr. Combs has a collection of more than 300 mountaineer songs. He placed at our disposal a number of them appearing in the section called Kentucky Blazing Star, which is the name of a "kiverlid" design that originated in some cabin alongside a Troublesome or Kingdom Come Creek.

SOURWOOD MOUNTAIN

This tune and text of Sourwood Mountain, which has so many versions, is another from the collection of Gilbert R. Combs of Lexington, Kentucky. It is as much a dance tune as a song, and is close to the style of the yodel.

Arr. A. G. W.

1 Chickens a-crowin' on Sourwood Mountain,
   Ho-dee-ing-dong-doodle allay day,
   So many pretty girls I can't count 'em,
   Ho-dee-ing-dong-doodle allay day.

2 My true love, she's a blue-eyed dandy,
   Ho-dee-ing-dong-doodle allay day,
   A kiss from her is sweeter than candy,
   Ho-dee-ing-dong-doodle allay day.

3 My true love lives over the river,
   Ho-dee-ing-dong-doodle allay day,
   A hop and a skip and I'll be with her,
   Ho-dee-ing-dong-doodle allay day.

4 My true love is a blue-eyed daisy,
   Ho-dee-ing-dong-doodle allay day,
   If she don't marry me I'll go crazy,
   Ho-dee-ing-dong-doodle allay day.

5 Back my jenny up the Sourwood Mountain,
   Ho-dee-ing-dong-doodle allay day,
   So many pretty girls I can't count 'em,
   Ho-dee-ing-dong-doodle allay day.

6 My true love is a sun-burnt daisy,
   Ho-dee-ing-dong-doodle allay day,
   She won't work and I'm too lazy,
   Ho-dee-ing-dong-doodle allay day.

THE LOVER'S LAMENT

Blendings from five or six old ballads are in this song of parting lovers. "Her lips was like some musical instrument," and other lines, are extraordinary. The pangs of separation find voice in an upward sliding wail. It is communicated by Neeta Marquis of Los Angeles, who says it is too finely sweet a song to be among the lost and forgotten things of melodic art.

Arr. A. G. W.

My dear-est dear, the time draws near When you and I must part; But lit-tle do you know the grief or woe Of my poor troub-led heart.

Oh hush, my love, you will break my heart, Nor let me hear you

THE LOVER'S LAMENT

cry; For the best of friends will have to part, And so must you and I.

A

1 My dearest dear, the time draws near
When you and I must part;
But little do you know the grief or woe
Of my poor troubled heart.

Refrain:
Oh hush, my love, you will break my heart,
Nor let me hear you cry;
For the best of friends will have to part,
And so must you and I.

2 As I walked out one clear summer night,
A-drinking of sweet wine,
It was then I saw that pretty little girl
That stole this heart of mine.
Refrain:

3 Her cheeks was like some pink or rose
That blooms in the month of June,
Her lips was like some musical instrument,
That sung this doleful tune.
Refrain:

4 Ah, who will shoe your feet, my love,
And who will glove your hands,
And who will kiss your red, rosy lips
When I am gone to the foreign land?
Refrain:

5 My father, he will shoe my feet,
My mother will glove my hands,
And you may kiss my red, rosy lips,
When you come from the foreign land.
Refrain:

6 You are like unto some turtle dove,
That flies from tree to tree,
A-mourning for its own true love
Just as I mourn for thee.
Refrain:

7 You are like unto some sailing ship
That sails the raging main,
If I prove false to you, my love,
The raging seas will burn.
Refrain:

B

1 I wish your breast was made of glass,
All in it I might behold;
Your name in secret I would write
In letters of bright gold.
Refrain.

2 Your name in secret I would write,
Pray believe in what I say;
You are the man that I love best
Unto my dying day.
Refrain.

127

HELLO, GIRLS

Girls who are thinking about getting married find advice here. The third verse carries a laugh, with a slight mourning border of sober second thought. Movers from Kentucky, probably, took the tune to Kansas, and gave it new verses as in text B, the song of Kansas Boys. "Puncheon floor" and "milk in the gourd" are clearly Kentucky inventions or importations. Planting corn in February "with a Texas pony and a grasshopper plow," however, is a farming trick the Kentuckians first heard of after they left "the Gascony of America" and took up claims in the Sunflower state. The verses traveled up into Nebraska districts where they pitch horseshoes and hold championship corn-husking contests, for Edwin Ford Piper, who lived on a farm near Auburn, wrote of Kansas Boys, "This ballad I found in my sister's note book. The older brothers and sisters used to sing it."

Arr. A. G. W.

A

1 Hello girls, listen to my voice,
   Don't you never marry no good-for-nothing boys.
   If you do your doom shall be
   Hoe-cake, hominy, and sassafras tea.

2 Young boys walking down the street,
   Young girls think they look mighty sweet.
   Hands in their pockets not a dime can they find,
   Oh, how tickled, poor girls mine.

3 When a young man falls in love,
   First it's honey and then turtle dove.
   After he's married no such thing,
   "Get up and get my breakfast, you good-for-nothing thing!"

128

B
KANSAS BOYS

1 Come, all young girls, pay attention to my noise,
  Don't fall in love with the Kansas boys,
  For if you do your portion it will be,
  Johnny cake and antelope is all you'll see.

2 They'll take you out on the jet black hill,
  Take you there so much against your will,
  Leave you there to perish on the plains,
  For that is the way with the Kansas range.

3 Some live in a cabin with a huge log wall,
  Nary a window in it at all,
  Sand stone chimney and a puncheon floor,
  Clapboard roof and a button door.

4 When they get hungry and go to make bread,
  They kindle a fire as high as your head,
  Rake around the ashes and in they throw,
  The name they give it is "doughboys' dough."

5 When they go to milk they milk in a gourd,
  Heave it in the corner and cover with a board,
  Some get plenty and some get none,
  That is the way with the Kansas run.

6 When they go to meeting the clothes that they wear
  Is an old brown coat all picked and bare,
  An old white hat more rim than crown,
  A pair of cotton socks they wore the week around.

7 When they go to farming you needn't be alarmed,
  In February they plant their corn,
  The way they tend it I'll tell you now,
  With a Texas pony and a grasshopper plow.

8 When they go a-fishing they take along a worm,
  Put it on the hook just to see it squirm,
  The first thing they say when they get a bite
  Is "I caught a fish as big as Johnny White."

9 When they go courting they take along a chair,
  The first thing they say is, "Has your daddy killed a bear,"
  The second thing they say when they sit down
  Is "Madam, your Johnny cake is baking brown."

RED RIVER VALLEY

The popular song In the Bright Mohawk Valley went through changes in the seaboard and mountain states of the South. It became The Red River Valley; it went west and became a "cowboy love song," the end line speaking of "the cowboy that's waiting for you" or "the half breed that's waiting for you." The version here is from Gilbert R. Combs as he heard it on Pine Mountain. Three final stanzas are added from the R. W. Gordon collection. I have heard it sung as if bells might be calling across a mist in a gloaming.

Arr. H. F. P.

From this val - ley they say you are go - ing, ... We will
Come and sit by my side if you love me, ... Do not

miss your bright eyes and sweet smile, For they say you are tak - ing the
has - ten to bid me a - dieu, But re - mem - ber the Red Riv - er

sun - shine That bright - ens our path - way a - while. ....
Val - ley And the girl that has loved you so true. ....

RED RIVER VALLEY

1 From this valley they say you are going,
We will miss your bright eyes and sweet smile,
For they say you are taking the sunshine
That brightens our pathway awhile.

Refrain:
   Come and sit by my side if you love me,
   Do not hasten to bid me adieu,
   But remember the Red River Valley
   And the girl that has loved you so true.

2 For a long time I have been waiting
For those dear words you never would say,
But at last all my fond hopes have vanished,
For they say you are going aawy.
Refrain:

3 Won't you think of the valley you're leaving?
Oh how lonely, how sad it will be.
Oh think of the fond heart you're breaking,
And the grief you are causing me to see?
Refrain:

4 From this valley they say you are going;
When you go, may your darling go too?
Would you leave her behind unprotected
When she loves no other but you?
Refrain:

5 I have promised you, darling, that never
Will a word from my lips cause you pain;
And my life, — it will be yours forever
If you only will love me again.
Refrain:

6 Must the past with its joys be blighted
By the future of sorrow and pain,
And the vows that was spoken be slighted?
Don't you think you can love me again?
Refrain:

7 As you go to your home by the ocean,
May you never forget those sweet hours,
That we spent in Red River Valley,
And the love we exchanged 'mid the flowers.
Refrain:

8 There never could be such a longing
In the heart of a pure maiden's breast,
That dwells in the heart you are breaking
As I wait in my home in the West.
Refrain:

9 And the dark maiden's prayer for her lover
To the Spirit that rules over the world;
May his pathway be ever in sunshine,
Is the prayer of the Red River girl.
Refrain:

LIZA JANE

The mountains are friendly and homelike to many who live there. Gilbert R. Combs tells of men leaving for a year or two of "ranching it" on the western plains, and then straggling back saying of the flat prairies and level horizons, "It was too lonesome, too l-o-n-e-s-o-m-e." They have their own ways. Some are told of in these lines from men who are a law unto themselves. There are as many Liza songs in the Appalachian mountains as there are species of trees on the slopes of that range. The one in text A is called Liza Jane and the one in text B is known as Mountain Top.

Arr. A. G. W.

I'll go up on the moun-tain top, And plant me a patch of cane, I'll make me a jug of mo-las-ses, For to sweet-en lit-tle Li-za Jane. O po' Li-za, po' gal,

O po' Li - za Jane, O po' Li - za, po' gal, She died on the train.

A

1 I'll go up on the mountain top,
And plant me a patch of cane,
I'll make me a jug of molasses,
For to sweeten little Liza Jane.

Refrain:
    O po' Liza, po' gal,
    O po' Liza Jane,
    O po' Liza, po' gal,
    She died on the train.

2 I'll go up on the mountain top,
Put up my moonshine still,
I'll make you a quart of old moonshine,
For just one dollar bill.
Refrain:

3 Head is like a coffee pot,
Nose is like a spout,
Her mouth is like an old fire-place,
With the ashes all raked out.
Refrain:

4 I went to see my Liza Jane,
She was standing in the door,
Her shoes and stockings in her hand,
And her feet all over the floor.
Refrain:

5 The hardest work that ever I did,
Was a-brakin' on the train,
The easiest work that ever I did,
Was a-huggin' little Liza Jane.
Refrain:

B

MOUNTAIN TOP

1 I'll go up on the mountain top
And grow me a patch of cane,
I'll make me a jug of molasses too,
For to sweeten up Liza Jane.

2 Come along, sweet Liza Jane,
Just come along with me,
We'll go up on the mountain top,
Some pleasures there to see.

3 I'll go up on this mountain top
Put out me a moonshine still,
I'll sell you a quart of old moonshine
Just for a one dollar bill.

4 I will eat when I am hungry
And drink when I am dry,
If a tree don't fall on me
I'll live until I die.

133

NEGRO REEL

This mountain piece comes from Neeta Marquis of Los Angeles, California, who recalls the singing of it in her family when she was a girl. It was a traditional tune of Kentucky and Tennessee that her father said went back to the Eighteen-forties. Alfred Wathall points out that the tune derives from an old English contra dance air.

Arr. A. G. W.

Laws - a - mas - sey, what have you done? You've mar - ried the old man in -

stead of his son! His legs are all crook - ed and wrong put on, They're

all a - laugh-ing at your old man. Now you're mar-ried you must o - bey. You

rit.   poco a poco

must prove true to all you say. And as you have prom-ised, so

now you must do,— Kiss him twice and hug him too.

1 Laws-a-massey, what have you done?
　You've married the old man instead of his son!
　His legs are all crooked and wrong put on,
　They're all a-laughing at your old man.

2 Now you're married you must obey.
　You must prove true to all you say.
　And as you have promised, so now you must do, —
　Kiss him twice and hug him, too.

135

ONE MORNING IN MAY

This is a mountain dance tune. One can see feet and fiddles, the bowing of lovers looking into each other's eyes, the exchange of glances as they go circling in "all hands around." Such a song was particularly useful when the fiddler failed to show up or went out of commission with a heavy cargo of "corn." This lineal descendant of old British balladry has many variants in America; an instance of certain English folk-songs which have a wider variety of text and tunes in the Appalachian Mountains of the United States than are to be found in the British Isles. The musical design here is cunning, and the skill of it grows on us as we become more familiar with it. This was heard by Gilbert R. Combs in his Pine Mountain years. He gives us two texts, One Morning In May and The Troubled Soldier, both of which can be managed to the one tune.

Arr. A. G. W.

One morn-ing, one morn-ing, one morn-ing in May I

met a fair cou-ple a-mak-ing their way, And one was a maid-en so

bright and so fair, And the oth-er was a sol-dier and a brave vol-un-teer.

ONE MORNING IN MAY

A

1 One morning, one morning, one morning in May
I met a fair couple a-making their way,
And one was a maiden so bright and so fair,
And the other was a soldier and a brave volunteer.

2 Good morning, good morning, good morning to thee,
O where are you going my pretty lady?
O I am a-going to the banks of the sea,
To see the waters gliding, hear the nightingale sing.

3 We hadn't been a-standing but a minute or two
When out from his knapsack a fiddle he drew,
And the tune that he played made the valleys all ring,
O see the waters gliding, hear the nightingale sing.

4 Pretty lady, pretty lady, it's time to give o'er,
O no, pretty soldier, please play one tune more,
I'd rather hear your fiddle or the touch of one string
Than to see the waters gliding, hear the nightingale sing.

5 Pretty soldier, pretty soldier, will you marry me?
O no, pretty lady, that never can be;
I've a wife in old London and children twice three;
Two wives in the army's too many for me.

6 I'll go back to London and stay there one year
And often I'll think of you my little dear,
If ever I return, 'twill be in the spring
To see the waters gliding, hear the nightingale sing.

B

THE TROUBLED SOLDIER

1 It was in the lovely month of May,
I heard a poor soldier lamenting and say,
I heard a poor soldier lamenting and moan,
"I am a troubled soldier, no friend and no home."

2 O Mary, O Mary, 'twas for your sake alone
I left my poor father and mother at home,
I left my poor father, my mother to roam, —
I am a troubled soldier, no friend and no home.

137

3 I'm troubled in trouble, I'm troubled, and why?
If trouble don't kill me I know I'll never die.
If Jesus don't hear me and help me to moan,
I am a troubled soldier, no friend and no home.

4 Go build me a castle on yon mountain high,
Where the wild geese can hear me as they do pass by,
Where the turtle dove can hear me and help me to mourn,
I am a troubled soldier, no friend and no home.

5 Don't you remember on one Friday night,
While by your side I sat, you said
You loved me, and my heart laid in your breast,
And if you didn't get married you never could rest?

6 Adieu to Old Kentucky I never more expect to see,
For love and misfortune has called me away,
For love and misfortune has called me to mourn,
I am a troubled soldier, no friend and no home.

POST-RAIL SONG

The post-rail fence in Kentucky has posts with holes bored in them, through which the fence rails run. Fence-builders chant these lines to the swing of their bodies as they "put 'em up solid." We have this on the authority of Charles Hoening of the University of Rochester faculty. He grew up in the blue grass region and when he had finished growing he was six feet four inches tall and put up solid.

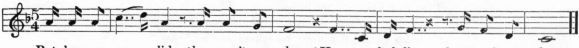

Put 'em up so - lid, they won't come down! Hey, ma lad-die, they won't come down.

Put 'em up solid, they won't come down!
Hey, ma laddie, they won't come down!

HAMMER MAN

The negro worker often makes songs on the job, whether in the white harvest of cotton or driving a railroad tunnel through a rock mountain. We are told of a research student who took a seat on a fence to listen to the singing of a negro work gang on a railroad. When he finally detected their words he found they were singing lines that sounded like, "See dat white man . . . sittin' on a fence . . . sittin' on a fence . . . wastin' his time . . . wastin' his time." This song from the Combs collection was probably made by negroes on the job and learned from the negroes by the mountain whites. Drivin' steel is hard work; the worker's stay on the job depends on whether he is treated right or wrong; the idea is big enough for a song whose tempo is hammer swing rhythms.

Arr. A. G. W.

1 Drivin' steel, drivin' steel,
   Drivin' steel, boys,
   Is hard work, I know;
   Drivin' steel, drivin' steel,
   Drivin' steel, boys,
   Is hard work, I know.

2 Treat me right, treat me right,
   Treat me right, boys,
   I am bound to stay all day;
   Treat me wrong, treat me wrong,
   Treat me wrong, boys,
   I am bound to run away.

3 Boss man, boss man,
   Boss man, boys,
   See the boss man comin' down the line,
   Boss man, boss man,
   Boss man, boys,
   See the boss man comin' down the line.

LOVE SOMEBODY, YES I DO

Fiddlers play this. Its timebeat is to "all hands circle round." If the fiddlers fail to come the dancers can sing their music. The word "love" is mentioned in every line but the last, "'Tween sixteen and twenty-two." It is for young folks, and has air and step from an old English contra dance, Wathall tells us. Also, for this we are indebted to the Combs collection.

Love some-bod - y, yes I do; love some-bod - y, yes I do;

Love some-bod - y, yes I do; Love some-bod - y, but I won't tell who.

Love some-bod - y, yes I do; Love some-bod - y, yes I do;

LOVE SOMEBODY, YES I DO

1 Love somebody, yes I do;
Love somebody, yes I do;
Love somebody, yes I do;
Love somebody, but I won't tell who.
Love somebody, yes I do;
Love somebody, yes I do;
Love somebody, yes I do;
And I hope somebody loves me too.

2 Love somebody, yes I do;
Love somebody, yes I do;
Love somebody, yes I do;
Love somebody, but I won't tell who.
Love somebody, yes I do;
Love somebody, yes I do;
Love somebody, yes I do,
'Tween sixteen and twenty-two.

AIN'T GONNA RAIN

This Iowa and Nebraska dance song has mountaineer and negro versions; it came west from Kentucky and other southern states according to Edwin Ford Piper; it is at least as old as the 1870's.

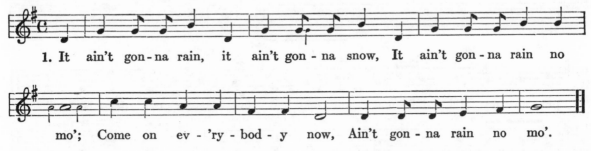

2 Oh, what did the blackbird say to the crow?
It ain't gonna rain no mo',
Ain't gonna hail, ain't gonna snow,
Ain't gonna rain no mo'.

3 Bake them biscuits good and brown,
It ain't gonna rain no mo'.
Swing yo' ladies round and round,
Ain't gonna rain no mo'.

KENTUCKY MOONSHINER

Gilbert R. Combs says that of all songs he heard as he grew up in the mountains, this is the most desolate and poignant. It wails; it brandishes sorrow; it publishes grief; it opens the final stop-gaps of lonely fate, staunchly vocal. This relates directly to ancient Gaelic lamentations over dead kings; it is "keening" of a sort and has the character of melody suitable to a wake over one with the lights gone from him. A "grocery," we note, is a general store keeping liquor among provisions and staples for sale.

142

1 I've been a moonshiner for seventeen long years,
I've spent all my money for whiskey and beers.
I'll go to some holler, I'll put up my still,
I'll make you one gallon for a two dollar bill.

2 I'll go to some grocery and drink with my friends,
No women to follow to see what I spends.
God bless those pretty women, I wish they were mine,
Their breath smells as sweet as the dew on the vine.

3 I'll eat when I'm hungry and drink when I'm dry,
If moonshine don't kill me, I'll live till I die.
God bless those moonshiners, I wish they were mine,
Their breath smells as sweet as the good old moonshine.

MISTER FROG WENT A–COURTING

"In continuous use for four hundred years," L. W. Payne tells us in a forty-four page history of the song in Publication No. 5 of the Texas Folk Lore Society; he prints sixteen tunes and has many more. The following is a Kentucky and Virginia version, with text additions from Payne. "Ah-hah" can be "uhn-huhn," "eh-heh," "och-kungh" (like a bull frog) and, as you please.

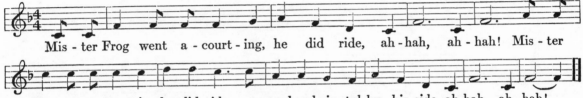

Mis - ter Frog went a - court - ing, he did ride, ah - hah, ah - hah! Mis - ter

Frog went a-court-ing, he did ride, a sword and pis - tol by his side, ah-hah, ah - hah!

1 Mister Frog went a-courting, he did ride, ah-hah, ah-hah!
Mister Frog went a-courting, he did ride, a sword and a pistol by his side, ah-hah, ah-hah!
2 He rode up to Miss Mousie's door, ah-hah, ah-hah!
He rode up to Miss Mousie's door, where he had often been before, ah-hah, ah-hah!
3 Now Uncle Rat when he came home says, "Who's been here since I been gone?"
4 "A very fine gentleman has been here who wishes me to be his dear."
5 Uncle Rat laughed and shook his side to think his niece would be a bride.
6 Uncle Rat on a horse he went to town to buy his niece a wedding gown.
7 Where shall the wedding supper be? Away down yonder in a hollow tree.
8 What shall the wedding supper be? Three green beans and a black-eyed pea.
9 Tell us, what was the bride dressed in? A cream gauze veil and a brass breastpin.
10 Tell us next what was the groom dressed in? Sky blue britches with silver stitches.
11 The first came in was a bumble bee, to play the fiddle upon his knee.
12 They all sat down and began to chat, when in walked the kitten and the cat.
13 Mrs. Cat she stepped to the supper and turned over the plate of butter.
14 Miss Mousie went a-tearing up the wall, her foot slipped and she got a fall.
15 They all went a-sailing across the lake, and they all were swallowed by a big black snake.
16 So here's the end of one, two, three, the cat, the frog and Miss Mousie.
17 There's bread and cheese upon the shelf, and if you want any just help yourself.

KIND MISS

"Did she marry him for love or money?" is about as old as the query, "Would you rather marry a handsome man who is poor or a man with lots of money and a face like a mud fence?" The answer among children is, "I'd rather have both." In the Kentucky song here we have an offer of marriage, even elopement. The girl refuses and tells why. . . . Ann Riddell Anderson of the University of Kentucky communicates this; her father, Hugh Riddell, is judge in a circuit of courts including "Bloody Breathitt" County.

Arr. A. G. W.

Kind miss, kind miss, go ask your moth-er If you, my bride shall ev - er be.

If she says "Yes," Come back and tell me, If she says "No," we'll run a - way.

1 Kind miss, kind miss, go ask your mother
If you, my bride shall ever be.
If she says "Yes," come back and tell me,
If she says "No," we'll run away.

2 Kind miss, I have much gold and silver,
Kind miss, I have a house and land,
Kind miss, I have a world of pleasure,
And all of these at thy command.

3 What do I care for your gold and silver,
What do I care for your house and land,
What do I care for your world of pleasure,
When all I want is a handsome man.

144

GOIN' DOWN TO TOWN

This is comic poetry, in a rough and tumble sense, put to a tune that is strictly rough and tumble. Millions of horses and mules have heard this, and the likes of it, from drivers on the wagon seat singing to themselves. It is a horse's earful.

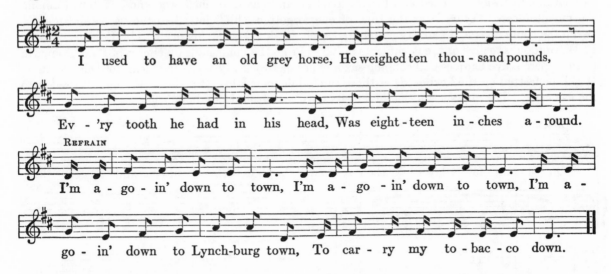

I used to have an old grey horse, He weighed ten thou - sand pounds,

Ev - 'ry tooth he had in his head, Was eight - teen in - ches a - round.

REFRAIN

I'm a - go - in' down to town, I'm a - go - in' down to town, I'm a -

go - in' down to Lynch-burg town, To car - ry my to - bac - co down.

1 I used to have an old grey horse,
He weighed ten thousand pounds,
Ev'ry tooth he had in his head,
Was eighteen inches around.

Refrain:
I'm a-goin' down to town,
I'm a-goin' down to town,
I'm a-goin' down to Lynchburg town,
To carry my tobacco down.

2 That horse he had a holler tooth,
He could eat ten bushels of corn,
Ev'ry time he opened his mouth,
Two bushels and a half were gone.
Refrain:

3 I had a yaller gal,
I brought her from the south,
All the fault I had with her,
She had too big a mouth.
Refrain:

4 I took her down to the blacksmith shop,
To get her mouth made small,
She opened her mouth to get a long breath,
And swallowed blacksmith, shop and all.
Refrain:

5 I'm a-goin' to get me some sticks and sand,
To make my chimney higher,
To keep that dog-goned old tom cat,
From puttin' out my fire.
Refrain:

145

THE SHIP THAT NEVER RETURNED

A Kentucky mountain version of a popular song of about 1870, we are told. Gilbert R. Combs heard it as a boy on Pine Mountain. The Prisoner's Song, a 1925–1926 "hit," got its melody from "The Ship that Never Returned" and its verses from another old timer, "Moonlight." That is, two songs Broadway launched and forgot, lived on and changed, mellowed and sweetened among the mountaineers. Years later the tune of one forgotten "hit" joined to the verses of another, sweep the country as a Broadway triumph. Such, in short, is the history of The Prisoner's Song; R. W. Gordon is to give us the documents in full. From the homemade dulcimers of Pine Mountain to the repercussive banjoes and sobbing saxophones of Broadway was a long leap for this old tune. It will be fretted on the keyboards of those same dulcimers when Broadway has again tossed it to the ash cans. The manner and method of its next comeback is anybody's guess.

Arr. H. F. P.

146

THE SHIP THAT NEVER RETURNED

nev-er returned,and her fate is still un-learned, . . . But a last poor man set

sail com-mand-er, on a ship that nev-er re-turned. . . . .

1 On a summer's day while the waves were rippling, with a quiet and a gentle breeze;
A ship set sail with a cargo laden for a port beyond the sea.

Refrain:
   Did she ever return?   No, she never returned, and her fate is still unlearned,
   But a last poor man set sail commander, on a ship that never returned.

2 There were sad farewells, there were friends forsaken, and her fate is still unlearned,
But a last poor man set sail commander on a ship that never returned.
Refrain:

3 Said a feeble lad to his aged mother, I must cross that deep blue sea,
For I hear of a land in the far off country, where there's health and strength for me.
Refrain:

4 'Tis a gleam of hope and a maze of danger, and our fate is still to learn,
And a last poor man set sail commander, on a ship that never returned.
Refrain:

5 Said this feeble lad to his aged mother, as he kissed his weeping wife,
"Just one more purse of that golden treasure, it will last us all through life.
Refrain:

6 "Then we'll live in peace and joy together and enjoy all I have earned."
So they sent him forth with a smile and blessing on a ship that never returned.
Refrain:

147

DOWN IN THE VALLEY

Here are nine verses of a poem as idle as the wind. It is an old fashioned lyric, simple in its stitches yet as fixed in its design as certain "kiverlids" made by housewives in the Kentucky mountains. I have heard the remark, "It is a good song to be singing while writing a love letter — it is full of wishes — and dances a little — and hopes a beloved dancing partner will come back." The text and tune are from Frances Ries of Batavia, Ohio.

Arr. A. G. W.

1 Down in the valley,
The valley so low,
Hang your head over,
Hear the wind blow.

2 Hear the wind blow, dear,
Hear the wind blow,
Hang your head over,
Hear the wind blow.

3 If you don't love me,
Love whom you please;
Throw your arms 'round me,
Give my heart ease.

4 Throw your arms 'round me,
Before it's too late;
Throw yours 'round me,
Feel my heart break.

5 Writing this letter,
Containing three lines,
Answer my question:
"Will you be mine?"

6 "Will you be mine, dear,
Will you be mine?"
Answer my question:
"Will you be mine?"

7 Go build me a castle
Forty feet high;
So I can see him,
As he goes by.

8 As he goes by, dear;
As he goes by;
So I can see him,
As he goes by.

9 Roses love sunshine,
Violets love dew,
Angels in heaven
Knows I love you.

I DREAMED LAST NIGHT OF MY TRUE LOVE

English travelers have said it is the 17th century language of England that is spoken in certain isolated mountain and seaboard corners of America. Among these pocketed populations they say "poke" for "pocket," "my may" for "my sweetheart," and asking a kiss, "Come buss me." . . . The mountaineer may remark of his horse, "That mare is the loveliest runner and the sensiblest animal I ever saddled," or he may give places names such as Shoo Bird Mountain, Shake-a-rag Holler, or Huggins Hell. Once in Kentucky a wanderer inquiring the route was told he was on the right road and to go on "about two screeches and a holler." . . . The independent lingo and manner of the mountaineer is in this text and tune from Mrs. Mark E. Hutchinson of Mount Vernon, Iowa.

Arr. A. G. W.

I dreamed last night of my true love All in my arms I had her Her
pret-ty yel-ler hair like strands of gold Lay dang-ling round my pil-ler.

1 I dreamed last night of my true love.
All in my arms I had her;
Her pretty yeller hair like strands of gold,
Lay dangling round my piller.

2 I waked in the morning and found her not.
I was forced to do without her;
I went unto her uncle's house,
Inquiring for this lady.

3 He said that she was not there,
And neither would he keep her.
I turned around to go away,
My love she come to the winder.

4 She said that she would come to me,
If doors nor locks did not hinder.
I turned around and broke them locks,
I broke 'em all asinder (asunder).

149

DRIVIN' STEEL

The mountaineers of East Tennessee have their own song of the steel driving man who toils in tunnels and on railroads. This version is from Gilbert R. Combs as he heard it from mountaineers. It is a working class song straight from men on the job, uttered to muscular body rhythms. We can almost hear the ring of steel on steel. There is heave of shoulders, deep breath control, the touch of hands on a familiar well-worn hammer handle.

Arr. A. G. W.

1 If I could drive steel like John Henry
  I'd go home, Baby, I'd go home.

2 If I had forty-one dollars
  I'd go home, Baby, I'd go home.

3 I'm goin' home and tell Little Annie,
  No mo' trials, Baby, no mo' trials.

4 Do you hear that rain crow hollerin'?
  Sign of rain, Baby, sign of rain.

5 This old hammer killed John Henry
  Can't kill me, Baby, can't kill me.

6 This old hammer killed Bill Dooley
  Can't kill me, Baby, can't kill me.

7 This old hammer weighs forty pounds, sah,
  Can't kill me, Baby, can't kill me.

THE LINCOLNS AND HANKSES

THE MISSOURI HARMONY

A famous oblong song book of the pioneer days in the middle west was "The Missouri Harmony," published in 1808 by Morgan and Sanxay of Cincinnatti. Young Abraham Lincoln and his sweetheart, Ann Rutledge, sang from this book in the Rutledge tavern in New Salem, according to old settlers there. It was used at camp meetings of Peter Cartwright and other circuit riding evangelists, and was highly thought of by many church members in the Mississippi Valley.

Though the volume included "Legacy" an Irish drinking song, praising "balmy drops of the red grape," the author in his instructions to singers, warned them: "A cold or cough, all kinds of spiritous liquors, violent exercise, bile upon the stomach, long fasting, the veins overcharged with impure blood, etc., etc., are destructive to the voice of one who is much in the habit of singing. A frequent use of spiritous liquors will speedily ruin the best voice."

In further advice on vocal hygiene, he declared, "A frequent use of some acid drink, such as purified cider, elixir of vitriol with water, vinegar, etc., if used sparingly is strengthening to the lungs."

The author of the "supplement" on how to sing, kept himself anonymous, the title page saying the book was "By An Amateur." He desired his readers to know "the superiority of vocal to instrumental music is, that while one only pleases the ear, the other informs the understanding." Under the head of "General Observations," he gave these hints on the frame of mind singers should try for: "There should not be any noise indulged in while singing (except the music) as it destroys entirely the beauty of harmony, and renders the performance (especially to learners) very difficult; and if it is designedly promoted, it is nothing less than a proof of disrespect in the singers to the exercise, to themselves who occasion it, and to the Author of our existence."

"All 'affectation' should be banished. It is disgusting in the performance of sacred music, and contrary to that solemnity which should accompany an exercise so near akin to that which will through all eternity engage the attention of those who walk 'in climes of bliss.'" "The great Jehovah, who implanted in our nature the noble faculty of vocal performance, is jealous of the use to which we apply our talents in that particular lest we exercise them in a way which does not tend to glorify his name."

The pages from the "Missouri Harmony," reproduced here, contain at least two songs with which Abraham Lincoln had close acquaintance. Dennis Hanks, a cousin of Lincoln, has related that in Spencer County, Indiana, the song, "How Tedious and Tasteless the Hours," (Greenfields), was well-known, and New Salem, Illinois, residents have told of how Lincoln parodied "Legacy."

THE MISSOURI HARMONY;

OR A COLLECTION OF

PSALM AND HYMN TUNES, AND ANTHEMS,

FROM EMINENT AUTHORS:

WITH AN INTRODUCTION TO THE GROUNDS AND RUDIMENTS OF MUSIC.

BY ALLEN D. CARDEN.

153

WINDSOR. C. M.

My God, how many are my fears; How fast my foes increase! Their number how it multi- plies: How fatal to my peace.

Above are lines from the title page of The Missouri Harmony, a songbook published in 1808 in Cincinnati, and widely used among midwest pioneers. Below is a photograph of the hymn music of Windsor.

GREENFIELDS. 8s.

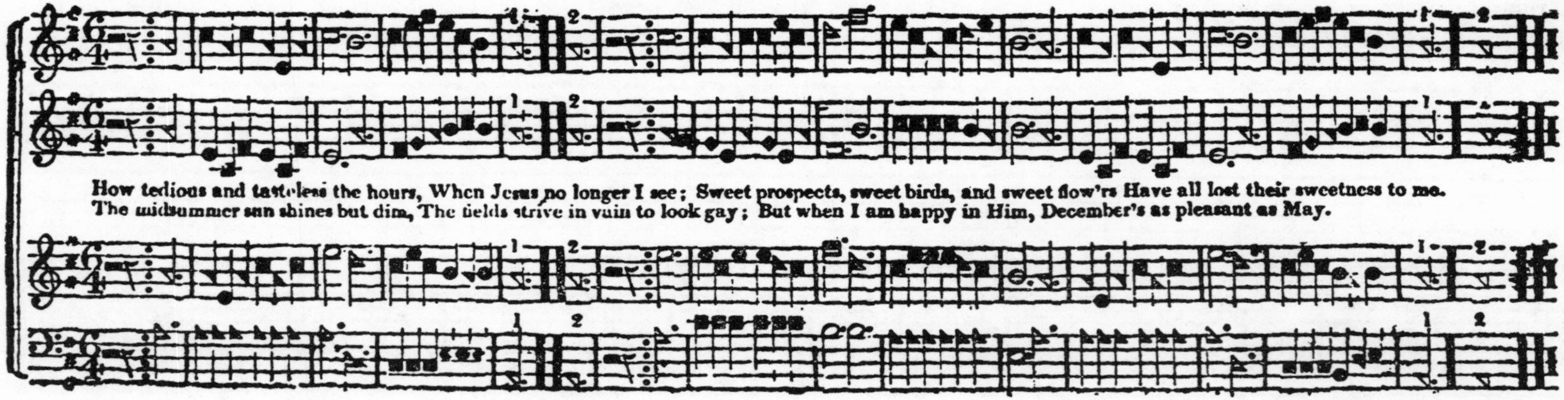

How tedious and tasteless the hours, When Jesus no longer I see;
Sweet prospects, sweet birds, and sweet flow'rs Have all lost their sweetness to me.
The midsummer sun shines but dim, The fields strive in vain to look gay;
But when I am happy in Him, December's as pleasant as May.

WORTHINGTON. C. M.

What dying worms, what dying worms, &c.

What dying worms are we,

Thou we adore eternal name,   How feeble is our mortal frame,   How feeble is our mortal frame,
And humbly own to thee;

154

When Dennis Hanks was asked what songs the Lincolns and Hankses sang in their years in Spencer County, Indiana, he said one was, "How tejus and tasteless the hours." The Missouri Harmony presented it as Greenfields, as above. The depths of humility in Worthington, below, is characteristic, with its cry, "What dying worms are we."

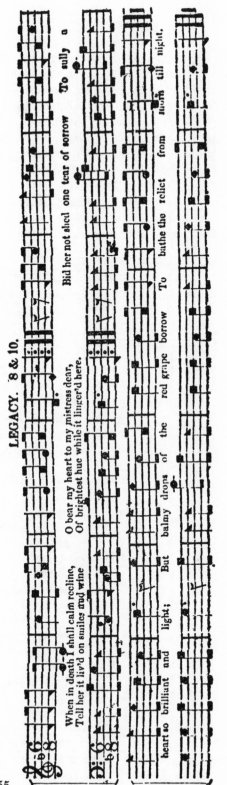

HIGHBRIDGE L. M.

148

Through ev'ry age eternal God, Thou art our rest, our safe abode: High was thy throne ere heav'n was made, Or earth thy humble footstool laid.

2 Long hast thou reign'd ere time began, Or dust was fashion'd into man; And long thy kingdom shall endure, When earth and time shall be no more.

3 But man, weak man, is born to die, Made up of guilt and vanity; Thy dreadful sentence, Lord, was just, "Return ye sinners to your dust."

4 Death, like an overflowing stream, Sweeps us away; Our life's a dream, An empty tale—a morning flow'r, Cut down and wither'd in an hour.

5 Teach us, O Lord, how frail is man. And kindly lengthen out his span, Till a wise career of piety Fit us to die and dwell with Thee.

LEGACY. 8 & 10.

155

When in death I shall calm recline, O bear my heart to my mistress dear, Tell her it liv'd on smiles and wine Of brightest hue while it linger'd here. Bid her not shed one tear of sorrow To sully a

heart so brilliant and light; But balmy drops of the red grape borrow To bathe the relict from morn till night.

The two songs on this page from The Missouri Harmony are opposites in tone and feeling. The one above, Highbridge, is solemn, pious, humble. The one below, Legacy, is an old Irish air with words by Thomas Moore; the tune was used by country fiddlers at dances.

THE BROWN GIRL OR FAIR ELEANOR

Nancy Hanks in her old Kentucky home, sang ballads the western pioneers brought through Cumberland Gap from the uplands and mountains farther east. The story of the Brown Girl stabbing Fair Eleanor, then having her head cut off by Lord Thomas, who killed himself and was buried with the two women, sounds almost like a grand opera plot. Grim and terrible though this ballad story is, the tune is even, comforting, a little like riding a slow galloping horse. It is still used in many a southern mountain home for rocking the children to sleep. Little Abe Lincoln, as a child, probably heard The Brown Girl, according to persons familiar with Kentucky backgrounds. This version is from the Reed Smith ballad group published by the University of South Carolina; it was heard by Tressie Pierce in Alexander County, North Carolina. The thirteenth verse is an interpolation from another text, to explain the killing of Lord Thomas by himself before he is buried with the two ladies who so suddenly met violent deaths. Where the singer is so inclined, the last lines of each verse are repeated.

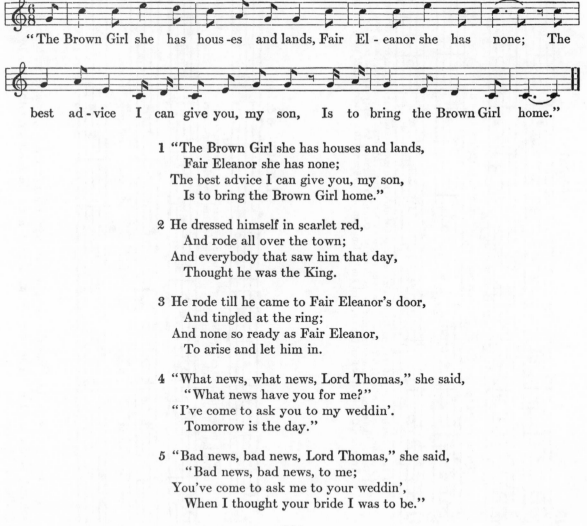

"The Brown Girl she has hous-es and lands, Fair El-eanor she has none; The best ad-vice I can give you, my son, Is to bring the Brown Girl home."

1 "The Brown Girl she has houses and lands,
   Fair Eleanor she has none;
   The best advice I can give you, my son,
   Is to bring the Brown Girl home."

2 He dressed himself in scarlet red,
   And rode all over the town;
   And everybody that saw him that day,
   Thought he was the King.

3 He rode till he came to Fair Eleanor's door,
   And tingled at the ring;
   And none so ready as Fair Eleanor,
   To arise and let him in.

4 "What news, what news, Lord Thomas," she said,
   "What news have you for me?"
   "I've come to ask you to my weddin'.
   Tomorrow is the day."

5 "Bad news, bad news, Lord Thomas," she said,
   "Bad news, bad news, to me;
   You've come to ask me to your weddin',
   When I thought your bride I was to be."

156

6 She dressed herself in scarlet red,
    And rode all over the town;
And everybody that saw her that day,
    Took her to be the Queen.

7 She rode till she came to Lord Thomas' door,
    And tingled at the ring;
And none so ready as Lord Thomas himself,
    To arise and let her in.

8 "Is this your bride? Lord Thomas," she cried,
    "I'm sure, she's wonderful brown;
You might have had as fair a young bride,
    As ever the sun shone on."

9 The Brown Girl, she had a long pen-knife,
    'Twas wonderful long and sharp;
Between the short ribs and the long,
    She pierced Fair Eleanor's heart.

10 "Fair Eleanor, what makes you look so pale?
    You used to look so red;
You used to have two rosy red cheeks,
    And now you've nary one."

11 "Oh, don't you see, or can't you see,
    The knife that was pierced in me?
Oh, don't you see my own heart's blood,
    A-tricklin' to my knee?"

12 Lord Thomas had a long broad-sword,
    It was wonderful long and sharp,
He cut the head of the Brown Girl off,
    And kicked it against the wall.

13 He pointed the handle toward the sun,
    The point toward his breast.
"Here is the going of three true loves,
    God send our souls to rest.

14 "Go dig my grave under yonder green tree,
    Go dig it wide and long;
And bury Fair Eleanor in my arms,
    And the Brown Girl at my feet."

HEY BETTY MARTIN

In the early 1890's, in the tank towns of the corn belt, few women bobbed their hair. Often when a woman who had taken this liberty walked along Main Street on a night when there was to be a band concert on the public square, she was an object of special scrutiny. Young men would sing at her:

> Chippy, get your hair cut, hair cut, hair cut,
> Chippy, get your hair cut, hair cut short.

The tune went back to a ditty sung in the 1860's during the War between the States, as follows:

> Johnny, git your gun and your sword and your pistol,
> Johnny, git your gun and come with me.

The tune is at least as old as the War of 1812, when drummer boys beat it on their drums and sang words about "Hey Betty Martin Tiptoe." We have that drummer's melody and words from A. T. Vance, a Long Island, New York, fisherman who was raised in Kansas, and whose great-grandfather was a drummer in the War of 1812. The tune is traditionary in the Vance family and is executed with variations by Comfort Vance, son of A. T. The tempo, Wathall indicates, is allegretto scherzando, which in 1812 meant "Make it snappy," or "Let's go."

Hey Bet-ty Mar-tin, tip-toe, tip-toe, Hey Bet-ty Mar-tin, tip-toe fine.

OLD BRASS WAGON

Indiana, Missouri and Iowa pioneers had this dance game. The note following the verses below is from The Play-Party in Indiana by Leah Jackson Wolford.

Arr. H. F.

Cir - cle to the left, the Old Brass Wag - on; Cir - cle to the left, the Old Brass Wagon, Cir - cle to the left, the Old Brass Wagon, You're the one, my dar - ling.

1 Circle to the left, Old Brass Wagon,
   You're the one, my darling.

2 Swing oh swing, Old Brass Wagon,
   You're the one, my darling.

3 Promenade home, Old Brass Wagon,
   You're the one, my darling.

4 Shoddish up and down, the Old Brass Wagon,
   You're the one, my darling.

5 Break and swing, the Old Brass Wagon,
   You're the one, my darling.

6 Promenade around the Old Brass Wagon,
   You're the one, my darling.

NOTE. — Repeat the first line of each stanza three times. During 1, all join hands, boys being at the left of their partners, and circle left. At 2, they drop hands and each boy swings his partner. During 3, partners promenade, circling to the right. Repeat from the beginning while singing stanzas 4, 5 and 6.

CUCKOO WALTZ

The tune here is ancient. Saxon, Teuton, Slav, Magyar, have used the likes of it in dance and folk song. . . . Hazel Felman gives it an old-fashioned music box setting. . . . Leah Jackson Wolford's book on "The Play-Party in Indiana," includes the tune and a description of the dance.

Arr. H. F.

Three times round the cuck-oo waltz, Three times round the cuck-oo waltz, Three times round the cuck-oo waltz, Love-ly Sus - ie Brown. Fare thee well, my charming girl, Fare thee well I'm gone, Fare thee well, my charming girl, With gold - en slip -pers on.

1 (a) Choose your pard as we go round,
       Choose your pard as we go round,
       Choose your pard as we go round,
  (b) We'll all take Susie Brown.

2 (c) Fare thee well, my charming girl,
  (d) Fare thee well I'm gone,
       Fare thee well, my charming girl,
       With golden slippers on.

Note. — A boy and a girl stand in the center. All of the others (irrespective of partners) circle to the left around them during (a). At (b) the girl chooses a boy, the boy a girl, and all four stand in the center. At (c) the two couples in the center form a circle, each boy opposite his partner. Partners cross hands forming a "star" and circle left. Repeat with left hands and circle right. At (d) each of the boys in the center swings the contrary girl, then two-steps with his partner.

160

WEEVILY WHEAT

"Way Down in the Paw Paw Patch," and "All Chaw Hay on the Corner," were play-party songs in early times in Indiana. Others were "Pig in the Parlor," "Pop, Goes the Weasel," "Old Bald Eagle Sail Around," "Old Sister Phoebe," "Skip to My Lou," "Thus the Farmer Sows His Seed." A dance somewhat like Virginia Reel went to the song of "Weevily Wheat." Indications are that the Charley of this song may be the Prince Charlie of Jacobite ballads; he figures in songs of the Scotch Highlanders who were harassed during Prince Charlie's time, left their homes to take up life in the Alleghanies and to spread westward.

It's step her to your weev'-ly wheat, It's step her to your bar - ley, It's step her to your weev - 'ly wheat, To bake a cake for Char - ley.

1 It's step her to your weev'ly wheat,
   It's step her to your barley,
   It's step her to your weev'ly wheat,
   To bake a cake for Charley.

   Refrain:
       O Charley he's a fine young man,
       O Charley he's a dandy,
       He loves to hug and kiss the girls,
       And feed 'em on good candy.

2 The higher up the cherry tree,
   The riper grow the cherries,
   The more you hug and kiss the girls,
   The sooner they will marry.
   Refrain:

3 Over the river to water the sheep,
   To measure up the barley,
   Over the river to water the sheep,
   To bake a cake for Charley.
   Refrain:

4 My pretty little Pink, I suppose you think,
   I care but little about you,
   But I'll let you know before you go
   I cannot do without you.
   Refrain:

161

EL-A-NOY

Among the pioneers were boomers, boosters. About the time this song came, the *Shawnee-town Advocate*, only newspaper in seven counties of southern Illinois, was proclaiming its ideal to be "universal liberty abroad, and an ocean-bound republic at home." In northern Illinois, the *Gem of the Prairie*, a weekly magazine published in Chicago, was declaring, "The West must have a literature peculiarly its own. It is here that the great problem of human destiny will be worked out on a grander scale than was ever before attempted or conceived." . . . John D. Black, a Chicago attorney-at-law, lived on the Ohio River as a boy and heard his father sing El-a-noy. . . . Shawnee Ferry was a crossing point for many who had come by the Ohio river route or on Wilderness Road through Cumberland Gap, headed for Illinois . . . The fourth verse is probably a later addition thrown in by some joker who felt challenged by the preceding verses.

Arr. H. F.

'Way down . up-on the Wa-bash, Sich land was nev-er known; If
Ad-am had passed o-ver it, The soil he'd sure-ly own; He'd think it was the
gar-den He'd played in when a boy, And straight pro-nounce it E-den, In the

State of El - a - noy. Then move your fam - ily west-ward, Good health you will en -

joy, And rise to wealth and hon - or In the State of El - a - noy.

1 'Way down upon the Wabash,
Sich land was never known;
If Adam had passed over it,
The soil he'd surely own;
He'd think it was the garden
He'd played in when a boy,
And straight pronounce it Eden,
In the State of El-a-noy.

Refrain:
    Then move your family westward,
    Good health you will enjoy,
    And rise to wealth and honor
    In the State of El-a-noy.

2 'Twas here the Queen of Sheba came,
With Solomon of old,
With an Ass load of spices,
Pomegranates and fine gold;
And when she saw this lovely land,
Her heart was filled with joy,
Straightway she said: "I'd like to be
A Queen in El-a-noy."
Refrain:

3 She's bounded by the Wabash,
The Ohio and the Lakes,
She's crawfish in the swampy lands,
The milk-sick and the shakes;
But these are slight diversions
And take not from the joy
Of living in this garden land,
The State of El-a-noy.
Refrain:

4 Away up in the northward,
Right on the border line,
A great commercial city,
Chicago, you will find.
Her men are all like Abelard,
Her women like Heloise;
All honest virtuous people,
For they live in El-a-noy.

Last Refrain:
    Then move your family westward,
    Bring all your girls and boys,
    And cross at Shawnee ferry
    To the State of El-a-noy.

HOOSEN JOHNNY

Lawyers sat around the wood stoves of the taverns and hotels of the Eighth Circuit in Illinois and sang this on many a winter night. Lincoln heard it often. It was a favorite of his singing friend with the banjo, Ward Hill Lamon. Col. Clark E. Carr, who came to Illinois in 1852 and was a first settler of Galesburg, tells us in his book "The Illini" of these verses, "The improvisor would go on singing as long as he could. The solo is a sort of droning chant; but the chorus, when sung by good voices, is superb. The song became a favorite with lawyers traveling the circuit in those days, and was often sung on convivial occasions. It is said that at one time, at Knoxville in our county, when some good news that caused universal rejoicing had been received, the court was adjourned, and judge, lawyers, jury, spectators, paraded around the public square singing, 'De ol' black bull kem down de medder.' It must be remembered that this was before the days of brass bands and other artificial contrivances for giving expression to tumultuous feeling."

Arr. A. G. W.

De lit-tle black bull kem down de med-der, Hoo-sen John-ny, Hoo-sen John-ny, De lit-tle black bull kem down de medder, Long time a-go. Long time a-go, long time a-go, De little black bull kem down de medder, Long time a-go.

HOOSEN JOHNNY

1 De little black bull kem down de medder,
    Hoosen Johnny, Hoosen Johnny.
De little black bull kem down de medder,
    Long time ago.

Chorus:
    Long time ago, long time ago,
    De little black bull kem down de medder,
    Long time ago.

2 Fust he paw and den he beller,
    Hoosen Johnny, Hoosen Johnny.
Fust he paw and den he beller,
    Long time ago.

3 He whet his horn on a white oak saplin',
    Hoosen Johnny, Hoosen Johnny.
He whet his horn on a white oak saplin',
    Long time ago.

4 He shake his tail, he jar de ribber,
    Hoosen Johnny, Hoosen Johnny.
He shake his tail, he jar de ribber,
    Long time ago.

5 He paw de dirt in de heifers' faces,
    Hoosen Johnny, Hoosen Johnny.
He paw de dirt in de heifers' faces,
    Long time ago.

MY PRETTY LITTLE PINK

A dance song known in Kentucky, Indiana and Illinois became a knapsack and marching tune with Mexican War references. . . . The line patrolled was about 2500 miles, from Santa Fe to Vera Cruz; young men, volunteers mostly, filled the ranks; they were a long ways from home and needed a quickstep tune with a don't-care lyric. . . . The first verse and melody are from Lillian K. Rickaby of Riverside, California, as she heard them when a girl in Galesburg, Illinois; the other two verses are from Neeta Marquis of Los Angeles as learned by her mother in Kentucky in the late 1840's.

Arr. A. G. W.

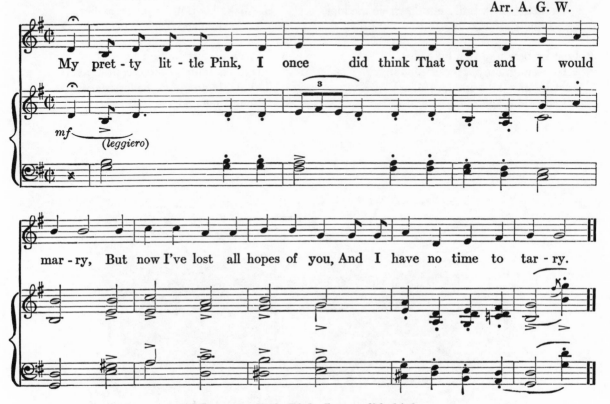

My pret-ty lit-tle Pink, I once did think That you and I would

mar-ry, But now I've lost all hopes of you, And I have no time to tar-ry.

1 My pretty little Pink, I once did think
   That you and I would marry,
   But now I've lost all hopes of you,
   And I have no time to tarry.

2 I'll take my knapsack on my back,
   My rifle on my shoulder,
   And I'll march away to the Rio Grande,
   To view the forest over;

3 Where coffee grows on white oak trees,
   And the river flows with brandy,
   Where the girls are sweet as sweet can be
   And the boys like sugar candy.

LINCOLN AND LIBERTY

This campaign ditty of 1860 has the brag and extravaganza of electioneering. The tune is from "Old Rosin the Bow" and served earlier for a Henry Clay candidacy in which was the salutation:

So, freemen, come on to the rally,
This motto emblazons your crest:
That lone star of Hope yet is shining,
It lightens the skies in the West.
Hark! freedom peals far in her thunder,
Her lightning no force can arrest,
She drives the foul army asunder.
"Hail, gallant old Hal of the West!"

In a later year when Horace Greeley was running for the Presidency against Gen. U. S. Grant, voters were reminded, "Then let Greeley go to the dickens, too soon he has counted his chickens."

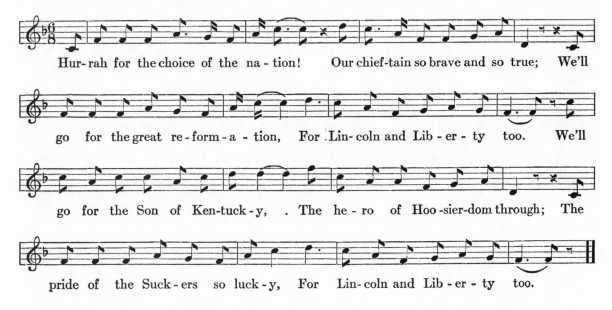

Hur-rah for the choice of the na - tion! Our chief-tain so brave and so true; We'll
go for the great re-form-a - tion, For Lin-coln and Lib - er - ty too. We'll
go for the Son of Ken-tuck-y, . The he - ro of Hoo-sier-dom through; The
pride of the Suck-ers so luck-y, For Lin-coln and Lib - er - ty too.

1 Hurrah for the choice of the nation!
Our chieftain so brave and so true;
We'll go for the great reformation,
For Lincoln and Liberty too.
We'll go for the Son of Kentucky,
The hero of Hoosierdom through;
The pride of the Suckers so lucky,
For Lincoln and Liberty too.

2 They'll find what by felling and mauling,
Our rail-maker statesman can do;
For the people are everywhere calling
For Lincoln and Liberty too.
Then up with our banner so glorious,
The star-spangled red, white and blue,
We'll fight till our banner is victorious,
For Lincoln and Liberty too.

OLD ABE LINCOLN CAME OUT OF THE WILDERNESS

Torchlight processions of Republicans sang this in the summer and fall months of 1860. The young Wide Awakes burbled it as the kerosene dripped on their blue oilcloth capes. Quartets and octettes jubilated with it in packed, smoky halls where audiences waited for speakers of the evening. In Springfield, Illinois, the Tall Man who was a candidate for the presidency of the nation, heard his two boys Tad and Willie, sing it at him. The tune is from negro spirituals, When I Come Out De Wilderness and Ol' Gray Mare Come Tearin' Out De Wilderness.

Arr. H. F.

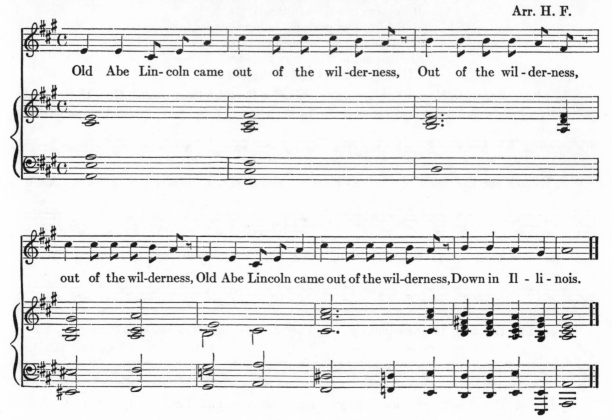

Old Abe Lin-coln came out of the wil-der-ness, Out of the wil-der-ness,

out of the wil-derness, Old Abe Lincoln came out of the wil-derness, Down in Il-li-nois.

Old Abe Lincoln came out of the wilderness,
Out of the wilderness, out of the wilderness,
Old Abe Lincoln came out of the wilderness,
Down in Illinois.

GREAT LAKES AND ERIE CANAL

THE ERIE CANAL

The Erie Canal, in its day, had dignity, almost majesty. Before railroads came, it was a great man-made transportation link connecting the Atlantic Ocean and the Great Lakes, a highway and common carrier for an immense flow of merchandise westbound and of products eastbound. It gave to the mid-west nails, steel, knives, scissors, fabrics, sewing machines in exchange for pork, beef, wheat, corn. It was celebrated as a thing of use and public utility. People were thankful for it as an achievement of human genius. A placid, even stream, its traffic ran quietly, softly, lazily. Navigation was easy. Men and horses took their jobs as monotonous, mild burdens. A day's travel, a walk, went with monotonous time-beats. The feel of this is in the best known Erie Canal song. I have heard George S. Chappell (Dr. Traprock) sing it movingly, meditatively, so that the Erie Canal took on the character of a symbol of life as a highway to be taken ploddingly with steady pulse. Railroads may fill rush orders; not so canals. To say that Chappell's performance of this song is as interesting and important as a star performer's rendition of the "Song of the Volga Boatmen," might be a misleading statement. Perhaps when certain American songs of vulgar birth are as much loved by American singers as are similar Slavic melodies by Russian vocalists, there may develop meditative airs and commonplace lyrics with the significant pauses and deeper tintings not given them now. . . . The opening line here is sometimes, "I've got a gal, she's Big Foot Sal." On close acquaintance, one may find in the melodic and lyric statements here the gravity, tenacity, and day-by-day responsibility that looks from the face of a faithful friendly mule. . . . An incomplete verse from Dr. T. L. Chapman of Duluth has the lines:

> Drop a tear for Big Foot Sal,
> The best dam cook on the Erie Canal.

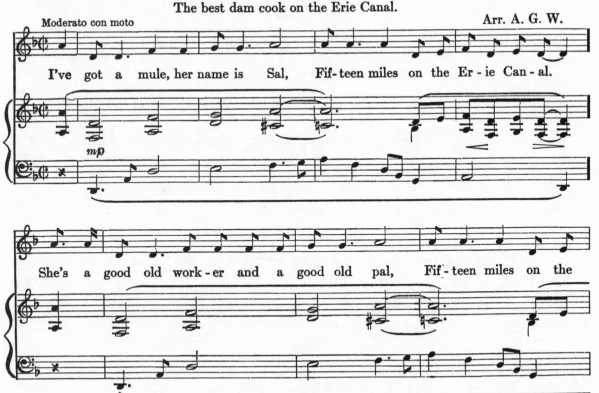

Er - ie Can - al. We've haul'd some barg - es in our day,

Fill'd with lum - ber, coal and hay, And we know ev - 'ry inch of the way From

Al - ban - y to Buf - fa - lo. . . . **Refrain** Low bridge, ev - 'ry - bod - y down!

Low bridge, for we're go - ing thro' a town, And you'll al - ways know your neigh - bor, You'll

172

al-ways know your pal, If you ev - er nav - i - gat - ed on the Er - ie Can - al.

1 I've got a mule, her name is Sal,
   Fifteen miles on the Erie Canal.
   She's a good old worker and a good old pal,
   Fifteen miles on the Erie Canal.
   We've haul'd some barges in our day,
   Fill'd with lumber, coal and hay,
   And we know ev'ry inch of the way
   From Albany to Buffalo.

   Refrain:
      Low bridge, ev'rybody down!
      Low bridge, for we're going through a town,
      And you'll always know your neighbor,
      You'll always know your pal,
      If you ever navigated on the Erie Canal.

2 We better get along on our way, old gal
   Fifteen miles on the Erie Canal,
   Cause you bet your life I'd never part with Sal,
   Fifteen miles on the Erie Canal.
   Git up there, mule, here comes a lock,
   We'll make Rome 'bout six o'clock,
   One more trip and back we'll go
   Right back home to Buffalo.
   Refrain:

BIGERLOW

We learn here the song of the Great Lakes boatmen, from the years when barges, "timber drovers," carried raw products east and brought manufactured goods west. It is lusty and gusty in such lines as, "Give her the sheet an' let her go. We're the boys to see her through!" and it has spray and wind magic in, "You should a'heard her howlin', When the wind was blowin' free!" I have this from Jack Raper, who writes the colyum in the *Cleveland, Ohio, Press* under the moniker of Josh Wise. He had served as marine editor of the *Cleveland Plaindealer* about the same time I was marine editor of the *Milwaukee Journal*. Our reunion was not as two old sea dogs but as two old marine editors. The piece is related to "The Bigler," sung on the Great Lakes and among lumberjacks.

Arr. L. S.

'Twas one Oc-to-ber morn-in' That I seen a wond'rous sight; 'Twas the

tim-ber drov-er Big-er-low, A-hail-in' from De-trite. Watch her!

Catch her! Jump up in her Ju-ju-ba-ju! Give her the sheet an' let her go, We're the

174

boys to see her through! You should a' heard her howlin' When the wind was blow-in'

free! 'Twas on the trip to Buf-fa-lo from Mil - wau - kee!

'Twas one October mornin'
That I seen a wond'rous sight;
'Twas the timber drover Bigerlow
A-hailin' from Detrite.
Watch her! Catch her!
Jump up in her Jujubaju!
Give her the sheet an' let her go,
We're the boys to see her through!
You should a' heard her howlin'
When the wind was blowin' free!
'Twas on the trip to Buffalo from Milwaukee!

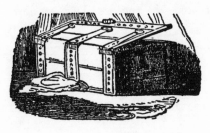

RED IRON ORE

Three of the Great Lakes (see any atlas) are traversed in this odyssey of red iron ore. It is a log, the diary of a ship and its men on one cruise. The facts are specific. The *E. C. Roberts* was a boat. So was *The Minch*. Riding up Lake Michigan, they passed through death's door; the lake storms were ugly. At Escanaba loading red ore, they "looked like red devils." The crew of *The Minch* thumbed their noses and taunted, "We'll see you in Cleveland next Fourth of July." But the *E. C. Roberts* got there ahead of the fleet. A crew of "bold boys" they were, even if they say so themselves. The singer is humble, "Now my song is ended, I hope you won't laugh." The tune is old Irish; the repeated line with each verse, "Derry down, down, down derry down," is in old ballads. It is a virile song, a tale of grappling with harsh elements and riding through, a rattling tune and a devil-may-care timebeat. It may, at first, seem just a lilt with a matter-of-fact story. It is more than that; it is a little drama; the singer should know what it is to shovel red iron ore; the singer should know the wide curves of that ship path from Chicago to Cleveland on three Great Lakes (see any atlas).

Arr. H. F. P.

Come all you bold sail-ors that fol-low the Lakes On an i-ron ore ves-sel your liv-ing to make. I shipp'd in Chi-ca-go, bid a-dieu to the shore, Bound a-way to Es-ca-na-ba for red i-ron ore. Der-ry down, down, down der-ry down.

RED IRON ORE

1 Come all you bold sailors that follow the Lakes
On an iron ore vessel your living to make.
I shipped in Chicago, bid adieu to the shore,
Bound away to Escanaba for red iron ore.
    Derry down, down, down derry down.

2 In the month of September, the seventeenth day,
Two dollars and a quarter is all they would pay,
And on Monday morning the *Bridgeport* did take
The *E. C. Roberts* out in the Lake.
    Derry down, down, down derry down.

3 The wind from the south'ard sprang up a fresh breeze,
And away through Lake Michigan the *Roberts* did sneeze.
Down through Lake Michigan the *Roberts* did roar,
And on Friday morning we passed through death's door.

4 This packet she howled across the mouth of Green Bay,
And before her cutwater she dashed the white spray.
We rounded the sand point, our anchor let go,
We furled in our canvas and the watch went below.

5 Next morning we hove alongside the *Exile*,
And soon was made fast to an iron ore pile,
They lowered their chutes and like thunder did roar,
They spouted into us that red iron ore.

6 Some sailors took shovels while others got spades,
And some took wheelbarrows, each man to his trade.
We looked like red devils, our fingers got sore,
We cursed Escanaba and that damned iron ore.

7 The tug *Escanaba* she towed out the *Minch*,
The *Roberts* she thought she had left in a pinch,
And as she passed by us she bid us good-bye,
Saying, "We'll meet you in Cleveland next Fourth of July!"

8 Through Louse Island it blew a fresh breeze;
We made the Foxes, the Beavers, the Skillageles;
We flew by the *Minch* for to show her the way,
And she ne'er hove in sight till we were off Thunder Bay.

9 Across Saginaw Bay the *Roberts* did ride
With the dark and deep water rolling over her side.
And now for Port Huron the *Roberts* must go,
Where the tug *Kate Williams* she took us in tow.

10 We went through North Passage — O Lord, how it blew!
And all 'round the Dummy a large fleet there came too.
The night being dark, Old Nick it would scare.
We hove up next morning and for Cleveland did steer.

11 Now the *Roberts* is in Cleveland, made fast stem and stern,
And over the bottle we'll spin a big yarn.
But Captain Harvey Shannon had ought to stand treat
For getting into Cleveland ahead of the fleet.

12 Now my song is ended, I hope you won't laugh.
Our dunnage is packed and all hands are paid off.
Here's a health to the *Roberts*, she's staunch, strong and true;
Not forgotten the bold boys that comprise her crew.
Derry down, down, down derry down.

RAGING CANAWL

America has no more genuine folk lore than is in the following recitative, Raging Canawl. It goes best when delivered for a small company by a performer who knows what he is doing. Drolleries lurk in every line. Only those who understand the perils of deep canal life can untie the hawsers of foolery here. The word "canal" is to be pronounced "canawl" so as to rhyme with "squall."

1 Come, listen to my story, ye landsmen, one and all,
And I'll sing to you the dangers of that raging canal;
For I am one of many who expects a watery grave,
For I've been at the mercies of the winds and the waves.

2 I left Albany harbor about the break of day,
If rightly I remember, 'twas the second day of May;
We trusted to our driver, altho' he was but small,
Yet he knew all the windings of that raging canal.

3 It seemed as if the devil had work in hand that night.
For our oil it was all gone, and our lamps they gave no light;
The clouds began to gather, and the rain began to fall,
And I wished myself off of that raging canal.

4 The Captain told the driver to hurry with all speed,
And his orders were obeyed, for he soon cracked up his lead;
With the fastest kind of towing we allowed by twelve o'clock,
We should be in old Schenectady, right bang against the dock.

5 But sad was the fate of our poor devoted bark,
For the rain kept a-pouring faster, and the night it grew more dark,
The horses gave a stumble, and the driver gave a squall.
And they tumbled head and heels into that raging canal.

6 The Captain came on deck, with a voice so clear and sound,
Crying, "Cut the horses loose, my boys, or I swear we'll all be drowned!"
The driver paddled to the shore, altho' he was but small,
While the horses sank to rise no more in that raging canal.

7 The cook she wrung her hands, and she came upon the deck,
Saying: "Alas! what will become of us, our boat it is a wreck?"
The steersman laid her over, for he was a man of sense,
When the bowsman jumped ashore he lashed her to the fence.

8 We had a load of Dutch, and we stowed them in the hole,
They were not the least concerned about the welfare of their soul;
The Captain went below and implored them for to pray,
But the only answer he could get was, "Nix come rous, nix fis staa."

9 The Captain came on deck with a spyglass in his hand,
But the night it was so dark he could not diskiver land;
He said to us with a faltering voice, while tears began to fall,
"Prepare to meet your death, my boys, this night on the canal."

10 The cook, she being kind-hearted, she loaned us an old dress,
Which we raised upon a setting pole as a signal of distress;
We agreed with restoration, aboard the boat to hide,
And never quit her deck whilst a plank hung to her side.

11 It was our good fortune about the break of day,
The storm it did abate, and a boat came by that way;
Our signal was discovered, and they hove alongside.
And we all jumped aboard and for Buffalo did ride.

12 I landed in Buffalo about twelve o'clock,
The first place I went to was down to the dock;
I wanted to go up the lake, but it looked rather squally,
When along came Fred Emmons and his friend, Billy Bally.

13 Says Fred, "How do you do, and whar have you been so long?"
Says I, "For the last fortnight I've been on the canal;
For it stormed all the time, and thar was the devil to pay.
When we got in Tonawandy Creek we thar was cast away."

14 "Now," says Fred, "Let me tell you how to manage wind and weather,
In a storm hug to the towpath, and then lay feather to feather;
And when the weather is bad, and the wind it blows a gale,
Just jump ashore, knock down a horse — that's taking in a sail.

15 And if you wish to see both sides of the canal,
To steer your course to Buffalo, and that right true and well,
And it be so foggy that you cannot see the track,
Just call the driver aboard and hitch a lantern on his back."

179

THE E–RI–E

When hard work and the monotony of life overshadowed the souls on the Erie Canal, the crew did what so many sailors and longshoremen ever have done. They took to drink and to song and to hopes for an end of the voyage, to voicing in a tune their feelings about how life used them up and left them unsung and unwept. The preacher, Koheleth, who sings so rhythmically in the Book of Ecclesiastes, "Vanity of vanities, all is vanity," or Omar in his short-spoken pessimism, arrive at a philosophy somewhat like that sung here. Some might call it "realistic in the method of approach." It tries for laughter at monotony and fate. We have this text and tune from Robert Wolfe and Oliver R. Barrett of Chicago. The canal's name is enunciated in three syllables, viz., "E-ri-e."

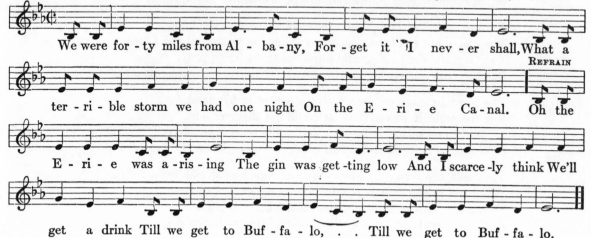

We were for - ty miles from Al - ba - ny, For - get it I nev - er shall, What a
ter - ri - ble storm we had one night On the E - ri - e Ca - nal. Oh the
E - ri - e was a - ris - ing The gin was get - ting low And I scarce - ly think We'll
get a drink Till we get to Buf - fa - lo, . . Till we get to Buf - fa - lo.

1 We were forty miles from Albany,
Forget it I never shall,
What a terrible storm we had one night
On the E-ri-e Canal.

Refrain:
  Oh the E-ri-e was a-rising
  The gin was getting low
    And I scarcely think
    We'll get a drink
  Till we get to Buffalo,
  Till we get to Buffalo.

2 We were loaded down with barley,
We were chuck up full of rye;
And the captain he looked down at me
With his goddam wicked eye.
Refrain:

3 Oh the girls are in the Police Gazette,
The crew are all in jail;
I'm the only living sea cook's son
That's left to tell the tale.
Refrain:

180

HOBO SONGS

SHOVELLIN' IRON ORE

"I got a snootful of it and I'll never go back," a fellow coal shoveler told me once in Omaha. He was speaking of iron ore, heavier, dirtier, more infiltrating than coal dust. . . . Those who sing this usually hook it up with We Are Four Bums.

Arr. A. G. W.

Some-thing hap-pened the oth-er day, that nev-er hap-pened be-

fore. A man tried to get me to shov-el i-ron ore. Says

I, "Old man now what will you pay?" Says he, "Two bits a ton." Says

I, "Old man, go did-dle your-self, I'd rath-er bum."

HALLELUJAH, I'M A BUM!

This old song heard at the water tanks of railroads in Kansas in 1897 and from harvest hands who worked in the wheat fields of Pawnee County, was picked up later by the I. W. W.'s, who made verses of their own for it, and gave it a wide fame. The migratory workers are familiar with the Salvation Army missions, and have adopted the Army custom of occasionally abandoning all polite formalities and striking deep into the common things and ways for their music and words. A "handout" is food handed out from a back door as distinguished from "a sit down" which means an entrance into a house and a chair at a table.

Arr. H. J.

Oh, why don't you work Like oth-er men do? How the hell can I work When there's no work to do? Hal-le-lu-jah, I'm a bum, Hal-le-lu-jah, bum a-gain, Hal-le-lu-jah, give us a hand-out, To re-vive us a-gain! gain!

1 Oh, why don't you work
  Like other men do?
  How the hell can I work
  When there's no work to do?
    Hallelujah, I'm a bum,
    Hallelujah, bum again,
    Hallelujah, give us a handout,
    To revive us again.

2 Oh, I love my boss
  And my boss loves me,
  And that is the reason
  I'm so hungry,
    Hallelujah, etc.

3 Oh, the springtime has came
  And I'm just out of jail,
  Without any money,
  Without any bail.
    Hallelujah, etc.

4 I went to a house,
  And I knocked on the door;
  A lady came out, says,
  "You been here before."
    Hallelujah, etc.

5 I went to a house,
  And I asked for a piece of bread;
  A lady came out, says,
  "The baker is dead."
    Hallelujah, etc.

6 When springtime does come,
  O won't we have fun,
  We'll throw up our jobs
  And we'll go on the bum.
    Hallelujah, etc.

TRAMP, TRAMP, TRAMP, KEEP ON A–TRAMPING

When W. P. Webb asked two hobos in the lockup in Cuero, Texas, "Where you from?" one shrugged his shoulders and said, "Oh, everywhere. We've been from the Atlantic to the Pacific, so we can't say where we're from." Then came an afterthought, "We been everywhere looking for work, and — never able to find it." In Denver they had picked up an I. W. W. song to the tune of Tramp, Tramp, Tramp, the Boys are Marching.

1 He walked up and down the street 'till the shoes fell off his feet,
Across the street he spied a lady cooking stew. And he said, "How do you do,
May I chop some wood for you?" But what the lady told him made him feel so blue.

Refrain:
  "Tramp, tramp, tramp, keep on a-trampin', There is nothing here for you;
  If I catch you round again, You will wear the ball and chain,
  Keep a-trampin', that's the best thing you can do."

2 Across the street a sign he read, "Work for Jesus," so it said.
And he said, "Here is my chance, I'll surely try." And he kneeled upon the floor
Until his knees got rather sore, But at eating time he heard the preacher cry:
Refrain:

3 Down the street he met a cop, And the copper made him stop,
And he said: "When did you blow into town?" And he took him to the judge,
But the judge he said, "Ah fudge! Bums that have no money need not come around."
Refrain:

THE DYING HOGGER

Once on a newspaper assignment during the copper mine strike in the Calumet region, I spent an hour with a "wobbly" who had been switchman, cowboy, jailbird. He sang this song. . . . "Hogger" is railroad slang for an engineer or "hoghead," while a "tallow-pot" is a fireman. "Snake" and "stinger" are pet names among switchmen and brakemen, whose two brotherhood organizations during a number of years have antagonized each other and engaged in jurisdictional disputes.

Arr. A. G. W.

A hog-ger on his death-bed lay. His life was ooz-ing fast a-way; The snakes and sting-ers round him pressed To hear the hog-ger's last re-quest. He said, "Be-fore I bid a-dieu, One last re-quest I'll make of you; Be-

fore I soar be-yond the stars, Just hook me on to nine-ty cars.

1 A hogger on his death-bed lay.
His life was oozing fast away;
The snakes and stingers round him pressed
To hear the hogger's last request.
He said, "Before I bid adieu,
One last request I'll make of you;
Before I soar beyond the stars,
Just hook me on to ninety cars.

2 "A marble slab I do not crave;
Just mark the head of my lonely grave
With a draw-bar pointing to the skies,
Showing the spot where this hogger lies.
Oh, just once more before I'm dead
Let me stand the conductor on his head;
Let me see him crawl from under the wreck
With a way-car window-sash around his neck.

3 "And you, dear friends, I'll have to thank,
If you'll let me die at the water-tank,
Within my ears that old-time sound,
The tallow-pot pulling the tank-spout down.
And when at last in the grave I'm laid,
Let it be in the cool of the water-tank shade.
And put within my cold, still hand
A monkey-wrench and the old oil can."

WANDERIN'

This peculiarly American song in text A is from Arthur Sutherland of Rochester, New York, as learned from comrades in the American Relief Expedition to the Near East. It is a lyric of tough days. The pulsation is gay till the contemplative pauses, the wishes and the lingerings, of that final line of each verse, and the prolonged vocalizing of "l-i-k-e." The philosophy is desperate as the old sailor saying, "To work hard, to live hard, to die hard, and then to go to hell after all, would be too damned hard." Text B, also a lyric of tough days, is from Hubert Canfield of Pittsford, New York.

Arr. H. F.

My dad-dy is an en-gin-eer, My broth-er drives a hack, My sis-ter takes in wash-in' An' the ba-by balls the jack, An' it looks like . . I'm nev-er gon-na cease my wan - - - der-in'.

188

WANDERIN'

A

1 My daddy is an engineer,
  My brother drives a hack,
  My sister takes in washin'
  An' the baby balls the jack,
  An' it looks like
  I'm never gonna cease my wanderin'.

2 I been a wanderin'
  Early and late,
  New York City
  To the Golden Gate,
  An' it looks like
  I'm never gonna cease my wanderin'.

3 Been a-workin' in the army,
  Workin' on a farm,
  All I got to show for it
  Is the muscle in my arm,
  An' it looks like
  I'm never gonna cease my wanderin'.

B

1 There's snakes on the mountain,
  And eels in the sea,
  'Twas a red-headed woman
  Made a wreck out of me,
  And it looks like
  I'm never gonna cease my wanderin'.

2 Ashes to ashes
  And dust to dust,
  If whiskey don't get you,
  Then the women must,
  And it looks like
  I'm never gonna cease my wanderin'.

A. R. U.

The American Railway Union strike of 1893, led by Eugene V. Debbs, paralyzed traffic on railways of the Northwest. As the concerted stoppage of work began, not a wheel moved on thousands of miles of right-of-way; it was a terrific tie-up, a red chapter in American transportation history. The railway managers blacklisted A. R. U. men; strikers drifted to other railroads, got jobs under new names, were detected, dropped from the pay rolls, and again put "on the hog," riding hog and cattle cars. These drifters made a song out of their grief. C. W. Loutzenhiser of Chicago met a brother A. R. U. man in the Illinois Central switchyards at Macomb, Mississippi; they held a little songfest; one song has verses flinging a switchman's gauntlet into the face of Fate. It is a gay-hearted tune asking Lady Luck, in plain railroad slang, not to be too hard. "Go screw your nut," in rail talk means, "Be on your way." Railway lines alluded to here can be located at any railway station information desk; also hotel porters are ready to assist. R. W. Gordon gave me the verses in Darien, Georgia, and sent me to Loutzenhiser in Chicago for the melody. A good man, with a brick-dust face and invincible Irish eyes, is Loutzenhiser. In the course of our acquaintance he made the casual remark, "The fellows that sing the songs I know have all gone where the woodbine twineth and bejeez maybe I ought to go too." He seemed a serene, self-contained soul, once laughing after singing a sweet Irish ditty, "I sing these songs to keep from goin' bugs."

Arr. H. F. P.

Been on the hum-mer since nine-ty-four, Last job I had was on the Lake Shore, Lost my of-fice in the A. R. U., And I won't get it back till nine-teen-two. And I'm still on the hog train

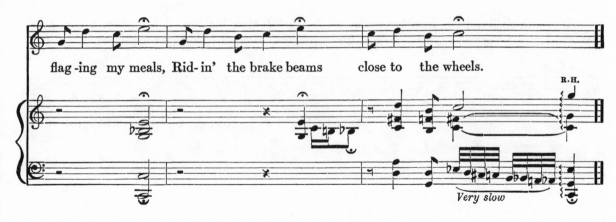

flag-ing my meals, Rid-in' the brake beams close to the wheels.

Very slow

Been on the hummer since ninety-four,
Last job I had was on the Lake Shore,
Lost my office in the A. R. U.
And I won't get it back till nineteen-two
And I'm still on the hog train flagging my meals,
Ridin' the brake beams close to the wheels.

WE ARE FOUR BUMS

If a man shall not work neither shall he eat. . . . Is that so? . . . A bums' song . . . heard among glee club boys and among persons who go to the Barber's College for a haircut. . . .

Arr. E. M.

We are four bums, four jol-ly good chums, We live like roy - al Turks; We're hav-ing good luck, in bum-ming our chuck, God bless the man that works!

1 We are four bums, four jolly good chums,
   We live like royal Turks;
   We're having good luck, in bumming our chuck,
   God bless the man that works!

2 We are four bums, four jolly good chums,
   We live like royal Turks;
   We're having good luck, in bumming our chuck,
   To hell with the man that works!

192

THE BIG BRUTAL CITY

THE POOR WORKING GIRL

This wastrel may be heard from the lips of factory girls in several scattered cities of the Union of States.   Some sing it as if it were true and after the fact, while others rattle it off as if there's nothing to it but a ditty to pass the time away.   Both may be correct.

Arr. L. S.

Slowly and mockingly angrily

The poor work - ing girl, May heav - en pro - tect her, She has such an aw - f'ly hard time;   The rich man's daugh - ter goes haugh - ti - ly by, My God! do you won - der at crime!

The poor working girl,
May heaven protect her,
She has such an awf'ly hard time;
The rich man's daughter goes haughtily by,
My God! do you wonder at crime!

ROLL THE CHARIOT

What would the big brutal city be without that international, interdenominational organization, The Salvation Army?   It is ready to take any popular song, any ragtime ditty or jazz tune, and tie it up to religion.   I have heard converts sing:

> "There are flies on you,
> There are flies on me,
> But there ain't no flies on Jesus."

Reading Bramwell Booth's memoirs, we notice that forty years ago, and more, the Army street meetings were broken up; singers of gospel hymns were pelted with bad eggs and worse tomatoes. Time has passed.   The Army is respectable now, is established, with million dollar real estate holdings.   When the big bass drum is laid flat and the public invited to throw dimes or dollars onto the drum, there is no outside interference.   They challenge the Devil and worship God in peace. An old Saturday night favorite in Fond du Lac, Wisconsin, and Waterloo, Iowa, is "The Chariot Song," trumpeted with jubilee voices as the bass drum invites contributions.   I heard it on the public square, in front of sample rooms and saloons on Prairie Street, in Galesburg, on nights when "the Q pay car" had come in.

Arr. A. G. W.

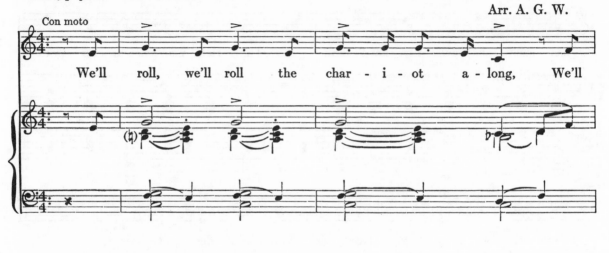

ROLL THE CHARIOT

char - i - ot a - long, And we won't drag on be - hind.

hind. . . . .

1 We'll roll, we'll roll the chariot along,
We'll roll, we'll roll the chariot along,
We'll roll, we'll roll the chariot along,
And we won't drag on behind.

2 If the Devil's in the way we will roll it over him,
If the Devil's in the way we will roll it over him,
If the Devil's in the way we will roll it over him,
And we won't drag on behind.

3 The collection will help us to roll it along,
The collection will help us to roll it along,
The collection will help us to roll it along,
And we won't drag on behind.

BRADY

A Nebraska-born woman, now practicing law in Chicago, gives us one verse and a tune from St. Louis. It is a tale of wicked people, a bad man so bad that even after death he went "struttin' in hell with his Stetson hat." Geraldine Smith, attorney-at-law in Chicago, heard it from Omaha railroad men. It is text A. Then from the R. W. Gordon collection we have text B. The snarl of the underworld, the hazards of those street corners and alleys "where any moment may be your next," are in the brawling of this Brady reminiscence.

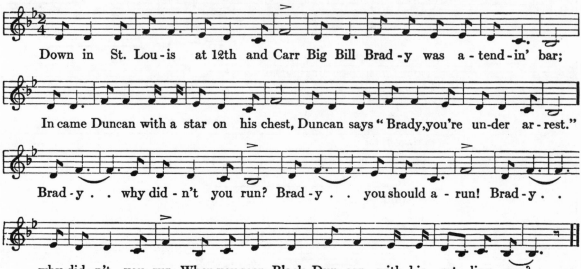

Down in St. Lou-is at 12th and Carr Big Bill Brad-y was a-tend-in' bar;

In came Duncan with a star on his chest, Duncan says "Brady, you're un-der ar-rest."

Brad-y . . why did-n't you run? Brad-y . . you should a-run! Brad-y . .

why did-n't you run When you seen Black Dun-can with his gat-ling gun?

A

Down in St. Louis at 12th and Carr
Big Bill Brady was a-tendin' bar;
In came Duncan with a star on his chest
Duncan says "Brady, you're under arrest."
Brady — why didn't you run?
Brady — you should a-run!
Brady — why didn't you run
When you seen Black Duncan with his gatling gun?

B

1 Duncan and his brother was playing pool
When Brady came in acting a fool;
He shot him once, he shot him twice,
Saying, "I don't make my living by shooting dice!"

Brady won't come no more!
Brady won't come no more!
Brady won't come no more!
For Duncan shot Brady with a forty-four!

198

2 "Brady, Brady, don't you know you done wrong
   To come in my house when my game was going on?
   I told you half a dozen times before,
   And now you lie dead on my barroom floor!"

3 Brady went to hell lookin' mighty curious,
   The devil says, "Where you from?" "East St. Louis."
   "Well, pull off your coat and step this way,
   For I've been expecting you every day!"

4 When the girls heard Brady was dead
   They went up home and put on red,
   And came down town singin' this song —
   "Brady's struttin' in hell with his Stetson on!

   "Brady, where you at?
   Brady, where you at?
   Brady, where you at?
   Struttin' in hell with his Stetson hat!"

ON TO THE MORGUE

We heard this travesty on the Chopin funeral march sung by two newspapermen, one an Irishman, the other an Icelander, in Atlantic City, during a convention of the American Federation of Labor.

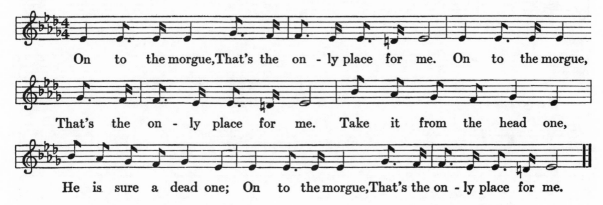

On   to   the morgue, That's the on - ly place for me. On   to   the morgue,

That's   the   on - ly place for me. Take   it   from the   head   one,

He   is   sure   a   dead one; On   to   the morgue, That's the on - ly place for me.

1 On to the morgue,
  That's the only place for me.
  On to the morgue,
  That's the only place for me.
  Take it from the head one.
  He is sure a dead one;
  On to the morgue,
  That's the only place for me.

2 Where will we all be
  One hundred years from now?
  Where will we all be
  One hundred years from now?
  Pushing up the daisies,
  Pushing up the daisies,
  That's where we'll all be
  One hundred years from now.

IT'S THE SYME THE WHOLE WORLD OVER

This tale of love's ironic pathways, as sometimes sung by soldiers, sailors, and travelling men, carries its main character through farther episodes in other cities. It was a favorite in The Black Watch and among Canadian and Anzac contingents during the World War. The melody comes here from Paul Boston, John Lock and Bert Massee of Chicago. The text was fortified in part by H. L. Mencken and a contributor to *The American Mercury*.

Arr. A. G. W.

1 It's the syme the whole world over,
　It's the poor what gets the blyme,
　While the rich 'as all the plysures.
　Now ain't that a blinkin' shyme?

2 She was a parson's daughter,
　Pure, unstyn-ed was her fyme,
　Till a country squire come courtin',
　And the poor girl lorst her nyme.

3 So she went aw'y to Lunnon,
  Just to 'ide her guilty shyme.
  There she met an Army Chaplain:
  Ornst ag'yn she lorst her nyme.

4 'Ear 'im as he jaws the Tommies,
  Warnin' o' the flymes o' 'ell.
  With 'er 'ole 'eart she had trusted,
  But ag'yn she lorst her nyme.

5 Now 'es in his ridin' britches,
  'Untin' foxes in the chyse
  W'ile the wictim o' his folly
  Makes her livin' by her wice.

6 So she settled down in Lunnon,
  Sinkin' deeper in her shyme,
  Till she met a lybor leader,
  And ag'yn she lorst 'er nyme.

7 Now 'es in the 'Ouse o' Commons,
  Mykin' laws to put down crime,
  W'ile the wictim of his plysure
  Walks the street each night in shyme.

8 Then there cyme a bloated bishop.
  Marriage was the tyle 'e tole.
  There was no one else to tyke 'er,
  So she sold 'er soul for gold.

9 See 'er in 'er 'orse and carriage,
  Drivin' d'ily through the park.
  Though she's myde a wealthy marriage
  Still she 'ides a brykin' 'eart.

10 In a cottage down in Sussex
   Live's 'er payrents old and lyme,
   And they drink the wine she sends them,
   But they never, never, speaks 'er nyme.

11 In their poor and 'umble dwellin'
   There 'er grievin' payrents live,
   Drinkin' champyne as she sends 'em
   But they never, never, can forgive.

12 It's the syme the whole world over,
   It's the poor what gets the blyme,
   While the rich 'as all the plysures.
   Now ayn't it a bloody shyme?

IN THE DAYS OF OLD RAMESES

In the years when Jack the Ripper was baffling the police of London with his murders of women, leaving mutilated victims in the Whitechapel district, there flourished in Chicago an organization of newspaper men known as the Whitechapel Club. Its rooms fronted on the alley at the rear of *The Chicago Daily News* office, between Fifth Avenue and La Salle Street. George Ade says of the club, "It was a little group of thirsty intellectuals who were opposed to everything. The fact that Jack the Ripper was their patron saint will give a dim idea of the hard-boiledness of the organization. They had kind words and excuses for many of the anarchists who had been hanged for the bomb-throwing at the Haymarket riot. They were social revolutionists and single-taxers and haters of the rich. They scoffed at the conventional and orthodox and deplored the cheap futility of their own slave-tasks as contributors to the daily press. They were young men enjoying their first revolt." Ade, James Keeley, Finley Peter Dunne, Brand Whitlock, John T. McCutcheon, Ben King, Drury Underwood and others were members. It was about the time of the Chestnut Bell, an attachment for men's vests; when a story that had been told many times before was narrated, it was the custom to give a ring or two on the bells, signifying that the hearers had heard the story once or twice. At the Whitechapel Club, however, instead of ringing Chestnut Bells, they sang a song. The verses, as given below, are jointly from James Keeley and George Ade while the melody is a Keeley reminiscence. Ade tells us that Rudyard Kipling remembered his evening at their club because, later on, he tried to recall and write the words of the club song.

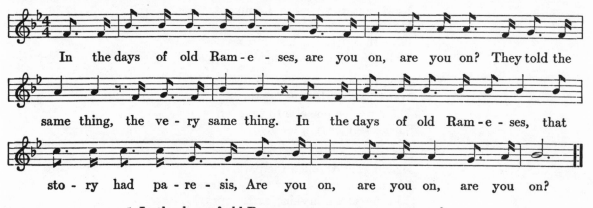

In the days of old Ram - e - ses, are you on, are you on? They told the
same thing, the ve - ry same thing. In the days of old Ram - e - ses, that
sto - ry had pa - re - sis, Are you on, are you on, are you on?

1 In the days of old Rameses, are you on, are you on?
   They told the same thing, the very same thing.
   In the days of old Rameses, that story had paresis,
   Are you on, are you on, are you on?

2 Adam told it to the beast before the fall, are you on?
   He told the same thing, the very same thing.
   When he told it to the creatures, it possessed redeeming features,
   But to tell it now requires a lot of gall.

3 Joshua told it to the boys before the wall, are you on?
   He told the same thing, the very same thing
   At the wall of Jericho before the wall began to fall,
   Are you on, are you on, are you on?

4 In the days of Sodom and Gomorrah, are you on?
  They told the same thing, the very same thing;
  In Sodom and Gomorrah, people told it to their sorrow,
  Are you on, are you on, are you on?

5 In the days of ancient Florence, are you on?
  They told the same thing, the very same thing;
  In the days of ancient Florence, it was held in great abhorrence,
  Are you on, are you on, are you on?

THE GOOD BOY

Lem Parton, a New York journalist who farms at Sneeden's Landing up the Hudson, gives the following version of a highbrow folk song which has several variants.

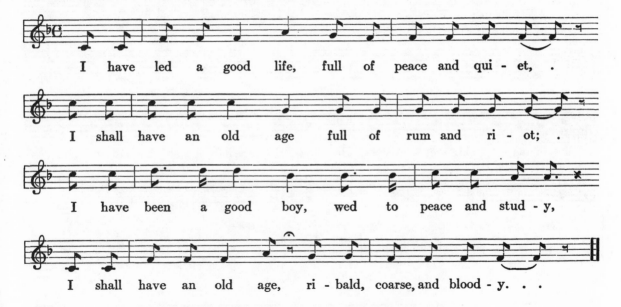

I have led a good life, full of peace and qui - et, .

I shall have an old age full of rum and ri - ot; .

I have been a good boy, wed to peace and stud - y,

I shall have an old age, ri - bald, coarse, and blood - y. . .

1 I have led a good life, full of peace and quiet,
  I shall have an old age full of rum and riot;
  I have been a good boy, wed to peace and study,
  I shall have an old age, ribald, coarse and bloody.

2 I have never cut throats, even when I yearned to,
  Never sang dirty songs that my fancy turned to;
  I have been a nice boy and done what was expected,
  I shall be an old bum loved but unrespected.

WILLY THE WEEPER

R. W. Gordon in his editorship of the Adventure magazine department "Old Songs That Men Have Sung" received thirty versions of Willy the Weeper, about one hundred verses different. Willy shoots craps with kings, plays poker with presidents, eats nightingale tongues a queen cooks for him; his Monte Carlo winnings come to a million, he lights his pipe with a hundred dollar bill, he has heart affairs with Cleopatra, the Queen of Sheba, and movie actresses.

As against versions of this heard in Detroit and New York, we prefer the one by Henry (Hinky) McCarthy of the University of Alabama. He gives it with pauses, with mellowed, mellifluous tones, with an insinuating guitar accompaniment. The lines "Teet tee dee dee dee dee," are lingering and dreamy, supposed to indicate regions where the alphabet is not wanted.

Arr. L. S.

Did you ev - er hear the sto - ry 'bout Wil - ly, the Weep - er? Made his

liv - in' as a chim-ney - sweeper. He had the dope hab -it an' he had it bad;

Lis - ten while I tell you 'bout the dream he had: Teet tee dee dee dee dee,

WILLY THE WEEPER

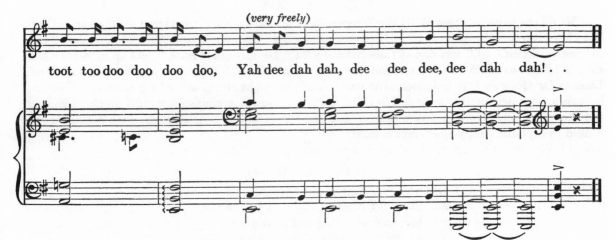

(very freely)

toot too doo doo doo doo,   Yah dee dah dah, dee   dee dee, dee dah   dah! . .

1 Did you ever hear the story 'bout Willy the Weeper?
Made his livin' as a chimney-sweeper.
He had the dope habit an' he had it bad;
Listen while I tell you 'bout the dream he had:
Teet tee dee dee dee dee, toot too doo doo doo doo,
Yah dee dah dah, dee dee dee, dee dah dah!

2 He went down to the dope house one Saturday night,
An' he knew that the lights would be burnin' bright.
I guess he smoked a dozen pills or mo';
When he woke up he wuz on a foreign sho':
Teet tee dee dee dee dee, toot too doo doo doo doo, etc.

3 Queen o' Bulgaria wuz the first he met;
She called him her darlin' an' her lovin' pet.
She promised him a pretty Fohd automobile,
With a diamond headlight an' a silver steerin'-wheel:
Teet tee dee dee dee dee, toot too doo doo doo doo, etc.

4 She had a million cattle, she had a million sheep;
She had a million vessels on the ocean deep;
She had a million dollahs, all in nickles an' dimes;
She knew 'cause she counted them a million times:
Teet tee dee dee dee dee, toot too doo doo doo doo, etc.

5 Willy landed in New York one evenin' late,
He asked his sugar baby for an after-date.
Willy he got funny, she began to shout:
Bim bam boo! — an' the dope gave out.
Teet tee dee dee dee dee, toot too doo doo doo doo, etc.

COCAINE LIL

We do not know whether Willy the Weeper and Cocaine Lil were ever introduced to each other. But they travelled the same route. Illusions, headaches, mornings after, soft fool fantasies, "and the rest is silence." Lil was one of those who say "I'll try any thing once." As an utterance the song of Lil has as much validity and more brevity than "The Confessions of an Opium Eater," by Thomas De Quincey. It is a document that rises from night life places of Chicago and Detroit. Besides a document it is a song-sketch. "Snow" is slang for a white flaky dust sniffed by drug addicts. Precisely how and why a cocaine dog and a cocaine cat fight all night with a cocaine rat is hard to explain. They symbolize a snarl.

Air: Willy the Weeper

1 Did you ever hear about Cocaine Lil?
She lived in Cocaine town on Cocaine hill,
She had a cocaine dog and a cocaine cat,
They fought all night with the cocaine rat.

2 She had cocaine hair on her cocaine head.
She wore a snowbird hat and sleigh-riding clothes.
She had a cocaine dress that was poppy red.
On her coat she wore a crimson, cocaine rose.

3 Big gold chariots on the Milky Way,
Snakes and elephants silver and gray,
O the cocaine blues they make me sad,
O the cocaine blues make me feel bad.

4 Lil went to a "snow" party one cold night,
And the way she "sniffed" was sure a fright.
There was Hophead Mag with Dopey Slim,
Kankakee Liz with Yen Shee Jim.

5 There was Hasheesh Nell and the Poppy Face Kid,
Climbed up snow ladders and down they slid;
There was Stepladder Kit, stood six feet,
And The Sleighriding Sisters that are hard to beat.

6 Along in the morning about half-past three
They were all lit up like a Christmas tree;
Lil got home and started to go to bed,
Took another "sniff" and it knocked her dead.

7 They laid her out in her cocaine clothes.
She wore a snowbird hat and a crimson rose;
On her headstone you'll find this refrain:
"She died as she lived, sniffing cocaine."

SHE PROMISED SHE'D MEET ME

It is believed this song originated in Chicago, the premier meat packing city of the round earth, the continents thereof, and the archipelagoes of the seven seas. However, it is also sung in Omaha, Cincinnatti, New York and San Francisco, as of local origin. In time seven cities may claim its author, though it is Aristophanic rather than Homeric in style. The second verse is more vulgar than the first. Both are sung with gusto at all our best universities. Footballs are made of pigskin. In Cincinnati, once nicknamed Porkopolis, we heard that the song "is best rendered when rendering lard or skinning a beef."

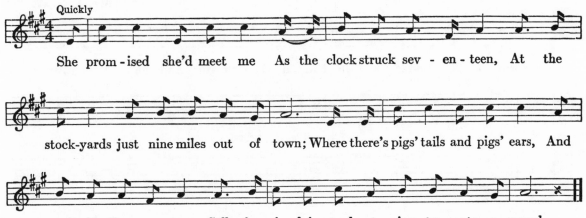

She prom-ised she'd meet me As the clock struck sev - en - teen, At the stock-yards just nine miles out of town; Where there's pigs' tails and pigs' ears, And tough old Tex - as steers Sell for sir - loin steak at nine-ty cents a pound.

1 She promised she'd meet me
  As the clock struck seventeen,
    At the stockyards just nine miles out of town;
  Where there's pigs' tails and pigs' ears,
  And tough old Texas steers
    Sell for sirloin steak at ninety cents a pound.

2 She's my darlin', my daisy,
  She's humpbacked, she's crazy,
    She's knock-kneed, bow-legged, and lame —
  (*Spoken:* Got the rheumatism!)
  They say her breath is sweet,
  But I'd rather smell her feet,
    She's my freckle-faced, consumptive Mary Jane.

NO MORE BOOZE (FIREMAN SAVE MY CHILD)

The phrase "rush the growler" here refers to any receptacle such as a pitcher, a pail, a bucket, or a tin can, in which draught beer was carried from the bar of a saloon to adjacent premises by consumers or agents of consumers. . . . About the time this song arose there were mainly three kinds of saloons in the United States: (1) saloons in bone-dry territory with the doors locked and a *For Sale* sign in front; (2) saloons where the doors never closed seven days in the week; (3) saloons where the doors closed only on Sundays. . . . The period was one provocative of vulgar proverbs, such as, "The coat and the pants do all the work but the vest gets all the gravy."

Arr. A. G. W.

There was a lit-tle man and he had a lit-tle can, And he used to rush the growl-er; He went to the sa-loon on a Sun-day af-ter-noon, And you ought to heard the bar-ten-der hol-ler:

CHORUS

No more booze, no more booze,

no more booze on Sun-day; No more booze, no more booze, Got to get your can filled

Mon-day. She's the on - ly girl I love, . . . With a face like a horse and

bug-gy. . . . Lean-ing up a-gainst the lake, O fire-man! save my child!

1 There was a little man and he had a little can,
   And he used to rush the growler;
   He went to the saloon on a Sunday afternoon,
   And you ought to heard the bartender holler:

Chorus:
   No more booze, no more booze,
   No more booze on Sunday;
   No more booze, no more booze,
   Got to get your can filled Monday.

She's the only girl I love,
With a face like a horse and buggy.
Leaning up against the lake,
O fireman! save my child!

2 The chambermaid came to my door,
   "Get up, you lazy sinner,
   We need those sheets for table-cloths
   And it's almost time for dinner."
   Chorus:

209

LYDIA PINKHAM

Only two of the many verses of this song are presented here.   As a satire the piece has its points and touches more than the surface of current life, manners and morals.

Arr. L. S.

Then we'll sing .. of Ly - di - a Pink - ham, And her

love .. for the hu - man race; How she sold .. her veg - 'ta - ble

com - pound And the pa - pers pub - lish'd her face.

1 Then we'll sing of Lydia Pinkham,
And her love for the human race;
How she sold her veg'table compound
And the papers publish'd her face.

2 Oh, it sells for a dollar a bottle
Which is very cheap you see,
And if it doesn't cure you
She will sell you six for three.

PRISON AND JAIL SONGS

BIRD IN A CAGE

In the mountains of Kentucky there was sung an old lyric of English origin, Down In The Valley. And there were jail-birds in Lexington, Kentucky, who built and wove from this older song with lines telling their sweethearts where to send letters. . . . Charles Hoening, working with a threshing crew near Lexington, heard four negroes, harvest hands, go off by themselves after supper, among strawstacks to sing. The gloaming crept on, an evening star came, a rising moon climbed the horizon dusk and mist. "They sang that song over and over and they knew how to sing it."

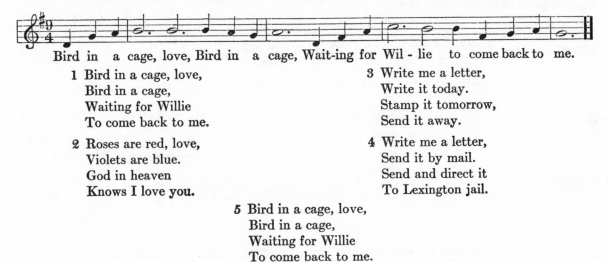

Bird in a cage, love, Bird in a cage, Wait-ing for Wil - lie to come back to me.

1 Bird in a cage, love,
   Bird in a cage,
   Waiting for Willie
   To come back to me.

2 Roses are red, love,
   Violets are blue.
   God in heaven
   Knows I love you.

3 Write me a letter,
   Write it today.
   Stamp it tomorrow,
   Send it away.

4 Write me a letter,
   Send it by mail.
   Send and direct it
   To Lexington jail.

5 Bird in a cage, love,
   Bird in a cage,
   Waiting for Willie
   To come back to me.

YONDER COMES THE HIGH SHERIFF

To the time-beats of galloping hoofs, the stride of horse and rider, convicts of the Kentucky penitentiary at Frankfort have made a song.

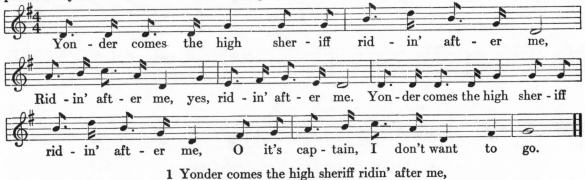

Yon - der comes the high sher - iff rid - in' aft - er me,
Rid - in' aft - er me, yes, rid - in' aft - er me. Yon - der comes the high sher - iff
rid - in' aft - er me, O it's cap - tain, I don't want to go.

1 Yonder comes the high sheriff ridin' after me,
   Ridin' after me, yes, ridin' after me.
   Yonder comes the high sheriff ridin' after me,
   O it's captain, I don't want to go.

2 Been down to Frankfort servin' out my time,
   Servin' out my time, yes, servin' out my time.
   Been down to Frankfort servin' out my time,
   O it's captain, I don't want to go.

PORTLAND COUNTY JAIL

A Chicago newspaperman who happened to do in real life what Paddy Flynn does in this song, got ten days, as Paddy Flynn did, in the Portland County jail. While recovering from his bootleg headache, he learned the first three verses of a song there. For the fourth, we are indebted to philosophers at the extreme left in the labor movement and in modernist art in Chicago. Whether sung solo or in ensemble or melee, the ungrammatical "A" in the last line is to be howled with high scorn. The word "trun" means "threw" or "throwed"; it rhymes with fun. A "can" signifies a jail or place of forcible detention.

Arr. L. S.

I'm a stran-ger in your cit-y, my name is Pad-dy Flynn.

I got drunk the oth-er night and the cop-pers run me in. I

had no mon-ey to pay my fine, no one to go my bail; So

PORTLAND COUNTY JAIL

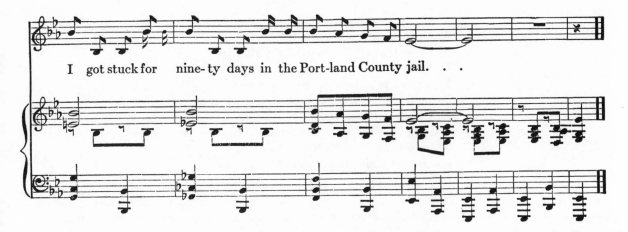

I got stuck for nine-ty days in the Port-land County jail. . .

1 I'm a stranger in your city, my name is Paddy Flynn.
  I got drunk the other night and the coppers run me in.
  I had no money to pay my fine, no one to go my bail;
  So I got stuck for ninety days in the Portland County jail.

2 Oh, the only friend that I had left was Happy Sailor Jack;
  He told me all the lies he knew, and all the safes he'd cracked;
  He'd cracked them in Seattle, he'd robbed the Western Mail.
  'Twould freeze the blood of an honest man in the Portland County jail.

3 Oh, such a bunch of devils no one ever saw,
  Robbers, thieves and highwaymen, breakers of the law;
  They sang a song the whole night long, the curses fell like hail;
  I'll bless the day that takes me away from the Portland County jail.

4 Finest friend I ever had was Officer McGurk.
  He said I was a lazy bum, a no-good and a shirk.
  One Saturday night when I got tight, he trun me in the can,
  And now you see he's made of me *A* honest workingman.

MOONLIGHT

Meet me by moon-light alone,
And then I will tell you a tale,
Must be told by the moon-light alone,
In the grove at the end of the vale;
You must promise to come, for I said
I would show the night-flowers their queen,
Nay turn not away that sweet head!
'Tis the loveliest ever was seen!
Oh! meet me by moonlight alone,
Meet me by moonlight alone!

The verse above is one of several in the popular song of many years ago, Meet Me by Moonlight. As it reached the Tennessee and Kentucky mountains and lived on there, the mountain people made adaptations till they had changed it into their own song and something else again. . . . See, in this connection, the note to The Ship That Never Returned, in this book. . . . The mountain lyrists who composed the verses to "Moonlight," as here given, eventually won an immense audience; desperate opera stars, hunting a composition that had a sure hold on American heart strings, put on its modern derivative, The Prisoner's Song, in their "popular performances," as the phrase goes. . . . The tune here is from Gilbert R. Combs and the text includes verses from Combs and from Mary Leaphart. . . . In singing the refrain may or may not be used with all stanzas.

1 Meet me to-night, lover, meet me,
O meet me in the moonlight alone,
I have a sad story to tell you,
Must be told in the moonlight alone.

The first verse serves as Refrain.

2 I'm going to a new jail to-morrow,
And leave my poor darlin' alone,
With the cold prison bars all around me,
And my head on a pillow of stone.

3 Your father and mother don't like me,
Or they never would have drove me from their
door;
If I had my life to live over
I would never go there any more.

216

4 I wish I had never been born
  Or had died when I was young.
  I would never have saw your sweet face
  Or heard your lyin' tongue.

5 If I had a-minded my mother
  I had been with her today,
  But I was young and foolish
  And you stole my heart away.

6 I have three ships on the ocean
  All laden with silver and gold;
  And before my darlin' should suffer
  I'd have them all anchored and sold.

7 If I had the wings of an eagle
  Across the wide sea I would fly.
  I would fly to the arms of my darling
  And there I would stay till I die.

MIDNIGHT SPECIAL.   (2)

A fast train, such as "The Midnight Special," means a getaway, outside air, freedom.   They sing about it in the Houston, Texas, jailhouse, and elsewhere.   The verses here can with little or no practice be adjusted to the tune of Midnight Special (1) in our folio of Dramas and Portraits.

1 If you evah go to Houston,
  You better walk right;
  You better not gamble
  And you better not fight.
  T. Bentley will arrest you,
  He'll surely take you down;
  Judge Nelson'll sentence you,
  Then you're jailhouse bound.

Refrain:
  O let the Midnight Special
  Shine a light on me,
  Let the Midnight Special
  Shine a evah lovin' light on me!

2 Every Monday mawnin',
  When the ding-dong rings,

You go to the table,
See the same damn things;
And on the table,
There's a knife an' pan,
Say anything about it,
Have trouble with a man.

3 Yondah come Miss Rosy;
  Oh, how do you know?
  By th' umbrella on her shoulder
  An' the dress that she woah!
  Straw hat on her head,
  Piece of paper in her hand,
  Says, "Look here, Mr. Jailer,
  I want's my life-time man."

217

SEVEN LONG YEARS IN STATE PRISON

A convict tells what life has done to him. . . . During the international imbroglio known as the Spanish-American War, I heard half of this song from a high private in the rear ranks; we went to Porto Rico and the oftener it rained between Guanica and Utuado, and the worse the mud and the higher the water in the pup tents at Adjuntas, the more Private Campbell sang "Sad, sad and lonely." . . . The other half of the song came to me at Denison College, Ohio, twenty-seven years later.

Arr. A. G. W.

Sev - en long years in state pri - son, Sev - en long years for to stay, For

knock - ing a man down the al - ley And tak - ing his gold watch and chain. . .

Sad, . . . sad and lone - ly, sit - ting in my cell All a - lone, all a - lone, .

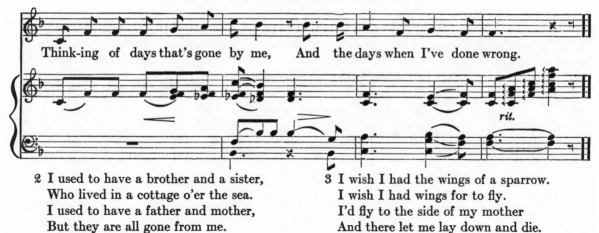

Think-ing of days that's gone by me, And the days when I've done wrong.

2 I used to have a brother and a sister,
Who lived in a cottage o'er the sea.
I used to have a father and mother,
But they are all gone from me.

3 I wish I had the wings of a sparrow.
I wish I had wings for to fly.
I'd fly to the side of my mother
And there let me lay down and die.

WHEN I WAS YOUNG AND FOOLISH

There are sailor and lumberjack, railroad and cowboy versions of this. New York, Atlanta, and Seattle have local variants. It is sung in jails and outside. The tune is from Albert Richard Wetjen, of Salem, Oregon, able seaman and story teller.

Arr. A. G. W.

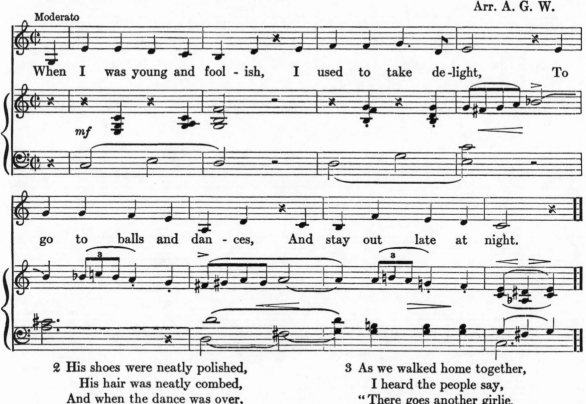

When I was young and fool-ish, I used to take de-light, To go to balls and dan-ces, And stay out late at night.

2 His shoes were neatly polished,
His hair was neatly combed,
And when the dance was over,
He asked to see me home.

3 As we walked home together,
I heard the people say,
"There goes another girlie,
That's being led astray."

BEEN IN THE PEN SO LONG

Three musketeers, regular army men en route to a fort in Texas, learned this in jail in Oklahoma. They "blued" it in unison, with harmonics, with a chromatic harmonica. They made a Santa Fe smoking car melodious. . . . A white man's rearrangement of a negro wail such as one recorded in a publication of the Texas Folk Lore Society.

Arr. A. G. W.

Been in the pen so long, Lawd, I got to go a - gain.

Been in the pen so long, O hon-ey, I'll be long gone.

Been in the pen so long,
O honey, I'll be long gone,
Been in the pen, Lawd,
I got to go again.
Been in the pen so long,
O honey, I'll be long gone.
Been in the pen so long,
Lawd, I got to go again.
Been in the pen so long,
O honey, I'll be long gone.

221

THE PREACHER AND THE SLAVE

When Joe Hill, the I. W. W. man, had the death sentence executed on him in Utah while the World War was on, his loss was mourned by the members of his organization. He was their star song writer and is the only outstanding producer of lyrics widely sung in the militant cohorts of the labor movement of America. Jails and jungles from the Lawrence, Massachusetts, woolen mills to the Wheatland, California, hop fields, have heard the rhymes and melodies started by Joe Hill. One of them is The Preacher and the Slave, going to the tune of Sweet By and By.

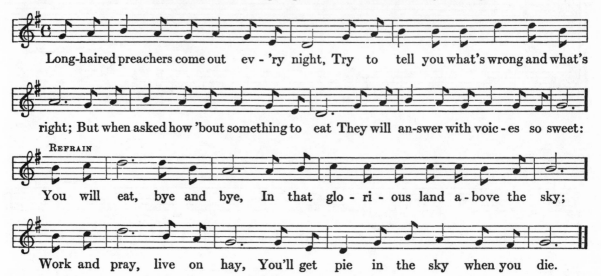

Long-haired preachers come out ev-'ry night, Try to tell you what's wrong and what's right; But when asked how 'bout something to eat They will an-swer with voic-es so sweet:

REFRAIN

You will eat, bye and bye, In that glo-ri-ous land a-bove the sky; Work and pray, live on hay, You'll get pie in the sky when you die.

1 Long-haired preachers come out every night, Try to tell you what's wrong and what's right;
But when asked how 'bout something to eat They will answer with voices so sweet:

Refrain:
   You will eat, bye and bye, In that glorious land above the sky;
   Work and pray, live on hay, You'll get pie in the sky when you die.

2 And the starvation army they play, And they sing and they clap and they pray.
Till they get all your coin on the drum, Then they'll tell you when you're on the bum:

3 Holy Rollers and jumpers come out, And they holler, they jump and they shout:
"Give your money to Jesus," they say, "He will cure all diseases today."

4 If you fight hard for children and wife — Try to get something good in this life —
You're a sinner and bad man, they tell, When you die you will sure go to hell.

5 Workingmen of all countries, unite, Side by side we for freedom will fight:
When the world and its wealth we have gained, To the grafters we'll sing this refrain:

Last Refrain:
   You will eat, bye and bye, When you've learned how to cook and to fry;
   Chop some wood, 'twill do you good, And you'll eat in the sweet bye and bye.

BLUES, MELLOWS, BALLETS

I dare hint delicately that while it is possible that neither the vocalist nor I might derive joy from singing *as singing*, yet as a folk-lorist I should experience delight at hearing a folk song put across in such a way that I could capture it. I urge that as a song hunter I should rather hear a Negro in the cornfield or on the levee or in a tobacco factory, than to hear Galli-Curci grand-operize.

DOROTHY SCARBOROUGH in *On the Trail of Negro Folk-Songs*.

LEVEE MOAN

Both Mississippi and Ohio river levees have had versions of this one, which reached up into the region roundabout Pendleton, Indiana, where it was heard by Lloyd Lewis, the Free Quaker pegged elsewhere in this book. A sonorous lament, is "Levee Moan," fully equal to many Gregorian chants that could be named. Some of its lines assuage the bitterness of our short mortal pilgrimage, some have an overtone aiming at the world beyond the flesh, while others are rooted amid such plain realities as the iron pathway of "dat ol' K. C. line."

Arr. L. S.

Ah'm go - in' whah no - bod - y knows my name, Lawd, Lawd, Lawd Lawd! Ah'm go - in' whah no - bod - y knows mah name, . . . Ah'm go - in' whah no - bod - y knows mah name! Ah'm go - in' whar dey don't shov - el no snow, Lawd, Lawd,

225

blow, . . .   Ah'm go - in' whah de chill - y wind don't blow!

1 Ah'm goin' whah nobody knows mah name, Lawd, Lawd, Lawd, Lawd!
   Ah'm goin' whah nobody knows mah name, Ah'm goin' whah nobody knows mah name!

2 Ah'm goin' whah dey don't shovel no snow, Lawd, Lawd, Lawd, Lawd!
   Ah'm goin' whah dey don't shovel no snow, Ah'm goin' whah dey don't shovel no snow!

3 Ah'm goin whah de chilly wind don't blow, Lawd, Lawd, Lawd, Lawd!
   Ah'm goin' whah de chilly wind don't blow, Ah'm goin' whah de chilly wind don't blow!

Note: Those who so choose may use the following "K. C. line" couplet in place of one the above stanzas; or the El Paso version (B) below.

Ah'm goin' on dat ol' K. C. line, Lawd, Lawd, Lawd, Lawd!
Ah'm goin' on dat ol' K. C. line, Ah'm goin' on dat ol' K. C. line!

B

1 O baby, where you been so long?   Lord, Lord, Lord, Lord,
   O baby, where you been so long?   O baby, where you been so long?

2 O honey, let your hair hang down, Lord, Lord, Lord, Lord,
   O honey, let your hair hang down, O honey, let your hair hang down.

3 O honey, your hair grows too long, Lord, Lord, Lord, Lord,
   O honey, your hair grows too long, O honey, your hair grows too long.

THOSE GAMBLER'S BLUES

This may be what polite society calls a gutter song. In a foreign language, in any lingo but that of the U. S. A., it would seem less vulgar, more bizarre. Its opening realism works on toward irony and fantasy, dropping in its final lines again to blunt realism. Texts and melody are from the song as given (A) by Henry McCarthy of the University of Alabama, and (B) by Jake Zeitlin and Jack Hagerty of Fort Worth and Los Angeles.

Arr. R. C.

1. It was down in old Joe's bar-room .. On a
   left stood Joe Mc-Ken-ny, ... His

cor-ner by the square, The drinks were served as us-u-al, And a
eyes blood-shot and red, He gazed at the crowd a-round him, And

good-ly crowd was there. 2. On my 3. As I
these are the words he said:

228

passed by the old in - fir - mar-y, . , I saw my sweet-heart there, . . All

stretched out on a ta - ble, . . So pale, so cold, so fair.

4. Six - teen coal - black hors - es, ... All hitched to a rub - ber - tired

hack, . . . Car - ried sev - en girls to the grave-yard, . . And on - ly

229

six of 'em com-in' . back. . . . .

5. O when I . die just bur-y me . In a box - back coat and hat, . . Put a
6. Six crap shooters as pall bearers, . . Let a cho-rus girl sing me a song With a

twent-y dol-lar gold-piece on my watch chain To let the Lord know I'm standin' pat.
jazz band on . my . hearse . . . To raise hell as we go a - long."

7. And now you've heard my sto-ry, . . . I'll take an-other shot o' booze; If

an - y - bod-y hap-pens to ask you, . . Then I've got those gambler's blues.

A

1 It was down in old Joe's bar-room
  On a corner by the square,
  The drinks were served as usual,
  And a goodly crowd was there.

2 On my left stood Joe McKenny,
  His eyes bloodshot and red,
  He gazed at the crowd around him
  And these are the words he said:

3 "As I passed by the old infirmary,
  I saw my sweetheart there,
  All stretched out on a table,
  So pale, so cold, so fair.

4 Sixteen coal-block horses,
  All hitched to a rubber-tired hack,

Carried seven girls to the graveyard,
And only six of 'em comin' back.

5 O, when I die, just bury me
  In a box-back coat and hat,   [chain
  Put a twenty dollar gold piece on my watch
  To let the Lord know I'm standin' pat.

6 Six crap shooters as pall bearers,
  Let a chorus girl sing me a song
  With a jazz band on my hearse
  To raise hell as we go along."

7 And now you've heard my story,
  I'll take another shot o' booze;
  If anybody happens to ask you,
  Then I've got those gambler's blues.

B

1 Went down to St. Joe's infirmary,
  To see my woman there;
  She was layin' on the table,
  So white, so cold, so fair.

2 Went up to see the doctor,
  "She's very low," he said;
  Went back to see my woman,
  Good God! she's layin' there dead,
  Spoken: She's dead!

3 Let her go, let her go, God bless her,
  Wherever she may be!
  There'll never be another like her,
  There'll never be another for me.

4 I may be killed on the ocean,
  I may be killed by a cannonball,
  But let me tell you, buddy,
  That a woman was the cause of it all.

5 Seventeen girls to the graveyard,
  Seventeen girls to sing her a song,
  Seventeen girls to the graveyard —
  Only sixteen of 'em comin' back.

6 O sixteen coal-black horses,
  To carry me when I'm gone.
  O flowers on the coffin,
  While the burial's carried on.

231

GOT DEM BLUES

"The very essence of the majority of blues," wrote Abbe Niles, "is found in the traditional line, common property of the race: 'Got de blues, but too dam' mean to cry.'" . . . One of the earliest blues is presented here, as heard, recorded, and harmonized by Henry Francis Parks, composer, music critic, theater console player, author of the book, "Jazzology of the Pipe Organ." It was moaned by resonant moaners in honky tonks of the southwest.

Arr. H. F. P.

Got dem blues, but I'm too mean, lordy,
I'm too damned mean to cry.
Oh! I got dem blues!
Got dem blues, but I'm too damned mean to cry.
Yes! I got dem dirty blues,
But I'm too damned mean to cry;
Yes! mean to cry.
Sweet Daddy! Uh-huh! Trun me down! Uh-huh!

DE BLUES AIN' NOTHIN'

This blues was sung in honky tonks of the southwest in years before the appearance of "mean moaners" in cafes where a tuxedo is requisite. . . . "B-l-u-e" at the close of each verse is sometimes "b-a-d."

Arr. L. S.

blues ain' noth-in' But a good man feel-in' b-l-u-e! . . .

draw this out . . . .

mf

p

1 Ah'm gonna build mahself a raft,
  An' float dat ribbah down.
  Ah'll build mahself a shack
  In some ol' Texas town,
    Mhm, mhm!
  'Cause de blues ain' nothin',
  No, de blues ain' nothin'
  But a good man feelin' b-l-u-e.

2 Ah'm goin' down on de levee,
  Goin' to take mahself a rockin' **chair.**
  If mah lovin' man don' come,
  Ah'll **rock** away from there,

  Mhm, mhm!
  'Cause de blues ain' nothin',
  No, de blues ain' nothin'
  But a good man feelin' b-l-u-e.

3 Why did you leave me blue?
  Why did you leave me blue?
  All **I** do is sit
  And cry for you,
    Mhm, mhm!
  'Cause de blues ain' nothin',
  No, de blues ain' nothin'
  But a good man feelin' b-l-u-e.

WHEN A WOMAN BLUE

This arrangement is based on the song as heard at the Wisconsin Players' House in Milwaukee, where it arrived through an Oklahoma poet named Ellis, who heard it from negroes in the cotton fields of Texas. It is an early blues, not to be hurried in its rendition; if you feel like giving it very slow and very draggy that is the way for you to give it; it is a massive, lugubrious gargoyle of a song.

Arr. L. S.

When a woman blue, when a woman blue,
She hang her little head and cry —
When a woman blue, when a woman blue,
She hang her little head and cry —
(Hah hah hah high!)
When a man get blue
He grab a railroad train and ride.

2 I'm go'n lay my head, I'm go'n lay my head,
Down on dat railroad line —
I'm go'n lay my head, I'm go'n lay my head,
Down on dat railroad line —
(Lah hah hah hine!)
Let de train roll by,
And dat'll pacify my min'.

COO-COO

(PEACOCK SONG)

An old negro voodoo woman in South Carolina told of all the animals holding a meeting. They elected the peacock to be queen. She sang an acknowledgment, spoke with music, her appreciation of the honor conferred on her. Thus we have the Coo-Coo murmur, moan and cry, presented here from Arthur Billings Hunt, baritone concert singer, and authority in several fields of American folk and art song.

Arr. Th. O.

GREAT GAWD, I'M FEELIN' BAD

A desolated heart trumpets humiliation. . . . Florence Heizer of Osage, Kansas, heard this often from a negro woman, who, over the ironing board, could reply to any mourning dove that sat in the cottonwoods.

Arr. A. G. W.

Great Gawd, I'm feel-in' bad, I ain't got the man that I

thought I had! . . . .

Great Gawd, I'm feelin' bad,
I ain't got the man that I thought I had!

238

O MY HONEY, TAKE ME BACK

Tubman K. Hedrick heard this often from a hotel kitchen in Memphis, over and over, day on day. He said of the lyric, "Love is not love that too openly proclaims itself," adding, "It is a solo with no audience intended or wanted but one person in the whole world. And as such, the melody carries the lyric persuasively."

Arr. A. G. W.

1 O my honey, take me back,
O my dahlin', I'll be true.
I am mo'nin' all day long,
O my honey, I love you.

2 I have loved you in joy and pain,
In de sunshine and de rain,
O my honey, heah me do,
O my dahlin', I love you.

WHAT KIN' O' PANTS DOES THE GAMBLER WEAR

The striped elegance of gamblers, the hazards of the meat supply, the troubles of money, love, and sleep, are themes here. The verses are casual, typical of the impromptu, the "make-up" song of the negro, "a product of economic and labor conditions," as Gates Thomas notes in No. 5 of the Publications of the Texas Folk Lore Society. His songs came from "shiftless and shifting day laborers and small croppers who follow Lady Luck, Aphrodite, and John Barleycorn." . . . The tune is close to certain Frog's Courting melodies. . . . "Gwain" is more accurate than "gwine" or "g'on." . . . When the wooden slats, on which a mattress lay, broke and went "blam-to-blam," it took a good sleeper to go on drowsing.

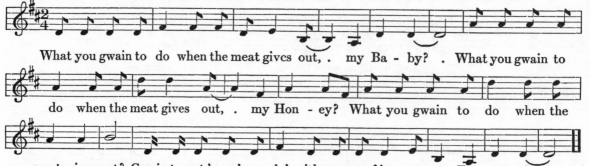

What you gwain to do when the meat gives out, . my Ba - by? . What you gwain to do when the meat gives out, . my Hon - ey? What you gwain to do when the meat gives out? Gwain to set 'roun' my do' with my mouf in a pout, For some - time.

1 What you gwain to do when the meat gives out, my Baby?
   What you gwain to do when the meat gives out, my Honey?
   What you gwain to do when the meat gives out?
   Gwain to set 'roun' my do' with my mouf in a pout,
       For sometime.

2 What kin' o' pants does the gambler wear, this mo'nin'?
   What kin' o' pants does the gambler wear, this evenin'?
   What kin' o' pants does the gambler wear?
   Big-legged stripes cost nine a pair
       This mo'nin'.

3 What kin' o' shoes does the gambler wear, this mo'nin'?
   What kin' o' shoes does the gambler wear, this evenin'?
   What kin' o' shoes does the gambler wear?
   Yaller toothpicks, cost 'leven a pair
       This evenin'.

4 Slats in the bed went blam-to-blam, this mo'nin';
   Slats in the bed went blam-to-blam, this evenin';
   Slats in the bed went blam-to-blam;
   Kep' on a-sleepin' like I didn't give a damn
       For sometime.

5 I'll be blamed ef I can see, my Baby,
   I'll be blamed ef I can see, my Honey,
   I'll be blamed ef I can see
   How all my money got away from me.
       For sometime.

JOE TURNER

W. C. Handy refers to Joe Turner as a grandaddy of blues. " In some sections it was called Going Down the River For Long, but in Tennessee it was always Joe Turner." Joe was a brother of Pete Turner, once governor of Tennessee, and clothed with police powers Joe Turner took prisoners from Memphis to Nashville, " handcuffed, to be gone no telling how long." Thus Handy explained the song to Dorothy Scarborough who recalled lines:

> Dey tell me Joe Turner's come to town.
> He's brought along one thousand links of chain;
> He's gwine to have one nigger for each link!
> He's gwine to have dis nigger for one link!

Handy used the old theme for building Joe Turner blues with such interesting lines as:

> Sweet Babe, I'm goin to leave you,
> And the time ain't long,
> No, the time ain't long,
> If you don't b'lieve I'm leavin'
> Count the days I'm gone.

Arr. A. G. W.

Dey tell me Joe Turn-ner he done come, . Dey tell me Joe
Tur-ner he done come, . (1) Got my man an' gone. . .
(2) Come with foh-ty links of chain. .

Dey tell me Joe Turner he done come,
Dey tell me Joe Turner he done come,
Got my man an' gone.

Dey tell me Joe Turner he done come,
Dey tell me Joe Turner he done come,
Come with fohty links of chain.

TIMES GETTIN' HARD, BOYS

When Rebecca Taylor sang her spirituals for us in Columbia, South Carolina, she was asked if she knew other songs, not spirituals. "When you were a girl wasn't there something that boys and girls would sing at each other for fun, for mischief?" Her eyes lighted, she gave a soprano chuckle, and sang this verse out of the years when she was young. The "yellow boy" amid the black girls made an impression; it started a song.

Arr. L. S.

Times get-tin' hard, boys, mon-ey get-tin' scarce; If times don't be no bet-ter hyar, boun' to leave dis place. Take my true love by de han' lead her roun' de town; When she see dat yel-low boy she al-mos' faint a - way.

Times gettin' hard, boys, money gettin' scarce;
If times don't be no better hyar, boun' to leave dis place.
Take my true love by de han' lead her roun' de town;
When she see dat yellow boy she almos' faint away.

I'M SAD AND I'M LONELY

How many lies will a free young man tell a young lady? As many as the cross-ties on the rail-road or as many as the stars in the sky. He will lie and lie. His lies are endless. Thus the cast-off woman speaks of him. She wants a mountain cabin. She wants to be so far away that she won't bother her friends, the blackbirds. She sings it slowly. There is time for deliberation. Yet a phrase now and then, shaded with hate or pity, comes swiftly, almost gutturally and as a threat. The song came to me from a Dallas, Texas, woman who got it from Tennessee folks.

Arr. L. S.

I'm sad and I'm lone-ly, my heart it will break; My
sweet-heart loves an-oth-er, Lord, I wish I wuz dead! . . My
cheeks once were red as the bud on the rose, But now they are whit-er than the

li - ly that grows. Young la - dies, tak' wahn -in', tak' a wahn-in' from

me. Don't waste your af - fec -tions on a young man so free. . He'll

hug you, he'll kiss you, he'll tell you mo' lies, Than the cross ties on the

rail- road or the stars in the sky. I'll build me a cab - in in the

I'M SAD AND I'M LONELY

moun-tains so high, Where the black-birds can't see me and hear my sad cry. I'm troub-led, I'm troub-led, I'm troub-led in mind; Ef trou-ble don' kill me, I'll live a long time. . . . . . .

1 I'm sad and I'm lonely, my heart it will break;
My sweetheart loves another, Lord, I wish I wuz dead!
My cheeks once were red as the bud on the rose,
But now they are whiter than the lily that grows.

2 Young ladies, tak' wahnin', tak' a wahnin' from me.
Don't waste your affections on a young man so free.
He'll hug you, he'll kiss you, he'll tell you mo' lies,
Than the cross-ties on the railroad or the stars in the sky.

3 I'll build me a cabin in the mountains so high,
Where the blackbirds can't see me and hear my sad cry.
I'm troubled, I'm troubled, I'm troubled in mind;
Ef trouble don' kill me, I'll live a long time.

C. C. RIDER

John Lomax and I heard this song (A) in Austin, Texas, in an old saloon, *The Silver King*, operated as a soft drink parlor by a Mexican negro, Martinez. After two negroes with guitars had sung "The Original Blues," "Franky and Johnny," "Boll Weevil," and other pieces, Martinez himself favored us with "C. C. Rider," which may derive from "easy rider." . . . The Sunshine Special, a crack railroad train, has crossed Texas every day for many years. . . . In the last line of the first verse the word "blowed" is given long, slow, controlled and powerful, like the whistle of an onrushing overland train on a southwestern prairie; likewise the word "shine" in the last line of the second verse. . . . Text B is from Gates Thomas and his south Texas negro songs.

246

C. C. RIDER

nev - ah blowed be - foh.

A

1 Dat Sunshine Special comin' around de bend,
It blowed jus' like it nevah blowed befoh,
It blowed jus' like it nevah blowed befoh,
It blowed jus' like it nevah blowed befoh.

2 If I had a head-light like on a passenger train,
I'd shine my light on cool Colorado Springs,
I'd shine my light on cool Colorado Springs,
I'd shine my light on cool Colorado Springs.

3 Oh C. C. Rider, now see what you done, done,
You made me love you, now your sweetheart's come,
You made me love you, now your sweetheart's come,
You made me love you, now your sweetheart's come.

B

1 C. C. Rider, just see what you have done!
You made me love you, now yo' woman's done come!
You made me love you, now yo' woman's done come!
You made me love you, now yo' woman's done come!

2 You caused me, Rider, to hang my head and cry;
You put me down; God knows I don't see why!
You put me down; God knows I don't see why!
You put me down; God knows I don't see why!

YOU FIGHT ON

Brave counsel and spacious melody for a pilgrim's progress. . . . A North Carolina woman at Purdue University heard this for years as a girl from a negro woman cook in her home. "Often when I was in the kitchen she would say to me, 'Come on, Miss Mary, get on de tune wagon, you ain't on de tune wagon.'"

Arr. E. M.

* The first eighth note is sung in the natural voice, the second eighth note in falsetto

swo'd in yo' han', You fight on, yes, you fight on.

Lawd-'y you fight on With yo' swo'd in yo' han', You fight on.

If yo' brother done you wrong
Take him to yo'self alone;
Tell him brother you done treated me wrong.
You fight on, you fight on,
With yo' swo'd in yo' han',
You fight on, yes, you fight on.
Lawdy you fight on
With yo' swo'd in yo' han'
You fight on.

SATAN'S A LIAH

In Duluth, Minnesota, I heard Margaret Moore Nye, of a Richmond, Virginia, family, deliver this spiritual as she heard it in the kitchen of her girlhood home. She seated herself in a chair, crossed her knees, threw her head back, closed her eyes, patted the time with a foot, impersonating the mammy in Richmond from whose lips she heard it many years.

Con moto tranquillo

Arr. A. G. W.

Sa - tan's a li - ah, . an' a con - juh too; . . If you don' watch out . he'll con - juh you; . . Sa-tan's a li - ah, an' a con - juh too; If you don' watch out he'll con - juh you.

SATAN'S A LIAH

Ain' gon-na wor-ry my Lawd no' mo', Ain' gon-na wor-ry my Lawd no mo'.

1 Satan's a liah, an' a conjuh too;
   If you don' watch out he'll conjuh you.
   Satan's a liah, an' a conjuh too;
   If you don' watch out he'll conjuh you.
   Ain' gonna worry my Lawd no mo',
   Ain' gonna worry my Lawd no mo'.

2 Satan's got a mighty big shoe,
   If you don' watch out he'll slip it on you.
   Satan's got a mighty big shoe,
   If you don' watch out he'll slip it on you.
   Ain' gonna worry my Lawd no mo', etc.

3 Goin' to heaven on a angel's wing,
   When I get there you'll hear me sing.
   Goin' to heaven on a angel's wing,
   When I get there you'll hear me sing.
   Ain' gonna worry my Lawd no mo', etc.

4 When I get to heaven goin' to sit yah down,
   Goin' to put on my robe an' starry crown.
   When I get to heaven goin' to sit yah down,
   Goin' to put on my robe an' starry crown.
   Ain' gonna worry my Lawd no mo', etc.

DE BALLET OF DE BOLL WEEVIL.

"What's the song you're singing?" John Lomax once asked a group of negroes, who answered, "Dat's de ballet of de boll weevil." They have "ballets" (narratives), "reels" (dance songs), and "mellows" (melodies), besides improvisations called "make-up" and "jump-up" songs. . . . There were planters who gazed on ravaged cotton fields and felt the multiplied myrmidons of the boll weevil to be as terrible as one of the Four Horsemen of the Apocalypse. The imagination of the negro field workers played shrewdly and whimsically on the phantom that came so silently to destroy the work of man on the land that man claims to own. . . . Gates Thomas recorded three boll weevil verses in 1897, many more in 1906, and wrote in 1926 as to calamity and destruction by the insect plague, that it had been "more than averted, thanks to the application of scientific findings to cotton-growing and to the practical and creative work of seed breeders; but the ballad is still imaginatively true to the time and region in which it arose communally." . . . Text and tune here are from Texas, Oklahoma, Mississippi and Alabama; we forego boll weevil blues heard in Nashville, Tennessee, and on Lang Syne Plantation at Fort Motte, South Carolina.

Goin' to have a home."

1 De farmer say to de weevil:
"What you doin' on de square?"
De li'l bug say to de farmer:
"Got a nice big fambly dere;
Goin' to have a home, goin' to have a home."

2 Farmer say to de boll weevil:
"You's right up on de square."
Boll weevil say to de farmer:
"Mah whole fambly's there,
I have a home, I have a home."

3 Boll weevil say to de lightnin' bug:
"Can I get up a trade wid you?
If I was a lightnin' bug,
I'd work the whole night through,
All night long, all night long."

4 Don' you see dem creepers
Now have done me wrong?
Boll weevil got my cotton,
An' de merchan' got my corn;
What shall I do? I've got de blues.

5 Boll weevil say to de merchan':
"Bettah drink yo' col' lemonade;
W'en I get through wid you,
Goin' to drag you out o' dat shade,
I have a home, I have a home."

6 Boll weevil say to de doctah:
"Bettah pull out all dem pills,
W'en I get through wid de farmer,
Can't pay no doctah's bills.
I have a home, I have a home."

7 Boll weevil say to de preacher:
"Bettah close up dem church doors,
W'en I get through wid de farmer,
Can't pay de preacher no mo'.
I have a home, I have a home."

8 Boll weevil say to de farmer:
"You can ride in dat Fohd machine.
But w'en I get through wid yo' cotton,
Can't buy no gasoline,
Won't have no home, won't have no home."

9 Boll weevil say to de farmer:
"I'm a sittin' here on dis gate,
W'en I get through wid de farmer,
He's goin' to sell his Cadillac Eight,
I have a home, I have a home."

10 Boll weevil say to his wife:
"Bettah stan' up on yo' feet,
Look way down in Mississippi,
At de cotton we'd got to eat,
All night long, all night long."

11 De farmer say to de merchan':
"I want some meat an' meal!"
"Get away f'm here, yo' son-of-a-gun,
Yo' got boll weevils in yo' fiel',
Goin' to get yo' home, goin' to get yo' home."

12 Boll weevil say to de farmer,
"I wish you all is well!"
Farmer say to de boll weevil:
"I wish you wuz in hell!
I'd have a home, I'd have a home."

253

DE TITANIC

The central facts of an immense sea tragedy are here.   The main narrative lines of each stanza cadence a proud ship sailing at high speed, ending with a slow drawn drag, the silence of the empty sea that follows the "sinkin' down."   As a poem, in accuracy of statement, in stresses of details, and in implicative quality, some would rate this above Longfellow's "Wreck of the Hesperus." The arrangement here is based on the singing of Miss Bessie Zaban, formerly of Georgia and now of Chicago; a number of verses were sent to her by C. H. Currie of Atlanta, Georgia. . . The dialect is imperfectly rendered.   Negro troops sang the song crossing the submarine zone and in the trenches overseas.   The verses move smoothly, in even pulsations, like the stride of a great ocean liner with its turbines in good working order.   The chorus words "ocean" and "Titanic" sway like a swiftly moving thing abruptly slowed down, struck, staggering and bewildered, while the words "sinkin' down" have the grave, quiet suspension of a requiem.

Arr. L. S

254

DE TITANIC

Out on dat o-o-cean, De great wide o - - cean, De

Ti - tan - ic, out on de o-cean, Sink-in' down! . . . .

1 De rich folks 'cided to take a trip
On de fines' ship dat was ever built.
De cap'n presuaded dese peoples to think
Dis Titanic too safe to sink.

Chorus:

    Out on dat ocean,
    De great wide ocean,
    De Titanic, out on de ocean,
    Sinkin' down!

2 De ship lef' de harbor at a rapid speed,
'Twuz carryin' everythin' dat de peeples need.
She sailed six-hundred miles away,
Met an icebug in her way.

DE TITANIC

3 De ship lef' de harbor, 'twuz runnin' fas'.
 'Twuz her fus' trip an' her las'.
 Way out on dat ocean wide
 An icebug ripped her in de side.

4 Up come Bill from de bottom flo'
 Said de water wuz runnin' in de boiler do'.
 Go back, Bill, an' shut yo' mouth,
 Got forty-eight pumps to keep de water out!

5 Jus' about den de cap'n looked aroun',
 He seed de Titanic wuz a-sinkin' down.
 He give orders to de mens aroun':
 "Get yo' life-boats an' let 'em down!"

6 De mens standin' roun' like heroes brave,
 Nothin' but de wimin an' de chillun to save;
 De wimin an' de chillun a-wipin' dere eyes,
 Kissin' dere husbands an' friends good-bye.

7 On de fifteenth day of May nineteen-twelve,
 De ship wrecked by an icebug out in de ocean dwell.
 De people wuz thinkin' o' Jesus o' Nazaree,
 While de band played "Nearer My God to Thee!"

THE GREAT OPEN SPACES

In only a few instances have I been able to discover the authorship of any song. They seem to have sprung up as quietly and mysteriously as does the grass on the plains. All have been popular with the range riders, several being current all the way from Texas to Montana, and quite as long as the old, old Chisholm Trail stretching between these states. Some of the songs the cowboy certainly composed; all of them he sang. Obviously, a number of the most characteristic cannot be printed for general circulation. To paraphrase slightly what Sidney Lanier said of Walt Whitman's poetry, they are raw collops slashed from the rump of Nature, and never mind the gristle. Likewise some of the strong adjectives and nouns have been softened—Jonahed, as George Meredith would have said. There is, however, a Homeric quality about the cowboy's profanity and vulgarity that pleases rather than repulses. The broad sky under which he slept, the limitless plains over which he rode, the big, open, free life he lived near to Nature's breast, taught him simplicity, calm, directness. He spoke out plainly the impulses of his heart. But as yet so-called polite society is not quite willing to hear.

JOHN A. LOMAX in *Cowboy Songs and Ballads.*

The big ranches of the West are now being cut up into small farms. The nester has come, and come to stay. Gone is the buffalo, the Indian warwhoop, the free grass of the open plain;—even the stinging lizard, the horned frog, the centipede, the prairie dog, the rattlesnake are fast disappearing. Save in some of the secluded valleys of southern New Mexico, the old-time round-up is no more; the trails to Kansas and Montana have become grass-grown or lost in fields of waving grain; the maverick steer, the regal longhorn, has been supplanted by his unpoetic but more beefy and profitable Polled Angus, Durham, and Hereford cousins from across the seas. The changing and romantic West of the early days lives mainly in story and song. The last figure to vanish is the cowboy, the animating spirit of the vanishing era. He sits his horse easily as he rides through a wide valley, enclosed by mountains, clad in the hazy purple of coming night, with his face turned steadily down the long, long road, "the road that the sun goes down." Dauntless, reckless, as gentle to a pure woman as King Arthur, he is truly a knight of the twentieth century. A vagrant puff of wind shakes a corner of the crimson handkerchief knotted loosely at his throat; the thud of his pony's feet mingling with the jingle of his spurs is borne back: and as the careless, gracious, lovable figure disappears over the divide, the breeze brings to the ears, faint and far yet cheery still, the refrain of a cowboy song:

Whoopee ti yi, git along, little dogies;
    It's my misfortune and none of your own.
Whoopee ti yi, git along, little dogies;
    For you know Wyoming will be your new home.

JOHN A. LOMAX in *Cowboy Songs and Ballads.*

WHEN THE CURTAINS OF NIGHT ARE PINNED BACK

The cowboys of Colorado took a garrulous popular song of the 1870's, and kept a fragment, the heart's essence of it. It is impressive when sung by a lone horseman silhouetted against a distant horizon. Given anywhere with ease, feeling, control, it may leave echoes as thin and air-hung as certain apparitions of a clear night's sky of stars. That is, it holds an honest and independent poetry. . . . Text and tune are from Jane Ogle of Rock Island, Illinois.

Arr. Th. O.

When the cur-tains of night Are pinned back by the stars, And the beau-ti-ful moon sweeps the sky, I'll re-mem-ber you, Love, In my prayers.

1 When the curtains of night
   Are pinned back by the stars,
   And the beautiful moon sweeps the sky,
      I'll remember you,
      Love,
      In my prayers.

2 When the curtains of night
   Are pinned back by the stars,
   And the dew drops of heav'n kiss the rose,
      I'll remember you,
      Love,
      In my prayers.

WHEN THE WORK'S ALL DONE THIS FALL

What the poet meant in his mention of "the short and simple annals of the poor," is fairly well delivered in the specific case told of here. It is a story sure of its main facts. Radio Mack of San Francisco, of the regular army and of western cattle ranches, communicated the tune and verses.

Arr. H. F. P.

A group of jol-ly cow-boys, dis-cus-sing plans at ease, Says one, "I'll tell you some-thing, boys, if you will lis-ten, please. I am an old cow-punch-er and hyer I'm dress'd in rags, I used to be a tough one and go on great big jags.

quasi guitar   *simile*

But I have got a home, boys, a good one, you all know, Al-

though I have not seen it since long, long a - go. I'm go - ing back to Dix - ie once

more to see them all, Yes, I'm go-ing to see my moth-er when the work's all done this fall.

WHEN THE WORK'S ALL DONE THIS FALL

1 A group of jolly cowboys, discussing plans at ease,
  Says one, "I'll tell you something, boys, if you will listen, please.
  I am an old cow-puncher and hyer I'm dressed in rags,
  I used to be a tough one and go on great big jags.
  But I have got a home, boys, a good one, you all know,
  Although I have not seen it since long, long ago.
  I'm going back to Dixie once more to see them all,
  Yes, I'm going to see my mother when the work's all done this fall.

2 "After the round-up's over and after the shipping's done,
  I am going right straight home, boys, ere all my money is gone.
  I have changed my ways, boys, no more will I fall;
  And I am going home, boys, when the work's all done this fall.
  When I left home, boys, my mother for me cried,
  Begged me not to go, boys, for me she would have died;
  My mother's heart is breaking, breaking for me, that's all,
  And with God's help I'll see her when the work's all done this fall."

3 That very night this cowboy went out to stand his guard;
  The night was dark and cloudy and storming very hard;
  The cattle they got frightened and rushed in wild stampede,
  The cowboy tried to head them, riding at full speed.
  While riding in the darkness so loudly did he shout,
  Trying his best to head them and turn the herd about,
  His saddle horse did stumble and on him did fall,
  The poor boy won't see his mother when the work's all done this fall.

4 His body was so mangled the boys all thought him dead,
  They picked him up so gently and laid him on a bed;
  He opened wide his blue eyes and looking all around
  He motioned to his comrades to sit near him on the ground.
  "Boys, send my mother my wages, the wages I have earned,
  For I am afraid, boys, my last steer I have turned.
  I'm going to a new range, I hyear my Master's call,
  And I'll not see my mother when the work's all done this fall.

5 "Bill, you may have my saddle; George, you may take my bed;
  Jack may have my pistol, after I am dead.
  Boys, think of me kindly when you look upon them all,
  For I'll not see my mother when the work's all done this fall."
  Poor Charlie was buried at sunrise, no tombstone at his head,
  Nothing but a little board and this is what it said,
  "Charlie died at daybreak, he died from a fall,
  The boy won't see his mother when the work's all done this fall."

AS I WALKED OUT IN THE STREETS OF LAREDO

A cowboy classic known in several tunes from the spaces patrolled by the Northwest Mounted to those where the Texas Rangers keep law and order, more or less.   The air is old Irish and many of the lines are almost literally from old broadsides peddled in Dublin these years now gone.

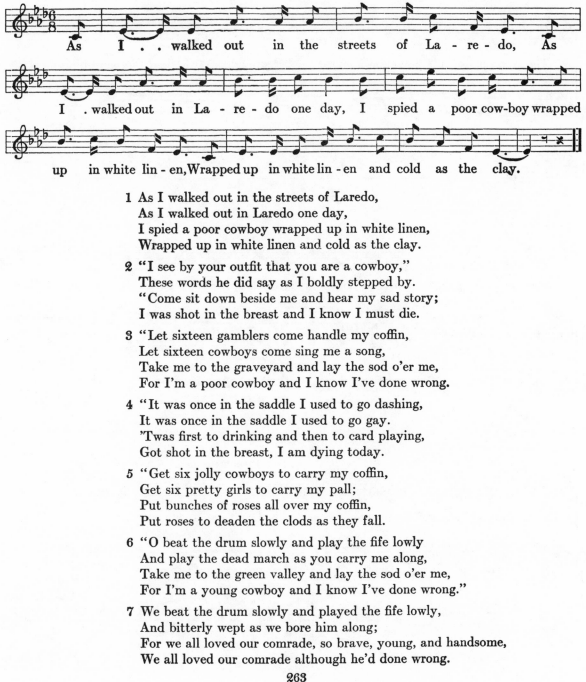

As I . . walked out in the streets of La - re - do, As
I . walked out in La - re - do one day, I spied a poor cow-boy wrapped
up in white lin - en, Wrapped up in white lin - en and cold as the clay.

1 As I walked out in the streets of Laredo,
   As I walked out in Laredo one day,
   I spied a poor cowboy wrapped up in white linen,
   Wrapped up in white linen and cold as the clay.

2 "I see by your outfit that you are a cowboy,"
   These words he did say as I boldly stepped by.
   "Come sit down beside me and hear my sad story;
   I was shot in the breast and I know I must die.

3 "Let sixteen gamblers come handle my coffin,
   Let sixteen cowboys come sing me a song,
   Take me to the graveyard and lay the sod o'er me,
   For I'm a poor cowboy and I know I've done wrong.

4 "It was once in the saddle I used to go dashing,
   It was once in the saddle I used to go gay.
   'Twas first to drinking and then to card playing,
   Got shot in the breast, I am dying today.

5 "Get six jolly cowboys to carry my coffin,
   Get six pretty girls to carry my pall;
   Put bunches of roses all over my coffin,
   Put roses to deaden the clods as they fall.

6 "O beat the drum slowly and play the fife lowly
   And play the dead march as you carry me along,
   Take me to the green valley and lay the sod o'er me,
   For I'm a young cowboy and I know I've done wrong."

7 We beat the drum slowly and played the fife lowly,
   And bitterly wept as we bore him along;
   For we all loved our comrade, so brave, young, and handsome,
   We all loved our comrade although he'd done wrong.

THE DREARY BLACK HILLS

Honest workmen, small business men, loafers and bummers, rainbow chasers, hopers and seekers, were in that roundhouse at Cheyenne. And one who was frozen plumb to the gills, who was called the orphan of the Black Hills, sketched the scenery.

Arr. M. L.

The round-house in Chey-enne is filled ev - 'ry night, With loaf-ers and bum-mers of

most ev - 'ry plight, On their backs is no clothes, in their pock - ets no bills, Each

day they keep start-ing for the drear-y Black Hills. Don't go a-way, stay at home if you can,

Stay a-way from that cit - y they call it Cheyenne, Where the blue wa - ters roll, and Co-

man - che Bills, They will lift up your hair, on the drea - ry Black Hills.

1 The roundhouse in Cheyenne is filled every night,
With loafers and bummers of most ev'ry plight,
On their backs is no clothes, in their pockets no bills,
Each day they keep starting for the dreary Black Hills.

Chorus:
  Don't go away, stay at home if you can,
  Stay away from that city they call it Cheyenne,
  Where the blue waters roll, and Comanche Bills,
  They will lift up your hair, on the dreary Black Hills.

2 I got to Cheyenne, no gold could I find,
I thought of the lunch route I'd left far behind;
Through rain, hail, and snow, frozen plumb to the gills, —
They call me the orphan of the dreary Black Hills.

3 Kind friend, to conclude, my advice I'll unfold,
Don't go to the Black Hills a-hunting for gold;
Railroad speculators their pockets you'll fill
By taking a trip to those dreary Black Hills.

Last Chorus:
  Don't go away, stay at home if you can,
  Stay away from that city, they call it Cheyenne,
  For old Sitting Bull or Comanche Bills
  They will take off your scalp on the dreary Black Hills.

265

THE LONE STAR TRAIL

A cowboy classic of saddle and trail, ranch and range. The verses are from John Lomax of Texas and Jay Monaghan of Wyoming. . . . The line "I got a gal, prettiest gal you ever saw," is sometimes sung, "I went to the reservation to see my squaw." Certain versions have extended and lurid conversations between the cowboy and the lady.

Arr. M. L.

I start-ed on the trail on June twen-ty-third, I been punch-in' Tex - as cat - tle on the Lone Star trail; Sing-in' Ki yi yip - pi yap - pi yay, yap-pi yay! Sing-in' Ki yi yip-pi yap-pi y - ay! . .

1 I started on the trail on June twenty-third,
 I been punchin' Texas cattle on the Lone Star trail;
  Singin' Ki yi yippi yappi yay, yappi yay!
  Singin' Ki yi yippi yappi yay!

THE LONE STAR TRAIL

2 It's cloudy in the west, a-lookin' like rain,
And my damned old slicker's in the wagon again;
    Singin' Ki yi yippi, etc.

3 My slicker's in the wagon, and I'm gettin' mighty cold,
And these long-horned sons-o'-guns are gettin' hard to hold;
    Singin' Ki yi yippi, etc.

4 I'm up in the mornin' before daylight,
And before I sleep the moon shines bright.

5 Oh it's bacon and beans 'most every day,
I'd as soon be a-eatin' prairie hay.

6 I went up to the boss to draw my roll,
He had it figgered out I was nine dollars in the hole.

7 I'll drive them cattle to the top of the hill,
I'll kiss that gal, gol darn I will.

8 My seat is in the saddle and my hand is on the horn,
I'm the best dam cowboy ever was born.

9 My hand is on the horn and my seat is in the saddle,
I'm the best dam cowboy that ever punched cattle.

10 My feet are in the stirrups and my rope is on the side,
Show me a hoss that I can't ride.

11 I herded and I hollered and I done very well,
Till the boss said, "Boys, just let 'em go to hell."

12 Stray in the herd and the boss said kill it,
So I shot him in the rump with the handle of the skillet.

13 I went up to the boss and we had a little chat,
I slapped him in the face with my big slouch hat.

14 O the boss says to me, "I'll fire you,
Not only you, but the whole dam crew."

15 I got a gal, prettiest gal y'u ever saw,
And she lives on the bank of the Deep Cedar Draw.

16 I'll sell my outfit just as soon as I can;
I won't punch cattle for no dam man.

17 Goin' back to town to draw my money,
Goin' back home to see my honey.

18 Well, I'll sell my saddle and I'll buy me a plow
And I'll swear begad, I'll never rope another cow.

19 With my knees in the saddle and my seat in the sky,
I'll quit punching cows in the sweet by and by.

WHOOPEE, TI YI YO, GIT ALONG, LITTLE DOGIES

This widely sung piece also has the smell of saddle leather and long reaches of level prairies in it. It is plainly of Irish origin, connecting with the lilts and the ballads that begin, "As I was a-walking one morning." The word "cholla" is Spanish and is pronounced as if spelled "choya." The "dogies" are the little yearling steers.

Arr. C. F. E.

As I was a-walk-ing one morn-ing for pleas-ure, I saw a cow-punch-er come rid-ing a-lone. His hat was throwed back and his spurs was a-jing-ling, And as he ap-proached he was sing-ing this song: Whoo-pee, ti yi yo, git a-long, lit-tle dog-ies! It's

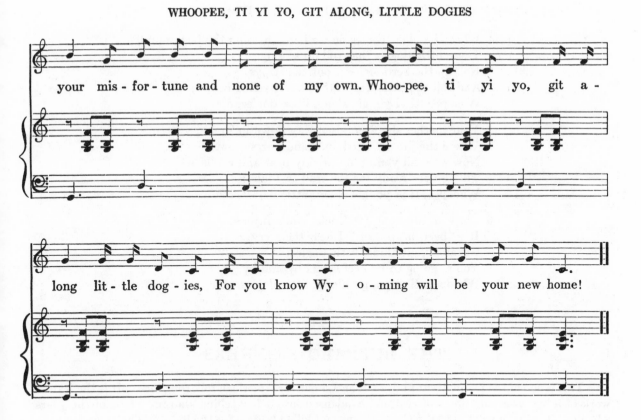

your mis-for-tune and none of my own. Whoo-pee, ti yi yo, git a-long lit-tle dog-ies, For you know Wy-o-ming will be your new home!

1 As I was a-walking one morning for pleasure,
I saw a cowpuncher come riding alone.
His hat was throwed back and his spurs was a-jingling,
And as he approached he was singing this song:

Refrain:
Whoopee, ti yi yo, git along, little dogies!
It's your misfortune and none of my own.
Whoopee, ti yi yo, git along, little dogies,
For you know Wyoming will be your new home!

2 Early in the spring we round up the dogies,
Mark and brand and bob off their tails,
Round up our horses, load up the chuck wagon,
Then throw the dogies up on the trail:
Whoopee, ti yi yo, git along, little dogies, etc.

3 It's whooping and yelling and driving the dogies;
O how I wish they would go on!
It's whooping and punching and go on little dogies,
For you know Wyoming will be your new home:
Whoopee, ti yi yo, git along, little dogies, etc.

4 When the night comes on we herd them on the bedground,
These little dogies that roll on so slow;
Roll up the herd and cut out the strays,
And roll the little dogies that never rolled before:
Whoopee, ti yi yo, git along, little dogies, etc.

5 Your mother she was raised way down in Texas,
Where the jimson weed and sand burrs grow.
Now we'll fill you up on prickly pear and cholla
Till you are ready for the trail to Idaho:
Whoopee, ti yi yo, git along, little dogies, etc.

6 Oh, you'll be soup for Uncle Sam's Injuns;
It's "beef, heap beef," I hear them cry.
Git along, git along, little dogies,
You're going to be beef steers by and by.
Whoopee, ti yi yo, git along, little dogies, etc.

THE BUFFALO SKINNERS

This is one of the magnificent finds of John Lomax for American folk song lore. It is the framework of a big, sweeping novel of real life, condensed into a few telling stanzas. It is of the years when outfits of men went onto the Great Plains and killed buffalo for the hides. The carcasses were skinned by thousands and left on the open prairies for the crows and buzzards to pick to the bone. We may hunt for a harder sardonic than that of Crego telling the men they had been "extravagant" and were in debt to him. They killed him; it is told as casually and as frankly as the doing of the bloody deed and their immediate forgetfulness about it except as one of many passing difficulties of that summer. Lomax speaks of this piece as having in its language a "Homeric quality." Its words are blunt, direct, odorous, plain and made-to-hand, having the sound to some American ears that the Greek language of Homer had for the Greeks of that time.

Arr. C. F. E.

'Twas in the town of Jacks - bo - ro in the spring of seven - ty - three, A

man by the name of Cre - go . . came step - ping up to me, Say - ing,

"How do you do, young fel - low, . and how would you like to go . And

spend one sum - mer pleas - ant - ly on the range of the buf - fa - lo?"

1 'Twas in the town of Jacksboro in the spring of seventy-three,
   A man by the name of Crego came stepping up to me,
   Saying, "How do you do, young fellow, and how would you like to go
   And spend one summer pleasantly on the range of the buffalo?"

2 "It's me being out of employment," this to Crego I did say,
   "This going out on the buffalo range depends upon the pay.
   But if you will pay good wages and transportation too,
   I think, sir, I will go with you to the range of the buffalo."

3 "Yes, I will pay good wages, give transportation too,
   Provided you will go with me and stay the summer through;
   But if you should grow homesick, come back to Jacksboro,
   I won't pay transportation from the range of the buffalo."

271

4 It's now our outfit was complete — seven able-bodied men,
With navy six and needle gun — our troubles did begin;
Our way it was a pleasant one, the route we had to go,
Until we crossed Pease River on the range of the buffalo.

5 It's now we've crossed Pease River, our troubles have begun.
The first damned tail I went to rip, Christ! how I cut my thumb!
While skinning the damned old stinkers our lives wasn't a show,
For the Indians watched to pick us off while skinning the buffalo.

6 He fed us on such sorry chuck I wished myself 'most dead,
It was old jerked beef, croton coffee, and sour bread.
Pease River's as salty as hell fire, the water I could never go —
O God! I wished I had never come to the range of the buffalo.

7 Our meat it was buffalo hump and iron wedge bread,
And all we had to sleep on was a buffalo robe for a bed;
The fleas and gray-backs worked on us, O boys, it was not slow,
I'll tell you there's no worse hell on earth than the range of the buffalo.

8 Our hearts were cased with buffalo hocks, our souls were cased with steel,
And the hardships of that summer would nearly make us reel.
While skinning the damned old stinkers our lives they had no show
For the Indians waited to pick us off on the hills of Mexico.

9 The season being near over, old Crego he did say
The crowd had been extravagant, was in debt to him that day,
We coaxed him and we begged him and still it was no go —
We left old Crego's bones to bleach on the range of the buffalo.

10 Oh, it's now we've crossed Pease River and homeward we are bound,
No more in that hell-fired country shall ever we be found.
Go home to our wives and sweethearts, tell others not to go,
For God's forsaken the buffalo range and the damned old buffalo.

272

POOR LONESOME COWBOY

An atmospheric sketch from Charles J. Finger, of Fayetteville, Arkansas, editor of "All's Well," and author of "Tales from Silver Lands" and other books. It is a species of Cowboy blues, the range rider's moan. Finger says, "It is strangely like a song I heard among the Argentine gauchos —

> No tengo padre, no tengo madre;
> No hermana, no hermano;
> O no! O no! O no!

Which may be translated, "I have no father, I have no mother, nor brother, nor sister, and so on." . . . The first verse here may be used as a chorus for all succeeding verses.

Arr. H. F.

Sad, and worse than sad

I'm a poor lone-some cow-boy, I'm a poor lone-some cow-boy, I'm a poor lone-some cow-boy, And a long way from home.

1 I'm a poor lonesome cowboy,
I'm a poor lonesome cowboy,
I'm a poor lonesome cowboy,
And a long way from home.

2 I ain't got no father,
I ain't got no father,
I ain't got no father,
To buy the clothes I wear.

3 I ain't got no mother,
I ain't got no mother,
I ain't got no mother,
To mend the clothes I wear.

4 I ain't got no sister,
I ain't got no sister,
I ain't got no sister,
To go and play with me.

5 I ain't got no brother,
I ain't got no brother,
I ain't got no brother,
To drive the steers with me.

6 I ain't got no sweetheart,
I ain't got no sweetheart,
I ain't got no sweetheart,
To sit and talk with me.

273

THE TENDERFOOT

A plain tale that has gravity and persuasion and belongs in the realistic school of narrative. We may laugh, as bystanders usually do, when somebody else's mortal frame and personal dignity are kicked around as with this tenderfoot. Text and tune are as sung by Norman Byrne of the University of Oregon, and as he learned it in Alberta, Canada.

Arr. H. F.

One day I thought I'd have some fun, And see how punch-ing cows was done; So when the round-up had be-gun I tack-led the cat-tle king. Says he, "My fore-man's gone to town, He's in a sa-loon and his name is Brown; If

THE TENDERFOOT

you see him he'll take you down." Says I, "That's just the thing." . (way.)

1 One day I thought I'd have some fun,
And see how punching cows was done;
So when the roundup had begun
I tackled the cattle king.
Says he, "My foreman's gone to town,
He's in a saloon and his name is Brown;
If you see him he'll take you down."
Says I, "That's just the thing."

2 We started out to the ranch next day.
Brown talked to me most all the way.
Says, "Punching cows is nothing but play,
It is no work at all."
Oh jimminy krissmas, how he lied!
He had a hell of a lot of gall,
He put me in charge of the cavvy hole,
Says Brown, "Don't work too hard."

3 Sometimes those cattle would make a break
And across the prairie they would take,
Just like they was running for a stake.
To them it was nothing but play.
Sometimes they would stumble and fall,
Sometimes you couldn't head 'em at all,
And we'd shoot on like a cannonball
Till the ground came in our way.

4 They saddled me up an old gray hack
With a great big seat fast on his back.
They padded him down with gunny sack
And with my bedding too.
When I got on him he left the ground,
Went up in the air and circled around
And when I came down I busted the ground.
I got a terrible fall.

5 They picked me up and carried me in
And rubbed me down with a picket pin.
Says, "That's the way they all begin."
"You're doing fine," says Brown.
"To-morrow morning if you don't die
I'll give you another hoss to try."
Says I, "Oh can't I walk? . . ."
Says Brown, "Yep, back to town."

6 I've travelled up, I've travelled down,
I've travelled this wide world all around,
I've lived in city, I've lived in town;
I've got this much to say:
Before you go to punching cows,   [your life,
Go kiss your wife, get a heavy insurance upon
And shoot yourself with a butcher knife,
For that is the easiest way.

LITTLE AH SID

A popular song, a black-face minstrel ballad, a favorite among chuck wagon cooks on the Chisholm Trail, as I am told by one of the cooks who had been a minstrel. From West Coast cities it traveled to gold diggings and cattle ranges.

Arr. M. L.

Lit - tle Ah Sid was a Chi - nese kid, A neat lit - tle cuss, I de -

clare, . . With eyes full of fun, And a nose that be - gun

REFRAIN

Way up in the roots of his hair. Ki - yee ki - yay, ki -

276

LITTLE AH SID

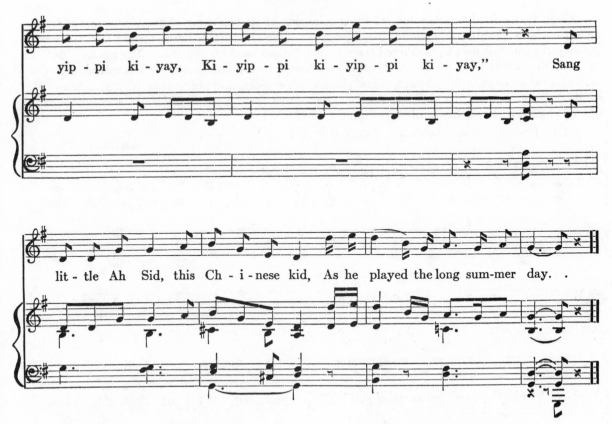

yip - pi ki - yay, Ki - yip - pi ki - yip - pi ki - yay," Sang

lit - tle Ah Sid, this Ch - i - nese kid, As he played the long sum - mer day. .

1 Little Ah Sid was a Chinese kid,
  A neat little cuss, I declare,
  With eyes full of fun,
  And a nose that begun
  Way up in the roots of his hair.

  Refrain:
    "Ki-yee ki-yay, ki-yippi ki-yay,
    Ki-yippi ki-yippi ki-yay,"
  Sang little Ah Sid, this Chinese kid,
  As he played the long summer day.

2 So jolly and fat was this innocent brat,
  As he played in the long summer day,
  And he braided his cue
  Like papa used to
  In Chinaland far away.

3 Once on a lawn that Ah Sid played on,
  A bumble-bee flew in the spring.
  "Ah, Mellicee bullifly!"

Cried he, winking his eye,
"Me ketch um and pull off um wing."

4 And then with his cap he hit it a rap,
  This innocent bumbley bee,
  And he put its remains
  In the seat of his janes
  For a pocket there had this Chinee.

5 Now little Ah Sid was only a kid;
  How could you expect him to guess
  What kind of a bug
  He was holding so snug
  In the folds of his loose-fitting dress.

6 "Ki-yee ki-yay, ki-yippi ki-yay,"
  As he hurriedly rose from the spot,
  "Ki-yee ki-yam,
  Um Mellican man,
  Um bullifly velly dam hot!"

277

THE KINKAIDERS

These verses, from the Edwin Ford Piper collection of pioneer songs at the University of Iowa, go to a melody based on Maryland, My Maryland, which in turn is based on the German song, O Tannenbaum, which in turn derived from an old Italian melody, Vittoria. The phrase "out of sight" in the late 1880's was slang indicating excellence or superfine quality. Homesteaders in the Nebraska sandhills sang this at old settlers' picnics, at reunions, and political gatherings. Moses P. Kinkaid, Congressman from the Sixth District, 1903–1919, introduced a bill for 640-acre homesteads and was hailed as a benefactor of the sandhill region.

Arr. A. G. W.

You ask what place I like the best, The sand hills, O the old sand hills; The

place Kin-kaid - ers make their home, And prai - rie chick - ens free - ly roam.

REFRAIN

In all Ne-bras - ka's wide do-main 'Tis the place we long to see a - gain; The

sand hills are the ver - y best, She is the queen of all the rest.

1 You ask what place I like the best,
  The sand hills, O the old sand hills;
  The place Kinkaiders make their home,
  And prairie chickens freely roam.

  Chorus:
    In all Nebraska's wide domain
    'Tis the place we long to see again;
    The sand hills are the very best,
    She is the queen of all the rest.

2 The corn we raise is our delight,
  The melons, too, are out of sight.
  Potatoes grown are extra fine
  And can't be beat in any clime.

3 The peaceful cows in pastures dream
  And furnish us with golden cream,
  So I shall keep my Kinkaid home
  And never far away shall roam.

  Chorus:
    Then let us all with hearts sincere
    Thank him for what has brought us here,
    And for the homestead law he made,
    This noble Moses P. Kinkaid.

DAKOTA LAND

Older nations have had peasant revolts and agrarian movements and parties. The United States has had its Greenback, Populist, Nonpartisan League and Farm Bloc movements, all of them western, and in part representative of strugglers in semi-arid areas where so often "the rain's just gone around." A poet of those strugglers, Edwin Ford Piper, in "Barbed Wire and Wayfarers," uses their lingo:

> *Run, you old stiff-kneed grasshopper,*
> *You spiral-spined jackrabbit, you!*
> *A-ho, whoopee!*
> Brown's Hotel we're bound to see,
> Swing them girls at the dance party,
> One-and-twenty on a moonlight spree —
> *A-ho, whoopee!*
> Whoa, Zebe, whoa!
> Whoa, 'till I hitch you, whoa!

In a piece on "The Drought," he tells how

> On the whitening grass,
> With bright and helpless eyes, a meadow lark
> Sits open-beaked and desperately mute.
> The thin, brown wheat that was too short to cut
> Stands in the field; the feeble corn, breast high,
> Shows yellowed leaf and tassel.

And from Piper's song collection we have a psalm of a desolate people, "Dakota Land," with an air somewhat after the gospel hymn, "Beulah Land."

Arr. A. G. W.

We've reached the land of des-ert sweet, Where noth-ing grows for man to eat, The wind it blows with fev-'rish heat A-cross the plains so hard to beat.

Legato sempre

280

DAKOTA LAND

O Da - ko - ta land, sweet Da - ko - ta land, As on thy fier - y

soil I stand, I look a - cross the plains, And won - der why it nev - er

rains, Till Ga - briel blows his trum-pet sound, And says the rain's just gone a-round.

1 We've reached the land of desert sweet,
  Where nothing grows for man to eat,
  The wind it blows with feverish heat
  Across the plains so hard to beat.

Refrain:

  O Dakota land, sweet Dakota land,
  As on thy fiery soil I stand,
  I look across the plains,
  And wonder why it never rains,
  Till Gabriel blows his trumpet sound
  And says the rain's just gone around.

2 We've reached the land of hills and stones
  Where all is strewn with buffalo bones.
  O buffalo bones, bleached buffalo bones,
  I seem to hear your sighs and moans.

3 We have no wheat, we have no oats,
  We have no corn to feed our shoats;
  Our chickens are so very poor
  They beg for crumbs outside the door.

4 Our horses are of broncho race;
  Starvation stares them in the face.
  We do not live, we only stay;
  We are too poor to get away.

THE FARMER

Fragments of this were heard in Illinois in the early 1890's. S. K. Barlow, a Galesburg milkman who used to be a fiddler at country dances near Galva, sang it for me as we washed eight- and two-gallon delivery cans and quart-measure cups on winter afternoons. W. W. Delaney said, "As near as I remember that song came out in the 1860's, just after the war."

Arr. L. R. G.

When the farm - er comes to town, With his wag - on bro - ken down, O, the
farm - er is the man who feeds them all! If you'll on - ly look and see, I . .
think you will a - gree That the farm - er is the man who feeds them all. . .

THE FARMER

1 When the farmer comes to town,
   With his wagon broken down,
   O, the farmer is the man who feeds them all!
   If you'll only look and see,
   I think you will agree
   That the farmer is the man who feeds them all.

   Refrain:
      The farmer is the man,
      The farmer is the man,
      Buys on credit till the fall;
      Then they take him by the hand,
      And they lead him to the land,
      And the merchant is the man who gets it all.

2 The doctor hangs around
   While the blacksmith heats his iron,
   O, the farmer is the man who feeds them all!
   The preacher and the cook
   Go strolling by the brook,
   And the farmer is the man who feeds them all.

   Refrain:
      The farmer is the man,
      The farmer is the man,
      Buys on credit till the fall.
      Tho' his family comes to town,
      With a wagon broken down,
      O, the farmer is the man who feeds them all!

RABBLE SOLDIER

This also travels under the names of "O Molly" and "My Horses Ain't Hungry." John Lomax gives a version called "Jack O' Diamonds," with one chorus going —

> If the ocean was whiskey, and I was a duck,
> I'd dive to the bottom to get one sweet sup;
> But the ocean ain't whiskey, and I ain't a duck,
> So I'll play Jack O' Diamonds and then we'll get drunk.
> O Baby, O Baby, I've told you before,
> Do make me a pallet, I'll lie on the floor.

Texts and tunes are related to southern mountain songs, to old English and Scotch ballads, blends of "Old Smokey," "Clinch Mountain," "Skew Ball," "Rebel Soldier," "I'm a Poor Troubled Soldier."

Liltingly

Arr. H. F.

I've ram-bled and gam-bled all my mon-ey a - way, And it's with the rab-ble

ar - my, O Mol - ly, I'll stay; I'll think of you, Mol - ly, you

caused me to roam, I'm an old rab - ble sol - dier and Dix -ie's my home.

284

1 I've rambled and gambled all my money away,
   And it's with the rabble army, O Molly, I'll stay;
   I'll think of you, Molly, you caused me to roam,
   I'm an old rabble soldier and Dixie's my home.

2 I'll build me a castle on a mountain so high,
   Where the bluebirds and white doves can't hear my cry;
   Your parents are against me, they say I'm too poor,
   They say I'm not worthy to enter your door.

3 My horses ain't hungry, they won't eat your hay,
   Farewell, little darling, I'll be on my way;
   As sure as the dew falls upon the green corn,
   Last night I was with her, to-night she is gone.

THE TRAIL TO MEXICO

We have this mixture of plain facts and romantic language from an informal gathering of newspaper workers in Fort Worth, Texas, when tune and text were made known by Jake Zeitlin, Frank Wolfe, and an oil driller. It is a cow trail classic, to be delivered earnestly like a witness who knows his names and dates and as though everybody knows who A. J. Stinson is. . . . "Get the hang of the tune and all the lines are easy to pucker in."

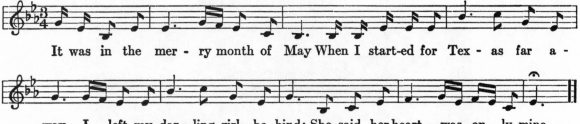

It was in the mer - ry month of May When I start-ed for Tex - as far a -
way, I left my dar - ling girl be- hind; She said her heart was on - ly mine.

1 It was in the merry month of May
   When I started for Texas far away,
   I left my darling girl behind;
   She said her heart was only mine.

2 O it was when I embraced her in my arms,
   I thought she had ten thousand charms;
   Her caresses were soft, her kisses were sweet,
   Saying, "We'll get married next time we meet."

3 It was in the year of 'eighty-three
   That A. J. Stinson hired me;
   He says, "Young man, I want you to go
   And follow this herd into Mexico."

4 Well, it was early in the year
　When I started out to drive those steers;
　Through sleet and snow 'twas a lonesome go
　As the herd rolled on into Mexico.

5 When I arrived in Mexico
　I wanted to see my girl but I could not go;
　So I wrote a letter to my dear
　But not a word for years did I hear.

6 Well, I started back to my once loved home,
　Inquired for the girl I had called my own;
　They said she had married a richer life,
　Therefore, wild cowboy, seek another wife.

7 "O buddie, O buddie, please stay at home,
　Don't forever be on the roam.
　There is many a girl more true than I,
　So pray don't go where the bullets fly."

8 "O curse your gold and your silver too.
　God pity a girl that won't prove true.
　I'll travel west where the bullets fly.
　I'll stay on the trail till the day I die."

MEXICAN BORDER SONGS

Child Drawings from *Mexican Folkways*

LA CUCARACHA (MEXICAN COCKROACH SONG)

Dark women are good as gold;
Brunettes like silver win;
The blondes are only copper,
And the light ones only tin.

God made the swarthy women;
A silversmith the white ones;
The dark brunettes, a tailor;
A cobbler the black-as-night ones.

In his book, "The Land of Poco Tempo," Charles Lummis gives these verses as instances of epigrammatic folk utterances, proverbial rhymes, *dichos*. Nearly every Mexican sometimes has made a *dicho*, and the fittest of them survive, Lummis tells us. They include offhand oddities such as this:

Lovable eyes
Of coffee hue,
Give me a kiss
Of faith all true.

And they may proclaim lines of highly serious mood:

There is no better friend than God,
This is clear and past denying;
For the dearest may betray,
The most truthful may be lying.

We are not surprised that in the song of La Cucaracha (The Cockroach), there is variety of theme. Sunny Spain heard the likes of some of the verses before they married a new tune in Mexico. And for understanding the banter and satire of other stanzas one would require knowledge of the careers of Pancho Villa and Zapata besides an acquaintance with Mexican political and revolutionary history. In 1916 in Chicago I heard the tune and two or three stray verses of La Cucaracha from Wallace Smith and Don Magregor, both of whom as newspaper correspondents with a streak of outlaw in them, had eaten frijoles with Villa and slept under Pancho's poncho, so to speak. Also T. K. Hedrick from down Texas way sang the Cockroach song in Mexican. However, we must not assume that a cockroach is what the Mexican means in singing these verses. It may be a pet name, "The Little Dancer," we are told by Alice Corbin. For F. S. Curtis, Jr., of the Texas Folk Lore Society observes, "A whole dissertation might be written upon the fact that a cucaracha may be either a cockroach or a little, dried-up old maid, and that the term was also used as a nickname for the late Venustiano Carranza; and considerable space might be devoted to explaining that marihuana is a weed, which, when smoked, is capable of producing serious narcotic effects and even causing a homicidal mania." Then he queries significantly, "But of what benefit is such stuff to the songs of New Mexico?" The text here is from Curtis. He says of the tune, "It strongly suggests a sixteenth century origin, especially with the guitar accompaniment usually used."

LA CUCARACHA

Arr. A. G. W.

Allegretto

When a fel-low loves a maid-en And that maid-en does-n't love him,

It's the same as when a bald man Finds a comb up-on the high-way.

CHORUS

The cu-ca-rach-a, the cu-ca-rach-a Does-n't want to trav-el

on Be-cause she has-n't Oh, no, she has-n't Ma-ri-hua-na for to smoke.

LA CUCARACHA

1 Cuando uno quiere a una
  Y esta una no lo quiere,
  Es lo mismo que si un calvo
  En la calle encuentr' un peine.

  Chorus:
    La cucaracha, la cucaracha,
    Ya no quieres caminar,
    Porque no tienes,
    Porque le falta,
    Marihuana que fumar.

2 Las muchachas son de oro;
  Las casadas son de plata;
  Las viudas son de cobre,
  Y las viejas oja de lata.

3 Mi vecina de enfrente
  Se llamaba Doña Clara,
  Y si no había muerto
  Es probable se llamara.

4 Las muchachas de Las Vegas
  Son muy altas y delgaditas,
  Pero son mas pedigueñas
  Que las animas benditas.

5 Las muchachas de la villa
  No saben ni dar un beso,
  Cuando las de Albuquerque
  Hasta estiran el pescuezo.

6 Las muchachas Mexicanas
  Son lindas como una flor,
  Y hablan tan dulcemente
  Que encantan de amor.

7 Una cosa me da risa —
  Pancho Villa sin camisa.
  Ya se van los Carranzistas
  Porque vienen los Villistas.

8 Necesita automóvil
  Par' hacer la caminata
  Al lugar a donde mandó
  La convención Zapata.

When a fellow loves a maiden
And that maiden doesn't love him,
It's the same as when a bald man
Finds a comb upon the highway.

Chorus:
  The cucaracha, the cucaracha,
  Doesn't want to travel on
  Because she hasn't,
  Oh no, she hasn't,
  Marihuana for to smoke.

All the maidens are of pure gold;
All the married girls are silver;
All the widows are of copper,
And old women merely tin.

My neighbor across the highway
Used to be called Doña Clara,
And if she has not expired
Likely that's her name tomorrow.

All the girls up at Las Vegas
Are most awful tall and skinny,
But they're worse for plaintive pleading
Than the souls in Purgatory.

All the girls here in the city
Don't know how to give you kisses,
While the ones from Albuquerque
Stretch their necks to avoid misses.

All the girls from Mexico
Are as pretty as a flower
And they talk so very sweetly,
Fill your heart quite up with love.

One thing makes me laugh most hearty —
Pancho Villa with no shirt on
Now the Carranzistas beat it
Because Villa's men are coming.

Fellow needs an automobile
If he undertakes the journey
To the place to which Zapata
Ordered the famous convention.

MAÑANITAS (de Jalisco)

(EARLY MORNINGS) (from Jalisco)

Verses and air were published in Mexican Folkways. Luis Morones, violinist and Chicagoan, made a literal translation which was freely rendered by Louis Untermeyer, poet and New Yorker.

Arr. A. G. W.

(1) El día en que tu na - cis - te na - cie - ron to - das las flo res, el día en que tu na - cis - te can - ta - ron los rui - se - ño - res.

(1) The day that my dear came to us, The flow'rs were a - born - ing, too; The day that my dear came to us, The night-in-gales trilled their songs.

Ya vie - ne a ma - ne - cien - do ya la

(REFRAIN)

Sun - rise is com-ing, is com - ing, The

MAÑANITAS

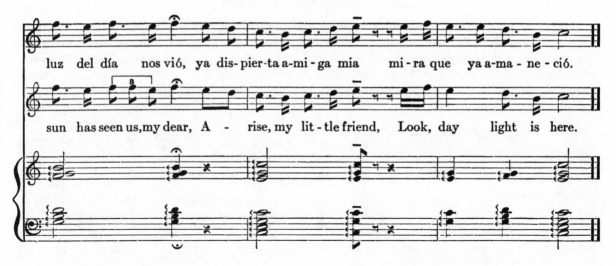

luz del día nos vió, ya dis-pier-ta a-mi-ga mia mi-ra que ya a-ma-ne-ció.

sun has seen us, my dear, A - rise, my lit-tle friend, Look, day light is here.

1 El día en que tu naciste
nacieron todas las flores,
el día en que tu naciste
cantaron los ruiseñores.

Refrain:
Ya viene a maneciendo,
ya la luz del día nos vió,
ya dispierta amiga mía
mira que ya amaneció.

2 Quisiera ser solecito
para entrar por tu ventana,

y darte los buenos días
acostadita en tu cama.

3 Por la luna doy un peso,
por el sol doy un tostón,
por mi amiga Marianita,
la vida y el corazón.

4 De las estrellas del cielo
quisiera bajarte dos,
una para saludarte
y otra pa decirte adiós.

EARLY MORNINGS

(English version by Louis Untermeyer)

1 The day that my dear came to us,
The flow'rs were a-borning too;
The day that my dear came to us,
The nightingales trilled their songs.

Refrain:
Sunrise is coming, is coming,
The sun has seen us, my dear,
Arise, my little friend,
Look, day-light is here.

2 If I were a yellow sunray
I'd sparkle about your head

And flicker a bright "Good Morning"
Before you were out of bed.

3 For the moon I'd give a dollar
For the sun a guinea of gold,
For my sweet friend Marianita
I'd give my heart and soul.

4 From all the stars in heaven
I'd like to bring down two;
With the one I'd say, "How are you?"
With the other, "Good bye to you."

LO QUE DIGO

Mexican Folkways, the magazine so ably and humanly edited by Frances Toor in Mexico City, published the lyric lines and lovely air of this song. Luis Morones, violinist and Chicagoan, presented the variant given here, as he heard it and sang it when a youth in Jalisco, Mexico. There, he informs us, it was known as the Venadito Song, venadito meaning little deer or offspring of parent deer. By many it is considered a characteristic specimen and a superb instance of the Latin-American love song.

Arr. A. G. W.

From Jalisco

1 Lo que digo de hoy en día,
  Lo que digo lo sostengo,
  Yo no vengo a ver si puedo,
  Yo no vengo a ver si puedo,
  Yo no vengo a ver si puedo,
  Sino porque puedo, vengo.

1 What I will say today
  I shall always maintain,
  I do not come to see,
  I do not come to see,
  I do not come to see,
  If I can, only because I can, I come.

294

2 Los higos y las naranjas
  En el árbol se maduran,
  Los ojitos que se queren,
  Los ojitos que se queren,
  Los ojitos que se queren,
  Dende lejos se saludan.

3 Y a mí me saludaron
  Aquellos que estoy mirando,
  Sin poderles contestar,
  Sin poderles contestar,
  Sin poderles contestar,
  Su mamá me está mirando.

4 A las once de la noche
  Allá te espero en el Kiosco,
  Pa que sepas que te quero,
  Pa que sepas que te quero,
  Pa que sepas que te quero,
  Y el miedo no lo conozco.

2 Figs and oranges
  In the tree mature,
  Little eyes that love each other,
  Little eyes that love each other,
  Little eyes that love each other,
  From afar they say "Hello!"

3 And they said hello to me,
  Those little eyes, I see,
  I can not answer though,
  I can not answer though,
  I can not answer though,
  For mother is watching.

4 At eleven o'clock tonight
  I shall be waiting in the Kiosco
  You will know I love you,
  You will know I love you,
  You will know I love you,
  And fear I do not know.

EL ABANDONADO

MEXICAN FOLK SONG

"The love song is by far the most common of all Mexican folk-songs. During the trail driving days many of the cowboys who drove herds from Southern Texas to Kansas and beyond were Mexicans. I have often asked old trail drivers if the *vaqueros* had any such songs as the Texas cowboys had. Invariably the answer has been that the vaqueros sang little else but love songs." Thus wrote Frank J. Dobie, Secretary of the Texas Folk Lore Society, in No. 3 of the publications of that organization. Of El Abandonado he wrote that it is one of the most popular of all Mexican songs, "is sung wherever Mexicans live," and is representative "of that large body of Mexican love songs to be heard day and night whether in camp or at fiesta." Each verse here is given in Mexican, followed by free translation into English, as presented by Dobie.

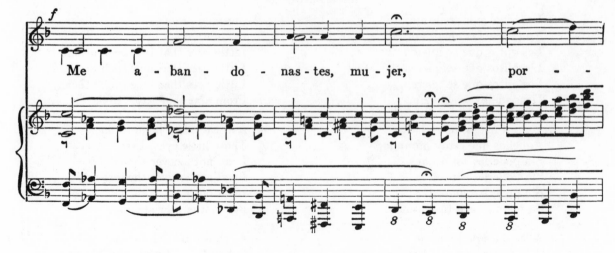

Me a - ban - do - nas - tes, mu - jer, por -

que soy muy po - bre . . . Y la des - gra - cia

es ser hom - bre a - pa - sion - a - do. Pues qué he de

ha - - cer, si yo soy el a - ban - do - na - do? . . .

Pues qué he de ha - cer, se - rá por el a - - mor de Dios.

1 Me abandonastes, mujer, porque soy muy pobre
   Y la desgracia es ser hombre apasionado.
   Pues qué he de hacer, si yo soy el abandonado?
   Pues qué he de hacer, será por el amor de Dios.

You abandon me, woman, because I am very poor; the misfortune is to be a man of passionate devotion. Then, what am I to do if I am the abandoned one? Well, whatever I am to do will be done by the will of God.

2 Tres vicios tengo, los tres tengo adoptados:
   El ser borracho, jugador, y enamorado.
   Pues qué he de hacer si soy el abandonado?
   Pues qué he de hacer, será por el amor de Dios.

Three vices I have cultivated: drunkenness, gambling, and love. Then what am I to do if I am the abandoned one? Well, whatever I am to do will be done by the will of God.

3 Pero ando ingrato si con mi amor no quedo;
   Tal vez otro hombre con su amor se habrá jugado.
   Pues qué he de hacer, si soy el abandonado?
   Pues qué he de hacer, será por el amor de Dios.

But I go unhappy if with my love I cannot remain. Perhaps another man has toyed with her love. Then what am I to do if I am the abandoned one? Well, whatever I am to do will be done by the will of God.

CIELITO LINDO

In the southwestern states on the Mexican border are a million or more citizens of the United States, having Latin, North American Indian, or Nordic mother tongues, who sing Cielito Lindo only in Spanish. The text and tune here are from Luis Morones of Chicago, in the version most familiar to him since birth and education in Mexico, and residence in border states.

Arr. A. G. W.

298

CIELITO LINDO

Ay! . . . Can - ta y no llo - res, . . por - que can - tan - do se a - le - gran Cie - li - to Lin - do los co - ra - zo - nes.

1 De la sierra morena,
   cielito lindo,
   vienen bajando
   un par de ojitos negros
   cielito lindo
   de contrabando.

   Chorus:
      ¡Ay, ay, ay, ay!
      canta y no llores,
      porque cantando se alegran
      cielito lindo
      los corazones.

2 Una flecha en el aire
   cielito lindo
   lanzó Cupido
   y como fué jugando,
   cielito lindo,
   yo fuí el herido.

3 Pájaro que abandona
   cielito lindo
   su primer nido,

vuelve y lo halla ocupado
cielito lindo
y muy merecido.

4 Ese lunar que tienes
   cielito lindo
   junto a la boca,
   no se lo des a nadie
   cielito lindo,
   que a mí me toca.

5 Todas las iluciones
   cielito lindo
   que el amor fragua,
   son como las espumas
   cielito lindo
   que forma el agua.

      ¡Ay, ay, ay, ay!
      suben y crecen
      y con el mismo viento
      cielito lindo,
      desaparecen.

ADELITA

The simple song of Adelita is widely known in the Southwest, survives time and usage, and takes added vitality from the infusion of new verses. I have heard it from the box-car bunk-houses of Mexican railroad workers in Elmhurst, Illinois, and from a singing guitar player who passed the hat in the Mexican quarter in Los Angeles, California. I heard the Mayor of Santa Fe, New Mexico, one afternoon command ten of his constituents and subjects to sing it in unison and in Spanish — which they did. . . . The text and air here are from F. S. Curtis, Jr., who notes that with the possible exception of stanzas 1 and 5, it is distinctly Mexican in subject matter. "The number of stanzas available is very nearly unlimited. The version given here was selected because there is a reasonable amount of connection between the stanzas."

Arr. A. G. W.

Con moto, ma con espressione

A - de - li - ta's the name of the la - dy . . Who was mis - tress of all my pleas - ures here. . . . . Nev - er think I can come to for - get her, . . Nor to change her for an - y oth - er dear. . . .

300

ADELITA

1 Adelita se llama la ingrata,
La qu' era dueña de todo mi placer.
Nunca piensas que llegue a olvidarla
Ní cambiarla por otra mujer.

Adelita's the name of the lady
Who was the mistress of all my pleasures here.
Never think I can come to forget her,
Nor to change her for any other dear.

2 Si Adelita quisiera ser mi esposa,
Si Adelita fuera mi mujer,
Le compraría un vestido de seda
Y la llevara a pasear el cuartel.

If Adelita would take me for a husband,
If Adelita would only be my wife,
I would buy her a costume of satin
And I'd give her a taste of barracks life.

3 Ya me llama el clarín de campaña
Como soldado valiente a pelear.
Correrrá por los calles la sangre
Pero olvidarte jamás me verá.

Now the trumpet to battle does call me
To fight as every valiant soldier should.
In the streets then the blood will be running,
But 'twill never see me forget thee.

4 Si acaso yo muero en campaña
Y mi cadaver en la tierra va a quedar,
Adelita, por Dos te la ruego
Que por mí muerte tu vayas a llorar.

If perhaps I should die in the battle,
And my poor corpse be left upon the field,
Adelita, for God's sake I pray thee
For my death thou wilt shed but one tear.

5 Adelita es una fronteriza
Con ojos verdes, color de la mar,
Que trae locos a todos los hombres
Y a todos les hace llorar.

Adelita's a desperate coquette
With deep green eyes, the color of the sea,
Who drives all the men to distraction
And makes them all weep bitterly.

6 Si Adelita se fuere con otro
La seguiría la huella sin cesar,
En aeroplanos y buques de guerra
Y por tierra hast' en tren militar.

Should Adelita run off with another,
I'd trail her always, forever, near and far,
Both in airplanes and ships of the navy,
And on land in a military train.

VERSOS DE MONTALGO

"In the year 1900, Encarnacion Garcia waylaid and killed another Mexican in Cameron County. Montalgo, a Mexican deputy sheriff, rode up on Encarnacion as the latter was burying his victim. Encarnacion resisted arrest, or at least Montalgo always so claimed, and Montalgo killed him. Ten years later to a day, Encarnacion's *gente* got their revenge by killing Montalgo." Thus Frank J. Dobie, of the Texas Folk Lore Society, gives in brief the facts leading to this ballad in its opening verses. As to the closing stanzas he notes, "Sandoval had a little ranch and herded goats. He sang this song to my brother and presumably had composed it, certainly the last three stanzas. Sandoval came up to the Granjeno gate while the crowd were viewing the *restos* of Montalgo. Hinojosa, a deputy sheriff from Brownsville, came up, did nothing about the murder but arrested poor old Sandoval for killing the *venaditas*." . . . "These people of Manoa" refers to a family of Mexicans that owned a little ranch near by; they were in sympathy with the sisters of the murdered Montalgo; authorities at Brownsville deputized the head of the Manoa family to act as sheriff. . . . *Edal* in the first stanza "seems to be a Mexicanism not recorded in the dictionaries," Dobie notes. Almazan is a ranch west of Lyford. *El puerto* (masculine) is irregularly used for *la puerta* (feminine) in the fourth and sixth stanzas; there seems to be authority for such interchange of usage in Spanish manuscripts dating as far back as 1760. . . . "*Versos*," Dobie also notes, "as understood and used by Texas Mexicans, are songs or verses, of folk composition in contradistinction to *canciones*, songs derived from more or less literary purveyors, though *cancion* (song or ballad) is also frequently applied to verses of local composition. For *Versos de Montalgo* I am indebted to my brother, Elrich H. Dobie, who learned them while he was *caporal* (boss of a cow outfit) on the King Ranch in South Texas, 1916–1917. He says the *vaqueros* frequently made up songs on local happenings. A white maverick bull killed two or three horses and had to be shot. A Mexican made up a song on the subject and for a while it was widely sung by the King Ranch Mexicans. A raid, a killing, a *ladino* (outlaw) horse or steer, a stampede, a daring rider — these are characteristic themes for *vaquero* improvisation." . . . The following is one of several stories of Lost Ballads that Frank Dobie tells: "In the summer of 1921, I was with Captain Will Wright's rangers, when they raided a band of *tequila* smugglers on the Nueces River in La Salle County. It was an interesting raid; one smuggler had to be killed and over a thousand quarts of *tequila* were captured. I am told that a very long song was composed on the subject, in which certain *gringos*, including myself, are not very well spoken of. Much to my disappointment, I have been unable to hear the song or secure a copy of it."

Arr. R. H.

VERSOS DE MONTALGO

En el mil nueve cien - tos y di -ez— Y los cuen - to sin e - dal—

A Mon-tal - go le ma - ta-ron Cer - ca del ca - mi - no re - al.

1 En el mil nueve cientos y diez —
  Y los cuento sin edal —
  A Montalgo le mataron
  Cerca del camino real.

2 A Montalgo le mataron,
  Le mataron sin razón,
  A los diez años cumplidos
  Que le mató a Encarnación.

3 Lunes en la mañana
  Salió del Almazan.
  Montalgo no sabía
  Que le tenían su plan.

4 A las tres salió de Lyford
  En su caballo bayito,
  En el Puerto del Granjeno
  Ahí le formaron sitio.

In the year 1910 — and I give the date without uncertainty — they killed Montalgo near
the public road.

They killed Montalgo, killed him without
reason, after ten years had passed from the
time he killed Encarnación.

Monday in the morning Montalgo left the
Almazan. He did not know that there was a
plot against him.

At three o'clock in the afternoon he left
Lyford on his dun horse. At the gate called
Granjeno his enemies had laid an ambush.

303

5 Cuando Montalgo cayó,
   El malhecho le decía:
   "No te asustas, Montalgo;
   Págaste lo que debías."

When Montalgo fell, murder said to him: "You need not be scared, Montalgo; pay what you owe."

6 Y perdido estuvo un mes,
   Eso dicen por cierto,
   Que en el Puerto del Granjeno
   Ahí le hallaron muerto.

He (that is, Montalgo's body) was lost for a month. This is said for a certainty; that at the Granjeno gate they found him dead.

7 Al mes hallaron los restos
   Envueltos en un costal;
   Arriba tenían hierbas,
   Y más arriba nopal.

At the end of a month they found the remains wrapped up in a sack; on top of them were weeds and on top of the weeds prickly pear was piled.

8 Cuando se juntó la gente,
   Estuvieron medio día;
   La mayor parte decía
   "¡Válgame Dios! ¿como sería?"

When the people got together, they remained assembled for half a day. "Good God!" most of them cried, "how did this come about?"

9 Las Hermanas de Montalgo
   Lloraron sin compasión
   "¡Oh, Montalgo, te mataron
   A traición!"

Montalgo's sisters wept most piteously. "Oh, Montalgo!" they cried, "they have murdered you through treason."

10 Esta gente del Manoa
   Ayudaron de corazón;
   Y a las seis u ocho días
   Le mandaron comisión.

These people of Manoa out of a good heart helped the sisters. In six or eight days they (the proper authorities) sent him (the head of the Manoa family) a commission.

11 Al pobre Sandoval
   Le pegaron sin tuerca;
   Le subieron a express
   Con dos venaditas muertas.

Poor Sandoval they nabbed without handcuffs, and hoisted him up on his wagon along with two little deer that he had killed.

12 En el camino arreglaron
   Con el señor Hinojosa
   Con veinticinco moneas
   Que le dieron.

On the road they fixed it up with Señor Hinojosa by paying him $25.

13 El que compuso esos versos
   No sabía lo que decía;
   Anda va cuidando cabras
   Que no se corta la guía.

The fellow who made these verses did not know what he was talking about. Let him care for his goats and see that some bell-wether does not cut off with a bunch of them.

SOUTHERN MOUNTAINS

In 1917 I met Cecil J. Sharp, Director of the Stratford-upon-Avon School of Folk Lore and Folk Dancing. He was at Knoxville, Tennessee, just back from the mountains, joyful over a book full of new ballads, copied down as people had sung them to him. "These missionaries with their schools!" he exclaimed indignantly. "I'd like to build a wall around these mountains and let the mountain people alone. The only distinctive culture in America is here. These people live. They sustain themselves on the meanest food. They are not interested in eating, but they have time to sing ballads." . . .

When these people emigrated to this continent, many of them landed at Philadelphia to join Penn's more tolerant colony. Gradually they pushed their way up the Cumberland Valley into Maryland, then up the valley of the Shenandoah and the narrow valleys of southwestern Virginia. Then they pressed beyond the Cumberland Gap and gradually took possession of the great region of the Southern Appalachians. As Bishop Burleson well puts it:

"Most of them broke through the barrier of the mountains and founded new commonwealths in Kentucky and Tennessee. But some stopped in the mountains. A horse died, a cart broke down, a young couple could not leave the little grave of their only child; fatigue, illness, the lure of the mountains—now it was one thing and now another; but when the host had passed, there were scattered dwellings being reared among the great hills, and a few hundreds—progenitors of many thousands—had begun a course of life which was to continue unchanged for generations. They came in poor, . . . and they are today the poorest people in America. As in all races, there are different grades among them, ranging from the fairly well-to-do farmers along the river valleys to the squatters in the cabins on the high mountains, where the cultivated land is often so steep that the harvested crops can only be brought down in sleds." . . .

Illiteracy is high in the Southern Highlands, but illiteracy does not prove anything about one's brain capacity. We were all recently illiterate, and furthermore, gentlemen are born, not made with print. Friends of the mountaineer state it thus:

"It is the fatal fallacy of a public-schooled world that literacy is counted the earmark of civilization. The keenest intelligence, the sweetest behavior, the most high-born distinction of manner are gifts of the gods to those who can neither read nor write. A dear friend once said: 'We-uns that cain't read or write have a heap of time to think, and that's the reason we know more than you-all.'"

"If the time ever comes when the requirements for citizenship are based on intelligence rather than on information, perhaps these people will make a better showing than the multitude in cities who have just enough education to read the sporting pages of the newspapers."

J. Russell Smith in *North America*.

A
WAY UP ON CLINCH MOUNTAIN

This song has a thousand verses, perhaps going back to the Scotch of the 17th century, we are told. It is the daddy, probably, of many of the Lulu songs. There is poetry, now wayward, now wild, in these stanzas, of moods like Robert Burns and like Provencal balladists of France. Usually singers keep to one tune throughout but I have heard singers make their independent variations with some stanzas. At its best it delivers a character and parts of a life story.

Arr. A. G. W.

Way up on Clinch Mountain, I wander a-lone; I'm as drunk as the dev-il, Oh, let me a-lone!

1 Way up on Clinch Mountain,
   I wander alone;
   I'm as drunk as the devil,
   Oh, let me alone!

2 I'll eat when I'm hungry,
   En drink when I'm dry;
   If whisky don't kill me,
   I'll live till I die.

3 Rye whisky, rye whisky,
   I know you of old,
   You rob my poor pockets
   Of silver and gold.

4 Rye whisky, rye whisky,
   You're no friend to me.
   You killed my old daddy,
   God damn you, try me.

5 Jack o' diamonds, jack o' diamonds,
   I know you of old,
   You rob my poor pockets,
   Of silver and gold.

B

Way up on Clinch Mountain where the wild geese fly high, I'll think of little Allie en lay down en die.

1 Way up on Clinch Mountain where the wild
   geese fly high,
   I'll think of little Allie en lay down en die.

2 You may boast of yore knowledge, en brag o'
   yore sense,
   'Twill all be forgotten a hundred years hence.

3 Oh Lulu, oh Lulu, oh Lulu, my dear,
   I'd give the whole world if my Lulu was hyer.

LIZA IN THE SUMMER TIME (She Died on the Train)

The arrangement of air and words here is based on a song heard by Charles Rockwood of Geneva, Illinois, during a residence in North Carolina mountains. Lines from old British ballads mingle with mountaineer lingo as in the word "mountings;" negro influence is not absent. This may be an instance of the song that starts among people who have a tune, who want to sing, who join together on an improvisation, reaching out for any kind of verses, inventing, repeating, marrying Scotch lyrics with black-face minstrel ditties; in the end comes a song that pleases them for their purposes. Its mood varies here from the lugubrious to the light-hearted. The way to sing it is "as you like it."

Arr. A. G. W.

Li - za in the sum - mer - time, Li - za in the fall,— If I

can't be Li - za all the time, I won't be Li - za 't all.

CHORUS:

Po' li'l' Li - za, po' gal, po' li'l' Li - za Jane, Po' li'l' Li - za, po' li'l' gal,

she died on the train, She died on the train, she died on .the train.

1 Liza in the summer time, Liza in the fall,
  If I can't be Liza all the time, I won't be Liza 't all.

  Chorus: Po' li'l' Liza, po' gal, po' li'l' Liza Jane,
           Po' li'l' Liza, po' li'l' gal, she died on the train,
           She died on the train, she died on the train.

2 When I go up in the mountings and give my horn a blow,
  I think I hear my true love say, "Yonder comes my beau."

  Chorus: Po' li'l' Liza, etc.

3 I wish I had my needle and thread fine as I can sew,
  I'd sew my true love to my side and down the road we'd go.

  Chorus: Po' li'l' Liza, etc.

4 Her face was of a ruddy hue, her hair a chestnut brown.
  Her eyes were like a thunder cloud before the rain comes down.

  Chorus: Po' li'l' Liza, etc.

COON CAN (POOR BOY)

Of Fort Smith, Arkansas, we have heard, "There is no fort there and they have forgotten which Smith it was named after." It is a town where they sing Coon Can and Poor Boy; either name is correct, according to Kate Webber of Fort Smith and Chicago, who communicated the tune and one verse, other verses coming by fast freight with no demurrage from Jack Hagerty of Los Angeles. Its moral is plain: retribution overtakes the wrongdoer; years in the penitentiary are long. Folk songs are often like this; they leave the hearer to piece out the story. . . . The boy is found guilty of killing a woman. Why he killed her, his excuses, and explanations, are not told. There must have been extenuating circumstances, or the jury was impressed by the youthful aspect of the prisoner at the bar, in addition to the mother's testimony that he was always a good boy.

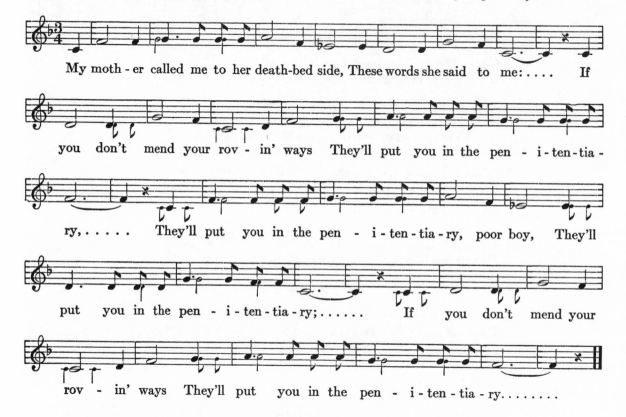

My moth - er called me to her death-bed side, These words she said to me: . . . . If you don't mend your rov - in' ways They'll put you in the pen - i - ten - tia - ry, ... They'll put you in the pen - i - ten - tia - ry, poor boy, They'll put you in the pen - i - ten - tia - ry; . . . . . . If you don't mend your rov - in' ways They'll put you in the pen - i - ten - tia - ry . . . .

1 My mother called me to her deathbed side, these words she said to me:
"If your don't mend your rovin' ways, they'll put you in the penitentiary,
They'll put you in the penitentiary, poor boy, they'll put you in the penitentiary,
If you don't mend your rovin' ways, they'll put you in the penitentiary."

2 I sat me down to play coon can, could scarcely read my hand,
A thinkin' about the woman I loved, ran away with another man.
Ran away with another man, poor boy, ran away with another man.
I was thinkin' about the woman I loved, ran away with another man.

3 I'm a standin' on the corner, in front of a jewelry store,
   Big policeman taps me on the back, says, "You ain't a goin' to kill no more."
   Says, "You ain't a goin' to kill no more, poor boy," says, "You ain't a goin' to kill no more."
   Big policeman taps me on the back, says, "You ain't a goin' to kill no more."

4 "Oh, cruel, kind judge, oh, cruel, kind judge, what are you goin' to do with me?"
   "If that jury finds you guilty, poor boy, I'm goin' to send you to the penitentiary.
   I'm goin' to send you to the penitentiary, poor boy, goin' to send you to the penitentiary.
   If that jury finds you guilty, poor boy, I'm goin' to send you to the penitentiary."

5 Well, the jury found him guilty, the clerk he wrote it down,
   The judge pronounced his sentence, poor boy; ten long years in Huntsville town.
   Ten long years in Huntsville town, poor boy, ten long years in Huntsville town;
   The judge pronounced his sentence, poor boy, ten long years in Huntsville town.

6 The iron gate clanged behind him, he heard the warden say,
   "Ten long years for you in prison, poor boy, yes, it's ten long years for you this day.
   Ten long years for you in prison, poor boy, yes, it's ten long years this day."
   As the iron gate clanged behind him, that's what he heard the warden say.

GYPSY DAVY

A fragment of an old ballad lives on in versions of two verses or ten, with many varying accounts of what happened between the two men and the one woman.

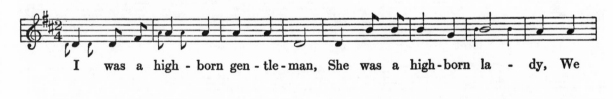

I was a high-born gen-tle-man, She was a high-born la - dy, We

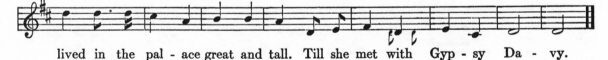

lived in the pal - ace great and tall. Till she met with Gyp - sy Da - vy.

1 I was a high-born gentleman,
   She was a high-born lady.
   We lived in a palace great and tall,
   Till she met with Gypsy Davy.

2 Last night she slept in a goose-feather bed,
   With her arms around her baby.
   To-night she lies in the cold, cold ground
   In the arms of her Gypsy Davy.

311

A
THE ROVING GAMBLER

Girls with a wild streak, in the farther yesterdays, often lost their hearts to the man in dapper clothes, with a big gold watch-chain across his vest, and with plenty of money. ("I don't care where he gets it.") That the man was a stranger in town, that he was a gambler, that he introduced himself saying, "Come with me, girlie"—were points in favor of his audacity, nerve. Such a couple, jack and queen, are briefly sketched in this song. The later chapters, whether she had to take in washing, whether he was converted at a religious revival and set himself up in a respectable business, we do not know. There is a swing and self-assurance to the tune and words, the swagger of the old-time minstrel troupe going down Main Street and around the public square, led by the high-hat drum-major holding aloft a long baton with a golden ball gleaming on the end. In the mischievous, Yonder Comes My Pretty Little Girl, text B, is an authentic folk song found by R. W. Gordon on a southern tour. From Delaney's Songbook No. 23, we give the text C, with repeated lines eliminated, of a piece called The Gamboling Man. This is evidently the popular song of English origin from which the southern and western minstrel troupes made their verses, Delaney tells us. We may note, in passing, that while gamblers may gambol and gambolers may gamble, the English version carries no deck of cards.

Arr. A. G. W.

1 I am a roving gambler, I've gambled all around,
   Wherever I meet with a deck of cards I lie my money down.

2 I've gambled down in Washington and I've gambled over in Spain;
   I am on my way to Georgia to knock down my last game.

3 I had not been in Washington many more weeks than three,
   Till I fell in love with a pretty little girl and she fell in love with me.

4 She took me in her parlor, she cooled me with her fan,
She whispered low in her mother's ears, "I love this gambling man!"

5 "O daughter, O dear daughter, how could you treat me so,
To leave your dear old mother and with a gambler go?"

6 "O mother, O dear mother, you know I love you well,
But the love I hold for this gambling man no human tongue can tell.

7 "I wouldn't marry a farmer, for he's always in the rain;
The man I want is the gambling man who wears the big gold chain.

8 "I wouldn't marry a doctor, he is always gone from home:
All I want is the gambling man, for he won't leave me alone.

9 "I wouldn't marry a railroad man, and this is the reason why;
I never seen a railroad man that wouldn't tell his wife a lie.

10 "I hear the train a-coming, she's coming around the curve,
Whistling and a-blowing and straining every nerve.

11 "O mother, O dear mother, I'll tell you if I can;
If you ever see me coming back again I'll be with the gambling man."

B

YONDER COMES MY PRETTY LITTLE GIRL

1 Yonder comes my pretty little girl,
She's a-goin' all dressed in red.
I looked down at her pretty little feet,
I wish my wife was dead.

2 Yonder comes my pretty little girl,
How do you know?
I know her by her bright apron strings
Hangin' down so low.

3 O, I've gambled in the wildwoods,
I've gambled in the Lane;
I've gambled in the wildwoods
And I never lost a game.

C

THE GAMBOLING MAN

1 I am a roving traveler and go from town to town,
Whene'er I see a table spread so merrily I sit down.

2 I had not been traveling but a few days, perhaps three,
When I fell in love with a London girl, and she in love with me.

3 She took me to her dwelling and cooled me with a fan.
She whispered low in her mother's ear, I love the gamboling man.

4 Oh, daughter, dear daughter, how could you treat me so,
To leave your poor old mother and with the gamboler go?

5 'Tis true I love you dearly, 'tis true I love you well,
But the love I have for the gamboling man no human tongue can tell.

6 So I'll bundle up my clothing, with him will leave my home,
I'll travel the world over wherever he may roam.

O BURY ME BENEATH THE WILLOW

"How does the tune go?" a mountaineer was asked about a song. "It's sad-like", was his reply. . . . Who that has looked at the night stars from under a weeping willow tree, can fail to find here its saturated mournfulness, almost murmuring, "Pity me, weep with me over what I had that's gone." The branches droop with a moist melancholy as though knowing a blessedness of tears. . . . Variants of this are heard in all states. . . . It is old. . . . The tune is from Jake Zeitlin, the text rounded out by verses from R. W. Gordon.

sleep-ing . . . . . . And per-haps he'll weep for me . . . .

1 O bury me beneath the willow,
 Beneath the weeping willow tree,
 And when he comes he'll find me sleeping
 And perhaps he'll weep for me.

2 Tomorrow was our wedding day,
 But God only knows where he is.
 He's gone, he's gone to seek another
 He no longer cares for me.

3 My heart's in sorrow, I'm in trouble,
 Grieving for the one I love
 For oh, I know I'll never see him
 Till we meet in Heaven above.

4 They told me that he did not love me,
 But how could I believe them true
 Until an angel whispered softly,
 "He will prove untrue to you."

5 Place on my grave a snow-white lily
 For to prove my love was true;
 To show the world I died to save him
 But his love I could not win.

6 So bury me beneath the willow,
 Beneath the weeping willow tree,
 And when he comes he'll find me sleeping
 And perhaps he'll think of me.

A

MAG'S SONG

The cold winter night, the falling snow, the poor girl outside looking in, the rich man, hard-hearted and comfortable, letting the girl outside freeze to death: these classic devices of melodrama are in Mag's Song. Kentuckians and Tennesseans, who formed a considerable part of the early settlers of Iowa, probably brought this song to that state, where it was heard by Edwin Ford Piper. It seems to be part of a ballad of thirty or forty stanzas of human woe from the Appalachians. Of course, farther back, it traces to a broadside or a popular ballad in England or Scotland. By cutting out all but two verses of this piece, we have the substance of a small melodrama that delivers swiftly. It erects an immense stage, puts the two chief puppets through their actions, and keeps "in character" to the finale. Alfred Wathall has created a tumultuous musical setting for it. The text B is a variant called The Orphan Girl or No Bread for the Poor.

Arr. A. G. W.

poor girl stood on the mar - ble step,   And

cried, "So cold,   so cold!" . . . .

Three years went by and the rich man died; . . .

1 The rich man lay on his velvet couch,
    He ate from plates of gold;
  A poor girl stood on the marble step,
    And cried, "So cold, so cold!"

2 Three years went by and the rich man died;
    He descended to fiery hell;
  The poor girl lay in an angel's arms
    And sighed, "All's well—all's well!"

B

THE ORPHAN GIRL or NO BREAD FOR THE POOR

1 "No home, no home," cried an orphan girl
    At the door of a princely hall,
  As she trembling stood on the polished steps
    And leaned on the marble wall.

2 Her clothes were torn and her head was bare
    And she tried to cover her feet
  With her dress that was tattered and covered with snow,
    Yes, covered with snow and sleet.

3 Her dress was thin and her feet were bare
    And the snow had covered her head.
  "Oh, give me a home," she feebly cried,
    "A home and a piece of bread."

4 "My father, alas, I never knew."
    Tears dimmed the eyes so bright.
  "My mother sleeps in a new-made grave,
    'Tis an orphan that begs to-night."

5 "I must freeze," she cried as she sank on the steps
    And strove to cover her feet
  With her ragged garments covered with snow,
    Yes, covered with snow and sleet.

6 The rich man lay on his velvet couch
    And dreamed of his silver and gold
  While the orphan girl in her bed of snow
    Was murmuring, "So cold, so cold."

7 The night was dark and the snow fell fast
    As the rich man closed his door,
  And his proud lips curled with scorn as he said,
    "No bread, no room, for the poor."

8 The morning dawned but the orphan girl
    Still lay at the rich man's door
  And her soul had fled to that home above
    Where there's bread and room for the poor.

I GOT A GAL AT THE HEAD OF THE HOLLER

This arrangement of Sourwood Mountain is based chiefly on one from Mary Leaphart. Company square dances, hoedowns, shindigs, or individual clogs and shuffles, work out to this tune. A yodel in steady staccato, a piece of mountain born pleasantry and jubilation, it is out of the human cloth from which Tom Jefferson wrote, "All men are free and equal", and should not be interfered with "in the pursuit of happiness." Those who make a song like this don't care a hoot whether it is called good music. Their answer to any criticism might be, "Ho-dee-ink-tum-diddle-ah-de-day." . . . This Kentucky version may trace to North Carolina mountains where R. W. Gordon heard a verse as follows:

> I have a lover in Sourwood,
> She's gone cripply and blind,
> She broke the heart of many a poor feller
> But she ain't broke this'n of mine.

Arr. H. F.

I got a gal at the head of the hol-ler, Ho-dee-ink-tum-did-dle-ah-dee-day;

She won't come and I won't fol-ler;

I GOT A GAL AT THE HEAD OF THE HOLLER

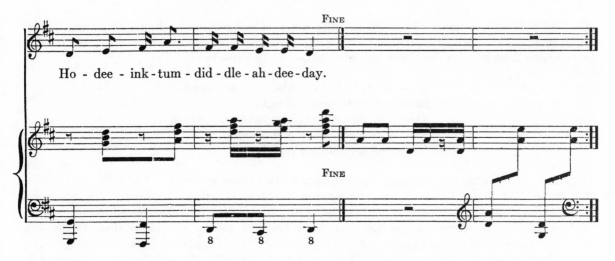

Ho - dee - ink - tum - did - dle - ah - dee - day.

1 I got a gal at the head of the holler,
Ho-dee-ink-tum-diddle-ah-dee-day;
She won't come and I won't foller;
Ho-dee-ink-tum-diddle-ah-dee-day.

2 She sits up with old Si Hall,
Ho-dee-ink-tum-diddle-ah-dee-day;
Me and Jeff can't go there at all.
Ho-dee-ink-tum-diddle-ah-dee-day.

3 Some of these days, before very long,
Ho-dee-ink-tum-diddle-ah-dee-day;
I'll get a gal and a-home I'll run,
Ho-dee-ink-tum-diddle-ah-dee-day.

4 Big dog bark an' the little one'll bite you,
Ho-dee-ink-tum-diddle-ah-dee-day;
Big gal court an' the little one'll marry you,
Ho-dee-ink-tum-diddle-ah-dee-day.

5 Geese in the pond and ducks in the ocean,
Ho-dee-ink-tum-diddle-ah-dee-day;
Devil's in the women when they take a notion,
Ho-dee-ink-tum-diddle-ah-dee-day.

LONESOME ROAD

The lyric of a desperate heart swings into a cry of self-pity and a hymn of personal hate. Waldron P. Webb of the Texas Folk Lore Society sang an early negro version of this for me one evening in a dormitory of the University of Chicago.   The verse ran—

> Look down, look down, dat lonesome road,
> Hang down yo' haid and sigh,
> You cause me to weep, you cause me to moan,
> You cause me to leave mah home.
> You cause me to leave mah home.

Webb sang it in imitation of an old negro woman he had heard as a boy.   The glides and twists, the snarls and moans, cannot be compassed in musical notation; the devices for measuring sound and indicating pitch are not yet available for writing scores for the more subtle negro vocal performances.   The white man, or the mulatto, takes such pieces and shades them to his own ways and likings.   We have Lonesome Road here as it came to Pendleton, Indiana, to people who passed it on to Lloyd Lewis. . . .   "Your" is "yo'."   "God" is "Gawd."   The "r" is silent in "'fore" and "heard."   "Head" is "haid." . . .   It goes lugubriously, interthreaded with a snarl.   As a theme it is slow, grave, "moanish."

Arr. R. C.

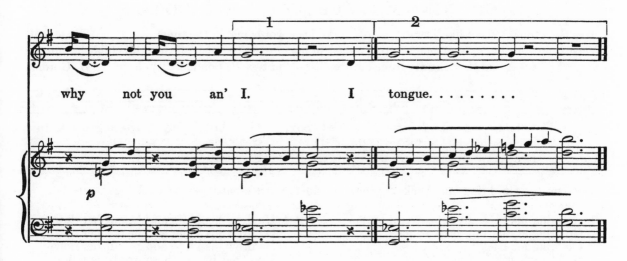

why   not you   an' I.   I   tongue. . . . .

1 Look down, look down that lonesome road,
   Hang down your head an' sigh;
   The best of friends must part some day,
   An' why not you an' I,
   An' why not you an' I?

2 I wish to God that I had died,
   Had died 'fore I was born,
   Before I seen your smilin' face
   An' heard your lyin' tongue,
   An' heard your lyin' tongue.

FOND AFFECTION

Sometimes it happens that lovely people write verses, lyrics, with inadequate melodies. The Kentucky mountain song, "Fond Affection," has a tune hardly worth record here but it does have these striking stanzas.

1 The world's so wide I cannot cross it,
   The sea's so deep I cannot wade,
   I'll just go hire me a little boatman,
   To row me across the stormy tide.

2 I give you back your ring and letters,
   And the picture I have loved so well,
   And henceforth we will meet as strangers,
   But I can never say farewell.

3 There's only three things that I could wish for,
   That is my coffin, shroud, and grave,
   And when I'm dead please don't weep o'er me,
   Or kiss the lips you once betrayed.

A
GO BRING ME BACK MY BLUE-EYED BOY

Here too is a "sad-like" tune. . . . And the words match the tune. . . . The seventh
verse is an addition by someone wanting a dash of horse sense to finish off the fatal childish romance.
. . . . Text A and the tune are from Frances Ries, and text B, London City, from R. W. Gordon.

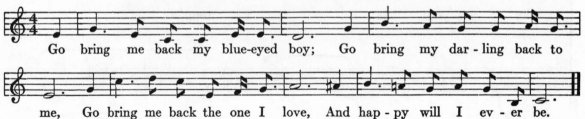

Go bring me back my blue-eyed boy; Go bring my dar - ling back to

me, Go bring me back the one I love, And hap - py will I ev - er be.

1 Go bring me back my blue-eyed boy,
Go bring my darling back to me,
Go bring me back the one I love,
And happy will I ever be.

2 Must I go bound while he goes free?
Must I love a man that don't love me?
Or must I act some childish part,
And die for the one that broke my heart?

3 Late one night when her father came home,
Inquiring where his daughter had gone,
He went upstairs and the lock he broke,
And found her hanging by a rope.

4 He drew his knife and he cut her down,
He drew his knife and he cut her down,
He drew his knife and he cut her down,
Upon her breast these words he found.

5 Go dig my grave, go dig it deep,
Go dig my grave, go dig it deep,
Go dig my grave, go dig it deep,
And plant a rose at my head and feet.

6 Upon my breast a turtle dove,
Upon my breast a turtle dove,
Upon my breast a turtle dove,
To show this world I died for love.

7 Around my grave go build a fence,
Around my grave go build a fence,
Around my grave go build a fence,
To show this world I had no sense.

B
LONDON CITY

1 London City where I used to dwell,
It's a railroad boy I loved so well,
He courted me my heart away,
And with me he would not stay.

2 Go out this fair little town,
Take him a chair and sit right down,
Take other strange girls upon his knee,
And tell them things he won't tell me.

3 I don't see the reason why
Unless they had more golden eyes.
Gold will melt, silver will fly,
I hope some day they will become as I.

4 She went off upstairs to fix her bed
Not a word to her mamma she said.
Mamma went off upstairs saying
Daughter dear, what is troubling you?

5 Oh, Mamma, Oh, Mamma, I dare to tell
It's the railroad boy I love so well,
He courted me my heart away
And with me would not stay.

6 Her papa came in from his work
Saying where is my daughter so dear,
Off upstairs he did go
And there found her hanging by a rope.

7 Upon her breast was a letter found
Saying, when you find me cut me down—
Go dig my grave both wide and deep
And place a marble stone at my head and feet.
Upon my breast place a turtle dove,
To show this world I died for love.

324

THE MIDNIGHT TRAIN

Railroad trains hurtling with smoke, fire, and thunder across peaceful landscapes at night, rushing remorseless as fate along the iron rail pathways, holding to a fixed timetable and repeating the performance every midnight or early morning "fo' day"—out of this the negro worker has made a song that pounds home with the beats and accents of a Limited Express. The grind of flanges, steel burnishing steel in a tireless syncopation, is here, in melody and overtone. . . . All night long the trains weave; every night they repeat the weave; civilization hangs on the time table. The "same train" runs, and always "all night long." . . . A smokestack with a maroon plume of sparks, a firebox square of crimson, the onrushing monotone of a strong, long-drawn locomotive whistle—thus the tempo. . . . In Montevallo at the State Teachers College of Alabama they sing it; and there are variants at the University of Georgia, and at the State Teachers College at Hattiesburg, Mississippi. . . . Additional verses may have the "same train" carrying "sister," "brother," and so on.

Arr. A. G. W.

1 The midnight train and the fo' day train
   Run all night long.
The midnight train and the fo' day train
   Run all night long,
They run until the break of day.

2 'Twas the same train carried yo' mother 'way
   Run all night long.
'Twas the same train carried yo' mother 'way
   Run all night long.
It run until the break of day.

I DON'T LIKE NO RAILROAD MAN

This arrangement is based on the song given by Mary Leaphart, whose husband is the head of the department of law at the University of Montana. Mrs. Leaphart is Kentucky born and spent years among the mountain people who sing this; her performance of it is an impersonation; she identifies herself with a character. It is to be sung staccato, nasal, abrupt, with contempt, yet with nice control as though railroads come and railroads go but the mountains and us, the mountaineers, live on. We can almost see the mountaineers sitting in their cabin doorways watching the railroad gangs come up the valley; they scorn the boasted oncoming civilization.

Arr. H. F.

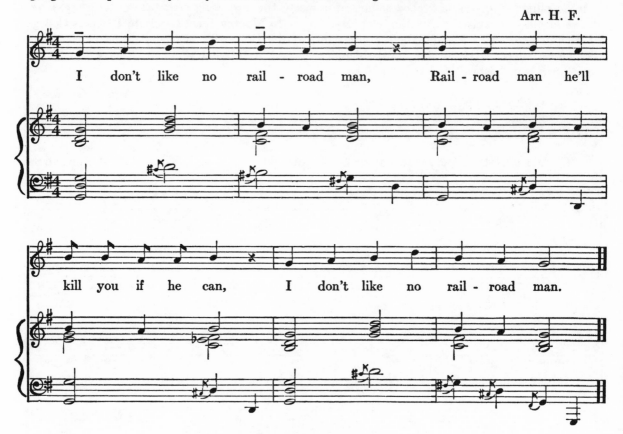

1 I don't like no railroad man,
   Railroad man he'll kill you if he can,
   I don't like no railroad man.

2 I don't like no railroad boss,
   Railroad boss got a head like a hoss,
   I don't like no railroad boss.

3 I don't like no railroad fool,
   Railroad fool got a head like a mule,
   I don't like no railroad fool.

326

PICNIC AND HAYRACK FOLLIES, CLOSE HARMONY, AND DARN FOOL DITTIES

From Old Songsters and Broadsides

SUCKING CIDER THROUGH A STRAW

H. Luke Stancil heard this from old men, his neighbors, in the mountains of Pickens County, Georgia. And Jess Ricks of Long Island heard it in Taylorville, Illinois, as a boy. R. W. Gordon surmises it may be early minstrel. . . . The syllable "ci" in "cider" is drawn out as if to indicate a prolonged sip.

Arr. H. F. P.

Drawlingly

The pret-ti-est girl ..... That ev-er I saw, ... Was sucking ci - der Thro' a straw.

1 The prettiest girl
That ever I saw,
Was sucking cider
Through a straw.

2 I told that gal
I didn't see how
She sucked the cider
Through a straw.

3 And cheek by cheek
And jaw by jaw,
We sucked that cider
Through that straw.

4 And all at once
That straw did slip;
I sucked some cider
From her lip.

5 And now I've got
Me a mother-in-law
From sucking cider
Through a straw.

DID YOU EVER, EVER, EVER?

A children's game rhyme, for counting out and finding who's going to be "It," is said to be as old as "eeny meeny miny mo" or "monkey, monkey, bottle of beer, how many monkeys are there here?"

Did you ever, ever, ever,
In your leaf, life, loaf,
See the deevel, divil, dovol,
Kiss his weef, wife, woaf?
No, I never, never, never,
In my leaf, life, loaf,
Saw the deevel, divil, dovol,
Kiss his weef, wife, woaf.

329

I WAS BORN ALMOST TEN THOUSAND YEARS AGO

Folk lore tells of giants and long-lived men. On far travels they saw and heard much. . . . Also hoary legends have dealt with the Champion Liar. . . . We have in this instance a vest pocket encyclopedia, an outline of history with numerous references to picturesque personages. . . . It packs a wicked lot of biography.

Arr. M. L.

I was born al-most ten thous-and years a-go; And there's noth-ing in the world that I don't know; I saw Pe-ter, Paul and Mo-ses, Play-ing ring-a-round the ros-es, And I'm here to lick the guy what says 'taint so.

1 I was born almost ten thousand years ago,
And there's nothing in the world that I don't
    know;
I saw Peter, Paul and Moses,
Playing ring-around-the-roses
And I'm here to lick the guy what says 'taint so.

2 I saw Satan when he looked the garden o'er,
Saw Adam and Eve driven from the door,
And behind the bushes peeping,
Saw the apple they were eating,
And I'll swear that I'm the guy what ate the core.

3 I saw Jonah when he embarked within the whale,
And thought he'd never live to tell the tale.
But old Jonah had eaten garlic
And he gave the whale a colic,
So he coughed up and let him out o' jail.

4 I saw Samson when he laid the village cold,
Saw Daniel tame the lions in the hold,
And helped build the Tower of Babel,
Up as high as they were able,
And there's lots of other things I haven't told.

5 I taught Solomon his little A-B-C's,
I helped Brigham Young to make Limburger
    cheese,
And while sailing down the bay
With Methusaleh one day,
I saved his flowing whiskers from the breeze.

6 Queen Elizabeth she fell in love with me
We were married in Milwaukee secretly,
But I schemed around and shook her,
And I went with General Hooker
To shoot mosquitoes down in Tennessee.

7 I remember when the country had a king,
I saw Cleopatra pawn her wedding ring,
And I saw the flags a-flying
When George Washington stopped lying,
On the night when Patti first began to sing.

331

GO GET THE AX

A bob-haired blond girl with a dirty face stood on a downtown street corner in Chicago singing this song; she wore green goggles and held out a tin cup to passers-by; she was being initiated. . . . We have heard the piece sung and giggled. . . . As to gigglers we quote Cherubini, "The only thing worse than one flute is two flutes."

Arr. H. F.

Peep-in' through the knot-hole Of grand-pa's wood-en leg, Who'll wind the clock when I am gone? . . . . Go get the ax, There's a flea in Liz-zie's ear, For a boy's . . . . . best friend is his moth-er. . . . .

1 Peepin' through the knot-hole
   Of grandpa's wooden leg,
Who'll wind the clock when I am gone?
   Go get the ax
There's a flea in Lizzie's ear,
   For a boy's best friend is his mother.

2 Peepin' through the knot-hole
   Of grandpa's wooden leg,
Why do they build the shore so near the ocean?
   Who cut the sleeves
Out of dear old daddy's vest,
   And dug up Fido's bones to build the sewer?

3 A horsey stood around,
   With his feet upon the ground,
Oh, who will wind the clock when I am gone?
   Go get the ax,
There's a fly on Lizzie's ear,
   But a boy's best friend is his mother.

4 I fell from a window,
   A second-story window,
I caught my eyebrow on the window-sill.
   The cellar is behind the door,
Mary's room is behind the ax,
   But a boy's best friend is his mother.

ABALONE

Monterey is a California town of Spanish streets lined with houses of a time when Proud Spain ruled the West Coast. Tourist cars run to the House Where Robert Louis Stevenson Lived. In the harbor one may see Italian fishermen mending nets, putting out to sea, coming home with toll taken from deep waters. And roundabout the pyramids of abalone shells are stacked high. It is a world capital of abalone. At the lunch counters abalone is a favorite dish, a nutritious mollusk. His shell makes shirt buttons by the carload. . . . From Monterey we go to Carmel-By-The-Sea, past cypress trees, tough twisted torsoes lashed by long winds, shapes of storm transfixed with a momentary peace, a picture for pilgrims. . . . Then at Carmel we may hear Abalone Song, its stanzas chiefly a bequest of George Sterling of San Francisco. . . . Beach fire singers have flung it with laughter at goblins of the half moon, the rising full moon, and the waning silver crescent.

Arr. H. F. P.

In Car-mel Bay the peo-ple say we feed the laz-za-ro-ni.... On
car-a-mels and cock-le-shells and hunks of Ab-a-lo-ne.....

1 In Carmel Bay the people say,
  We feed the Lazzaroni
  On caramels, and cockle-shells
  And hunks of abalone.

2 O, some folks boast of quail on toast,
  Because they think it's tony;
  But my tom-cat gets nice and fat
  On hunks of abalone.

3 He hides in caves, beneath the waves,
  His ancient patrimony:
  Race suicide will ne'er betide
  The fertile abalone.

4 I telegraph my better half
  By Morse or by Marconi
  But when in need of greater speed
  I send an abalone.

5 Some folks say that pain is real
  And some say that it's phoney;
  But as for me, when I can't agree,
  I eat an abalone.

6 Our naval hero, best of all,
  His name was Pauley Joney;
  He sailed the seas as he darn pleased,
  But he never ate abalone.

333

IN DE VINTER TIME

This is sung by superincumbent cucumbers in Iowa and elsewhere. We have it from students and faculty members of Cornell College. The tempo is mazurka and came with Polish and Czeko-Slovak emigration to the Corn Belt.

In de vinter, in de vinter-time,
Ven de vin' blows on de vindow-pane,
An' de vimmen, in de vaud'vil
Ride de veloc'pede in de vestibule,
Ah, vimmens! Ah, mens!

334

CIGARETTES WILL SPOIL YER LIFE

Two newspapermen, working for the Boston *Post*, took a poor poet around the town in a motor car, showing him Faneuil Hall, Bunker Hill, Charlestown Jail, Harvard University. They made inquiries, the poet gave guarded replies, but was twice caught napping. They wrote notes for an interview. Then they fed the poet and sang this modern Boston ditty.

Arr: H. J.

Cigarettes will spoil yer life,
Ruin yer health and kill yer baby,
Poor little innocent child.

335

MARY HAD A WILLIAM GOAT

We have heard of a man who bet he could eat two dozen raw oysters. Before putting up the money he excused himself, left the room, came back and won the bet. "But why did you leave the room?" he was asked. He replied, "I went out and ate two dozen raw oysters to make sure I could do it." Then they all joined hands and sang a tune that used to have words about Mary and her little lamb.

Arr. A. G. W.

Ma - ry had a Will-iam goat, Will-iam goat, Will-iam goat, Ma-ry had a Will-iam goat, his

stom-ach lined with zinc. One day he ate an oys - ter can, oys-ter can, oys-ter can, One

day he ate an oyster can, and a clothesline full of shirts. Oh, the shirts can do no harm inside,

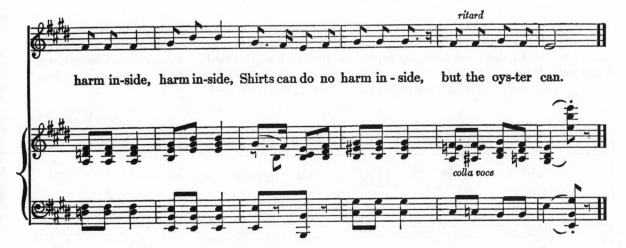

harm in-side, harm in-side, Shirts can do no harm in - side, but the oys-ter can.

Mary had a William goat, William goat, William goat,
Mary had a William goat, his stomach lined with zinc.
One day he ate an oyster can, oyster can, oyster can,
One day he ate an oyster can, and a clothesline full of shirts.
Oh, the shirts can do no harm inside, harm inside, harm inside,
Shirts can do no harm inside, but the oyster can.

337

I WISH I WAS A LITTLE BIRD

Suppose a bashful girl and a backward young man are lonesome at a party or picnic. Can they do better than to sing this just to see how it goes as a duet? . . . The spoken line can be varied to "But I don't see how you expect me to stay here deserted, forlorn, isolated, eating my heart out, all by myself." . . . A Hudson river steamboat deck favorite on moonlight nights. . . . Text and tune from Magda Brooks of New Paltz, New York.

Arr. H. F.

I wish I was a lit - tle bird, I'd fly up in a tree. I'd

(Spoken)

sit and sing my sad lit - tle song, But I can't stay here by my - self!

1 I wish I was a little bird,
  I'd fly up in a tree.
  I'd sit and sing my sad little song,
    But
       I
         can't
           stay
             here
               by
                 myself!

2 I wish I was a little fish,
  I'd swim way down in the sea.
  I'd sit and sing my sad little song,
    But
       I
         can't
           stay
             here
               by
                 myself!

OLD ADAM

Sympathy for The First Man is here. . . . College girls sing it. . . . Text and tune are from the State Teachers College at Harrisonburg, Virginia.

Arr. M. L.

I'm so sor - ry for old Ad - am,— Just as sor - ry as can be;— For he nev - er had no Mam - my For to hold him on her knee.

1 I'm so sorry for old Adam,
   Just as sorry as can be;
For he never had no mammy
   For to hold him on her knee.

2 For he never had no childhood,
   Playin' round the cabin door,
And he never had no daddy
   For to tell him all he know.

3 And I've always had the feelin'
   He'd a let that apple be,
If he'd only had a mammy
   For to hold him on her knee.

339

THE HORSE NAMED BILL

The tempo for this song is indicated as "with lucid intervals if possible." It is a highbrow folk song disbursed in many places where the higher learning is sought. The text is from Red Lewis of Sauk Center, Minnesota, who got the last verse from George Sterling of San Francisco, and one or two other verses from an Englishman in Italy returning from a cruise to Bombay. On the same boat was a rah-rah boy from Walla Walla, Washington, who asked the Englishman, "What is a caterpillar?" and answering his own riddle, said, "A caterpillar is a worm in a raccoon coat going for a college education." Also he told the Englishman, "Walla Walla is named twice for the sake of those who didn't hear the first time."

Arr. A. G. W.

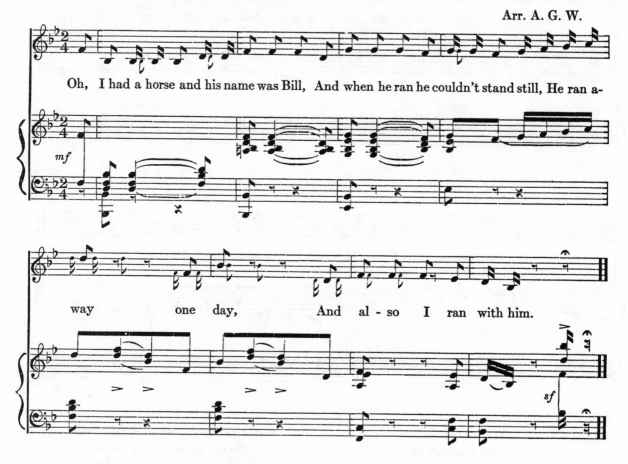

Oh, I had a horse and his name was Bill, And when he ran he couldn't stand still, He ran a-way one day, And al-so I ran with him.

1 Oh, I had a horse and his name was Bill.
   And when he ran he couldn't stand still.
   He ran away—one day—
   And also I ran with him.

2 He ran so fast he could not stop.
   He ran into a barber shop,
   And fell exhaustionized—with his eyeteeth—
   In the barber's left shoulder.

340

3 I had a gal and her name was Daisy
  And when she sang the cat went crazy
  With deliriums—St. Vituses—
  And all kinds of cataleptics.

4 One day she sang a song about
  A man who turned himself inside out
  And jumped—into the river—
  He was so very sleepy.

5 I'm going out in the woods next year
  And shoot for beer—and not for deer—
  I am — I ain't —
  I'm a great sharpshootress.

6 At shooting birds I am a beaut.
  There is no bird I cannot shoot
  In the eye, in the ear, in the teeth,
  In the fin(g)ers.

7 Oh, I went up in a balloon so big,
  The people on the earth they looked like a pig,
  Like a mice—like a katydid—like flieses—
  And like fleasens.

8 The balloon turned up with its bottom side higher.
  It fell on the wife of a country squire.
  She made a noise like a dog hound, like a steam whistle,
  And also like dynamite.

9 Oh, what could you do in a case like that?
  Oh, what could you do but stamp on your hat,
  And your toothbrush—and everything—
  That's helpless.

CRAZY SONG TO THE AIR OF "DIXIE"

We present here lines written by Andy Lee, a pen name of W. W. Delaney, as published in the Delaney Song Book No. 33. Our guess may be that his "Crazy Song to the Air of 'Dixie'" was the beginning of the highbrow folk song perpetrated and perpetuated by Sinclair Lewis, George Sterling and others. The text of it in full is here, so that each individual singer can figure it out for himself. Some of the logic is on the order of that of the member of Congress who expostulated, "Mr. Speaker, I smell a rat. I see him floating in the air. But I will nip him in the bud." Nor is it in tone above or below that of the orator addressing the House of Commons regarding certain thieves in high places, saying, "Sir, put these men on an uninhabited island and they would not be there an hour before they would have their hands in the pockets of the naked savages." . . . With but slight practice any of the verses will go to the tune of Dixie. And they are nearly as silly if read instead of sung.

1 Way down South in the land of cotton,
 I wrote this song and wrote it rotten;
 I did, I didn't—you don't believe me,
 The reason why I cannot sing,
 I have no chestnuts for to spring,
 O, me! Did we? She don't. Why does she?
 I just come back from Mobile, I did, I didn't!
 I just come back from Mobile,
 And I don't care to go anywhere—
 I do, I don't. Oh, Lizzie sells the peanuts.

2 I used to live down on a farm,
 And one bright night, when the day was warm,
 I swiped some cheese from off the table,
 The farmer chased me, but the night was damp,
 And the farmer got such an awful cramp
 In his necktie, in his feet, in his eye, oh, Heinie!
 I just come back from Cuba! Hurrah! Hurree!
 I just come back from Cuba,
 And I don't know which way to go—
 I do, I don't, I go out bicycle walking.

3 I like to sit down by the brook,
 Take a fishing line and hook,
 And fish for clams, for worms and sausages;
 And when I see a sign so near
 That says: "No fishing goes on here."
 I hunt for fleas, for flies and lobsters,
 I am an Irish hunter, I am, I ain't,
 I am an Irish hunter;
 I hunt for beer, but not for deer,
 I do, I don't. Now can you know the difference?

4 I once went up in a big balloon
 To get some cheese from off the moon;
 But the moon was full and I was fuller.
 I don't forget I took a drop,
 I fell kerflop in a barber shop,
 And got a shave—a shampoo—that's all.
 I'd like to see you after the show—I will—I won't.
 I'd like to know which way to go;
 For I can't know the wrong direction—
 I do. I don't. She was bred in old Kentucky

342

A BOY HE HAD AN AUGER

An old English song is revamped in American colleges. Spoken final lines are improvised, as
follows, "The Q is silent as in electricity," or "The bee is not mentioned as in bumble or honey,"
and so on.

Arr. A. G. W.

A boy, he had an au - ger, It bored two holes at once; A
boy, he had an au - ger, It bored two holes at once; And some were eat - ing
pop - corn, And some were eat-ing pick-les. (And the G is si - lent as in "Fish.")

A boy, he had an auger,
It bored two holes at once;
A boy, he had an auger,
It bored two holes at once;
And some were eating pop-corn,
And some were eating pickles—
Spoken (And the G is silent as in "Fish.")

343

ABDUL, THE BULBUL AMEER

When the Ahkoond of Swat passed away after a lingering illness, his last words were a message of felicitation to Abdul the Bulbul Ameer, his kinsman and host, that the reign and sway of that potentate might be long, illustrious, and filled with deeds of distinguished valor.   This wish would have come true, in all likelihood, but for the sudden and dramatic entrance on the scene of Ivan Petruski Skivah, whose knife proved superior to the chibouque in the culmination of the violent conflict, the finish contest, or knockdown and dragout affair, as one might say, which ensued between these two bitter opponents in classical language and diplomatic procedure. · . . .   Of the victor's Muscovite morganatic bride, little is known save the fact that while prone on her couch and fast in the arms of Morpheus she was heard frequently to pronounce the words "Ivan Petruski Skivah." . . .   The song in which is enshrined this legend of two embittered opponents, is a familiar of robustuous and grandiloquent men in both metropolitan centers of urban activity and in wilderness outposts of the Northwest Mounted, so to speak; it is vocalized con amore equally well in tuxedo vest, flannel shirt or duck canvas pants. . . .   As a serial tale it creates a climax which is hoist by its own petard . . .   The plot gets thicker and thicker till it runs out of gas, discombobulates, and leaves two stuffed shirts in the wind.

Arr. A. G. W.

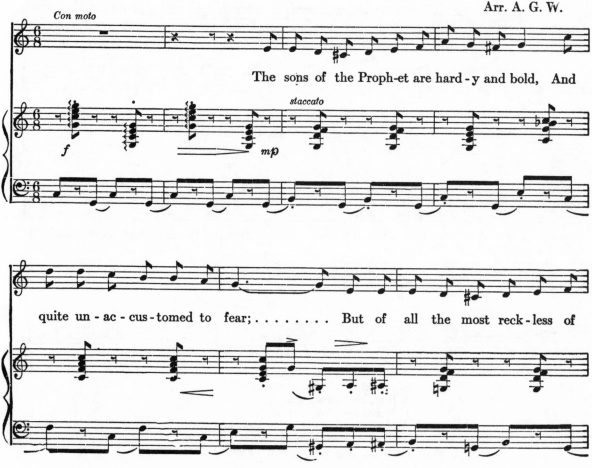

life or of limb, Was Ab - dul, the Bul - bul A - meer. . . . . . . When they

want - ed a man to en - cour - age the van, Or to shout "Hul - la - loo!" in the

rear, ... Or to storm a re - doubt, they straight-way sent out For

Ab - dul, the Bul - bul A - meer, ... For Ab - dul, the Bul - bul A - meer. . . . .

ABDUL, THE BULBUL AMEER

1 The sons of the Prophet are hardy and bold,
   And quite unaccustomed to fear;
But of all, the most reckless of life or of limb,
   Was Abdul, the Bulbul Ameer.
When they wanted a man to encourage the van,
   Or to shout "Hull-a-loo!" in the rear,
Or to storm a redoubt, they straightway sent out
   For Abdul, the Bulbul Ameer,
   For Abdul, the Bulbul Ameer.

2 There are heroes in plenty and well-known to fame
   In the ranks that are led by the Czar;
But among the most reckless of name or of fame
   Was Ivan Petruski Shivah.
He could imitate Irving, play euchre or pool,
   And perform on the Spanish guitar;
In fact, quite the cream of the Muscovite team,
   Was Ivan Petruski Skivah.

3 One morning the Russian had shouldered his gun
   And put on his most cynical sneer,
When, going down town, he happened to run
   Into Abdul, the Bulbul Ameer.
Said the Bulbul, "Young man, is your life then so dull,
   That you're anxious to end your career?
For, infidel, know that you've trod on the toe
   Of Abdul, the Bulbul Ameer.

4 Said the Russian, "My friend, your remarks in the end
   Will only prove futile, I fear;
For I mean to imply that you're going to die,
   Mr. Abdul, the Bulbul Ameer."
The Bulbul then drew out his trusty chibouque,
   And, shouting out "Allah Aklar,"
Being also intent upon slaughter he went
   For Ivan Petruski Skivah.

5 When, just as the knife was ending his life—
   In fact, he had shouted "Huzza!"—
He found himself struck by that subtle Calmuck,
   Bold Ivan Petruski Skivah.
There's a grave where the wave of the blue Danube flows,
   And on it, engraven so clear,
Is, "Stranger, remember to pray for the soul
   Of Abdul, the Bulbul Ameer."

6 Where the Muscovite maiden her vigil doth keep
   By the light of the true lover's star,
The name she so tenderly murmurs in sleep
   Is "Ivan Petruski Skivah."
The sons of the Prophet are hardy and bold;
   And quite unaccustomed to fear;
But of all, the most reckless of life or of limb,
   Was Abdul, the Bulbul Ameer.

GREENS

"What is close harmony?" was asked a glee club boy with fair Yale locks. He vouchsafed reply, "Close harmony is so called because the singers stand close to each other and watch each other closely." . . . Explaining why its music was not written in four parts, editors of the book of Columbia University Songs declared, "The musical contortionists will get in their fine work anyhow, and can always be relied on to contribute their improvisations regardless of the arrangement." . . . The following quartet, octette or double octette affair, is a "mellow" (negro for melody) from Southern Methodist University, Dallas, Texas—air and words as sung by Loia Magnuson.

Arr. A. G. W.

Greens, greens, good old culluhed greens,
I eats 'em in the mohnin',
I eats 'em in the night,
I eats 'em all the time;
They makes me feel just right.

347

ANIMAL FAIR

"All the old minstrels, Dan Rice, Dan Emmett, and all of them, sang it," said Delaney about Animal Fair. . . . "The monk, the monk, the monk," may be repeated till out of breath.

Arr. M. L.

I went to the an - i - mal fair, The birds and beasts were there. The

big ba - boon by the light of the moon Was comb - ing his au - burn hair. The

mon - key he got drunk And sat on the el - e - phant's trunk, The

el - e-phant sneezed and fell on his knees And what be-came of the monk, the monk?

I went to the animal fair,
The birds and beasts were there.
The big baboon by the light of the moon
Was combing his auburn hair.

The monkey he got drunk
And sat on the elephant's trunk,
The elephant sneezed and fell on his knees
And what became of the monk, the monk?

CALLIOPE

This is customarily rendered as a stunt without words, as indicated, in falsetto, soprano register, and in imitation of that mammoth, invincible, crowning feature of the three-ring circus, the last wagon in the parade, the steam "kallyope." Some quartets prefer singing it straight with words, This House Is Haunted. It was widely known across the Corn Belt in the 1890's. The version here is from Knox County, Illinois.

Arr. A. G. W.

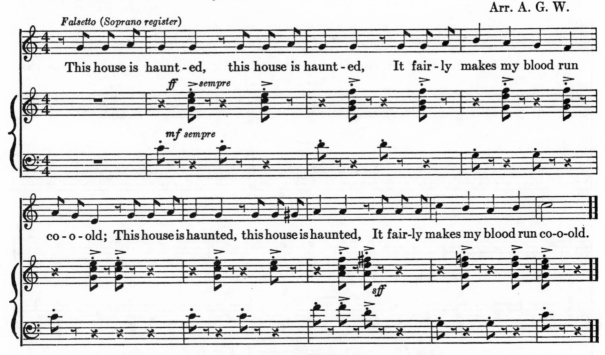

This house is haunt-ed, this house is haunt-ed, It fair-ly makes my blood run

co-o-old; This house is haunted, this house is haunted, It fair-ly makes my blood run co-o-old.

This house is haunted, this house is haunted,
It fairly makes my blood run co-o-old;
This house is haunted, this house is haunted,
It fairly makes my blood run co-o-old.

SI HUBBARD

Circus barkers made up as "hayseeds" sang and recited this piece in the 'Eighties. It was published in the early 'Seventies with the title Hey Rube. Three boys in Pittsfield, Illinois, asked a barker to teach them the words. He refused. The boys took turns listening, wrote down the words, joined the three parts and thus had the whole song. One of the boys grew up, became a Peoria lawyer, then a Chicago lawyer, and now on cold winter nights when there is no circus to go to, he sings it for his own boy.

Arr. A. G. W.

It wuz one day, I be-lieve in May, When old Si Hub-bard to me did say, "Bar-num's cir-cus has come to town, Let's you an' I go see the clowns."

350

It wuz one day, I believe in May, when old Si Hubbard to me did say,
"Barnum's circus has come to town, let's you an' I go see the clowns."

So we sold our barley, oats an' corn; in fact, we most cleaned out the barn;
Then went an' bought two bran' new suits, with white plug hats an' red top-boots.

An' when that circus got around, we two wuz the fust ones on the ground.
Sez Si to me, "Let's go get tight, pull down the tent an' have a fight."

"Not much," sez I, "I'll raise no feud," for you see I wuz skeered of the old 'Heye Rube!'
So I proposed some red lemonade an' goober peas for which I paid.

'Twuz a jolly good cuss who kept the store, so we thought when he asked us to have some more.
Sez he, "I like you boys fust rate, so don't stand back; I'll stand the treat."

So Si an' I jist pitched right in, an' the way we ate an' drank wuz a sin;
But when we turned to go away we heard that gosh-durned sharper say:

"Four dollars, quick! you Rubes! Don't wait, or else to the side-show you'll be late."
So I paid the cash like a durn fool cuss, an' off to the side-show we did rush.

When we got inside what sights we seen wuz enough to turn our whiskers green.
There wuz a tattooed man all covered with ink, an' a dog-faced boy called the 'missing link.'

But the sight that fairly made us shake wuz a great big sleepy-lookin' snake.
Si pulled his jack-knife out right quick an' up to the cage he then did slip,

An' he stabbed that snake an' jumped away, but I laughed for the critter wuz stuffed with hay.
Now a parrot in a cage close by soon caught the gaze of foolish Si;

Si didn't know this bird could talk an' when it called him a country gawk
He got right mad an' jist for spite, he knocked that bird clean out of sight.

But a monkey who wuz in the cage, at Si's conduct got in a rage,
An' to show his love for his feathered friend, a helping hand he allowed to lend.

So he grabbed poor Si by his red goatee an' it made the whole crowd laugh to see
Si tug an' pull to get away, but the pesky monkey had come to stay.

An' he pulled Si's whiskers so all-fired hard that his chin wuz as long as the neck of a gourd;
All at once I seed Si smile an' grin an' I knew his troubles wuz at an end.

An' sure enough, with his knife so keen, he'd cut them whiskers off close to his chin.
When I seed that face with the goatee off, I coughed an' laughed an' laughed an' coughed.

An' two girls fainted at the terrible sight, an' the rest of the crowd all took to flight;
Then the showmen threw us out in a hurry an' the gosh-durned band played "Annie Laurie."

Sez I: "What's the next thing on the docket?" for we both had money in our pocket.
As if in answer to my question, we both looked in the one direction,

An' there, before our very eyes, wuz a big balloon of enormous size.
An' a man in the basket in skin-tight clothes sez, "Cut the rope an' let her go."

Sez Si to me, "I'll spoil his racket," an' he grabbed a rope that wuz hitched to the basket,
An' he tried to hold the balloon to the ground, but the balloon wuz the strongest, so Si soon found.

An' to the horror of the lookers-on, up went poor Si tied to the balloon.
When I seed Si goin' I rushed to his aid, an' a sudden dash for the rope I made,

But my feet got tangled in the coil, an' I, like Si, left native soil.
Then up in the air like a rocket we shot, an' I called to the man in the balloon to stop;

But he only smiled into my face, an' asked me how I liked my place.
"Not much," sez I, "you skinny dude." "Then call me down," sez he, "you rube."

Sez I to Si, "Take out your knife an' cut the rope an' save our lives."
An' Si in his pocket his hand did slip, to get his knife, but he lost his grip,

An' he lit right square upon my face an' then we both fell into space.
"Look out! We're comin'," I cried out loud; "Oh, we don't care." came back from the crowd.

But instead of alighting on the spot I meant, we came smack down on the animal tent;
When we lit the tent began to tear, an' to save my life I grabbed Si's hair;

But his hair broke off an' down I went with Si on top, inside the tent.
An' we lit so hard on a candy-shop that the whole durned band in the circus stopped.

An' then the folks came running out to see what the racket wuz all about;
An' one of the troupers wanted to know if we had paid to get into the show.

"Why, no," sez I, "We just dropped in to try an' hear a circus ring."
He up with a club an' he hit me a crack which nearly broke my pesky back.

This made me mad an' up I rose an' I hit him square upon the nose.
He cried, "Hey Rube!" an' to my surprise, Hey Rubes came arunning thick as flies.

An' they grabbed us both an' tore our clothes, an' said they'd teach us to steal in shows.
"We didn't steal in," sez I to the crowd. "Why, no," sez Si, "We dropped from the clouds."

But a constable who had a badge on, an' like a dog's tail he kept a wagon,
Told Si an' I to get inside an' with him take a little ride.

When at the calaboose he stopped, he showed us in an' the door he locked,
An' said for being two big Jays, he'd have to give us sixty days—

But once wuz enough for us, once wuz enough for us, we'll never go to another show,
For once wuz enough for us.

352

RAILROAD AND WORK GANGS

The wish to gather and preserve popular song may be viewed as accompanying or growing out of the trend toward democracy. It parallels for literary history the change taking place in the history of society in general. Since the eighteenth century the attention of political thinkers has descended through the various strata of society until the lowest strata are now in the foreground of interest. It has often been pointed out that contemporary historians endeavor to chronicle the common man as well as the hero. The lowly may now serve as central characters in fiction and drama which were once concerned solely with patricians. Similarly, the interest of literary historians and of students and readers has extended downward from the masterpiece till it embraces the humble and unrecorded literature of the folk.

LOUISE POUND in *American Songs and Ballads.*

BOLSUM BROWN

Who he was, this Bolsum Brown, and who she was, the Sister Mary referred to, we do not know.
And nobody cares. But the song passes the time among the people who work for a living.

Arr. M. L.

There's a red light on the track for Bolsum Brown,   For Bolsum Brown,   for Bolsum

Brown. . . . . .   There's a   red   light on   the track,   and it'll   be

there when he comes back, There's a   red light   on   the track for Bol - sum Brown.

1 There's a red light on the track for Bolsum
    Brown,
  For Bolsum Brown, for Bolsum Brown.
  There's a red light on the track,
  And it'll be there when he comes back.
  There's a red light on the track for Bolsum
    Brown.

2 Hop along, Sister Mary, hop along,
    Hop along, hop along.
  There's a red light on the track,
  And it'll be there when he comes back.
  There's a red light on the track for Bolsum
    Brown.

355

POOR PADDY WORKS ON THE RAILWAY

Gangs of pick and shovel men from Ireland made the dirt and gravel fly in the years named in this song, as they were building the many little stub line railroads that were later connected into trunk lines. Emerson wrote then, "The poor Irishman — a wheelbarrow is his country." It is a considerable song and has been widely sung and known since its publication in sheet music in the early 1850's. Since then, too, the Irish have had a high percentage of railway executives; they have a faculty for railroading.

Arr. L. S.

Oh . . in eigh - teen hun-dred and for - ty one My cor - du-roy britch - es

I put on, My cor - du-roy britches I put on, To work up - on the rail - way, the

rail - way, I'm wea-ry of the rail - way; Oh poor Pad-dy works on the rail - way!

POOR PADDY WORKS ON THE RAILWAY

1 Oh in eighteen hundred and forty-one
  My corduroy britches I put on,
  My corduroy britches I put on,
  To work upon the railway, the railway,
  I'm weary of the railway;
  Oh poor Paddy works on the railway!

2 Oh in eighteen hundred and forty-two
  I did not know what I should do,
  I did not know what I should do,
  To work upon the railway, the railway,
  I'm weary of the railway;
  Oh poor Paddy works on the railway!

3 Oh in eighteen hundred and forty-three
  I sailed away across the sea,
  I sailed away across the sea,
  To work upon the railway, the railway,
  I'm weary of the railway;
  Oh poor Paddy works on the railway!

4 Oh in eighteen hundred and forty-four
  I landed on Columbia's shore,
  I landed on Columbia's shore,
  To work upon the railway, the railway,
  I'm weary of the railway;
  Oh poor Paddy works on the railway!

5 Oh in eighteen hundred and forty-five
  When Daniel O'Connell he was alive,
  When Daniel O'Connell he was alive,
  To work upon the railway, the railway,
  I'm weary of the railway;
  Oh poor Paddy works on the railway!

6 Oh in eighteen hundred and forty-six
  I changed my trade to carrying bricks,
  I changed my trade to carrying bricks,
  From working on the railway, the railway,
  I was weary of the railway;
  Oh poor Paddy worked on the railway!

7 Oh in eighteen hundred and forty-seven
  Poor Paddy was thinking of going to Heaven,
  Poor Paddy was thinking of going to Heaven,
  After working on the railway, the railway,
  He was weary of the railway;
  Oh poor Paddy worked on the railway!

THE RAILROAD CARS ARE COMING

Federal government experiments with camels in the 1850's were no go. The hope was that caravans of dromedaries might carry freight traffic from New Orleans to the west coast. . . . Horse, mule, burro, were good overland freighters. But the box car was better; it gave cruel desert spaces a friendly and human look. . . . As the work gangs spiked rails to ties and the eastern and western gangs came closer, this song arose, one verse with jubilation, one with laughter at the prairie dog, the rattlesnake and owl having their dominion of the desert interrupted. . . . We have this text and tune from Margery K. Forsythe of Chicago, who learned it from her pioneer mother.

Arr. H. F. P.

The great Pa-cif-ic rail-way, for Cal-i-for-ni-a hail! Bring on the lo-co-mo-tive, Lay

down the i-ron rail; A-cross the roll-ing prair-ies, By Steam we're bound to go, The

rail-road cars are com-ing, hum-ming Through . . . New Mex-i-co, ... The

358

rail - road cars are com-ing, hum-ming Through . . . . New Mex - i - co.

sfz

1 The great Pacific railway,
   For California hail!
Bring on the locomotive,
   Lay down the iron rail;
Across the rolling prairies
   By steam we're bound to go,
The railroad cars are coming, humming
   Through New Mexico,
The railroad cars are coming, humming
   Through New Mexico.

2 The little dogs in dog-town
   Will wag each little tail;
They'll think that something's coming
   A-riding on a rail.
The rattle-snake will show its fangs,
   The owl tu-whit, tu-who,
The railroad cars are coming, humming
   Through New Mexico,
The railroad cars are coming, humming
   Through New Mexico.

JERRY, GO AN' ILE THAT CAR

In 1884 Charles Lummis heard Gunnysack Riley sing this at Albuquerque, New Mexico. Later, as an editor, he wanted the verses and put the matter up to Santa Fe railroad officials, who sent out a general order covering the whole system, calling for verses to Jerry Go An' Ile That Car. A lost song was dug up. . . . Of the text here, Lummis says, "The words are pretty nearly conclusive, but any one who can round them out will do service to history." . . . The tune is given as notated by Arthur Farwell from Charles Lummis as learned from Gunnysack Riley.

Arr. A. F.

Come all ye rail-road sec-tion men, An' lis-ten to my song, It
is of Lar-ry O' Sul-li-van, Who now is dead and gone. For
twin-ty years a sec-tion boss, He niv-er hired a tar— Oh, it's

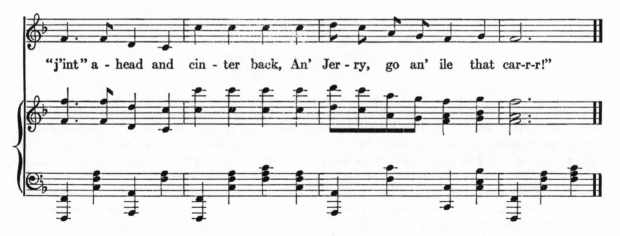

"j'int" a-head and cin-ter back, An' Jer-ry, go an' ile that car-r-r!"

1 Come all ye railroad section men,
   An' listen to my song;
It is of Larry O'Sullivan,
   Who now is dead and gone.
For twinty years a section boss,
   He niver hired a tar—
Oh, it's "j'int ahead and cinter back,
   An' Jerry, go an' ile that car-r-r!"

2 For twinty years a section boss
   He worked upon the track,
And be it to his cred-i-it,
   He niver had a wrack,
For he kept every j'int right up to the p'int
   Wid the tap of the tampin'-bar-r;
And while the byes was a-shimmin' up the ties,
   It's "Jerry, wud yez ile that car-r-r!"

3 God rest ye, Larry O'Sullivan,
   To me ye were kind an' good;
Ye always made the section men
   Go out and chop me wood;
An' fetch me wather from the well,
   An' cut the kindlin' fine;
And anny man that wudn't lind a han'
   'Twas Larry'd give him his Time.

4 And ivery Sunday marni-i-ing
   Unto the gang he'd say:
"Me byes, prepare—yez be aware
   The ould lady goes to church the day.
Now I want ivery man to pump the best that
   For the distance it is far-r-r;   [he can,
An' we have to get in ahead of Number 10—
   So, Jerry, go an' ile that car-r-r!"

5 'Twas in November, in the winter time,
   An' the ground all covered wid snow,
"Come, putt the hand-car-r on the track,
   An' over the section go!"
Wid his big sojer coat buttoned up to his t'roat,
   All weathers he wud dare—
An' it's "Paddy Mack, will yez walk the track,
   An' Jerry, go an' ile that car-r-r!"

6 "Give my rispicts to the Roadmas-ther,"
   Poor Larry he did cry,
"And lave me up, that I may see
   The ould hand-car-r before I die.
Then lay the spike-maul upon his chist,
   The gauge an' the ould claw-bar-r,
And while the byes do be fillin' up the grave,
   Oh, Jerry, go and ile that car-r-r!"

IF I DIE A RAILROAD MAN

O Lord, let it rain,
Wet my little dress!
So that corn will be cheaper
And I can fill my belly!

This translation from hieroglyphics on an ancient Egyptian temple is among the oldest known songs of working people. It is not a far cry from such lines to the replies of a witness before the industrial relations commission, who told the commission's examiner, Frank P. Walsh, that he and other railroad men had at a certain time been "sitting and talking." "What were you talking about?" "Oh, just railroad talk." "Anything particular in railroad talk." "No, just railroad talk." "Well, could you tell us just what you mean by railroad talk?" "Oh—whiskey—and women—and higher wages and shorter hours.". . . . The lyric here is a white and negro blend in its making; it was heard at the University of Kentucky; the young man who sang it said the notes are sometimes "blued" and it is then called The Louisville & Nashville Blues.

Arr. H. F.

They took John Hen-ry to the steep hill-side; He looked to the heav-en a-

bove. He says: "Take my ham-mer and wrap it in gold And

1 They took John Henry to the steep hillside;
He looked to the heaven above.
He says: "Take my hammer and wrap it in gold
And give it to the girl I love,
And give it to the girl I love.

2 "If I die a railroad man,
Go bury me under the tie,
So I can hear old No. 4
As she goes rolling by,
As she goes rolling by.

3 "If I die a railroad man,
Go bury me under the sand,
With a pick and a shovel at my head and feet,
And a nine-pound hammer in my hand,
And a nine-pound hammer in my hand."

CAP'N, I BELIEVE

When Tubman K. Hedrick, poet and philosopher, was a water boy on a building construction job in a Texas town, he heard negroes, going up a ladder with hods of mortar, chanting "Cap'n, I believe" to the bricklayers above who replied as our text indicates. It reminds us of one Pat who told one Mike, "All I do is carry the bricks up the ladder—the man on top does all the work."

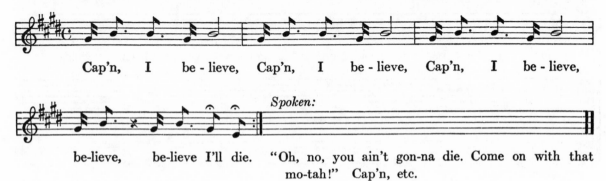

be-lieve,   be-lieve I'll die.   "Oh, no, you ain't gon-na die. Come on with that mo-tah!" Cap'n, etc.

JAY GOULD'S DAUGHTER and ON THE CHARLIE SO LONG

The Goulds and the Vanderbilts were big names in railroading in the 1880's. Daughters in both families found their way into railroad and hobo songs. . . . The "blind" baggage car, with a platform but no front door, hooked on just back of the engine tender, was a place bums rode; engine crews sometimes gave them hot water. . . .Smoke, dust, gravel, get into the nose and eyes, and grind into the skin of those riding the rods under a box car or in the trucks of a passenger coach; loosening a hold or going to sleep means death. . . . The same tune goes for Jay Gould's daughter and that train wreck ballad On The Charlie So Long (B). Both texts are from the collection of John Lomax while the tune is from the singing of Mrs. Lomax.

Rather fast

Arr. H. F.

On a Mon-day morn-in' it be-gan to rain; A-roun' the bend come a pass-en-ger train. On the bump-ers was a ho-bo John; He's a good old ho-bo, but he's dead an' gone. Dead an' gone,

dead and gone, He's a good old ho-bo, but he's dead and gone.

1 On a Monday mornin' it began to rain;
   Aroun' the bend come a passenger train.
   On the bumpers was a hobo John;
   He's a good old hobo, but he's dead and gone.
     Dead and gone, dead and gone,
   He's a good old hobo, but he's dead and gone.

2 Charley Snyder was a good engineer,
   He told his fireman not to fear,
   All he needed was water and coal;
   Put your head out the window, see the drivers roll,
     See the drivers roll, see the drivers roll,
   Put your head out the window, see the drivers roll.

3 Jay Gould's daughter said before she died:
   "There's one more road I'd like to ride."
   "Tell me, daughter, what can it be?"
   "It's in southern California on the Santa Fe,
     On the Santa Fe, on the Santa Fe,
   It's in southern California on the Santa Fe."

4 Jay Gould's daughter said before she died,
   "Father, fix the blind so the bums can't ride;
   If ride they must, let them ride the rod,
   Let 'em put their trust in the hands of God,
     In the hands of God, in the hands of God,
   Let 'em put their trust in the hands of God."

ON THE CHARLIE SO LONG

1 On a Monday morning it began to rain,
   Around the bend come a passenger train;
   On the bumpers was an old Jimmie Jones,
   He's a good old porter but he's dead and gone;
     Dead and gone, dead and gone,
   'Case he been on the Charlie so long.

2 Joseph Mickle was a good engineer,
   Told the fireman never to fear;
   All he wanted was to get her good and hot,
   "We'll make Paris 'bout four o'clock,
     'Bout four o'clock, 'bout four o'clock,
   'Case we been on the Charlie so long."

3 When we got within a mile of the place,
   Number One stared us right in the face;
   The conductor pulled his watch, and mumbled
     and said,
   "We may make it but we'll all be dead,
     We'll all be dead, we'll all be dead,
   'Case we been on the Charlie so long."

4 As the two locomotives was about to bump,
   The fireman prepared to make his jump;
   The engineer blowed the whistle, and the fire-
     man bawled,
   "Please, Mr. Conductor, won't you save us all?
     Won't you save us all? Won't you save us all?
   'Case you been on the Charlie so long."

5 O you ought to been there for to see the sight,
   Screaming and yelling, both colored and white;
   Some were crippled and some were lame,
   And the six-wheel driver had to bear the blame,
     Had to bear the blame, had to bear the
   'Case he been on the Charlie so long. [blame,

6 O ain't it a pity, ain't it a shame?
   The six-wheel driver had to bear the blame.
   Some were crippled, and some were lame,
   And the six-wheel driver had to bear the blame,
     Had to bear the blame, had to bear the
   'Case he been on the Charlie so long. [blame,

CASEY JONES[1]

At Dodge City, Kansas, in the Santa Fe railway station grass and flower plot, stands a plain memorial, a wooden post painted white with the reminder in black letters: Lest We Forget. Fastened to the post is an old time, cast-iron Link-and-Pin, the slaughterer, the crepe hanger, the maker of one-armed men peddling lead pencils on payday night, the predecessor of the beneficent Safety Coupler. . . . The laughter of the railroad man at death and mutilation runs through many of his songs. The promise of a wooden kimono, a six foot bungalow, is with him on every trip whether he's on a regular run or the extra list, and no matter what his seniority. . . . Verses sung by railroad men were printed in that remarkably American periodical, The Railroad Man's Magazine, under the editorship of Robert Davis. . . . Then came the sheet music version, widely popular. Lumberjacks, college girls, aviators, and doughboys, have made versions of their own. . . . Songs are like people, animals, plants. They have genealogies, pedigrees, thoroughbreds, cross-breeds, mongrels, strays, and often a strange love-child. . . . The Casey Jones song may stem from several earlier pieces that have the same gait, freckles, disposition, color of hair and eyes. Among such earlier pieces are Brady Why Didn't You Run?, Jay Gould's Daughter, On The Charlie So Long, Vanderbilt's Daughter, Mama Have You Heard the News? and all the earlier known songs in which figure Casey Jones, K. C. Jones, David Jones, and still other Joneses. . . . Two melodies are presented here. One is the traditional Casey Jones, the other (B) is the lesser known Mama Have You Heard the News? Some verses of the two songs are as interchangeable as standard box cars; others are narrow gauge and dinky. The second tune (B) is one notated in Ohio by Josephine Winston of the University of North Carolina.

Arr. R. E. K.

Come, all you round-ers, for I want you to hear The sto-ry of a brave en-gi-neer.... Cas-ey Jones ... was the

round-er's name. On a heav-y big eight wheeler of a might - y fame.

1 Come all you rounders, for I want you to hear,
   The story of a brave engineer.
   Casey Jones was the rounder's name.
   On a big eight wheeler of a mighty fame.

2 Caller called Casey 'bout half-past four,
   He kissed his wife at the station door,
   Climbed to the cab with the orders in his hand,
   He says, "This is my trip to the holy land."

3 Out of South Memphis yard on the fly,
   Heard the fireman say, "You got a white eye."
   Well, the switchmen knew by the engine moan
   That the man at the throttle was Casey Jones.

4 The rain was comin' down five or six weeks.
   The railroad track was like the bed of a creek.
   They slowed her down to a thirty mile gait
   And the south-bound mail was eight hours late.

5 Fireman says, "Casey, you're runnin' too fast,
   You run that block board the last station you passed."
   Casey says, "I believe we'll make it though,
   For she steams a lot better than I ever know."

6 Casey says, "Fireman, don't you fret,
   Keep knockin' at the fire door, don't give up yet,
   I'm going to run her till she leaves the rail,
   Or make it on time with the south-bound mail."

7 Around the curve and down the dump,
   Two locomotives was a bound to jump,
   Fireman hollered, "Casey, it's just ahead,
   We might jump and make it but we'll all be dead."

8 Around the curve comes a passenger train,
   Casey blows the whistle, tells the fireman, "Ring the bell,"
   Fireman jumps and says "Good-by,
   Casey Jones, You're bound to die."

9 Well Casey Jones was all right.
   He stuck to his duty day and night.
   They loved his whistle and his ring number three,
   And he came into Memphis on the old I. C.

10 Fireman goes down the depot track,
   Begging his honey to take him back,
   She says, "Oranges on the table, peaches on the shelf,
   You're a goin' to get tired sleepin' by yourself."

11 Mrs. Casey Jones was a sittin' on the bed.
   Telegram comes that Casey is dead.
   She says, "Children, go to bed, and hush your cryin',
   'Cause you got another papa on the Frisco line."

12 Headaches and heartaches and all kinds of pain.
   They ain't apart from a railroad train.
   Stories of brave men, noble and grand,
   Belong to the life of a railroad man.

B

MAMA HAVE YOU HEARD THE NEWS?

Arr. H. G.

Ma-ma, ma-ma, ma-ma have you heard the news? Dad-dy got killed on the C - B - and Q's;

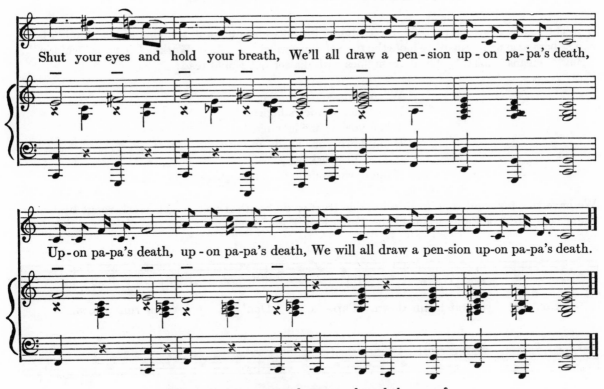

Shut your eyes and hold your breath, We'll all draw a pen-sion up-on pa-pa's death,

Up-on pa-pa's death, up-on pa-pa's death, We will all draw a pen-sion up-on pa-pa's death.

1 Mama, mama, mama have you heard the news?
Daddy got killed on the C-B-and Q's.
Shut your eyes and hold your breath,
We'll all draw a pension upon papa's death.
Upon papa's death, upon papa's death,
We will all draw a pension upon papa's death.

2 Early in the morning when it looked like rain
Around the curve came a gravel train;
On the train was Casey Jones,
He's a good old rounder but he's dead and gone,
But he's dead and gone, he's dead and gone,
He's a good old rounder but he's dead and gone.

3 All the way by the last board he passed,
Thirty-five minutes late with the U. S. mail,
Casey Jones to his fireman said,
"We'll make it into Canton or leave the rail,
Or leave the rail, or leave the rail,
We'll make it into Canton or leave the rail."

4 When Casey's family heard of his death
Casey's daughter fell on her knees,
"Mama, mama, how can it be
Papa got killed on the old I. C.?"
"O hush your mouth and hold your breath,
"We'll all draw a pension from Casey's death."

DON' LET YO' WATCH RUN DOWN

The toiling negro on railroad, levee, dump, his knees in mud, and thinking of his "luluh", begs cap'n (boss or gang foreman) to have the time of day correct. . . . "Workin'" may be "wukhin'". "Haist" means "hoist." Third verse lines with dialect out would read:

> When you see me coming
> Hoist your windows high;
> When you see me leaving
> Hang down your heads and cry,
>   Brownskins,
> Hang down your heads and cry.

We have this text and tune from a notable treatise on South Texas Negro Work-Songs by Gates Thomas in No. 5 of Publications of the Texas Folk Lore Society.

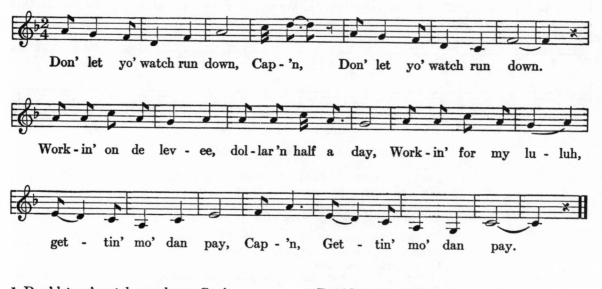

Don' let yo' watch run down, Cap - 'n, Don' let yo' watch run down.

Work - in' on de lev - ee, dol - lar 'n half a day, Work - in' for my lu - luh,

get - tin' mo' dan pay, Cap - 'n, Get - tin' mo' dan pay.

1 Don' let yo' watch run down, Cap'n,
  Don' let yo' watch run down.
  Workin' on de levee, dollar 'n half a day,
  Workin' for my luluh, gettin' mo' dan pay,
      Cap'n,
  Gettin' mo' dan pay.

2 Don' let yo' watch run down, Cap'n,
  Don' let yo' watch run down.
  Workin' on de railroad, mud up to my knees,
  Workin' for my luluh, she's a hard ole gal to
      please, Cap'n,
  She's a hard ole gal to please.

3 Don' let yo' watch run down, Cap'n,
  Don' let yo' watch run down.
  When you see me comin' haist yo' windo's high,
  When you see me leavin' hang down yo' heads an' cry, brownskins,
  Hang down yo' heads an' cry.

THERE'S MANY A MAN KILLED ON THE RAILROAD

The crying out loud is heard here; over smash-ups, head-on collisions, cow-catchers telescoped in cabooses, the iron horse meeting a broken rail and taking a tumble down an enbankment, the undertakers' harvest that came after someone was asleep at the switch—the crying out loud is heard here. . . . It is the landlubber brother of the sailor windlass song A Hundred Years Is A Very Long Time. . . . The prolonged repetitions of the word "r-a-i-l-r-o-a-d" go with a crying out loud.

Arr. H. F.

There's many a man killed on the railroad, railroad, railroad,
There's many a man killed on the railroad,
An' cast in a lonely grave.

SHE'LL BE COMIN' ROUND THE MOUNTAIN

An old-time negro spiritual When the Chariot Comes (B) was made by mountaineers into She'll Be Comin' Round the Mountain, and the song spread to railroad work gangs in the midwest in the 1890's.

Arr. H. F.

She'll be com-in' round the mountain, When she comes.   She'll be com-in' round the

moun-tain, When she comes.   She'll be com-in' round the moun-tain, She'll be

com-in' round the mountain, She'll be com-in' round the mountain, When she comes.

1 She'll be comin' round the mountain,
    When she comes.
She'll be comin' round the mountain,
    When she comes.
She'll be comin' round the mountain,
She'll be comin' round the mountain,
She'll be comin' round the mountain,
    When she comes.

2 She'll be drivin' six white horses,
    When she comes.
She'll be drivin' six white horses,
    When she comes.
She'll be drivin' six white horses,
She'll be drivin' six white horses,
She'll be drivin' six white horses,
    When she comes.

3 Oh we'll all go to meet her,
    When she comes.
Oh we'll all go to meet her,
    When she comes.
We will kill the old red rooster,
We will kill the old red rooster,
And we'll all have chicken and dumplin',
    When she comes.

B

1 O, who will drive the chariot when she comes?
O, who will drive the chariot when she comes?
O, who will drive the chariot, O who will drive the chariot,
O, who will drive the chariot when she comes?

2 King Jesus, he'll be driver when she comes,

3 She'll be loaded with bright angels,

4 She will neither rock nor totter,

5 She will run so level and steady,

6 She will take us to the portals.

I WENT DOWN TO THE DEPOT

This is the negro version of the Jesse James ballad, as heard by Charles Rockwood in work gangs of the south.

Arr. M. L.

I went down to the de-pot, not man-y nights a-go, And there I done something I

nev-er done be-fore. I got down on my knees And de-liv-ered up the keys To

Frank and his bro-ther Jes-se James. Po' Jes-se James, po' Jes-se James, I'll

I WENT DOWN TO THE DEPOT

nev - er see my Jes-se an - y more; 'Twas a dirt-y lit-tle cow-ard He

shot Mis - ter How-ard An' he laid Jes - se James in his grave.

1 I went down to the depot, not many nights ago,
And there I done something I never done before.
   I got down on my knees
   And delivered up the keys
To Frank and his brother Jesse James.
    Po' Jesse James, po' Jesse James,
    I'll never see my Jesse any more;
    'Twas a dirty little coward
    He shot Mister Howard
    An' laid Jesse James in his grave.

2 Jesse James was a man and he had a robber band,
And he flagged down the east bound train.
   Robert Ford watched his eye,
   And he shot him on the sly,
And they laid Jesse James in his grave.
    Po' Jesse James, po' Jesse James
    I'll never see my Jesse any more.
    'Twas a dirty little coward
    That shot Mister Howard
    And laid Jesse James in his grave.

3 Jesse James' little wife was a moaner all her life
When they laid Jesse James in his grave.
   She earned her daily bread
   By her needle and her thread
When they laid Jesse James in his grave.
    Po' Jesse James, po' Jesse James,
    I'll never see my Jesse any more.
    Robert Ford's pistol ball
    Brought him tumbling from the wall
    And laid Jesse James in his grave.

EVER SINCE UNCLE JOHN HENRY BEEN DEAD

This, as sung on western railroads, probably derives from the famous John Henry ballad. It may be sung with pick and shovel motions for the tamping of railroad ties or the swings of a hammer breaking hard rock, "ever since" for one stroke, "Uncle John" with another stroke, "Henry been" once more, "dead" once more, and so on.

Arr. H. F.

Ever since Uncle John Henry been dead
All of the women are wearin' red.
Dis yere hammer, nine-pound hammer,
Kill mah partner, kill John Henry,
Kill him dead.

GO 'WAY F'OM MAH WINDOW

This negro woodchopper's song came up from Arkansas and the Ozarks to Tubman K. Hedrick, author of "The Orientations of Hohen," when he was a newspaperman in Memphis, Tennessee. . . . Phrases of it time with ax-strokes. "Go 'way" sinks the ax, "f'om my window" sinks it again, and so on.

Arr. L. S.

1 Go 'way f'om mah window,
  Go 'way f'om mah doh,
  Go 'way f'om mah bedside,
  Don' you tease me no mo'.

2 Go 'way in de springtime,
  Come back in de fall,
  Bring you back mo' money
  Dan we bofe can haul.

MY LULU

Cowboys, loggers, pick and shovel stiffs, leathernecks, scissorbills, bootleggers, beer runners, hijackers, traveling men, plasterers, paperhangers, hogheads, tallowpots, snakes and stingers, and many men who carry gadgets and put on gaskets, have different kinds of verses about Lulu. Since the Chicago fire, the St. Louis cyclone and the Chatsworth wreck, she is the most sung about female character in American singing. We present nine of the nine hundred verses.

Arr. A. G. W.

My Lu-lu hugged and kissed me, She wrung my hand and cried, She
said I was the sweet-est thing That ev-er lived or died.

1 My Lulu hugged and kissed me,
　She wrung my hand and cried,
　She said I was the sweetest thing
　That ever lived or died.

2 My Lulu's tall and slender,
　My Lulu gal's tall and slim;
　But the only thing that satisfies her
　Is a good big drink of gin.

3 If you go monkey with my Lulu gal
　I'll tell you what I'll do,
　I'll carve your heart out with my razor,
　I'll shoot you with my pistol, too.

4 My Lulu gal's a daisy,
　She wears a big white hat;
　I bet your life when I'm in town
　The dudes all hit the flat.

5 I ain't goin' to work on the railroad,
    I ain't goin' to lie in jail,
But I'm goin' down to Cheyenne town
    To live with my Lulu gal.

6 My Lulu, she's an angel,
    Only she aint got no wings.
I guess I'll get her a wedding ring,
    When the grass gets green next spring.

7 My Lulu, she's a dandy,
    She stands and drinks like a man,
She calls for gin and brandy,
    And she doesn't give a damn.

8 Engineer blowed the whistle,
    Fireman rang the bell,
Lulu, in a pink kimona
    Says, "Baby, oh fare thee well."

9 I seen my Lulu in the springtime,
    I seen her in the fall;
She wrote me a letter in the winter time,
    Says, "Good-by, honey," that's all.

THE WIND IT BLEW UP THE RAILROAD TRACK

This is for cold weather, around the stove in the switch shanty.

The wind it blew up the rail-road track, It blew, it blew, The
wind it blew up the rail-road track, It blew,... it blew;... The
wind it blew up the rail-road track, It blew way up and
half way back, And the wind it blew, Ho-ly Jim-i-ny! how it blew!

The wind it blew up the railroad track,
    It blew, it blew,
The wind it blew up the railroad track,
    It blew, it blew;
The wind it blew up the railroad track,
    It blew way up and half way back,
        And the wind it blew,
        Holy Jiminy! how it blew!

HOG-EYE

A lusty and lustful song developed by negroes of South Carolina, who had it from sailors originally, is Hog-Eye. In themes it is primitive, anatomical, fierce of breath, aboriginal rather than original. One lone verse, passing any censor, is presented, with a tune notated by Julia Peterkin.

Hog-eye gal am a deb-bil of a gal. What de deb-bil ail 'em? 'E drinked a pint ob but-ter-milk An swear, by gosh, it killed 'em! Ro-ly-bo-ly sho-ly, hog-eye!.... Ro-ly-bo-ly sho-ly hog-eye!

Hog-eye gal am a debbil of a gal.
What de debbil ail 'em?
'E drinked a pint ob' butter-milk
An swear, by gosh, it killed 'em!
Ro-ly-bo-ly sho-ly hog-eye!
Ro-ly-bo-ly sho-ly hog-eye!

MY SISTER SHE WORKS IN A LAUNDRY

This is a bitter ditty of low life, a rhyme of things beyond statistics, epitomized autobiography wondering what it is laughing at.

Arr. H. F.

My sister she works in a laundry,
My father he fiddles for gin,
My mother she takes in washing,
My God, how the money rolls in.

381

I FOUND A HORSESHOE

Railroad switchmen at Illinois and Iowa division points sang this on nights in the 1890's when their gloves froze to the coupling pins between coal cars, and it was fun to reach a shanty stove. . . . Paperhangers, icewagon drivers, hash slingers and short order cooks have joined up and sung it on summer evenings for good people gathered under the Chinese lanterns of a lawn sociable, with ice cream served by the Ladies' Aid Society. . . . Henry Joslyn sets it here as a four-part piece for quartets.

Arr: H. J.

horse,   The man who owned the horse,   The man who owned the horse he lived in New York.

horse, The   man who owned the horse,The   man who owned the horse he lived in New York.

1 I found a horseshoe, I found a horseshoe.
I picked it up and nailed it on the door;
And it was rusty and full of nail holes,
Good luck 'twill bring to you forevermore.

2 The man who owned the horse he lived in New York,
The man who owned the horse he lived in New York,
    The man who owned the horse,
    The man who owned the horse,
The man who owned the horse he lived in New York.

3 The horse that wore the shoe his name was Mike,
The horse that wore the shoe his name was Mike,
    The horse that wore the shoe,
    The horse that wore the shoe,
The horse that wore the shoe his name was Mike.

RAILROAD BILL

Whereas John Henry was strong at driving steel and was a kindly family man, Railroad Bill is fierce and deep in sin and cussedness, "a mighty bad man." He carries mean hardware, steals the wives of men, and is a man-killer with the police after him. . . . There was an actual Railroad Bill who shot to kill and was feared and hunted. Southern negro work gangs have fixed him in a ballad of hundreds of lines. . . . The verses couple onto each other like fast mail coaches. Singers hesitate nowhere and stride through this with the clip of a non-stop train.

Arr. A. G. W.

1 Railroad Bill, Railroad Bill,
  He never work and he never will;
  Well, it's bad Railroad Bill.

2 Railroad Bill, Railroad Bill,
  Took ev'thing that the farmer had;
  That bad Railroad Bill.

3 Railroad Bill had no wife,
  Always looking for somebody's wife;
  Then it's ride, ride, ride.

4 Kill me a chicken, send me the wing,
  They think I'm working but I ain't done a thing;
  Then it's ride, ride, ride.

5 Railroad Bill, mighty bad man,
  Shoot the lantern out the brakeman's han',
  Bad Railroad Bill.

6 Railroad Bill, desp'rate an' bad,
  Take ev'thing po' women's had;
  Then it's ride, ride, ride.

7 Railroad Bill, coming home soon,
  Killed MacMillan by the light o' the moon;
  Then it's ride, ride, ride.

8 MacMillan had a special train,
  When he got there it was spring,
  Well, it's ride, ride, ride.

9 Two policemen, dressed in blue,
  Come down the street in two and two;
  Well, it's looking for Railroad Bill.

10 Ev'body tol' him he better turn back,
  Bill was a-going down the railroad track;
  Well, it's ride, ride, ride.

HANGMAN

As they sang in that Santa Fe smoker in Texas, I did not ask them why they joked about being in jail in Oklahoma nor why they enlisted in the regular army. They wore bib overalls, their hands were acquainted with shovels, and they told Lengthy, a Tennessee boy, to sing this or they would knock his block off.

Arr. A. G. W.

Hang-man, hang-man, slack up on your rope. Sweet-heart, sweet-heart, can you give me any hope? You've broke a heart a-many a time; But you'll never break this heart of mine.

1 Hangman, hangman, slack up on your rope.
  Sweetheart, sweetheart, can you give me any hope?
  You've broke a heart a-many a time;
  But you'll never break this heart of mine.

2 Hangman, hangman, slack up on your rope.
  Sister, sister, can they give me any hope?
  She broke a heart a-many a time;
  She'll never break this heart of mine.

TIMBER

An old negro on an Indiana farm near Porter had sung many spirituals and was asked, "Did you ever make up a song while working with other workers on a job?" He said that near Lynchburg, Virginia, when he was young they were cutting down timbers and hauling to a building under construction, and they made a hundred verses to this tune. . . . In his notable series of articles in the *New York Times* on "Folk Songs of America," R. W. Gordon says of work chanteys, "The solo lines are sung by one man, a leader or 'foresinger,' and the crowd joins in on the refrain. The task may be one that calls for a series of heavy pulls on a rope or of successive heaves when moving a heavy piece of timber. . . . A song often used on the docks is composed out of fragments loosely strung together. Tomorrow, or at a different task, it will be sung differently. Local allusions may at any time be introduced, but the tune and the refrain will remain the same. The very looseness of form in these work chanteys gives the leader a wonderful opportunity for directing the work without seeming to do so. If he is clever he will take advantage of many facts. To keep his men working steadily over long periods without feeling fatigue, he will choose a song that seems endlessly monotonous and count on its hypnotic power. Whenever a specially heavy heave is needed he will introduce a humorous verse or one that will appeal to the imagination of the men. Unconsciously, they will shout the refrain louder and at the same time pull harder. A good leader will always be careful to choose a song fitted to the task, one that has just the proper resting period in proportion to the frequency and the strength of the required pulls. He will pick a slow rhythm for continued work, a quick one for a sudden burst of energy." . . . In the following work chantey the singers took turns improvising solo lines, the group joining in on "Hallelujah, I don't know."

Arr. A. G. W.

1 We are trying to carry this timber to the building.
   Hallelujah, I don't know.

2 We will make doors and windows in that building.
   Hallelujah, I don't know.

3 We will build it to the glory of the Lord.
   Hallelujah, I don't know.

LUMBERJACKS, LOGGERS, SHANTY-BOYS

Science, invention, new machinery, the I. W. W., the Y. M. C. A., phonograph, radio, movies, and welfare organizations, have changed logging camp conditions, so that singing and singers are not what they used to be.   The old-time shanty boy in Michigan, Wisconsin and Minnesota, is gone. Franz Rickaby walked across the old lumber region from Charlevoix, Michigan, to Grand Forks, North Dakota, one summer, carrying a violin and a packsack, stopping where night found him, playing his violin and asking people, "What are the old songs you sing here?"   And the ballads he picked up were all from old men.   The pioneer lumberjacks cut the trees that made the frame houses of pioneer prairie farmers.   Rickaby met W. N. Allen of Wausau, Wisconsin, who sang of the cut-down pine tree made into sawlogs, sent on a river to a mill, and of how

> "Then they'll sell you to some farmer
> To keep his wife and children warmer.
> With his team he'll haul you home
> To the prairie drear and lone.
> Into a prairie house he'll make you,
> Where the prairie winds will shake you.
> There'll be little rest for thee,
> O ye noble Big Pine Tree.
> The prairie winds will sing around you.
> The hail and sleet and snow will pound you,
> And shake and wear and bleach your bones,
> On the prairie drear and lone."

Still other conditions have changed.   In Stewart Edward White's "The Blazed Trail" an old timer says, "The towns of Bay City and Saginaw alone in 1878 supported over fourteen hundred tough characters.   Block after block was devoted entirely to saloons.   In a radius of three hundred feet from the famous old Catacombs could be numbered forty saloons where drinks were sold by from three to ten 'pretty waiter girls.'   When the boys struck town, the proprietors and waitresses stood in their doorways to welcome them.   . . .   If Jack resisted temptation and walked resolutely on, one of the girls would remark audibly to another, 'He ain't no lumberjack! You can see that easy 'nuff. He's just off the hay trail'.   Ten to one that brought him."

Rickaby's "Ballads and Songs of the Shanty-Boy" has in it the big woods silence, the spray of white water, the roar of log jams, besides many things brawny, reeking and raucous out of the bunkhouse.   He understood rough men, their rough work, words, weather.   He was the first to put the singing lumberjack into an adequate document and book.   Of the logging camp fiddler it was remarked, "He gets the swing of the tune and then plays it to suit himself." and to this Rickaby adds: "Getting the swing of the melody of a song, and then bending both melody and words into satisfactory union, is fundamental in folk-song.   The singing of a ballad is a free and unconfined process. The story is the clear unmortgaged possession of the personality whose lips happen to be forming it at the time; word and note must serve, but they must not get in the way.   Thus it is that a singer, in three successive renditions of the same line, may sing it no twice alike.   Not only may the melody vary slightly, but 'they' may become 'we,' 'though' may become 'although,' 'Willie' may become 'William,' or even another person entirely.   'Oh' may be omitted, or supplied; or 'it's' or 'then' or 'now'; and so on through a hundred similar or greater possibilities.   This may all sound slovenly and unkempt to the conscious artist; but in the realm of popular balladry, until one does it, the ballad is not truly his."

JAMES WHALAND

Slow, ponderous, inevitable, this proceeds like a witness whose testimony is unshakable. He saw what he tells, knows how it happened, and is sure it is the truth. . . . Edwin Ford Piper of the University of Iowa, heard this in the 1890's from farmhands who had been up in a Minnesota logging camp.

Arr. A. G. W.

Moderato con moto. Lugubre

Come all you brave young shan-ty-boys, I pray you all draw near, ... 'Tis of a fright-ful ac-ci-dent, That I would have you hear. . . .

1 Come all you brave young shanty-boys,
I pray you all draw near,
'Tis of a frightful accident
That I would have you hear.

2 'Tis of a young and comely youth,
James Whaland he was called,
Got drownded from Le Claron's raft,
All on the upper falls.

3 The water being in its raging course,
The river rolling high,
When the foreman to young Whaland said,
"The jam you'll have to try."

4 As they were rolling off the logs,
Young Whaland made a shout:
"To shore, to shore, my shanty-boys,
The jam is going out!"

5 Those mighty logs went end on end,
With fearful crashing sound,
And when the shanty-boys looked back,
Young Whaland had gone down.

6 The foaming waters tore and tossed
The logs from shore to shore,
And here and there his body lies,
A-tumbling o'er and o'er.

THE SHANTY-MAN'S LIFE

Franz Rickaby heard from an old shanty-boy, A. C. Hannah at Bimidji, Minnesota, the same tune that John Lomax met in Texas. The cowpuncher of the southwestern plains and the lumberjack of the north woods strung on the same old Irish melody verses telling of similar troubles and like gaiety. Though they have "a wearisome life" it is "void of all slavish fear."

Arr. C. F. E.

Oh, a shanty-man's life is a wearisome life, although some think it

void of care, Swing-ing an ax from morn-ing till night, in the midst of the for-ests so

drear. Ly-ing in the shan-ty bleak and cold while the cold storm-y win-try winds

THE SHANTY-MAN'S LIFE

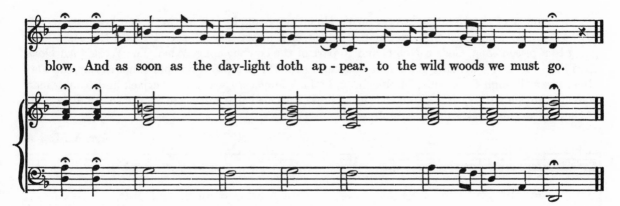

blow, And as soon as the day-light doth ap - pear, to the wild woods we must go.

1 Oh, a shanty-man's life is a wearisome life, although some think it void of care,
Swinging an ax from morning till night in the midst of the forests so drear.
Lying in the shanty bleak and cold while the cold stormy wintry winds blow,
And as soon as the daylight doth appear, to the wild woods we must go.

2 Oh, the cook rises up in the middle of the night saying, "Hurrah, brave boys, it's day."
Broken slumbers ofttimes are passed as the cold winter night whiles away.
Had we rum, wine or beer our spirits for to cheer as the days so lonely do dwine,
Or a glass of any shone while in the woods alone for to cheer up our troubled minds.

3 But when spring it does set in, double hardships then begin, when the waters are piercing cold,
And our clothes are dripping wet and fingers benumbed, and our pike-poles we scarcely can hold.
Betwixt rocks, shoals and sands give employment to all hands our well-banded raft for to steer,
And the rapids that we run, oh, they seem to us but fun, for we're void of all slavish fear.

4 Oh, a shanty lad is the only lad I love, and I never will deny the same.
My heart doth scorn these conceited farmer boys who think it a disgraceful name.
They may boast about their farms, but my shanty-boy has charms so far, far surpassing them all,
Until death it doth us part he shall enjoy my heart, let his riches be great or small.

FLAT RIVER GIRL

A member of the Great Lakes Seamen's Union sang this for me at the Union headquarters in Milwaukee, Wisconsin, when I was marine editor of a newspaper. Later I found the same tune going to a prison song, Cousin Nellie, and to part of the cowboy song, When The Work's All Done This Fall. . . . Rickaby gives four texts and tunes to this piece, one old timer saying the Flat River flows through Greenville, Michigan, and "Jack Haggerty was a lumberjack and from a man who used to run a livery stable and rent him horses I learned that he was not quite so rough as most of those birds, and was a little more dressy."

Arr. M. L.

Come all you fine young fel-lows with hearts so warm and true,

Nev-er be-lieve in a wom-an; you're lost if you do. But

if you ev-er see one with long brown chest-nut curls, Just

392

FLAT RIVER GIRL

think of Jack Hag-ger-ty and his Flat Riv-er girl.

1 Come all you fine young fellow with hearts so warm and true,
Never believe in a woman; you're lost if you do.
But if you ever see one with long brown chestnut curls,
Just think of Jack Haggerty and his Flat River girl.

2 Her form was like the dove, so slender and so neat,
Her long brown chestnut curls hung to her tiny feet,
Her voice it was like music or murmurs of the breeze
As she whispered that she loved me as we strolled among the trees.

3 She was a blacksmith's daughter from the Flat River side,
And I always had intended for to make her my bride;
But one day on the river a letter I received:
She said that from her promise herself she had relieved.

4 To her mother, Jane Tucker, I lay all the blame.
She caused her to leave me and to blacken my name.
I counted her my darling, what a lady for a wife!
When I think of her treachery it nearly takes my life.

5 Come all you fine young fellows with hearts so warm and true.
Never believe in a woman; you're lost if you do.
But if you ever see one with long brown chestnut curls,
Just think of Jack Haggerty and his Flat River girl.

THE JAM ON GERRY'S ROCK

On a melodious winter evening in Salem, Oregon, Charles Olaf Olsen, logger and poet, was asked to tell a lie that had few words and much imagination. He said, "Once there was a logger who had a trunk." . . . Then James Stevens, logger and author, sang "The Jam on Gerry's Rock," sonorously, rockingly, beating time with a sure, unfailing foot that slammed the floor with accurate measures. . . . It is a heavy, brooding ballad, portentous as a log boom on an ice locked river. . . . Rickaby, in an extended note, says it was born in Canada or Michigan, with the odds of witnesses in favor of Michigan. He observes, "Old fellows told me anyone starting Gerry's Rock in the shanties was summarily shut off because the song was sung to death; others vow that of all songs it was ever and always the most welcome." . . . "Deacon seat" was shanty lingo for a seat, or board, extending from the lower tier of bunks and running square or oblong around the bunkhouse; it was where they sat between suppertime and bedtime and smoked, talked, sang, and told Paul Bunyan stories.

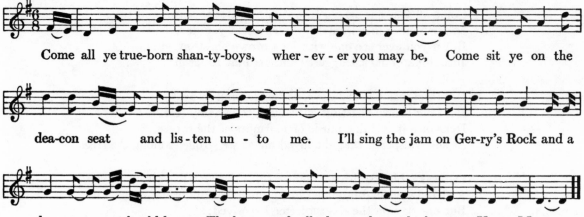

Come all ye true-born shan-ty-boys, wher-ev-er you may be, Come sit ye on the
dea-con seat and lis-ten un-to me. I'll sing the jam on Ger-ry's Rock and a
he-ro you should know, The bravest of all shan-ty-boys, the foreman, Young Mun-ro.

1 Come all ye true-born shanty-boys, wherever you may be,
   Come sit ye on the deacon seat and listen unto me.
   I'll sing the jam on Gerry's Rock and a hero you should know,
   The bravest of all shanty-boys, the foreman, Young Munro.

2 'Twas on a Sunday morning, ere daylight did appear.
   The logs were piling mountain-high: we could not keep them clear.
   "Cheer up! Cheer up, my rivermen, relieve your hearts of woe!
   We'll break the jam on Gerry's Rock!" cried our foreman, Young Munro.

3 Now some of them were willing, while others hid from sight.
   To break a jam on Sunday they did not think it right.
   Till six of our brave shanty-boys did volunteer to go
   And break the jam on Gerry's Rock with our foreman, Young Munro.

394

4 They had not picked off many logs till Munro to them did say,
"I must send you back up the drive, my boys, for the jam will soon give way!"
Alone he freed the key-log then, and when the jam did go
It carried away on the boiling-flood our foreman, Young Munro.

5 Now when the boys up at the camp the news they came to hear,
In search of his dead body down the river they did steer;
And there they found to their surprise, their sorrow, grief and woe,
All bruised and mangled on the beach, lay the corpse of Young Munro.

6 They picked him up most tenderly, smoothed down his raven hair.
There was one among the watchers whose cries did rend the air.
The fairest lass of Saginaw let tears of anguish flow;
But her moans and cries could not awake her true love, Young Munro.

7 The Missus Clark, a widow, lived by the riverside;
This was her only daughter, Munro's intended bride.
So the wages of her perished love the boss to her did pay
And a gift of gold was sent to her by the shanty-boys next day.

8 When she received the money she thanked them tearfully,
But it was not her portion long on the earth to be;
For it was just six weeks or so when she was called to go
And the shanty-boys laid her at rest by the side of Young Munro.

9 They decked the graves most decently—'twas on the fourth of May—
Come all ye true-born shanty-boys and for a comrade pray!
Engraven on a hemlock tree which by the beach did grow,
Are the name and date of the mournful fate of the foreman, Young Munro.

DRIVING SAW-LOGS ON THE PLOVER

Winter was the big time for work in the logging camps. The logs cut during winter were floated to the saw mills as the frozen rivers loosened up for the "drive" in the spring. Boys needed on the farms in summer and fall took a turn at logging in the winter. So there was plenty of argument on whether a farm hand or a shanty-boy had the better of it, in pay and cash or in favor with the girls. . . . In M. C. Dean's collection The Flying Cloud is an old song I Love My Sailor Boy, with a mother's advice and a daughter's scorn in two verses:

"Then wed a steady farmer's son that whistles at the plow,
And then you will have time enough to tend both sheep and cows.
But your sailor he'll carouse and drink whenever he comes on shore,
And when his money is spent and gone, he'll sail the seas for more."

"A fig for all your farmer's sons! Such lovers I disdain.
There is not one among them dare face the raging main.
And when the winds are howling and the billows are white as snow,
I'll venture my life with the lad that dare go where stormy winds do blow."

The text and tune here were notated by Franz Rickaby from W. N. Allen of Wausau, Wisconsin. Allen composed the verses in 1873, using the tune of an old song about a mother's words to her son as he went away to the Crimean War.

Arr. C. F. E.

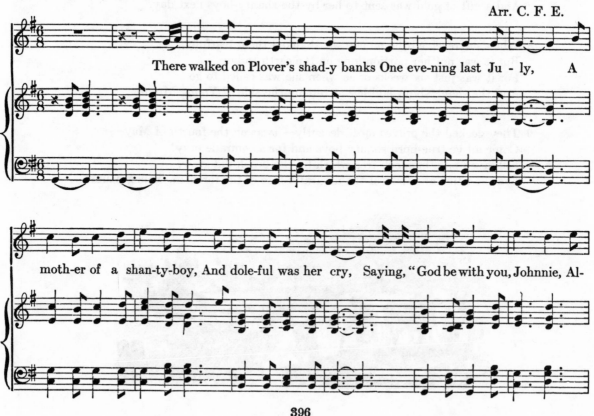

There walked on Plover's shad-y banks One eve-ning last Ju - ly, A

moth-er of a shan-ty-boy, And dole-ful was her cry, Saying, "God be with you, Johnnie, Al-

though you're far a - way Driving saw-logs on the Plo-ver, And you'll never get your pay.

1 There walked on Plover's shady banks
  One evening last July,
  A mother of a shanty-boy,
  And doleful was her cry,
  Saying, "God be with you, Johnnie,
  Although you're far away
  Driving saw-logs on the Plover,
  And you'll never get your pay.

2 "O Johnnie, I gave you schooling,
  I gave you a trade likewise;
  You need not been a shanty-boy
  Had you taken my advice.
  You need not gone from your dear home
  To the forest far away,
  Diving saw-logs on the Plover?
  And you'll never get your pay.

3 "O Johnnie, you were your father's hope,
  Your mother's only joy.
  Why is it that you ramble so,
  My own, my darling boy?
  What could induce you, Johnnie,
  From your own dear home to stray,
  Driving saw-logs on the Plover?
  And you'll never get your pay.

4 "Why didn't you stay upon the farm,
  And feed the ducks and hens,
  And drive the pigs and sheep each night
  And put them in their pens?
  Far better for you to help your dad
  To cut his corn and hay
  Than to drive saw-logs on the Plover,
  And you'll never get your pay."

5 A log canoe came floating
  Adown the quiet stream.
  As peacefully it glided
  As some young lover's dream.
  A youth crept out upon the bank
  And thus to her did say,
  "Dear mother, I have jumped the game,
  And I haven't got my pay.

6 "The boys called me a sucker
  And a son-of-a-gun to boot.
  I said to myself, 'O Johnnie,
  It is time for you to scoot.'
  I stole a canoe and started
  Upon my weary way,
  And now I have got home again,
  But nary a cent of pay.

7 "Now all young men take this advice:
  If e'er you wish to roam,
  Be sure and kiss your mothers
  Before you leave your home.
  You had better work upon a farm
  For half a dollar a day
  Than to drive saw-logs on the Plover,
  And you'll never get your pay."

397

MORRISSEY AND THE RUSSIAN SAILOR

A biography titled "Life of John Morrissey, the Irish Boy Who Fought His Way to Fame and Fortune" tells about a prize fighter, gambler, politician who became state senator and Member of Congress. His big fights were in the 1850's and he defeated Thompson, the Yankee Clipper, the Benicia boy, in the squared circle, as related in this song. He was a "Paddy" and a ring hero, too, as related. But sporting authorities consulted on the point fail to find that he ever planted his knuckles in a Russian sailor's face nor fought any such thirty-eight-round contest as here described. Yet the song delivers the atmosphere of the old-time bare-fisted ring fight. . . . It is presented here as sung by M. C. Dean, of Virginia, Minnesota, author of "The Flying Cloud," a collection of lumberjack and Great Lakes songs and American ballads. On the currency of this and similar ballads Franz Rickaby wrote this eloquent and informative note: "In the logging camp the hegemony in song belonged to the Irish. Although the Scotch and French-Canadian occur occasionally, the Irish were dominant, and the Irish street-song was the pattern upon which a liberal portion of the shanty-songs were made. Irishmen sailed the seas of the world. In the armies of England they fought against Russia and died on the fields of Indian insurrection. In Canada and the United States, whither they migrated in hordes, they fought wherever there was fighting. And in this New World those of them who were thrifty and provident laid foundations of homes; and those who were not, didn't. But whatever they did, they made and sang songs; and wherever they went roving, they took them along. Thus it was that the shanties rang with songs of ships and piracy, of American battle charges, and of prize-fights in far-lying ports of the world; of charging the heights of Alma, of dying in India for Britannia and Britannia's Queen, and of sailing the lakes with red iron ore—of all these, as well as of harvesting the mighty pine."

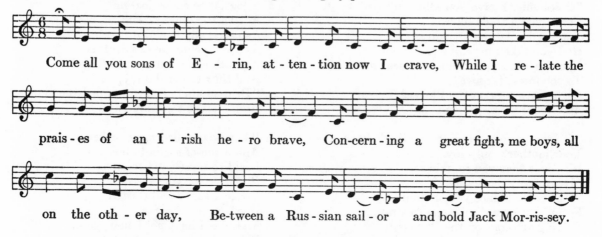

Come all you sons of E - rin, at - ten - tion now I crave, While I re - late the
prais - es of an I - rish he - ro brave, Con-cern - ing a great fight, me boys, all
on the oth - er day, Be-tween a Rus - sian sail - or and bold Jack Mor-ris-sey.

1 Come all you sons of Erin, attention now I crave,
   While I relate the praises of an Irish hero brave,
   Concerning a great fight, me boys, all on the other day,
   Between a Russian sailor and bold Jack Morrissey.

2 It was in Terra del Fuego, in South America,
   The Russian challenged Morrissey and unto him did say
   "I hear you are a fighting man, and wear a belt I see.
   What do you say, will you consent to have a round with me?"

398

3 Then up spoke bold Jack Morrissey, with a heart so stout and true,
Saying, "I am a gallant Irishman that never was subdued.
Oh, I can whale a Yankee, a Saxon bull or bear,
And in honor of old Paddy's land I'll still those laurels wear.

4 These words enraged the Russian upon that foreign land,
To think that he would be put down by any Irishman.
He says, "You are too light for me. On that make no mistake.
I would have you to resign the belt, or else your life I'll take."

5 To fight upon the tenth of June these heroes did agree,
And thousands came from every part the battle for to see.
The English and the Russians, their hearts were filled with glee;
They swore the Russian sailor boy would kill bold Morrissey.

6 They both stripped off, stepped in the ring, most glorious to be seen,
And Morrissey put on the belt bound round with shamrocks green.
Full twenty thousand dollars, as you may plainly see,
That was to be the champion's prize that gained the victory.

7 They both shook hands, walked round the ring, commencing then to fight.
It filled each Irish heart with joy for to behold the sight.
The Russian he floored Morrissey up to the eleventh round,
With English, Russian, and Saxon cheers the valley did resound.

8 A minute and a half our hero lay before he could rise.
The word went all around the field: "He's dead," were all their cries.
But Morrissey raised manfully, and raising from the ground,
From that until the twentieth the Russian he put down.

9 Up to the thirty-seventh round 'twas fall and fall about,
Which made the burly sailor to keep a sharp lookout.
The Russian called his second and asked for a glass of wine.
Our Irish hero smiled and said, "The battle will be mine."

10 The thirty-eighth decided all. The Russian felt the smart
When Morrissey, with a fearful blow, he struck him o'er the heart.
A doctor he was called on to open up a vein.
He said it was quite useless, he would never fight again.

11 Our hero conquered Thompson, the Yankee Clipper too;
The Benicia boy and Shepherd he nobly did subdue.
So let us fill a flowing bowl and drink a health galore
To brave Jack Morrissey and Paddies evermore.

MULE SKINNER'S SONG

"When the rosy fingers of dawn came stealing on soft feet along the eastern horizon, and it was time to get up and go to work, we sometimes heard a negro mule skinner singing of himself, of George McVane, and of three mules, two with names and one anonymous." Thus James Stevens, author of "Brawnyman" and other books, tells how in a Puget Sound logging camp he heard the musical fragment given here. . . . Stevens tells how he often met Mr. Puget, the contractor who hired Paul Bunyan to bring Babe the Blue Ox and dig out Puget Sound. Mr. Puget told Stevens how rain was interfering with Paul and Babe on the excavating work, and one day when a waterspout came traveling up as far as the Sound had been dug then, Paul dived deep, swum till he was under the waterspout, and then climbed with powerful overhand strokes till he reached the top. When Paul came down the waterspout was gone. "What did you do?" asked Mr. Puget, Paul answering, "I turned it off." . . . Though there are many stories there seem to be no songs of or by Paul Bunyan. . . . There is, however, one of and by a black mule skinner.

Arr. H. F. P.

O ah drove three mules foh Gawge Mc-Vane,   An' ah drove them three mules on a chain.

Nigh one Jude, . . . an' de middle one Jane, An' de one on de stick she did-n't have no name.

O ah drove three mules foh Gawge McVane,
An' ah drove them three mules on a chain.
Nigh one Jude, an' de middle one Jane,
An' de one on de stick she didn't have no name.

SAILOR MAN

WHISKY JOHNNY

Once when the night was wild without and the wintry winds piled snowdrifts around the traffic signals on Cottage Grove Avenue, Chicago, we sat with Robert Frost and Padraic Colum. The Gael had favored with Irish ballads of murder, robbery, passion. And Frost offered a sailorman song he learned as a boy on the wharves of San Francisco.

Arr. H. F.

As we sailed on the wa - ter blue, Whis-ky John-ny! A

good long pull and a strong one too, Whis-ky for my John - ny!

1 As we sailed on the water blue,
  Whisky Johnny,
  A good long pull and a strong one too,
  Whisky for my Johnny.

2 Whisky killed my brother Tom,
  Whisky Johnny,
  I drink whisky all day long,
  Whisky for my Johnny.

3 Whisky made me pawn my clothes,
  Whisky Johnny,
  Whisky gave me this red nose,
  Whisky for my Johnny.

4 Whisky stole my brains away,
  Whisky Johnny,
  The bos'n pipes and I'll belay,
  Whisky for my Johnny.

BLOW THE MAN DOWN

Robert Frost as a boy in San Francisco learned shanties from listening to sailors and dock-wal-lopers along the water front. He saved these tunes and verses in his heart. A favorite with him is Blow The Man Down. It has the lurch of ships, tough sea legs, a capacity for taking punishment and rising defiant of oppression and tyranny.

Arr. M. N.

As I was a-walk-in' down Par-a-dise Street To me aye, aye,

blow the man down! A sau-cy po-lice-man I chanced for to meet; Blow the man

down to me aye, aye, blow the man down! Wheth-er he's white man or

BLOW THE MAN DOWN

black man or brown,　Give me some time　to blow the man down,　Give me some

time　to blow　the man down,　Blow　the man down!　bul - lies!

1 As I was a-walkin' down Paradise Street
  To me aye, aye—blow the man down!
  A saucy young p'liceman I chanced for to meet;
  Blow the man down to me aye, aye, blow the man down!
  Whether he's white man or black man or brown,
  Give me some time to blow the man down,
  Give me some time to blow the man down,
  Blow the man down! bullies!

2 You're off from some clipper that flies the Black Ball,
  To me aye, aye—blow the man down!
  You've robbed some poor Dutchman of coat, boots, and all;
  Blow the man down, &c.

3 P'liceman, p'liceman, you do me much wrong
  To me aye, aye—blow the man down!
  I'm a peace party sailor just home from Hong Kong;
  Blow the man down, &c.

4 They gave me six months in Ledington jail
  To me aye, aye—blow the man down!
  For kickin' and fightin' and knockin' 'em down;
  Blow the man down, &c.

THE DEAD HORSE

The seamen on the old sailing vessels drew a month's pay before sailing. This was, as the folk proverbs of many nations have it, a dead horse to be paid for. At the end of the first sailing month, a canvas bag shaped like a horse was stuffed with straw, hoisted to the main yardarm, and given a sea burial. The ceremonial and its sung and spoken lines varied. Those below were given me in Philadelphia, by the daughter of a sailing master. Joanna Colcord designates it as a shanty used for halliards and capstan on American ships.

Arr. M. L.

1 They say, old man, your horse will die.
   And they say so and they hope so.
   They say, old man, your horse will die.
   O, poor old horse!

2 And if he dies they'll tan his hide,
   And they say so and they hope so.
   And if he dies they'll tan his hide,
   O, poor old horse!

3 And now he's gone he's buried deep,
   And they say so and they hope so.
   And now he's gone he's buried deep,
   O, poor old horse!

HEAVE AWAY

The name of Henry Clay rhymes with "heave away." What more was wanted? He was the idolized "Handsome Harry of the West" in the 1840's. This is among the few known work songs of the slave days of the American negro. It is not a ditty but a sonorous, flexible melody.

Heave a - way, heave a - way! I'd ra - ther court a yel - low gal Than work for Hen - ry Clay, Heave a - way, heave a - way!..... Yel - low gal, I want to go. I'd rath - er court a yel - low gal Than work for Hen - ry Clay. Heave a - way! Yel - low gal, I want to go!

Heave away, heave away!
I'd rather court a yellow gal
Than work for Henry Clay,
Heave away, heave away!
Yellow gal, I want to go.
I'd rather court a yellow gal
Than work for Henry Clay.
Heave away! Yellow gal, I want to go!

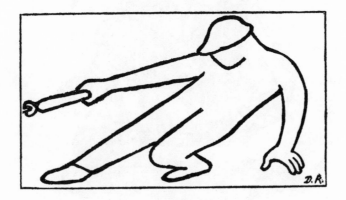

THE WIDE MIZZOURA

Regular army men were singing this in 1897. Many years earlier sailormen were singing it their way. . . . Shannadore, I am told, may have been the name of a ship. Or it may be the old time pronunciation of the name of an Indian chief or the historic Virginia valley. When I asked Joseph B. Fifer, former governor of Illinois about his early life, he said, "I was born in the Shannadore Valley." That was in the early 1840's. . . . The song was used as a capstan shanty, Joanna Colcord tells us. She notates it with varied time in her book "Roll and Go," and comments, "The tune is very free in its rhythms and cannot be written in one tempo." How that comment does go for so many good songs!

O Shan-na-dore, I love your daugh-ter, Hi-oh, you roll-ing riv-er, I'll take her 'cross the roll-ing wa-ter, Ah—hah, I'm bound a-way 'cross the wide Miz-zou-ra.

1 O Shannadore, I love your daughter,
Hi-oh, you rolling river,
I'll take her 'cross the rolling water,
Ah-hah, I'm bound away 'cross the wide Miz-zoura.

2 For seven years I courted Sally,
Hi-oh, you rolling river,
For seven more I longed to have her,
Ah-hah, I'm bound away 'cross the wide Miz-zoura.

3 She said she would not be my lover,
Hi-oh, you rolling river,
Because I was a dirty sailor,
Ah-hah, I'm bound away 'cross the wide Miz-zoura.

4 A-drinkin' rum and a-chewin' t'baccer,
Hi-oh, you rolling river,
A-drinkin' rum and a-chewin' t'baccer,
Ah-hah, I'm bound away 'cross the wide Miz-zoura.

I CATCH-A DA PLENTY OF FEESH

At Fishermen's Wharf and on Telegraph Hill in San Francisco they sing in such lingo as the heart commands. Harry Dick, Lillian Bos, and other occupants of crow nests on the topmost crags and crannies of Telegraph Hill, have heard this air and verse and have hunted a missing stanza about the selling of the fish.

Arr. H. F. P.

I sail o-ver the o - cean blue, I catch-a da plen-ty of feesh; The rain come down like hell, And the wind blow thro' my wheesk. O Mar - i - an, my good com-pan, O Vi - va le Gar - i - bal - di! Vi - va, vi - va, vi - va l'I-tal - i - ane!

Jubilantly

I sail over the ocean blue,
I catch-a da plenty of feesh;
The rain come down like hell,
And the wind blow through my wheesk.
O Marian, my good compan,
O Viva le Garibaldi!
Viva, viva, viva l'Italiane!

409

THE HOG-EYE MAN

A "hog-eye" was sailor slang in the 1850's for a barge that cruised around Cape Horn to San Francisco, where a dirty, tumultuous little Babylon met all newcomers and offered them a "good time." Spenders with nuggets of gold and sacks of gold dust met gamblers and women from nowhere, not telling their real names. It was a lighted town that beckoned seamen from afar; it crept into a sea song, of how the hog-eye men were all the go when they came down to old San Francisco. I heard the cracked voice of an old time sailor sing it, in 1922, just after R. W. Gordon had him make a phonograph cylinder record. The singer put in a high falsetto chuckle once in a while as if the song meant there was joy to come or mischief ahead or happiness remembered.

Arr. E. C.

O, the hog-eye men are all the go, When they come down to old San Fran-cis-co. And a hog-eye, rail-road nig-ger with his hog-eye, Row the boat a-shore, and a hog-eye, O, She wants the hog-eye man.

410

THE HOG-EYE MAN

1 O the hog-eye men are all the go,
  When they come down to old San Francisco.

  Chorus:
  And a hog-eye, railroad nigger with his hog-eye,
  Row the boat ashore, and a hog-eye, O,
  She wants the hog-eye man.

2 O the hog-eye man is the man for me,
  He works all day on the big levee.

3 Now who's been here since I been gone?
  A railroad nigger with his sea-boots on.

4 Go bring me down my riding cane,
  For I'm going to see my darling Jane.

5 O Sally in the garden picking peas,
  Her golden hair hanging down to her knees.

LEAVE HER, BULLIES, LEAVE HER

Text A is a hauling song as heard in the port of San Francisco. An earlier version (B), called Across the Western Ocean, from the R. W. Gordon collection, dates about 1850, after the Irish potato famine; packet ships carried thousands from Liverpool across to where there was "the Irish army," the many immigrants to America. "Amelia" is said to trace to the Irish name O'Melia.

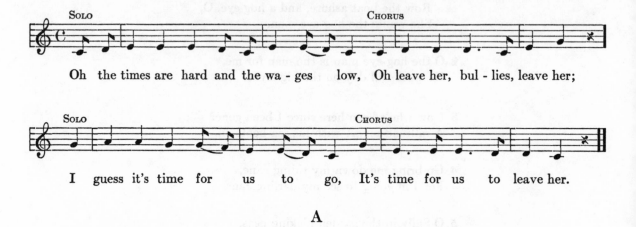

Oh the times are hard and the wa-ges low, Oh leave her, bul-lies, leave her;

I guess it's time for us to go, It's time for us to leave her.

A

1 Oh the times are hard and the wages low,
   Oh leave her, bullies, leave her;
   I guess it's time for us to go,
     It's time for us to leave her.

2 Oh don't you hear our old man say,
   Oh leave her, bullies, leave her;
   To-morrow you will get your pay,
     It's time for us to leave her.

ACROSS THE WESTERN OCEAN

B

1 Oh, the times are hard and the wages low—
   Amelia, whar you bound to?
   The Rocky Mountains is my home,
   Across the Western Ocean.

2 The Land of Promise there you'll see—
   Amelia, whar you bound to?
   I'm bound across the western sea,
   To join the Irish army.

3 To Liverpool I'll take my way—
   Amelia, whar you bound to?
   To Liverpool that Yankee school,
   Across the Western Ocean.

4 There's Liverpool Pat with his tarpaulin hat—
   Amelia, whar you bound to?
   And Yankee Jack the packet rat,
   Across the Western Ocean.

5 Beware these packet ships, I say—
   Amelia, whar you bound to?
   They steal your hide and soul away,
   Across the Western Ocean.

BANDIT BIOGRAPHIES

JIM FISK

Jim Fisk was an American business man who rose from Vermont country peddler to be a Civil War government supply contractor, a cotton speculator, a Wall Street broker, owner of the Narragansett Steamship Lines, owner of the Grand Opera House of New York, Colonel of the Ninth Regiment of the New York National Guard, director of the Erie railroad—and nicknamed "Prince Erie." He joined Jay Gould and others in a conspiracy to corner the gold of the United States in 1869, was instrumental in bringing on the financial crash of Black Friday, bought and sold judges, courts, decisions and writs of injunction, was a participant in the corruption of Tweed and Tammany. He drove a coach and eight horses around New York soliciting supplies for the Chicago fire sufferers, sent a carload of provisions and clothes to the stricken city, dispensed charity and won a large following of people who believed him a hero of proportions and heart.

He managed all things for worldly success till he met Helen Josephine Mansfield. He bought her a house with the winnings of one night's gambling, gave her horses, jewels, opera box tickets, and sent her funny, pompous love letters. She was his plaything; he was her pocketbook. She gave his letters to Edward S. Stokes of Philadelphia, who was the Other Man and who came and lived with her in the house that was a free gift and token. Newspapers published an affidavit of a negro butler of this house telling of a plot of Miss Mansfield and Stokes to force Fisk to pay $200,000 to get his letters back, his chuckling, pompous love letters.

When Miss Mansfield sued for libel, Fisk's lawyer declared at the trial, "I expect to show that Mr. Fisk found this lady without a dollar; that after lavishing upon her means enough to have satisfied Cleopatra herself, when the supply ceased, means were resorted to for the purpose of renewing them. Our defense is that this prosecution has no basis in good faith, nothing but an attempt to extort money. And have I not a right to show, if such be the fact, that finding this lady without a dollar, and having enriched her—although like most riches obtained in this way, it is rapidly disappearing—that she has had resort to this means to replenish her treasury? Cleopatra—aye, like unto her; for as the Egyptian siren queen is spoken of by the grandest of poets, 'age cannot wither her, nor custom stale her infinite variety.' "

The defense won. Stokes with a gun met Fisk in the Grand Central Hotel one afternoon and sent two bullets into his victim, who died that night. Stokes was tried and given a life sentence. Melodramatic newspaper and pulpit comment followed. Of the three actors in the tragedy, a writer declared, "One goes, how unprepared! to his long home—one goes to the solitary gloom of a murderer's cell—one to a life of deep, dark, ungovernable remorse." Henry Ward Beecher turned loose an invective declaring:

"And that supreme mountebank of fortune—the astounding event of his age: that a man with some smartness in business, but absolutely without moral sense, and as absolutely devoid of shame as the desert of Sahara is of grass—that this man, with one leap, should have vaulted to the very summit of power in New York, and for seven to ten years should have held the courts in his hands, and the Legislature and the most consummate invested interest of the land in his hands, and laughed at England and laughed at New York, and matched himself against the financial skill of the whole city, and outwitted the whole, and rode out to this hour in glaring and magnificent prosperity— shameless, vicious, criminal, abominable in his lusts, and flagrant in his violation of public decency —that this man should have been the supremest there; and yet in an instant, by the hand of a fellow culprit, God's providence struck him to the ground! And yet I say to every young man who has looked upon this glaring meteor, and seen his course of prosperity, and thought that perhaps integrity was not so necessary, 'Mark the end of the wicked man,' and turn back again to the ways of integrity."

415

And there came a song registering its own viewpoint, using the memory of Jim Fisk, a briber and corruptionist of courts, as an instance in which to lament the ancient fact that the poor get the worst of it when they go into court against the rich. . . . Text and tune here are from N. D. Cochran of Toledo, Ohio, who knows much more than most men do about corrupt courts, fixed juries, and crooked judges. The song is melodramatic and has maudlin lines. Yet it has been widely known and sung across decades in which Jim Fisk, his woman, his assassin, and all their follies were forgotten and being forgotten were forgiven. It has lived on and had a certain folk song vitality as a cry for justice, as a moan over money and cunning, greed and hypocrisy, so often winning the authorities and the decisions, the power and the glory.

Arr. A. G. W.

If you'll lis-ten a while, I'll sing you a song Of this glo-ri-ous land of the free;.......... And the dif-fer-ence I'll show 'twixt the rich and the poor, In a tri-al by the ju-ry, you'll see........ If you've plen-ty of stamps you can hold up your

416

head, And walk from your own pris - on door,............ But they'll hang you up

high, if you've no friends or gold, Let the rich go, but hang up the poor.........

In the tri - als for mur - der we have now - a - days, The rich ones get

JIM FISK

off swift and sure;............. If you've thou - sands to pay to the

ju - ry and judge, You may bet they'll go back on the poor...........

1 If you'll listen a while, I'll sing you a song
Of this glorious land of the free;
And the difference I'll show 'twixt the rich and the poor,
In a trial by the jury, you'll see.
If you've plenty of stamps, you can hold up your head
And walk from your own prison door,
But they'll hang you up high, if you've no friends or gold,
Let the rich go, but hang up the poor.

Refrain:—In the trials for murder we have nowadays,
The rich ones get off swift and sure;
If you've thousands to pay to the jury and judge,
You may bet they'll go back on the poor.

2 I'll sing of a man who's now dead in his grave,
A good man as ever was born;
Jim Fisk he was called and his money he gave
To the outcast, the poor, and forlorn.
We all know he loved both women and wine,
But his heart it was right, I am sure;
Though he lived like a prince in his palace so fine,
Yet he never went back on the poor.

Refrain:—If a man was in trouble, Fisk helped him along,
To drive the grim wolf from the door;
He strove to do right, though he may have done wrong,
But he never went back on the poor.

3 Jim Fisk was a man wore his heart on his sleeve,
No matter what people might say;
And he did all his deeds, both the good and the bad,
In the broad open light of the day.
With his grand six-in-hand, on the beach at Long Branch,
He cut a big dash to be sure;
But Chicago's great fire showed the world that Jim Fisk,
With his wealth, still remembered the poor.

Refrain:—When the telegram came that the homeless that night
Were starving to death slow but sure,
His lightning express manned by noble Jim Fisk
Flew to feed all the hungry and poor.

4 Now what do you think of the trial of Stokes,
Who murdered this friend of the poor?
When such men get free, is there anyone safe
To step outside their own door?
Is there one law for the poor and one for the rich?
It seems so, at least so I say;
If they hang up the poor, why surely the rich
Ought to swing up the very same way.

Refrain:—Don't show any favor to friend or to foe;
The beggar or prince at your door.
The big millionaire you must hang up, also,
But never go back on the poor.

JESSE JAMES

There is only one American bandit who is classical, who is to this country what Robin Hood or Dick Turpin is to England, whose exploits are so close to the mythical and apocryphal that to get a true picture of him we must read a stern inquiry such as Robertus Love's book, "The Rise and Fall of Jesse James." For the uninformed it should be stated that Jesse was living in St. Joseph, Missouri, under the name of Howard, when, unarmed, he was shot in the back of the head, and killed, by his supposed young friend, Robert Ford.

Arr. M. L.

It was on a Wednesday night, the moon was shining bright, They robbed the Glendale train, And the

peo-ple they did say, for man-y miles a-way, 'Twas the out-laws Frank and Jes-se James.

REFRAIN

Jes-se had a wife to mourn all her life, The chil-dren they are brave. 'Twas a

dirt - y lit - tle cow-ard   shot Mis-ter How-ard, And laid Jes-se James in his grave.

1 It was on a Wednesday night, the moon was shining bright,
    They robbed the Glendale train.
  And the people they did say, for many miles away,
    'Twas the outlaws Frank and Jesse James.

Refrain—Jesse had a wife to mourn all her life,
      The children they are brave.
    'Twas a dirty little coward shot Mister Howard,
      And laid Jesse James in his grave.

2 It was Robert Ford, the dirty little coward,
    I wonder how he does feel,
  For he ate of Jesse's bread and he slept in Jesse's bed,
    Then he laid Jesse James in his grave.—*Refrain*

3 It was his brother Frank that robbed the Gallatin bank,
    And carried the money from the town.
  It was in this very place that they had a little race,
    For they shot Captain Sheets to the ground.—*Refrain*

4 They went to the crossing not very far from there,
    And there they did the same;
  And the agent on his knees he delivered up the keys
    To the outlaws Frank and Jesse James.—*Refrain*

5 It was on a Saturday night, Jesse was at home
    Talking to his family brave,
  When the thief and the coward, little Robert Ford,
    Laid Jesse James in his grave.—*Refrain*

6 How people held their breath when they heard of Jesse's death,
    And wondered how he ever came to die.
  'Twas one of the gang, dirty Robert Ford,
    That shot Jesse James on the sly.—*Refrain*

7 Jesse went to his rest with his hand on his breast.
    The devil will be upon his knee.
  He was born one day in the county of Clay,
    And came from a solitary race.—*Refrain*

SAM BASS

"If a man knows any secrets he should die and go to hell with them in him," said Sam Bass as he lay bleeding from bullet wounds, and Texas Rangers and officers of the law asked him who were his partners. He and three of his boys, all handy with their six-shooters, on July 20, 1878, were in Round Rock, Texas, loafing sort of careless in a cigar store next to a bank they had their eye on to rob. Officers of the law, who had been tipped off by the squealer Murphy, spoke to Sam and his boys asking who they were, where they came from, how they made their living, and other questions often asked of strangers by men wearing stars and badges. Shooting began. One officer dropped dead. So did Seaborn Barnes, "right bower to Sam Bass." Sam got away, was found in woods near by next day, and died of his wounds on the day after that; it was his 27th birthday anniversary. In the woods, knowing he couldn't live, he gave Frank Jackson his horse and told him to make a get-away, though Jackson begged to stay and fight. Like other bandits of legend and fame Sam Bass was good to the poor. "He would give a poor woman a twenty-dollar gold piece for a dinner and take no change," wrote W. P. Webb in No. 3 of the Texas Folk Lore Society publications. "He paid farmers well for the horses he took from them, though sometimes he did not have time to see the farmer. . . . Sam Bass relics are scattered over the country, everywhere. His belt with some cartridges in it is in the library of the University of Texas. A carpenter at Snyder has a horseshoe from Bass's best race horse nailed to the top of his tool chest. Near Belton are some live oak trees that Bass is said to have shot his initials in while riding at full speed. Horns of steers supposed to have been killed by Bass sell over the country at fancy prices. In Montague County, there is a legend of $30,000 of loot buried by Sam Bass. Again, he is supposed to have left treasure in the Llano country. At McNeill, near Austin, there is a cave in which Sam Bass hid when he was in retirement. There he kept his horses and from there made his forays". . . . Legend wrote an epitaph on his monument which is not there: Would That He Were Good as He was Brave. Near Sam's pretentious monument, mutilated by souvenir collectors, is a rough sandstone memorial to Seaborn Barnes, with the inscription: He Was Right Bower to Sam Bass. Of this, Webb, a Texan, commented, "It is written in language Bass would have loved; it has a certain impertinence to law abiding people in the nearby graves, a certain pride in the leader at whose heels Barnes died. The spirit of the person who wrote the seven words of that epitaph is the spirit that has created the legend of Sam Bass in Texas." And, of course, some such spirit has kept the biographic Sam Bass ballad alive and going these many years since he met his doom at Round Rock.

Arr. A. G. W.

Sam Bass was born in In-di-an - a,— it was his na-tive home, And at the age of

422

gliss.

sev - en - teen young Sam be - gan to roam. Sam first came out to Tex - as a

cow - boy for to be, A kind - er - heart - ed fel - low you sel - dom ev - er see.

1 Sam Bass was born in Indiana, it was his native home,
   And at the age of seventeen young Sam began to roam.
   Sam first came out to Texas a cowboy for to be,
   A kinder-hearted fellow you seldom ever see.

2 Sam used to deal in race stock, one called the Denton mare,
   He matched her in scrub races, and took her to the fair.
   Sam used to coin the money and spent it just as free,
   He always drank good whiskey wherever he might be.

3 Sam left the Collins ranch in the merry month of May
   With a herd of Texas cattle the Black Hills for to see,
   Sold out in Custer City and then got on a spree,
   A harder set of cowboys you seldom ever see.

4 On their way back to Texas they robbed the U. P. train,
   And then split up in couples and started out again.
   Joe Collins and his partner were overtaken soon,
   With all their hard-earned money they had to meet their doom.

5 Sam made it back to Texas all right side up with care;
   Rode into the town of Denton with all his friends to share.
   Sam's life was short in Texas; three robberies did he do,
   He robbed all the passenger, mail, and express cars too.

6 Sam had four companions—four bold and daring lads—
   They were Richardson, Jackson, Joe Collins, and Old Dad;
   Four more bold and daring cowboys the rangers never knew,
   They whipped the Texas rangers and ran the boys in blue.

7 Sam had another companion, called Arkansas for short,
   Was shot by a Texas ranger by the name of Thomas Floyd;
   O, Tom is a big six-footer and thinks he's mighty fly,
   But I can tell you his racket,— he's a deadbeat on the sly.

8 Jim Murphy was arrested, and then released on bail;
   He jumped his bond at Tyler and then took the train for Terrell;
   But Mayor Jones had posted Jim and that was all a stall,
   'Twas only a plan to capture Sam before the coming of fall.

9 Sam met his fate at Round Rock, July the twenty-first,
   They pierced poor Sam with rifle balls and emptied out his purse.
   Poor Sam he is a corpse and six foot under clay,
   And Jackson's in the bushes trying to get away.

10 Jim had borrowed Sam's good gold and didn't want to pay,
   The only shot he saw was to give poor Sam away.
   He sold out Sam and Barnes and left their friends to mourn,—
   O what a scorching Jim will get when Gabriel blows his horn.

11 And so he sold out Sam and Barnes and left their friends to mourn,
   O what a scorching Jim will get when Gabriel blows his horn.
   Perhaps he's got to heaven, there's none of us can say,
   But if I'm right in my surmise he's gone the other way.

FIVE WARS

THE HUNTERS OF KENTUCKY or HALF HORSE
AND HALF ALLIGATOR

These verses done in the style of polite poetry were first sung to the air of Miss Baily. They were written by Samuel Woodworth, and published in 1826 by James M. Campbell in a book, Melodies, Duets, Trios, Songs, and Ballads. Under the title of Hunters of Kentucky, or Half Horse and Half Alligator, the song was published in Boston as a broadside. In singing, the pronunciation "Kaintucky" seems to be preferred to that of "Kentucky" among those who have perpetuated the song. It has been heard among the mountaineers and cowboys; Franz Rickaby found it among lumberjacks, and the air here is from the singing of George M. Hankins of Gordon, Wisconsin, as notated by Rickaby. The text is from a broadside in the Congressional Library, Washington, D. C.

Arr. A. G. W.

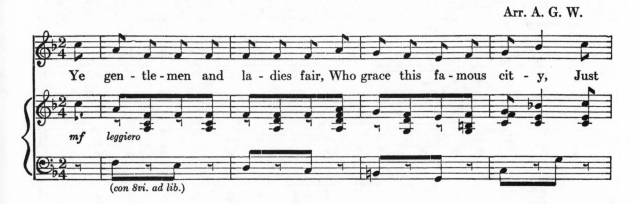

Ye gen-tle-men and la-dies fair, Who grace this fa-mous cit-y, Just

428

1 Ye gentlemen and ladies fair,
   Who grace this famous city,
Just listen if you've time to spare,
   While I rehearse a ditty;
And for the opportunity
   Conceive yourselves quite lucky,
For 'tis not often that you see
   A hunter from Kentucky.
Oh Kentucky, the hunters of Kentucky!
Oh Kentucky, the hunters of Kentucky!

2 We are a hardy, free-born race,
   Each man to fear a stranger;
Whate'er the game we join in chase,
   Despoiling time and danger,
And if a daring foe annoys,
   Whate'er his strength and forces,
We'll show him that Kentucky boys
   Are alligator horses.
         Oh Kentucky, &c.

3 I s'pose you've read it in the prints,
   How Packenham attempted
To make old Hickory Jackson wince,
   But soon his scheme repented;
For we, with rifles ready cock'd,
   Thought such occasion lucky,
And soon around the gen'ral flock'd
   The hunters of Kentucky.
         Oh Kentucky, &c.

4 You've heard, I s'pose how New-Orleans
   Is fam'd for wealth and beauty,
There's girls of ev'ry hue it seems,
   From snowy white to sooty.
So Packenham he made his brags,
   If he in fight was lucky,
He'd have their girls and cotton bags,
   In spite of old Kentucky.
         Oh Kentucky, &c.

5 But Jackson he was wide awake,
   And was not scar'd at trifles,
For well he knew what aim we take
   With our Kentucky rifles.
So he led us down to Cypress swamp,
   The ground was low and mucky,
There stood John Bull in martial pomp
   And here was old Kentucky.
Oh Kentucky, the hunters of Kentucky !
Oh Kentucky, the hunters of Kentucky !

6 A bank was rais'd to hide our breasts,
   Not that we thought of dying,
But that we always like to rest,
   Unless the game is flying.
Behind it stood our little force,
   None wished it to be greater,
For ev'ry man was half a horse,
   And half an alligator.
         Oh Kentucky, &c.

7 They did not let our patience tire,
   Before they show'd their faces;
We did not choose to waste our fire,
   So snugly kept our places.
But when so near we saw them wink,
   We thought it time to stop 'em,
And 'twould have done you good I think,
   To see Kentuckians drop 'em.
         Oh Kentucky, &c.

8 They found, at last, 'twas vain to fight,
   Where *lead* was all the *booty*,
And so they wisely took to flight,
   And left *us* all our *beauty*.
And now, if danger e'er annoys,
   Remember what our trade is,
Just send for us Kentucky boys,
   And we'll protect ye, ladies.
         Oh Kentucky, &c.

JACKSON

On his walking trip from the Great Lakes to the Great Plains Franz Rickaby met this survivor of the years of the War with Mexico.

Arr. A. G. W.

Jack-son is on sea,— Jack-son is on shore,— Jack-son's gone to Mex-i-co to fight the bat-tles o'er.— "Wel-come home, my Jack - son, oh, wel-come home," said she,— Last night my daught-er Ma-ry lay dream-ing of thee.—

1 Jackson is on sea, Jackson is on shore,
  Jackson's gone to Mexico to fight the battles o'er.
  "Welcome home, my Jackson, oh welcome home," said she,
  Last night my daughter Mary lay dreaming of thee.

430

2 "What news, Jackson?" "Very poor," says he.
"I lost all my money while crossing the sea.
Go bring your daughter Mary and get her down by me,
We'll drown our melancholy and married we will be."

3 "Oh Mary's not at home, Jack, nor has not been to-day;
And if she was at home, Jack, she would not let you stay.
For Mary's very, very rich and you are very poor,
And if she was at home, Jack, she'd show you the door."

4 Jackson bein' drowsy hung down his head,
He called for a candle to light him off to bed.
The beds are full of strangers, and have been so this week—
And now for your lodging, poor Jack, you'll have to seek.

5 Jack looked upon the strangers, upon them one and all,
He looked upon the landlady and in reckoning he did call.
Twenty shillings of the new and twenty of the old.
With this Jack pulled out his two hands full of gold.

6 The sight of the money made the old woman rue:
"Mary is at home, Jack, and she'll return to you.
I hope you're not in earnest, for I only spoke in jest.
Without any exception she loves you the best."

7 Mary came downstairs with a smiling face,
First a sweet kiss, then a fond embrace:
"Oh, welcome home, my Jackson, oh welcome home, my dear.
The big beds are empty and you shall lie there."

8 "Before I'd lie within your beds I'd lie within the street,
For when I had no money, my lodging I must seek.
But now I've plenty money I'll make the tavern hurl,
A bottle of good brandy and on each arm a girl."

POOR KITTY POPCORN

"A tragic little ballad of the Civil War which we children cried over many times. I recall it only in fragments, the story of a cat that joined a regiment of soldiers marching south. She perished in the snow on the grave of the one to whom she had become most attached." Thus the history of this verse from Neeta Marquis who as a girl grew up in Tennessee.

Poor Kitty Popcorn, buried in a snow drift now!
Never more we'll hear the music of her gladsome song,
"Me-o-o-o-w!"
Oh, she had a happy home beneath the Southern sky,
But she packed her goods and left it when our troops came by,
And she fell into the column with a low, glad cry,
"Me-o-o-w!"

THERE WAS AN OLD SOLDIER

A leading favorite of the Grand Army of the Republic, one of the healthiest survivors of the contest between the Blue and the Gray, and a widely known piece of American folk lore.

Arr. R. C.

O there was an old sol-dier and he had a wood-en leg, He had no to-bac-co but to-bac-co he could beg. An-oth-er old sol-dier, as sly as a fox, He al-ways had to-bac-co in his

old to - bac - co box.

1 O there was an old soldier and he had a wooden leg,
He had no tobacco but tobacco he could beg.
Another old soldier as sly as a fox,
He always had tobacco in his old tobacco box.

2 Said the one old soldier, "Won't you give me a chew?"
Said the other old soldier, "I'll be hanged if I do,
Save up your pennies and put away your rocks,
And you'll always have tobacco in your old tobacco box."

3 Well, the one old soldier was a feelin' very bad,
He says, "I'll get even, I will, begad!"
He goes to a corner, takes a rifle from his peg,
And stabs the other soldier with a splinter from his leg.

4 There was an old hen and she had a wooden foot,
And she made her nest by a mulberry root,
And she laid more eggs than any hen on the farm;
And another wooden foot wouldn't do her any harm.

433

A FILIPINO HOMBRE

Soldiers and sailors of conquering races and nations, in all times, it seems, have had songs kidding the language, manners, and customs, of the invaded, subjugated, and pacified races and nations. . . . An old song with a Spanish tune opens with the lines, "I am a gay cavalierio, on my way to Rio De Janierio." Verses going to that tune arose out of the Spanish-American War and the campaign in the Philippine Islands, and they constitute the song called A Filipino Hombre or The Philippine Family. The Book of Navy Songs says, "It was composed and first sung by the late Captain Lyman A. Cotten, U. S. N., about 1900, when Navy, Army and Marine Corps were busy 'pacifying' the newly acquired Philippines." . . . . It is a rough, gay fandango. All present may join in a shouted repeat of the last word of each verse.

Arr. A. G. W.

1 There was once a Filipino hombre
  Who ate rice pescado y legumbre.
  His trousers were wide, and his shirt hung out-
  And this, I may say, was costumbre.   [side,

2 He lived in a nipa bahay
  Which served as a stable and sty;
  He slept on a mat with the dogs and the cat
  And the rest of the family near by.

3 His daddy, un buen' Filipino
  Who never mixed tubig with bino,
  Said, "I am no insurrecto—no got gun or bolo,"
  Yet used both to kill a vecino.

4 His mujer once kept a tienda
  Underneath a large stone hacienda;
  She chewed buyo and sold for jawbone and gold
  To soldades who said, "No intienda."

5 Of ninos he had dos or tres,
  Good types of the Tagalo race;
  In dry or wet weather, in the altogether,
  They'd romp and they'd race and they'd chase.

6 Su hermana fue lavandera,
  And slapped clothes in fuerte manera
  On a rock in a stream where the carabaos dream,
  Which gave them a perfume lijera.

7 His brother, who was a cochero,
  Buscare in Manila dinero;
  His prices were high when a cop was near by
  To help scare the poor pasajero.

8 He once owned a bulic manoc
  With a haughty, valorous look
  Which lost him a name, y mil pesos tambien,
  So he changed to monte for luck.

9 When his pueblo last had a fiesta
  His family tried to digest a
  Mule that had died of glanders inside—
  And now his familia no esta.

THE SERGEANT, HE IS THE WORST OF ALL

The buck private's private opinion publicly expressed, and that ain't all.

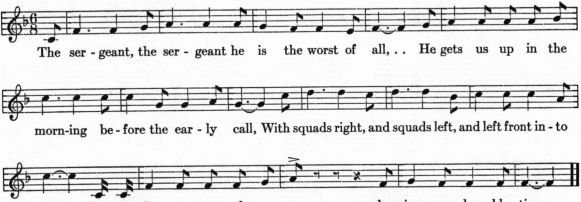

The ser-geant, the ser-geant he is the worst of all, .. He gets us up in the morn-ing be-fore the ear-ly call, With squads right, and squads left, and left front in-to line; Then the slim-y son of a gun, he gives us dou-ble time.

The sergeant, the sergeant he is the worst of all,
He gets us up in the morning before the early call,
With squads right, and squads left, and left front into line;
Then the slimy son of a gun, he gives us double time.

WRAP ME UP IN MY TARPAULIN JACKET

and

THE HANDSOME YOUNG AIRMAN

One of several in the R. W. Gordon collection, this version (A) is from Frank Haworth of the British Club, Havana, Cuba, while (B) is from Abbe Niles who comments on how landlubber songs often are in active duty on the high seas and vice versa. "Any living tune is a jack of all trades. This variant of Tarpaulin Jacket ten years ago on the flying fields was current among men who had never heard its original."

Arr. A. G. W.

Moderato

Wrap me up in my tar - pau - lin jack - et . . . . . And say a poor buff- er lies

low, lies low; And six stal-wart lanc - ers shall car-ry me . . . . With steps mourn-ful,

sol-emn, and slow . . . . . . I know I shan't get to Heav-en, ...

.... And I don't want to go ... be - low - ow - ow Oh, ain't there some

place in be - tween them .... Where this poor old buff-er can go? .....

A

Wrap me up in my tarpaulin jacket
And say a poor buffer lies low, lies low;
And six stalwart lancers shall carry me
With steps mournful, solemn, and slow.
I know I shan't get to Heaven,
And I don't want to go below-ow-ow—
Oh, ain't there some place in between them
Where this poor buffer can go?

B

A handsome young airman lay dying,
And as on the airdrome he lay,
To mechanics who 'round him came sighing
These last parting words he did say:
"Take the cylinders out of my kidneys,
The connecting rods out of my brain,
The crank-shaft out of my backbone,
And assemble the engine again."

437

A WAR BIRD'S BURLESQUE

In that revealing and vivid diary of an unknown aviator "War Birds," we learn of a flyer whose father was a cotton mill owner and, as the diarist tells us, "There was a bomb raid on last night and the dugout was stuffy so he and I went out and crawled under a box car on the siding. It's about as good shelter as you can get. We got to talking about home. . . I asked him what he wanted to do. He said he wanted to write but his father is determined to make a horny-handed hardboiled superintendent out of him. He's all the time scribbling now. He's always stopping something important to jot down a plot, as he calls it, for future reference. He's got a brief case full of them already,— plays, short stories, poems, sketches or what have you. He's tried to read me some of them several times." He lost one eye, was wounded, battered, made all sacrifices asked. In an interlude of the program of hell and death, he had an affair "with a very charming young lady who more or less owed allegiance to a big diplomat. We were all kidding him about it one night and after listening awhile he retired and penned a poem on the subject.". . . Nine of the verses are presented here with the melody given them by Chicago overseas service men, Paul Boston and John Locke.

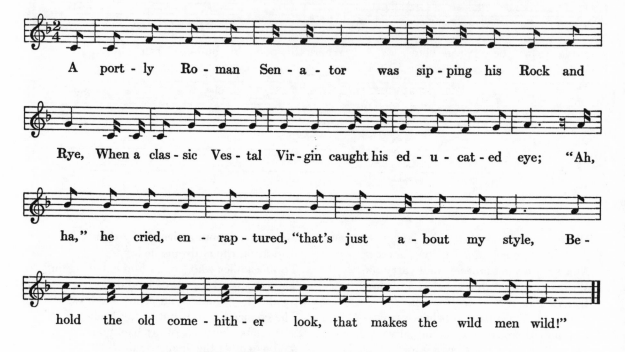

1 A portly Roman Senator was sipping his Rock and Rye,
   When a classic Vestal Virgin caught his educated eye;
   "Ah, ha," he cried enraptured, "that's just about my style,
   Behold the old come-hither look, that makes the wild men wild."

2 The old boy was no novice, for he'd served his time in Gaul,
   And he saw she was a chicken and the flapper pose a stall,
   So he flashed a roll of talents and she flashed him back a smile,
   And she shrugged her architecture in a manner to beguile.

3 But he had to go to Naples, where some rents were overdue,
   While she lingered by the Tiber, complaining of the flu.
   And no great time elapsed ere the wise ones slyly winked,
   And they whispered "Habeas Corpus," as their golden goblets clinked.

4 For it was whispered at the banquets and told o'er games of cards,
   That a certain dashing Shavetail of Julius Caesar's Guards,
   Was bringing home the bacon, had a latchkey to the flat,
   Had soused himself in pre-war stock and was staging a terrible bat.

5 He broke the records back to Rome and arrived with a terrible shout,
   But the Shavetail heard him on the stairs and escaped by the gutter spout,
   The Senator surveyed his flat, with bottles everywhere,
   And picked up some scattered plumage and bits of odd tinware.

6 The lady wept in anguish, but he only mocked her cries,
   "I gave you rings for your fingers, now they're beneath your eyes."
   The sweet young thing was cagy, she'd expected his return,
   And she explained, "Semper fidelis, won't you ever learn!

7 "Dear Caesar came to see me, said Pompey's getting hot,
   And the Legion's drilling badly and the Navy's gone to pot:
   So to stimulate recruiting, I've been flirting with this Wop."
   And she slipped her toga's shoulder strap, and displayed a fancy clock.

8 His thoughts went back to Britain, and he stroked a scarred chin,
   Where an angry Celtic husband had expressed his deep chagrin.
   He recalled how his upright figure and the polish his armor bore,
   Had intrigued the Spanish maidens on that temperamental shore.

9 And his anger soon abating, he replaced the truant strap,
   And she said, "Carpemus diem," as he gave her cheek a slap;
   He patted the tousled curly locks, that on his shoulder lay,
   And thought, "She's not hors de combat, 'tis part of an Officer's Pay."

HINKY DINKY, PARLEE-VOO

Among the American Expeditionary Forces in Europe during the world war this was a high spot favorite, sung more often, perhaps, and with more verses, than any other song. . . . It resembles an English pre-war song, and also an old American ditty, Snappoo Snappoo.

Arr. A. G. W.

440

HINKY DINKY, PARLEE-VOO!

Hin - ky din - ky, Par - - lee - - voo.............

1 Two German officers crossed the Rhine, parlee-voo,
Two German officers crossed the Rhine, parlee-voo,
Two German officers crossed the Rhine
To kiss the women and drink the wine, hinky dinky, parlee-voo.

2 "Oh farmer, have you a daughter fair, parlee-voo,
Oh farmer, have you a daughter fair, parlee-voo,
Oh farmer, have you a daughter fair
Who can wash a soldier's underwear, hinky dinky, parlee-voo.

3 Mademoiselle from Armentieres, parlee-voo,
Mademoiselle from Armentieres, parlee-voo,
Mademoiselle from Armentieres
She ain't even heard of underwear, hinky dinky, parlee-voo.

4 Mademoiselle from Armentieres, parlee-voo,
Mademoiselle from Armentieres, parlee-voo,
If you never wash your underwear
You'll never get the Croix de Guerre, hinky dinky, parlee-voo.

5 Many and many a married man, parlee-voo,
Many and many a married man, parlee-voo,
Many and many a married man
Wants to go back to France again, hinky dinky, parlee-voo.

6 The captain he's carrying the pack, parlee-voo,
The captain he's carrying the pack, parlee-voo,
The captain he's carrying the pack,
Hope to Lord it breaks his back, hinky dinky, parlee-voo.

7 The officers get all the steak, parlee-voo,
The officers get all the steak, parlee-voo,
The officers get all the steak,
And all we get is the belly-ache, hinky dinky, parlee-voo.

441

8 The M. P.s say they won the war, parlee-voo,
The M. P.s say they won the war, parlee-voo,
The M. P.s say they won the war
Standing on guard at a cafe door, hinky dinky, parlee-voo.

9 The little marine in love with his nurse, parlee-voo.
The little marine in love with his nurse, parlee-voo,
The little marine in love with his nurse,
He's taken her now for better or worse, hinky dinky, parlee-voo.

10 Mademoiselle all dressed in white, parlee-voo,
Mademoiselle all dressed in blue, parlee-voo,
Mademoiselle all dressed in black,
'Cause her little marine he didn't come back, hinky dinky, parlee-voo.

11 You might forget the gas and shell, parlee-voo,
You might forget the gas and shell, parlee-voo,
You might forget the gas and shell,
You'll never forget the mademoiselle, hinky dinky, parlee-voo.

WHERE THEY WERE

This is a little tough on the Brass Hats but they are used to it. . . . The text is from Harold and Verner Johnson of New York City.

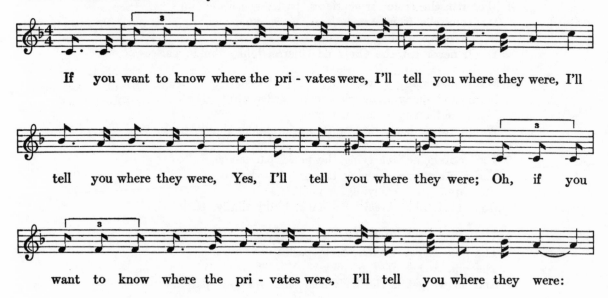

If you want to know where the pri - vates were, I'll tell you where they were, I'll tell you where they were, Yes, I'll tell you where they were; Oh, if you want to know where the pri - vates were, I'll tell you where they were:

WHERE THEY WERE

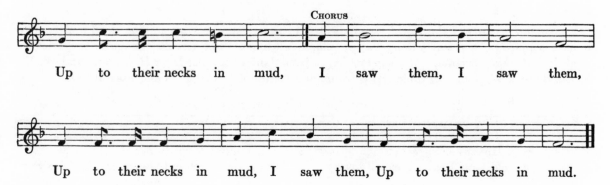

CHORUS

Up to their necks in mud, I saw them, I saw them,

Up to their necks in mud, I saw them, Up to their necks in mud.

1 If you want to know where the privates were,
I'll tell you where they were,
I'll tell you where they were,
Yes, I'll tell you where they were;
Oh, if you want to know where the privates were,
I'll tell you where they were:
    Up to their necks in mud,
      I saw them, I saw them,
    Up to their necks in mud, I saw them
      Up to their necks in mud.

2 If you want to know where the sergeants were,
I'll tell you where they were,
I'll tell you where they were,
Yes, I'll tell you where they were;
Oh, if you want to know where the sergeants
I'll tell you where they were: [were,
    Clipping the old barbed-wire,
     . I saw them, I saw them,
    Clipping the old barbed-wire, I saw them
      Clipping the old barbed-wire.

3 If you want to know where the captains were,
I'll tell you where they were,
I'll tell you where they were,
Yes, I'll tell you where they were;
Oh, if you want to know where the captains were,
I'll tell you where they were:
    Drinking the privates' rum,
      I saw them, I saw them,
    Drinking the privates' rum, I saw them
      Drinking the privates' rum.

4 If you want to know where the officers were,
I'll tell you where they were,
I'll tell you where they were,
Yes, I'll tell you where they were;
Oh, if you want to know where the officers were,
I'll tell you where they were:
    Down in their deep dugout,
      I saw them, I saw them,
    Down in their deep dugout, I saw them
      Down in their deep dugout.

5 And if you want to know where the generals were,
    I'll tell you where they were,
I'll tell you where they were,
    Yes, I'll tell you where they were;
Oh, if you want to know where the generals were,
    I'll tell you where they were:
        Back in gay Paree,
          I saw them, I saw them,
        Back in gay Paree, I saw them
        Back in gay Paree.

THE HEARSE SONG

Casualty records of the world war indicated in round numbers ten million dead and twenty million crippled. The Hearse Song was popular in all branches of service, though in the aviation corps it had more variants. The version (A) is from James Stevens, Irma H. Thrane and W. W. Woodbridge of Washington, while (B) is from Jake Zeitlin of Los Angeles and Fort Worth.

The old Grey Hearse goes roll-ing by, You don't know wheth-er to laugh or cry, For you

know some day it-'ll get you too, And the hearse's next load may con-sist of—you.

A

1 The old Grey Hearse goes rolling by,
 You don't know whether to laugh or cry;
 For you know some day it'll get you too,
 And the hearse's next load may consist of—you.

2 They'll take you out and they'll lower you down,
 While men with shovels stand all a-round;
 They'll throw in dirt and they'll throw in rocks,
 And they won't give a dam-m-m if they break the box.

3 The worms crawl in and the worms crawl out,
 They crawl all over your chin and mouth,
 They invite their friends and their friends' friends too,
 And you look like hell when they're—through—with you.

B

1 Did you ever think as the hearse rolls by
 That some of these days you must surely die?
 They'll take you away in a big black hack,
 They'll take you away but won't bring you back.

2 The men with shovels stand all around.
 They shovel you into that cold, wet ground.
 They shovel in dirt and they throw in rocks.
 They don't give a dam if they break the box.

3 And your eyes drop out and your teeth fall in
 And the worms crawl over your mouth and chin;
 And the worms crawl out and the worms crawl in
 And your limbs drop off of you limb by limb.

444

LOVELY PEOPLE

Things in a picture must not have the appearance of being brought together by chance or for a purpose, but must have a necessary and inevitable connection.

I desire that the creations which I depict should have the air of being dedicated to their situation, so that one could not imagine that they would dream of being anything else than what they are. A work of art ought to be all one piece, and the men and things in it should always be there for a reason.

It were better that the things weakly said should not be said at all, because in the former case they are only, as it were, deflowered and spoiled.

Beauty does not consist so much in the things represented, as in the *need* one has of expressing them; and this need it is which creates the degree of force with which one acquits oneself of the work. One may say that everything is beautiful provided the thing turns up in its own proper time and in its own place; and contrariwise, that nothing can be beautiful arriving inappropriately

Let Apollo *be Apollo*, and Socrates Socrates.

Which is more beautiful, a straight tree or a crooked tree?

Whichever is most in place.

This then is my conclusion: The beautiful is that which is in place.

JEAN FRANÇOIS MILLET.

MAN GOIN' ROUN'

At first glance this may seem a whimsical reference to the census taker going from door to door and taking the names of all people without regard to sex, color, race, or previous condition of servitude. Then we come to the line, "an' he leave my heart in pain," and we know it is a more august and austere Enumerator than any employed in the transient and temporal governments of man. Each verse deals with a relative, mother, father, sister, brother, or other dear one, checked off from the list of the living. A true instance of the poetry "to be overheard rather than heard," it keeps for those of long acquaintance with it, an overtone of a reverie on the riddles of death and the frail permits by which any one generation walks before the mirrors of life. I heard it in Columbia, South Carolina, sung for a group including Julia Peterkin, Danny and Isadora Bennett Read, and Prof. and Mrs. Taylor in whose family Rebecca, the singer, was a servant since a child. Rebecca was far in years but had a young singing heart and a clear singing voice. She was bashful, hesitant, at times, about going on with the songs, giving a silvery chuckle with a sidewise turn of her head as she took up the lines of a new song. There were moments when I felt about this homely, rather slightly built, black woman, the strength of earth and the patience of large, slow-changing landscapes.

Arr. H. F.

There's a man go-in' roun' tak-in' names, There's a man go-in' roun' tak-in' names, An' he took my mother' name, An' he leave my heart in pain, There's a man go-in' roun' takin' names.

1 There's a man goin' roun' takin' names,
There's a man goin' roun' takin' names,
An' he took my mother' name,
An' he leave my heart in pain,
There's a man goin' roun' takin' names.

2 There's a man goin' roun' takin' names,
There's a man goin' roun' takin' names,
An' he took my father' name,
An' he leave my heart in pain,
There's a man goin' roun' takin' names.

3, 4, etc.   Sister, brother, etc.

447

ALL NIGHT LONG

This is the second of a trilogy from Rebecca Taylor. It comes speaking in parables joined
to an air that is stately even though simple.

Arr. H. F.

Paul and Si - las, bound in jail, All...... night long..... One foh to sing an' de
oth-ah foh to pray, All night long....... One foh to sing an' de oth-ah foh to pray,
All........ night long. Do, Lawd, de - lib - bah po' me!...............

2 Straight up to heaven, straight right back,
All night long.
'Tain' but de one train on dis track,
All night long.
'Tain' but de one train on dis track,
All night long.
Do, Lawd, delibbah po' me!

3 Nebah seen de like since I ben born,
All night long.
People keep comin' an' de train done gone,
All night long.
People keep comin' an' de train done gone,
All night long.
Do, Lawd, delibbah po' me!

ZEK'L WEEP

This is the third number of the majestic trilogy from Rebecca Taylor.

Arr. H. F.

Zek - 'l weep, Zek - 'l mo'n, Flesh come a-creep-in' off o' Zek - 'l bones;

Church, I know you go'n to miss me When I'm gone................ When I'm

gone, gone, gone, When I'm gone to come no mo',

Church, I know you go'n to miss me When I'm gone.................

1 Zek'l weep, Zek'l mo'n,
 Flesh come a-creepin' off o' Zek'l bones;
 Church, I know you go'n to miss me
  When I'm gone.
 When I'm gone, gone, gone,
 When I'm gone to come no mo',
 Church, I know you go'n to miss me
  When I'm gone.

2 Star in the east, star in the west,
 Wish that star was in my breast,
 Church, I know you go'n to miss me
  When I'm gone.
 When I'm gone, gone, gone,
 When I'm gone to come no mo',
 Church, I know you go'n to miss me
  When I'm gone.

3 Hush, little baby, don' you cry,
 Know that yo' mother done born to die,
 Chillun, I know you go'n to miss me
  When I'm gone.
 When I'm gone, gone, gone,
 When I'm gone to come no mo',
 Chillun, I know you go'n to miss me
  When I'm gone.

I KNOW MOONLIGHT

An arrangement of lines from a slave day spiritual.

Arr. H. F.

1 I know moonlight,
  I know starlight,
  I lay this body down.

2 I walk in the moonlight,
  I walk in the starlight,
  I lay this body down.

3 I go to judgment
  In the evenin' of the day,
  When I lay this body down.

451

BLIND MAN LAY BESIDE THE WAY

A brief story . . . compact in diction . . . useless to add or subtract words.

Arr. A. G. W.

2 A man he died, was crucified,
  They hung a thief on either side;
  One lifted up his voice and cried:
  "O Lord, won't you help-a me!
  O Lord, won't you help-a me!"

3 A blind man lay by the way and cried,
  "O Lord, won't you help-a me."
  And the thief cried out before he died,
  "O Lord, won't you help-a me!
  O Lord, won't you help-a me!"

BY'M BY

The stealth and mystery of the coming out of the stars one by one on the night sky . . . a
fragment of a spiritual heard in Texas in the early 1880's by Charley Thorpe of Santa Fe.

Arr. M. L.

By'm by, by'm by, Stahs shin-in', Num-bah, num-bah one, Num-bah two, num-bah three, Good Lawd, by'm by, by'm by, Good Lawd, by'm by.

By'm by, by'm by,
Stahs shinin',
Numbah, numbah one,
Numbah two, numbah three,
Good Lawd, by'm by, by'm by,
Good Lawd, by'm by.

GO TO SLEEPY

A traditional lullaby in the City of Athens, State of Georgia, as written, words, air, and harmonization by Maybelle Stith of that city and state. She commented, "In the left hand I tried to get the effect of a cradle rocking. It was rather difficult to indicate the time as it varies with the mood of the singer."

Arr. M. S.

Go to sleep - y, lit - tle ba - by, 'Fo' de boo-ger man ketch you.

When you wake you'll have a piece of cake And a whole lot of lit - tle hors - es.

When you wake you shall have a cake, coach and four lit - tle pon - ies.

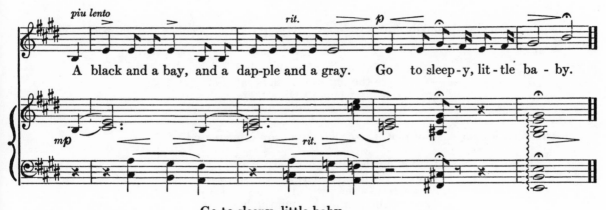

A black and a bay, and a dap-ple and a gray. Go to sleep-y, lit-tle ba - by.

Go to sleepy, little baby,
'Fo' de booger man ketch you.
When you wake you'll have a piece of cake
And a whole lot of little horses.
Go to sleepy, little baby,
'Fo' de booger man ketch you.
When you wake you shall have a cake,
Coach and four little ponies,
A black and a bay, and a dapple and a gray.
Go to sleepy, little baby.

JUNGLE MAMMY SONG

Margaret Johnson of Augusta, Georgia, heard her mother sing this, year on year, as the mother had learned it from the singing, year on year, of a negro woman who comforted children with it. The source of its language may be French, Creole, Cherokee, or mixed. The syllables are easy for singing; so is the tune. It may be, as provisionally titled, a Jungle Mammy Song, in the sense that all mothers are primitive and earthy even though civilized and celestial.

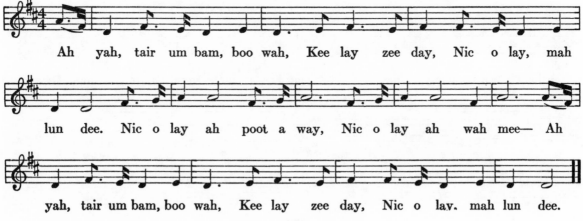

Ah yah, tair um bam, boo wah, Kee lay zee day, Nic o lay, mah

lun dee. Nic o lay ah poot a way, Nic o lay ah wah mee— Ah

yah, tair um bam, boo wah, Kee lay zee day, Nic o lay. mah lun dee.

TEN THOUSAND MILES AWAY FROM HOME

This may be one of the many Po' Boy songs, carrying its own peculiar load of grief. Verse 2 sometimes goes—

> I went down to the railroad
> Where the big six-wheelers ran;
> I saw my woman sitting there
> In the arms of another man.

And occasionally, for the sake of plot, these two verses are interspersed—

> I stood on the street corner;
> It was shortly after dark;
> Along came a man with the woman I love,
> And I stabbed him through the heart.

> "Well, it's please, Mr. Judge, now please, Mr. Judge,
> It's what are you goin' to do with me?"
> He says, "If I find you guilty, dear boy,
> I'm goin' to send you to the penitentiary."

Arr. R. C.

Ten thou-sand miles a - way from home And I don't e-ven know my name, For think-in' a - bout the wom-an I love, Ran a-

way with an-oth-er man..........

2 I went down to the old depot,
  The trains were a-passin' by;
  Looked through the bars, saw the woman I love,
  And I hung my head and cried.

3 Standing on the street corner,
  And the girl I loved passed by;
  She shrugged her shoulder and passed me by,
  And I tucked my head and cried.

MY OLD HAMMAH

The power and restraint of art and genius lurk in the lines and melody of this song from the negro hard rock gangs of Georgia and Alabama. The air is to be freely rendered. It is strictly one with variations, glides, blue notes, as you choose at moments. It relates directly to an older piece known in the mountains as Swannanoa Town. Sharp and Campbell present a fine air and ten verses of the latter in "English Folk Songs from the Southern Appalachians," of which these are four specimen verses:

When you hear my bull-dog barking,
Somebody round, baby, somebody round.

When you hear my pistol firing,
Another man dead, baby, another man dead.

Look for me till your eye runs water,
I'll be at home, baby, I'll be at home.

Don't you remember last December,
The wind blowed cold, baby, the wind blowed cold.

In accompaniment Henry Francis Parks indicates, "The hammer stroke motive should quite predominate."

MY OLD HAMMAH

Arr. H. F. P.

My old ham-mah.... Shin-a like

sil - vah,.... Shin-a like gol',............ Yes, shin-a like gol'.............

1 My old hammah
Shina like silvah,
Shina like gol',
Yes, shina like gol'.

2 Dere ain' no hammah
Ina this old mountain,
Shina like mine,
Yes, shina like mine!

3 This old hammah
Kill my pahtnah,
But it can't kill me,
No, it can't kill me!

4 I ben a-workin',
Ona this hyer railroad,
Fo' long year, boys,
Yes, fo' long year!

5 O next winter
Be so col',
Be so col',
Yes, be so col'!

CHAHCOAL MAN

Once the comment was heard on this, "It is a delicate imprint on a field of silence." . . . An old man selling charcoal used to proclaim himself to the residents of Springfield, Missouri, with this morning cry. . . . I notated it, hazardously, from the singing of a faculty member of the state teachers' college at Greeley, Colorado. She came from Missouri.

Arr. Th. O.

O-o-o-oh, lil' man,
Go get yo' pan;
Tell-a yo' mam
Hyeh come de chahcoal man-n-n-n.
Chahcoal!

459

THE WEAVER

A variant of Foggy Foggy Dew, or I Am A Bachelor, a song that stands against time and weather, tells a short-spoken story and ends with no more to say.

Arr. A. G. W.

Moderato con espressione

I was a bach-e-lor, I lived by my-self, I worked at the weav-er's trade; ...... The on—ly thing I did that was wrong Was to woo a pret-ty maid...... I wooed her in the sum-mer time And in the win-ter, too;...... And

mp Dolce

sostenuto

460

THE WEAVER

all night long I held her in my arms, Just to shield her from the foggy, foggy dew.

1 I was a bachelor, I lived by myself,
   I worked at the weaver's trade;
   The only thing I did that was wrong
   Was to woo a pretty maid.
   I wooed her in the summer-time
   And in the winter, too;
   And all night long I held her in my arms,
   Just to shield her from the foggy, foggy dew.

2 I am a bachelor, I live with my son;
   We work at the weaver's trade;
   And ev'ry single time I look into his eyes
   He reminds me of the fair young maid.
   He reminds me of the winter-time
   And of the summer, too;
   And the many, many times that I held her in my arms,
   Just to shield her from the foggy, foggy dew.

THE COLORADO TRAIL

A hoss wrangler brought a car of ponies to Duluth, Minnesota. The next day, after brave stunt riding, he was laid in a hospital bed with "ruptures on both sides." He told the surgeon Dr. T. L. Chapman, in a soft, forgiving voice, "That was a terribly bad hoss—not only throwed me, but he trompled me." Out of past years this rider had, Dr. Chapman's examination disclosed, "bones of both upper and lower legs broken, fractures of collar bone on both sides, numerous fractures of both arms and wrists, and many scars from lacerations and tramplings, the bones knit any way that God and Nature let them heal." As his strength came back he sang across the hospital ward in a mellowed tenor voice. And they always called for more. One song was The Colorado Trail remembered by Dr. Chapman as here set down.

Arr. A. G. W.

1 Eyes like the morning star,
   Cheek like a rose,
   Laura was a pretty girl,
    God Almighty knows.

Weep, all ye little rains,
   Wail, winds, wail,
   All along, along, along
    The Colorado trail.

I MET HER IN THE GARDEN WHERE THE PRATIES GROW

A quizzical, round-the-corner laughter at trouble that started where the potato blossoms grow. C. W. Loutzenhiser, the old railroad man of Chicago, who as a boy traveled with his father's circus, said he often sang this with an Irish girl, and the both of them used to wonder as the years went by, why they met only this one verse.

Arr. A. G. W.

O, have ye been in love, me boys, And have ye felt the pain? I'd rath-er be in jail, me boys, Than be in love a-gain; O, I met her in the morn-in', And I'll have yez all to know— That I met her in the gar-den Where the pra-ties grow.

O, have ye been in love, me boys,
And have ye felt the pain?
I'd rather be in jail, me boys,
Than be in love again;
O, I met her in the mornin'
And I'll have yez all to know
That I met her in the garden
Where the praties grow.

SOMEBODY

A fugitive little lyric heard by Edwin Ford Piper from the singing of his pioneer mother in the 1880's on a farm near Auburn, Nebraska. . . . At the University of Virginia, a lad from near Lynchburg, Virginia, said he had heard it from old people and it had been sung roundabout that neighborhood a long time.

Arr. E. M.

Some - bod-y's tall and hand-some,......

.... Some - bod-y's brave and true................

Some - bod-y's hair is ver - y fair,

Some - bod-y's eyes are blue.

1 Somebody's tall and handsome,
  Somebody's brave and true.
  Somebody's hair is very fair,
  Somebody's eyes are blue.

2 Somebody comes to see me,
  Somebody came last night.
  Somebody asked me to marry him,
  'Course I said, "All right."

I DON'T WANT TO BE A GAMBLER

1. Oh, I don't want to be a gam-bler, An' I'll tell you the rea-son why:

CHORUS

My Lord sit-tin' in his King-dom, Got his eyes on me, God got his eyes on

me, God got his eyes on me, My Lord sit-tin' in his Kingdom, Got his eyes on me.

2 Oh, I don't want to be a liar,
  An' I'll tell you the reason why: *Chorus.*

3 Oh, I don't want to be a drunkard,
  An' I'll tell you the reason why: *Chorus.*

WHEN POOR MARY CAME WANDERING HOME

This too was heard from Senour at Indiana University on the evening told of in the note to "Who Will Shoe Your Pretty Little Foot?" It is a fragment, a little make-over, from the mawkish popular song, "Mary of the Wild Moor." The mother of Senour sang it often. A wisp of melody, it is, five brief lines as implicative as a Chinese poem.

L. S.

It was on a cold winter's night
When poor Mary came wandering home.
And the watch-dog did howl,
And the village bell did toll,
And the wind blew across the wild moor.

ROAD TO HEAVEN

JESUS, WON'T YOU COME B'M-BY?

One of the lasting creations of the negro of slave days.

Arr. C. F. E.

You ride dat horse, you call him Macadoni; Jesus, won't you come b'm-

by? You ride him in de mornin' And you ride him in de eve-nin'; Jesus, won't you come b'm-

by? De Lord knows de world's gwine to end up, Jesus, won't you come b'm-by? De by?

You ride dat horse,
You call him Macadoni;
Jesus, won't you come b'm-by?
You ride him in de mornin'
And you ride him in de evenin';

Jesus, won't you come b'm-by?
De Lord knows de world's gwine to end up,
Jesus, won't you come b'm-by?
De Lord knows de world's gwine to end up,
Jesus, won't you come b'm-by?

DESE BONES GWINE TO RISE AGAIN

A retold story of the First Man, the First Woman, and the events of their Paradise Lost. It is comic, paradoxical, mystic, in the manner of some of the tumultuous imagery hurled forth from "God's Trombones" as written by James Weldon Johnson. Two or three generations of white people have cherished this creation of the Dark Brother. I have heard it in cities and on farms, in factories and pitching hay. For assistance in the text we are indebted to Lloyd Lewis, the Free Quaker. The harmonization is by Hilbert G. Stewart, a young colored composer, of Chicago.

Arr. H. G. S.

Lord, he thought he'd make a man, Dese bones gwine to rise a-gain;

Made him out of mud and a lit-tle bit of sand, Dese bones gwine to rise a-gain.

REFRAIN, *tenuto*

I know it, 'deed I know it, Dese bones gwine to rise a-gain.

470

1 Lord, he thought he'd make a man,
  Dese bones gwine to rise again;
  Made him out of mud and a little bit of sand,
  Dese bones gwine to rise again.

Refrain:

  I know it, 'deed I know it,
  Dese bones gwine to rise again.

2 "Adam, Adam, where art thou?"
  Dese bones gwine to rise again;
  "Here, Marse Lord, I'se comin' down."
  Dese bones gwine to rise again.

3 Thought he'd make a woman too;
  Dese bones gwine to rise again;
  Didn't know 'xactly what to do.
  Dese bones gwine to rise again.

4 Took a rib from Adam's side;
  Dese bones gwine to rise again;
  Made Miss Eve for to be his bride.
  Dese bones gwine to rise again.

5 Put 'em in a garden rich an' fair;
  Dese bones gwine to rise again;
  Tole 'em to eat what they found dere.
  Dese bones gwine to rise again.

6 To one tall tree dey mus' not go;
  Dese bones gwine to rise again;
  Dere mus' de fruit forever grow.
  Dese bones gwine to rise again.

7 Ol' Miss Eve come a-walkin' roun';
  Dese bones gwine to rise again;
  Spied dat tree all loaded down.
  Dese bones gwine to rise again.

8 Sarpent he came roun' de trunk.
  Dese bones gwine to rise again;
  At Miss Eve his eye he wunk.
  Dese bones gwine to rise again.

9 Firs' she took a little pull;
  Dese bones gwine to rise again;
  Den she filled her apron full.
  Dese bones gwine to rise again.

10 Adam he come prowlin' roun';
   Dese bones gwine to rise again;
   Spied dem peelin's on de groun'.
   Dese bones gwine to rise again.

11 Den he took a little slice;
   Dese bones gwine to rise again;
   Smack his lips an' said 'twas nice.
   Dese bones gwine to rise again.

12 Lord, he spoke with a mighty voice.
   Dese bones gwine to rise again;
   Shook de heavens to de joists.
   Dese bones gwine to rise again.

13 "Adam! Adam! Where are thou?"
   Dese bones gwine to rise again;
   "Yes, Marse Lord, I'se a-comin' now."
   Dese bones gwine to rise again.

14 "You et my apples, I believe?"
   Dese bones gwine to rise again;
   "Not me, Lord, but I 'spec 'twas Eve."
   Dese bones gwine to rise again.

15 Lord den rose up in his wrath;
   Dese bones gwine to rise again;
   Tole 'em beat it down de path.
   Dese bones gwine to rise again.

16 "Out of my garden you mus' git,"
   Dese bones gwine to rise again,
   "For you an' me has got to quit."
   Dese bones gwine to rise again.

Refrain:

  I know it, 'deed I know it,
  Dese bones gwine to rise again.

TWO WHITE HORSES

The white horses go in a sort of hoof-beat time; the "rassling" of Zek'l with sin is swift and dexterous, as also is his entrance into "heb'n." It is one of the gayer and more accelerated spirituals, and was heard by Dr. Ernest Horn, head of the College of Education, University of Iowa, when a boy in Missouri.

Arr. A. G. W.

2 Daniel was a man, Daniel was a man,
  In de lion's den;
  Daniel was a man, Daniel was a man,
  In de lion's den;
  Daniel was a man, Daniel was a man,
  In de lion's den;
  De good Lawd proved to be Daniel's frien'.

3 Zek'l was a man, Zek'l was a man,
  And he rassled wid sin;
  Zek'l was a man, Zek'l was a man,
  And he rassled wid sin;
  Zek'l was a man, Zek'l was a man,
  And he rassled wid sin;
  Heb'n gate opened, and he rolled right in.

WAY OVER IN THE NEW BURYIN' GROUN'

This negro spiritual to be heard on the coast of Georgia is from a series of negro spirituals recorded on phonograph cylinders for the extensive collection of R. W. Gordon. The time of it goes a little as though one heard a distinct hammering of curious incessancy.

Arr. A. G. W.

The hammer keeps a-ring-in' on some-bod-y's cof-fin, The hammer keeps a ring-in' on some-bod-y's cof-fin, Way o-ver in the new bur-yin' groun'.

2 Somebody's dying way over yonder,
  Somebody's dying way over yonder,
  Way over in the new buryin' groun'.

MARY WORE THREE LINKS OF CHAIN

One of the sublime creations of the negro race in America. . . mystic, simple, poetic, elusive, tinted with shadings of the light that never was on land or sea. . . . "I'm" is "Ahm," "wore" is "woh," and so on.

Arr. L. S.

Ma-ry wore............ three links of chain,......... Ma-ry

wore........... three links of chain,........... Ma-ry wore three links of

chain, Ev-'ry link bear-in' Je-sus' name; All my sins been tak-en a-way,...

tak - en a - way.................

2 Mary weeped and Martha mourned,
  Mary weeped and Martha mourned,
  Mary weeped and Martha mourned,
  Gabriel stood and blowed his horn;
  All my sins been taken away, taken away.

3 I don't know but I've been told,
  I don't know but I've been told,
  I don't know but I've been told,
  The streets in heaven are paved with gold;
  All my sins been taken away, taken away.

4 Can't you hear dem horses' feet?
  Can't you hear dem horses' feet?
  Can't you hear dem horses' feet
  Slippin' and slidin' on de golden street?
  All my sins been taken away, taken away.

5 My feet got wet in de midnight dew,
  My feet got wet in de midnight dew,
  My feet got wet in de midnight dew,
  An' de mornin' star was a witness too;
  All my sins been taken away, taken away.

6 I'm go'n home on de mornin' train,
  I'm go'n home on de mornin' train,
  I'm go'n home on de mornin' train,
  All don't see me go'n to hear me sing:
  All my sins been taken away, taken away.

PHARAOH'S ARMY GOT DROWNDED

Arr. L. S.

Slowly

If I could I sure-ly would Stan' on de rock where Mos-es stood, Pharaoh's

ar - my got drown-ded. O Ma - ry, don' you weep, don' you mo'n...... O

Ma - ry,... don' you weep, don' you mo'n, O Ma - ry, don' you weep, don' you mo'n, Pharaoh's

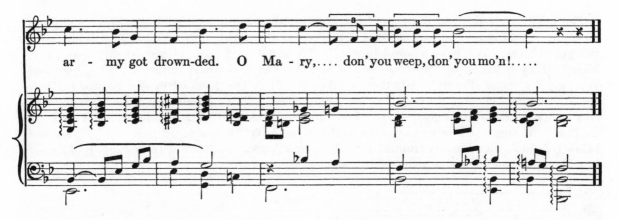

ar - my got drown-ded. O Ma - ry,.... don' you weep, don' you mo'n!.....

1 If I could I surely would
Stan' on de rock where Moses stood.
Pharaoh's army got drownded,
O Mary, don' you weep, don' you mo'n.
O Mary, don' you weep, don' you mo'n.
O Mary, don' you weep, don' you mo'n.
Pharaoh's army got drownded.
O Mary, don' you weep, don' you mo'n.

2 Some o' these nights about twelve o'clock
Dis ol' worl' gwine to reel an' rock.
Pharaoh's army got drownded,
O Mary, don' you weep, don' you mo'n.
O Mary, don' you weep, don' you mo'n.
O Mary, don' you weep, don' you mo'n.
Pharaoh's army got drownded.
O Mary, don' you weep, don' you mo'n.

GOOD-BYE, BROTHER

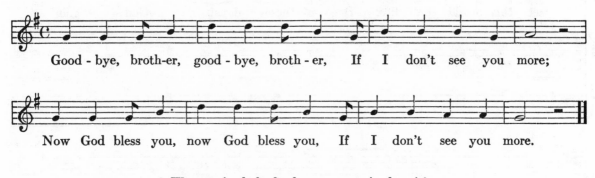

Good - bye, broth-er, good - bye, broth - er, If I don't see you more;

Now God bless you, now God bless you, If I don't see you more.

2 We part in de body, but we meet in de spirit,
If I don't see you more;
We'll meet in de heaben, in de blessed kingdom,
If I don't see you more.

3 So good-bye brother, good-bye sister,
If I don't see you more;
Now God bless you, now God bless you,
If I don't see you more.

GOD'S GOIN' TO SET THIS WORLD ON FIRE

The I. W. W. (Industrial Workers of the World) nailed the word "Solidarity" high and issued a call for "One Big Union." It shouted, "Workers of the world, unite! You have nothing to lose but your chains. You have a world to win." Those with red cards of membership were "wobblies." They belonged in "jungles," camps and hobo hangouts near railroads. They were outlaws, gypsies, vags. Several times they wrecked jails, tore the doors off hinges, twisted the bars, spoiled the plumbing, and defied all law and government. While in jail they often made the walls ring with a negro spiritual given here. Their favorite verse was "God's Goin' to Set This World on Fire." It suggests Fire wrecking the world as the I. W. W.'s wrecked jails . . . The text B below is from Arthur Billings Hunt of Brooklyn, New York, who heard it from a group of negroes in a Virginia farm house five years ago.

Arr. L. S.

478

A

1 God's goin' to set this world on fire,
   God's goin' to set this world on fire,
   One o' these days!
   God's goin' to set this world on fire,
   One o' these days!

2 I'm goin' to walk an' talk with Jesus,
   I'm goin' to walk an' talk with Jesus,
   One o' these days!
   I'm goin' to walk an' talk with Jesus,
   One o' these days!

3 I'm goin' to climb up Jacob's ladder,
   I'm goin' to climb up Jacob's ladder,
   One o' these days!
   I'm goin' to climb up Jacob's ladder,
   One o' these days!

4 All you sinners gonna turn up missing,
   All you sinners gonna turn up missing,
   One o' these days!
   All you sinners gonna turn up missing,
   One o' these days!

B

1 God don't want no coward soldiers,
   God don't want no coward soldiers,
       Some o' these days.
   He wants valiant hearted soldiers
       Some o' these days.

2 We are climbin' Jacob's ladder,
   We are climbin' Jacob's ladder,
       Some o' these days.
   Every round goes higher and higher,
       Some o' these days.

AIN' GO'N' TO STUDY WAR NO MO'

Among spirituals used by negroes as work songs this is to be mentioned. "They sing it by the hour," students at the University of Alabama told me, referring to "Ain' Go'n' to Study War No Mo'." As they go on, hour by hour, they bring in lines from many other spirituals. The tempo is vital, never actually monotonous, never ecstatic, yet steady in its onflow, sure of its pulses. It is a work song-spiritual. War is pronounced "wah" or "waw" as if to rhyme with "saw." Horse is "hawss." And so on with negro economy of vocables in speech and song.

Arr. L. S.

480

AIN' GO'N' TO STUDY WAR NO MO'

1 I'm go'n' to lay down my sword and shield, I'm go'n' to lay down my sword and shield,
Down by de ribber-side, down by de ribber-side, I'm go'n' to lay down my sword and shield.
I ain' go'n' to study war no mo', I ain' go'n' to study war no mo',
I ain' go'n' to study war no mo', I ain' go'n' to study war no mo'.

2 I'm go'n' to ride on a milk-white horse, I'm go'n' to ride on a milk-white horse,
Down by de ribber-side, down by de ribber-side, I'm go'n' to ride on a milk-white horse.
I ain' go'n' to study war no mo', I ain' go'n' to study war no mo',
I ain' go'n' to study war no mo', I ain' go'n' to study war no mo'.

3 I'm go'n' to wear a starry crown, I'm go'n' to wear a starry crown,
Down by de ribber-side, down by de ribber-side, I'm go'n' to wear a starry crown.

4 I'm go'n' to wear a snow-white robe, I'm go'n' to wear a snow-white robe,
Down by de ribber-side, down by de ribber-side, I'm go'n' to wear a snow-white robe.

5 I'm go'n' to ride with my King Jesus, I'm go'n' to ride with my King Jesus,
Down by de ribber-side, down by de ribber-side, I'm go'n' to ride with my King Jesus.

481

THINGS I USED TO DO

Texas camp meetings have heard these testimonies of an old way of life abandoned and a new one adopted.

Arr. A. G. W.

2 Chickens I used to steal, I don't steal no mo', (*3 times*)
There's been a great change since I been bohn.

3 Whisky I used to drink, I don't drink no mo', (*3 times*)
There's been a great change since I been bohn.

IN MY FATHER'S HOUSE

This spiritual comes from negroes of Fort Worth, Texas, through the medium of Jake Zeitlin, a poet who used to send me each year a horned toad from the Great Staked Plains. The list of occupations named in these verses can be extended according to desire or whim.

Arr. A. G. W.

There ain' no li - ars there In my Fa - ther's house; There

(Spoken)

ain' no li - ars there In my Fa - ther's house. Ain' no li - ars there,

(Spoken)

In my Fa - ther's house; O there's peace, peace, ev - 'ry - where!

2 There ain' no crapshooters there In my Father's house. (*3 times*)
O there's peace, peace, ev'rywhere!

3 There ain' no cardplayers there In my Father's house. (*3 times*)
O there's peace, peace, ev'rywhere!

STANDIN' ON THE WALLS OF ZION

The barber shop harmonizers of midwest towns used to make up their own melodies and then mix in the words. In Galesburg, boys from the Q. railroad shops, from Colton's foundry and the Purington brickyards, would meet in front of Brown's hotel or the Union hotel, practice with their voices as they strolled off Main Street, and then make the rounds of the ice-cream "sociables" held by various churches on a summer evening. Some boys would find the girls they were looking for. Others stayed with the bunch and sang. One of the favorite pieces, about the time of the Chicago anarchist case, was this white man's spiritual.

Arr. L. S.

Then it's a hooraw, and a hooraw,
Thru the merry green fields, hooraw!
Standin' on the walls of Zion, Zion,
See my ship come sailin', sailin',
Standin' on the walls of Zion,
See my ship come sailin' home.

A HUNDRED YEARS AGO

The high and prolonged declaration of a heart wanting to be home, having been away so long, yet it has a sea health. Wilbert Snow, the Maine poet who sailed before the mast when young and husky, knew this as a windlass song. . . . Air and accompaniment run without strict regard to rhythm. . . . as a meditation. . . . and of varied pulses.

Arr. H. F.

1 A hundred years is a very long time,
   Oh, yes, oh.
 A hundred years is a very long time,
   A hundred years ago.

2 A hundred years have passed and gone,
   Oh, yes, oh.
 A hundred years have passed and gone,
   A hundred years ago.

3 A hundred years will come once more,
   Oh, yes, oh.
 A hundred years will come once more,
   A hundred years ago.

YOU GOT TO CROSS IT FOH YOHSELF

This spiritual from the negroes of Texas, is a contemplation, a prayer, and an outcry.

Arr. A. G. W.

1 You got to cross that River Jordan,
You got to cross it foh yohself;
O there cain't nobody cross it foh you;
You got to cross it foh yohself,
Cain't yoh brothah cross it foh you,
You got to cross it foh yohself.

2 You got to stand that test of judgment,
You got to stand it foh yohself;
O there cain't nobody stand it foh you;
You got to stand it foh yohself,
Cain't yoh pahson stand it foh you,
You got to stand it foh yohself.

I GOT A LETTER FROM JESUS

This may be heard on Lang Syne Plantation, Fort Motte, South Carolina. It is sometimes sung by sinners or worldly negroes to persuade church members that they too shall receive salvation at the Throne of Grace.

Arr. A. G. W.

I got a letter from Jesus,
Ahah, ahah!
I got a letter, I got a letter,
I got a letter from Jesus,
'Mm,— 'Mm.—

487

EZEKIEL, YOU AND ME

The author's arrangement of lines and airs from five negro spirituals that have for many years given musical enjoyment and spiritual sustenance, with harmonization by Alfred G. Wathall.

Arr. A. G. W.

wheel,   'Way up   in de mid-dle of de air.   A wheel in   a wheel,   a

wheel in   a   wheel,   Ez-e-k'l saw de wheel, 'Way up   in de mid-dle of de air.

Keep a-inch-in,'   keep a-inch-in,'   Je-sus will come by and

by;   Inch by inch,   inch by inch,   Like a po' inch

EZEKIEL, YOU AND ME

491

Ho - pin' on de moun - tain,...... ho - pin' in de

val - ley,........ I'm go'n to reap.... jus' what I sow............

1 Ezek'l saw de wheel, Ezek'l saw de wheel,
'Way up in de middle of de air.
De big wheel move by faith;
De little wheel move by de grace of God;
A wheel in a wheel,
'Way up in de middle of de air.
A wheel in a wheel, a wheel in a wheel,
Ezek'l saw de wheel,
'Way up in de middle of de air.

2 Keep a-inchin', keep a-inchin',
Jesus will come by and by;
Inch by inch, inch by inch,
Like a po' inch worm,
Jesus will come by and by.

3 It's me, O Lord; it's me, it's me,
It's me, O Lord;
Standin' in de need of prayer;
It's me, it's me, it's me, O Lord;
Standin' in de need of prayer.

4 Chilly water, chilly water,
Hallelujah to dat Lamb!
I know dat water am chilly and cold,
And a Hallelujah to dat Lamb!

5 Prayin' on de mountain, prayin' in de valley,
We're go'n to reap jus' what we sow;
Hopin' on de mountain, hopin' in de valley,
I'm go'n to reap jus' what I sow.

492

INDEX